Testing Adults

Contributors

Melvin Berg, Ph.D.

Daniel C. Claiborn, Ph.D.

Dennis M. Dailey, D.S.W.

Terrie Fisk, M.A.

Nancy J. Garfield, Ph.D.

Carl J. Getto, M.D.

Charles J. Golden, Ph.D.

Lawrence C. Hartlage, Ph.D.

Robert K. Heaton, Ph.D.

Mark R. Lovell, Ph.D.

William J. Lynch, Ph.D.

Christopher H. North, Ph.D.

Carroll D. Ohlde, Ph.D.

Tom W. Patterson, Ph.D.

Thomas Reilly, Ph.D.

Douglas E. Robbins, Ph.D.

Andrew H. Schauer, Ph.D.

Fred D. Strider, Ph.D.

Mary Ann Strider, Ph.D.

Dennis P. Swiercinsky, Ph.D.

Testing Adults

A REFERENCE GUIDE FOR SPECIAL
PSYCHODIAGNOSTIC ASSESSMENTS

Dennis P. Swiercinsky, Ph.D.
General Editor

Foreword by William H. Smith, Ph.D.

TEST CORPORATION OF AMERICA
KANSAS CITY

LIBRARY OF CONGRESS CATALOGING IN PUBLICATION DATA
Main entry under title:

Testing adults.

    Includes bibliographies and index.
    1. Psychodiagnostics. 2. Diagnosis, Differential. 3. Psychological tests.
I. Swiercinsky, Dennis.
RC469.T47   1985   616.89'075   85-17341
ISBN 0-9611286-9-0

Printed in the United States of America

Contents

III. ISSUES IN SOCIAL/VOCATIONAL ASSESSMENTS

Foreword

WILLIAM H. SMITH, PH.D.

Diagnostic psychological testing remains a potent force in psychology despite some ebb and flow in its popularity. Critics periodically have announced that some if not all testing was about to disappear from the professional scene, but, as in Mark Twain's well-known retort, the news of its demise has been greatly exaggerated. Tests have been attacked as unfair and discriminatory, as so lacking in validity and reliability as to be unscientific, and as growing out of an undesirable medical model that puts patients or clients into passive, even helpless roles as objects of scrutiny by authoritarian evaluators. Social trends such as civil rights and patients' rights movements have seemed antagonistic to testing, and trends within psychology such as behavior therapy and community approaches have appeared to weaken the case for diagnostic appraisal. Seeking professional parity with psychiatrists, some psychologists have felt a need to "outgrow" testing, as if that task were tainted as subordinate, an activity incompatible with professional dignity and autonomy.

Despite such attacks, the head of psychological testing remains unbowed if bloodied at all, gaining momentum as psychological services continue to expand into wider applications in medicine, law, education, rehabilitation, and industry. The word "testing" carries certain unfortunate connotations: having one's abilities or qualities judged or even challenged. In its best sense, though, diagnostic psychological testing is done to promote the welfare of those tested, and is done for and with them, not to them. Our "consumers" are often the patients or clients themselves, or arise from a vast array of referral sources eager to benefit from what we have to offer. Of course we still work with physicians—not just psychiatrists but almost every specialty—and not as lab technicians but as consultants with special expertise to offer.

As the profession of psychology has evolved, so has our diagnostic function, growing into a rich and challenging activity that certainly need not be abandoned in the name of professional progress. But to consider oneself a diagnostician, a consultant, an expert in psychological evaluation requires paying certain dues for membership in such a high-sounding club. Taking a course or two in graduate school and doing a few supervised evaluations during an internship are no longer (not to say they ever were) a sufficient base for the practice of testing. There is a vast gulf between the role of psychometrician and that of psychological diagnostician, a gulf bridged only by training, experience, and extensive study. Like musical instruments that can be played poorly or with virtuosity, psychological tests are tools of the clinician who selects, applies, interprets, and conveys their meaning to others. To risk straining a metaphor, a musician is seldom proficient with all music, with blues as well as baroque. Mastering the instrument is one thing; mastering the music, another. Psychologists, then, must not just master their instruments, but be able to apply them to a variety of clinical needs, must be knowledgeable about a range of human problems and their related diagnostic and treatment issues.

In this volume are 17 contributions to the diversification of diagnostic knowledge. Not a primer in any sense, this collection is like a handbook that can be read selectively or piecemeal. It presumes knowledge of the basics of testing, and offers intermediate and advanced levels of knowledge about particular diagnostic problems or applications. The theoretical orientation of the authors varies, though most are eclectic enough to be understood by practitioners of any persuasion. Some chapters offer new ideas based on research, most provide a summary of accumulated facts and wisdom. They range from the somewhat familiar territory of anxiety and depression to newer concerns with pain, sexual dysfunction, and adjustment to alternative life-styles. Each chapter portrays for the reader how the author(s) have come to understand and meet the challenges posed by the topics under study, and in that sense are documents of personal conviction, a sharing of what has been experienced and learned.

Building on the pioneering efforts of key figures like Hermann Rorschach, David Wechsler, Henry Murray, David Rapaport, and Roy Schafer, these authors add new dimensions to our understanding of complex psychological phenomena and how they can be understood through the medium of psychological tests. In general, all the authors espouse a multifaceted approach, whereby data from history, interviews, and collateral sources are integrated with those from tests, blending information into a usable synthesis. Never resorting to a simplistic "sign approach," the various writers alert us to what can be expected as typical patterns or constellations. Their efforts guide us in widening our horizons and utilizing our test instruments in more refined, more diverse, more creative ways. All of the contributors, under the energetic and thoughtful leadership of the editor, are to be commended for these additions to our diagnostic knowledge.

The Menninger Foundation
Topeka, Kansas
August, 1985

Preface

The intent of *Testing Adults* is to provide categories of thinking about adjustment problems and the associated psychological assessment strategies and tests that are appropriate for sharpening clinical skills in dealing with those problems. As students and professionals read this book, we hope the presentations will reflect our being ever-critical of our task. We do not here concern ourselves directly with psychometric theory; these chapters represent psychology applied. However, in our changing profession we strive constantly to improve our skill and knowledge.

This book provides the clinician with fundamental knowledge and resources for understanding behavior problem areas and approaching diagnostic tasks with psychological tests and related procedures. As Dr. Weaver pointed out in his preface to *Testing Children*, the testing movement in psychology only rather recently has gained a resurgence of interest and appreciation as a medium that offers crucial procedures for attaining a level of understanding of behavior expeditiously and thoroughly, so that the intricate complexities of maladaptive behavior can be recognized and treated appropriately.

To make the most of this volume, readers should be minimally familiar with fundamental test construction theory and issues of validity, reliability, item construction, and norms. Similarly, fundamental principles of clinical psychology, psychopathology, psychodiagnostics, and personality theory are assumed. With this knowledge and the structure of thinking in terms of problems as they relate to tests, our presentations should provide a perspective on assessment and testing that is not only state-of-the-art but which offers a springboard for further innovation in testing.

The broad scope of this book is the assessment process in 1) problem definition, 2) preassessment, 3) testing, 4) integration of findings, and 5) communicating results and recommendations. The narrower focus is the description of tests and procedures that complement the assessment. Each contributor has defined a problem area, provided a conceptual foundation for the area, elaborated on the testing tools that help the clinician develop the area, and then summarized the integrative and reporting procedure. As most psychological reports are structured, each chapter is like dual funnels with a long connecting stem in between. It is this stem that represents the narrow focus and emphasis on tests. Our intent is not to be encyclopedic regarding tests, but to offer a foundation based on the most useful test strategies recommended by our contributors.

Certainly there are limits to the amount of information, particularly regarding numbers of tests, that a clinician may wish to gather. Psychological tests have proliferated in recent years, and there are hundreds of well-researched and validated instruments currently available. The clinician must be familiar with a sufficient variety of these measures to use them intelligently in completing a diagnostic study. With the number of published assessments well over 3,000, seasoned practitioners and students alike need a mechanism for being updated on recognized tests and on expert recommendations concerning good tools with which to provide diagnostic services. As these tests become comfortably and skillfully applied, one becomes more adept at evaluating new or otherwise unfamiliar tests. Thus, the purpose of this volume is to provide a contextual description of tests appropriate in a variety of diagnostic problem situations, in order to help the clinician avoid the errors and oversights that potentially exist with every patient.

Psychological assessment must be client-centered. Too frequently a mental health professional will ask another for a "Rorschach," or a "Halstead-Reitan," or a "Bender." If an assessor wants to respond to a request to administer a specific test to a client or patient, there are numerous excellent texts available that step through a variety of instruments, one-by-one. *Testing Adults* focuses on problems and the *assessment* perspective around those problems. Tests (often similar from problem to problem) are described in these chapters that focus on the scope of the behavior or problem area under consideration. Test results are interpreted in light of the whole range of data available about the client. The composite person is never lost in a test score; virtually every contributor to this volume has demonstrated that.

There is a matter-of-fact attitude reflected in the contributions to this volume regarding the inevitability of problems and our need to address them candidly and forthrightly. All families will likely experience communication problems from time to time; sexual dysfunction may be as common, and as transitory, as the flu; the "upward mobility" syndrome may be pushing record numbers of young adults to dangerous stress levels; nearly 20% of the adult population will experience mental health problems at any given time. We won't, however, stop forming families, making love, pushing career objectives to further and further limits, and so on; the concomitant problems are a natural part of life. Mental health professionals come to accept this as a given, yet must never lose respect for the help people want in solving these problems and returning their lives to balance.

As these chapters are read it becomes evident that many of the contributing experts rely on a similar core of tests (e.g., the Wechsler scales, the MMPI, the Rorschach) to provide a global understanding of the whole person. Then, as a problem area begins to emerge more clearly, specialized tests are used in the progressive refinement and definition of the adjustment problem, and special interpretive techniques using the core battery are described.

An assumption also is implied in these chapters that a clinician who knows how to administer a core set of complex tests (such as the Wechsler and the

Rorschach) very well, almost automatically, is freed-up from the mechanics to begin analyzing client responses from presentation of the first stimulus. In fact, it is this artistic-clinical quality in using a standardized basis for observation that characterizes the expert assessment, as opposed to a blind reliance on "tests."

Over 120 tests are highlighted within the various chapters, and the majority are further described in the volume's Appendix. Four instruments (two are projective tests) are cited almost universally by the contributors as providing a comprehensive foundation for assessment. There is a very good explanation for this phenomenon. Each contributor was asked to describe an assessment foundation for a problem area with which they are extremely familiar. Nearly all start with a core set of tests appropriate to the specific problem area, or broad enough to be used in a number of areas though interpreted uniquely in each. It is this "tried and true" approach that is the hallmark of excellence in testing. It is also interesting that nearly every contributor begins his or her advice with tests that require depth interpretation, not merely deriving a score that allows a dichotomous or other simplistic diagnosis. Process and product are emphasized, complementarity of findings is required, recursive investigation is forced. The use of established, multifactorial tests start the inferential process, which can then be augmented with additional procedures. If these procedures contribute to an understanding, then the assessment is progressing satisfactorily; if they muddy the understanding, one must return to the foundation data to find out what is wrong with the inferences.

For example, one might use the Beck Depression Inventory as an adjunct to a much broader, psychodynamic understanding of the *symptom* of depression. Problems such as those defining the chapter topics in this book are essentially symptoms or syndromes embedded within a whole personality, which in turn exists within a physiological entity. Diagnoses represent the fundamental problem that explains the symptom(s) within a unique-person context. A sexual dysfunction may be a symptom of anxiety, pain may be a symptom of an intractible physiological condition, attention deficit may be a symptom of brain-stem injury, or these symptoms may represent completely different etiologies. Through multimethod, inferential, and recursive procedures, tests make their contribution in assessment. Skilled diagnosticians (really, assessors) appreciate the multiple contributing causes of behavior and recognize that a diagnosis cannot be taken out of context, but is isolated to provide manageability.

Undertaking the task of editing a work of this scope requires the constant effort and vigilance of several people to see that contributors are conceptually consistent, timely, and unified in approach. The unity, continuity, and emphasis of our mission has been achieved only through the persistent efforts of our editors at Test Corporation of America, Terry Faulkner and Jane Guthrie. Their "gentle firmness" with regard to deadlines, suggestions for structure, technical editing, and keeping track of the venture's unfolding has made the project finally quite rewarding.

Each contributor deserves special acknowledgement as well, for faithfulness in adhering to our goals and deadlines. Their willingness to write chapters in a matter of weeks and to complete revisions in a matter of days truly reflects their commitment to our mission.

Although we had Dr. Weaver's book on *Testing Children* as an excellent model, the unique task we defined for ourselves in writing *Testing Adults* was an evolving one, completed much as we complete a psychological assessment. As chapters were received from contributors, we constantly checked back with our original scope, did some refining and redefining and molded the book into what we hope is a unified whole. The book reflects our dedication to excellence in clinical psychology.

1

The Role of Testing in Adult Assessments

DENNIS P. SWIERCINSKY, PH.D.

Understanding human behavior is an infinitely complex task. The mental health professional who is called upon to assess the structure and etiology of problematic or maladaptive behavior and to render a summary diagnosis is faced with a responsibility that is rarely appreciated in its procedural, integrative, and consequential demands. All psychological theories attempt to explain and predict the relationship between behavior and a variety of factors, including physiological, neurological, intellectual, developmental, psychodynamic, educational, social, and so on. Using a theoretical foundation, the clinician focuses on certain observations, history, and hypotheses, uses select test instruments, and finally synthesizes the information into a communicable form. Each diagnostic problem is unique and must be approached in progressively narrower working levels, providing a baserate of sorts that helps the clinician narrow his or her working foundation.

At the most general level is the chronological age group that represents the client. Most theories deal with at least three developmental stages: child, adolescent, and adult. Distinct from the assessment concerns of the child and adolescent, the adult client represents *relative* developmental stability. There are, of course, the natural aging concerns of the older individual, sometimes addressed as a factor with adults, especially in neuropsychological evaluation or in problems of depression. For the individual under approximately age 20, the intensity of physiological, sexual, social, and career development plays a greater relative role in accounting for behavior than it does in the adult client.

There are particular problem areas that face adults more strikingly than younger individuals: longer lives; new anxieties of work and career stresses; environmental threats and experiences such as war, nuclear waste, poisoned water and air, terrorism; physiological failings such as cancer, AIDS, heart disease, or conditions that cause lingering pain and suffering; changing values regarding sex roles; divorces and family splitting; threats of and involvement in legal disputes; changing acceptance of work roles and career as well as career mobility; sexual life-style adjustments—and so on. There is a growing psychological sophistication and recognition of complexity regarding adult life-styles and personal characteristics,

1

as well as the problem adjustment areas. Not only are homosexuals "coming out of the closet," so are adults with learning disabilities, persons with physical and neurological limitations, those experiencing serious medical maladies, and those who are "burned out" on their jobs or whose marriage has not worked and are willing to risk change. Former "mental patients," crime and rape victims, war veterans, and others are emerging to form support groups united to win back their lost individuality, to re-enter active social roles while diminishing prejudice and discrimination. People in general and mental health professionals in particular are recognizing that individuals do not fit convenient pigeonholes that describe their "type." New syndromes (e.g., post-traumatic stress disorder, ego-dystonic homosexuality) and diagnostic understandings (e.g., borderline personality, family systems) are emerging to provide us comprehensive and inclusive structures for understanding people instead of reducing them to narrow categories. Even the concepts of "depression" and "anxiety," still considered discrete categories according to common diagnostic nomenclature, are challenged as able to exist separately, concurrently, or complementarily, always parts of a larger personality complex.

Another concern for the mental health practitioner in working with adults is the growing rate of litigation involving psychological and neuropsychological damage. If nowhere else, it is in the courtroom that the true test of the mental health professional's commitment to maintaining the whole individual while satisfying the explicit requests of the court is made. The unique role of psychological tests, offering "objective" and "scientific" foundation to an argument of loss, tempts the expert witness, the adversaries, and the court in general to relinquish the concept of the composite person. Nearly everyone can expect to be a litigant in a dispute sometime in his or her life; for the mental health professional, this poses special responsibilities that are sometimes critical.

Mental health and problems coexist. Mental illness is not merely coming out into the open; it is being redefined to reflect a respect for whole persons. Referrals for mental health assistance, to private agencies and to public institutions, are at record numbers. The mental health profession has progressed a long way from the simplistic diagnosis of "mental illness" to an appreciation of the complexities of human problems. No mental health practitioner can address adult assessments in the same ways anymore, nor can he or she simply start with tests or types of tests and proceed directly to a categorical conclusion. Mental health professionals must define problems that encompass unique knowledge and procedures. The information explosion is occurring in psychology as intensely as it is in aeronautics.

HISTORICAL PERSPECTIVE

The "testing movement" in education and psychology began with the development of intelligence tests designed to produce a reductionistic or comprehensive value (i.e., IQ) for making interpersonal comparisons and educational placements. During the past 50 years this approach has evolved into procedures that produce arrays of subscales and psychometrically derived scores for examining a wide range of intrapersonal cognitive functions, contributing to the appreciation of the complexities of intelligence and the recognition and respect of individual uniqueness. Today, many psychological evaluations are based on Wechsler subscale scores, where the interest is in understanding an individual's cognitive part-processes and their interrelationships rather than in making simplistic interpersonal comparisons along global dimensions. The focus has shifted from measuring individual differences to exploring the complex intrapersonal characteristics that demonstrate individual uniqueness.

Similarly, personality evaluation has evolved from loosely structured, constructed, and applied word association or free association tests and from objective inventories designed to categorize people into nomothetically based diagnoses. Such approaches have been replaced with theoretically based projective techniques and actuarial methods leading to profile analyses, where the interest, again, is in intrapersonal characteristic comparisons. Psychological assessment has evolved to represent the foundation of clinical psychology; as such it is continually under scrutiny to reflect the scientific and sophisticated quality demanded by the profession.

Structured interviews, multidimensional rating scales, and complex scoring procedures for projective tests recently have augmented the resources of the mental health professional. (A recognition of the value of psychodynamic approaches, such as with projective tests, to complement more objective techniques is reflected strongly among the chapters in this volume; this is in contrast to Goldstein and Hersen [1984, p. 6] who believe there is evidence that the excitement for projective tests no longer exists.) In addition to the development and professional acceptance of a variety of scales, indices, and so on, the role of the projective test is still strongly felt. Such instruments offer a wealth of data and impressions that force the integrative process of assessment. They are invaluable in providing the information that is drawn together, along with other data and test scores, to a consolidated, "makes sense" picture. It is this global comprehensiveness that characterizes modern assessment.

With the use of tests in psychodiagnostic assessments firmly established, there is more interest than ever before in developing sophisticated new tests, in designing scoring and norming techniques (e.g., Embretson, 1985; Gorsuch, 1983), and in applying computer technology to improve standardization and efficiency and to obtain score forms unavailable by other techniques (Swiercinsky, 1983a, 1983b). In fact, a revived interest is evident in test design theory that examines substantive item properties by unique psychometric methods while preserving the objective quality of tests. It is in a sense bridging projective and objective tests.

ASSESSMENT PERSPECTIVE

Throughout the years psychological tests have cycled in popularity through bane and panacea. As with most ideas, extremes of fervor produce a loss of perspective. Those who would consider tests useless and those who regard them as diagnostic magic are wrong. Tests are tools of the clinician, as are pad and pen. The skill and sensitivity of the professional involves applying the tools appropriately, within the context of clinical art. It is a poor clinician who blames diagnostic failures entirely on his tests, or who relies on tests without the skill to use them wisely. The professional who performs psychological assessments must develop a clear attitude about tests that respects their usefulness and limitations, and respects the multi-faceted and multifactorial nature of behavior—even behavior segments. Testing is a procedure for segmenting and managing complexity, not denying or reducing it. Tests define behavior or personality and cognitive segments; assessments put this together within a coherent whole.

Weaver (1984) provides an excellent, two-part concept of the psychological assessment that places testing in perspective. By emphasizing the holistic and integrative aspect of an assessment, the practitioner is reminded to include informa-tion regarding the physical, intellectual, emotional, educational, and social areas of functioning at each stage of the assessment—from history review to communication of results. In addition to this parallel process, there is a sequential process that lends order and perspective: 1) prediagnostic considerations based on history and initial impressions, whereby the dimensions of the assessment are defined and procedures selected; 2) administration of tests and procedures; 3) interpretation and integra-tion of findings, whereby interaction among findings is stimulated to avoid sim-plistic explanations; and 4) the communication of results to patients, family, and other professionals.

Too often clinicians approach each new diagnostic problem in the same manner as all those that came before. If limited to a narrow and/or single theoretical basis, the understanding of the patient that is yielded can be simplistic and narrow. It is unsettling to hear colleagues describe a patient as "organic" or "psychotic" or "depressed," without being able to offer much additional explanation of the broad physiological and psychological dynamics behind those labels. Using a variety of tests that progressively change appropriate to the emerging nature of the problem helps the clinician avoid this simplicity by forcing a multifaceted and structured clinical look at patients from different perspectives. Our task is to encourage this approach. By learning about a variety of tests and procedures, and learning to discern problem areas that focus the assessment, the clinician improves on the probability of accomplishing a more complete understanding of a patient. That understanding then becomes invaluable in treatment, which is, after all, usually the reason we test in the first place.

Figure 1 provides a diagrammatic representation of the nature of assessment

FIGURE 1. PSYCHODIAGNOSTIC ASSESSMENT PERSPECTIVE

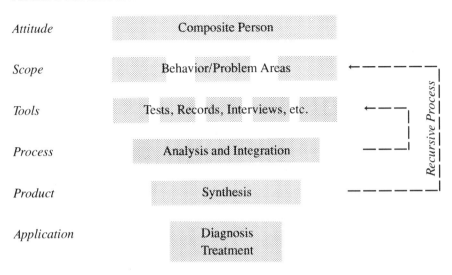

Attitude	Composite Person
Scope	Behavior/Problem Areas
Tools	Tests, Records, Interviews, etc.
Process	Analysis and Integration
Product	Synthesis
Application	Diagnosis Treatment

Recursive Process

and the place of tests. The fundamental approach to understanding human behavior is to understand the behavior or problem area being extracted from the composite person, to amass information from a variety of sources, and then to seek an integrated understanding of that information that can be encapsulated and communicated to be useful for changing maladaptive, dangerous, or unhappy behavior. The objective of tests is to provide the basis for inferring antecedent, maintenance, and dynamic factors that bear on the problem behaviors.

Once the scope of the assessment is defined, an economical yet comprehensive approach to data collection is begun. Background information, physical and neurological tests, psychological test scores, behavior observations, interview impressions, educational background and characteristics, behavioral characteristics, socioeconomic experiences, and so on are gathered. From these ingredients the clinician formulates an understanding of the multifactorial and dynamic causes or personality bases of current behavior. If any of the data are contradictory or somehow do not fit in that understanding, reconciliation is sought. This recursive process is crucial in understanding complex processes. Just as recursive mathematical processes allow the statistician to extract psychometric profiles from data by progressive recombinations, so mental recursion produces coincidence of impressions and hence understanding about people. Too frequently clinicians gather too little information or lose track of the composite person, thus making it too easy for their limited data to "hang together." This, of course, is at the risk of missing important observations and unjustly simplifying the assessment problem.

Certainly there are limits to the amount of information, particularly from the number of psychological tests, that a clinician may wish to gather. There are hundreds of well-researched, validated psychological tests available. The clinician must be familiar with a sufficient variety of these tests to use them intelligently in completing a diagnostic study. Facility with a few tests that yield maximum opportunity for impressionistic and objective data are usually the best with which to start. The examiner who can administer such tests automatically, with ease, is free to observe and note the limitless nuances of behavior that become data for the assessment. Tests provide the structured observations that lead to organized and cohesive thinking about a client.

There is, however, almost a natural tendency toward reductionism in the use of tests in psychological assessments. Tests often are selected to answer diagnostic questions, but that is not what they do; tests contribute the necessary quantity of global as well as discrete data for the *clinician* to answer diagnostic questions. Tests are to assessment as techniques (such as visual guided imagery) are to psychotherapy. Therapy is certainly more than "tricks." It is a process whereby a variety of procedures may be used sequentially or simultaneously, in which the outcome is more than the sum of the parts.

The broad scope of assessment is problem definition, preassessment screening, testing, integration of findings, communicating results, and making recommendations. The narrower scope is the use of tests and procedures that complement the assessment. Problem areas that form the reason for an assessment provide the starting point for thinking, for selecting tests and procedures, and for guiding the analysis and synthesis of the assessment.

FITTING TEST RESULTS TO THE PROBLEM SCOPE

Once a set of test scores and impressions is obtained, the clinician is faced with understanding the results in light of the presenting problem. Herein lies a major failing in assessments—the presenting problem. One wonders how many people referred for assessment were referred for the wrong problem: the young man who spent months in vocational assessment and counseling who never got around to addressing the real reason he sought professional help—his homosexuality; the late-middle-aged woman referred for depression over the loss of her husband, when the real problem was a precipitated catastrophic reaction to early-onset presenile dementia; or the young man referred for counseling after a lightning strike caused paraplegia, only to find out that a hysterical conversion reaction had taken place so he would never again have to work and reveal his profound learning disability, which had become extremely embarrassing to him. An accurate definition of the presenting problem is not only the first stage in making sense of test results, but is also an ongoing consideration that must be monitored as the assessment progresses.

Often an assessment begins with merely one or two presenting complaints. Being cautious not to take these at face value, the clinician judiciously redefines problems to address the primary problem category. Sensitivity to people and flexibility in exploring a wide range of possibilities with each client are the most valuable resources the clinician has in accomplishing this. The importance of knowing what the real problem is, however, cannot be overstated. One certainly is not going to interpret the MMPI results the same way in two cases if the presenting problems are vastly different yet the profiles similar. Tests are not magic. Obviously, the same or similar tests may be used for widely different problems; it is the interpretation that counts, however, not the use of the test to define the problem.

Weaver (1984) describes a model in which the data from various sources are laid out in rows on a table for the clinician (and student) to examine successively and begin formulating hypotheses. Each new set of data either leads to hypothesis confirmation or hypothesis reformulation. Eventually, this sequential logic process leads to a conclusion supported essentially by all the information. Similarly, in examining test results in light of continual monitoring of the problem area, the clinician must be willing to shift his or her thinking to sharpen the assessment understanding. This is analysis and integration.

The previously mentioned middle-aged woman who could not after two years shake the depression over the death of her husband demonstrated *most* of the clinical signs of depression, and thus her referral. However, early in the course of assessment her anxiety became obvious, as did her extremely poor memory. History recall was erratic, "why" questions perseverated, and subtle unnoticed mistakes in arithmetic were sufficient to prevent confirmation of the hypothesis of exogenous, event-related depression. Neuropsychological tests were inconclusive, yet were revealing in being inconsistent with simple depression (e.g., psychomotor speed was normal). Finally, extended family involvement and close observation revealed marked anxiety reaction in that the patient finally admitted she knew she was failing in her "mental powers." Alzheimer's disease was diagnosed eventually and appropriate treatment for anxiety initiated. The holes in the initial data were more important than the more abundant parts that did, indeed, fit together.

This, then, is a brief example of the use and place of tests in assessment. A major value in using tests lies on either side of their actual application (refer to Figure 1). The assessment scope must be evaluated continuously as the testing and analysis progress. Similarly, the analysis process will refine the selection of test procedures so that eventually the synthesis—the pulling together of all the information consistent with presenting problems—is reached. Then communication of findings can take place and treatment recommended or initiated.

Clinical psychology has long sought better and clearer formulations and procedures. The process just described is essentially a clinical form using as much scientific, objective basis as possible. The value therein is to assist the clinician in avoiding premature or biased conclusions. (In fact, it is inappropriate to use the term "conclusion"; what is desired is a synthesis—of all the data—not merely a conclusion that arbitrarily can exclude some data.) Clinicians should strive not only to perfect the assessment process by understanding more clearly the problem areas and dynamics, but also to re-refine the tools used to discover the clinical knowledge.

THE FUTURE OF TESTING

There are four areas of knowledge that bear on future developments in testing. First, and already discussed abundantly, is the matter of foundations. Clinicians who give psychological tests successfully do not rely on any approach exclusively. Signs, normative comparisons, patterns of strengths and weaknesses (cognitive and psychosocial), actuarial category predictions, and other techniques are used concurrently. Tests that rely on a narrow interpretation or unitary score and do not allow the clinician to "move around" in the data produced by the test (quantitatively or qualitatively) are not recommended or are used secondarily.

A second, re-emerging area is the sophistication of psychometrics. The use of derived scores, time series analyses in repeated measures, discriminant function analyses, and continuous norms allow the clinician greater opportunity to quantify previously qualified information; hence, rather than reducing its potential, this increases the information's reliability and lends it to empirical investigation.

Embretson's (1985) text reflects another advance in the future of testing. Many of its concepts are included in current research in computer-administered neuropsychological testing (Swiercinsky, 1983b). In one research test battery, for example, a series of nine short tests yields 84 score forms, many of which simply could not be obtained without the benefit of a computer, yet would have been derived as impressions only when administered "by hand." This is not computer-aided testing, this is computer-enhanced testing. McSweeny and Swiercinsky (1985) have demonstrated the potential for many computer-produced scores for understanding neurofunctional behaviors and for drawing inferences about the neurofunctional operation and status of the brain. Use of a mechanical finger tapper (from the Halstead-Reitan Neuropsychological Test Battery) and a stopwatch was once the only way to get average finger tapping speed on the right and left hands, and was obtained crudely at that. Computer-enhanced finger tapping allows precise counting of number of taps in exactly delimited 10-second trials, but such application also allows intertap latencies to be measured in milliseconds. Arrays of these values can then generate average intertap latency, deviations and statistics regarding normal distribution of those latencies, and time trends (series analyses). These values are determined for each tapping trial for each hand. Measures may then be calculated to indicate motor smoothness, fatigue, and subtle apraxia. Whereas mechanical finger tapping yields an average tapping speed for each hand, computer-enhanced tapping test yields 22 derived scores.

Finally, a growing trend in assessment is to make it intervention-based rather than status-descriptive. Tests can be used as an integral part of psychotherapy, for unveiling progressively identified areas of concern and for structuring feedback for clients. This technique is used frequently in working with families. Other applications involve serial testing, which not only evolves to clarify assessment understanding for the clinician, but provides feedback for clients regarding their changes over the course of therapy. Tests selected for this application are specific to the problems being addressed as opposed to the global tests with which most assessors start.

No clinician is sufficiently skilled or immune from bias and misperception to ply the diagnostic craft without the tools. Nor are the clinician's mind and memory capable, in one look, of capturing the complexities of human adjustment, compartmentalizing its multifaceted aspects, and knowing the changes that must be sought to improve that adjustment. Juggling and appreciating the individual's idiosyncratic nuances while respecting the nomothetic boundaries of acceptable adjustment is not easy—which is why most of us spend years in graduate school attempting this understanding.

There is an excitement in the blend of clinical art and science. Psychological assessment and the use of tests represent such an excitement re-emerging.

REFERENCES

Embretson, S. E. (1985). *Test design: Developments in psychology and psychometrics.* New York: Academic Press.

Goldstein, G., & Hersen, M. (Eds.). (1984). *Handbook of psychological assessment.* New York: Pergamon Press.

Gorsuch, R. L. (1983, August). *Continuous norming: Estimation of test statistics for norming purposes.* Paper presented at the annual meeting of the American Psychological Association, Anaheim, CA.

McSweeny, A. J., & Swiercinsky, D. P. (1985). *Computer-based neuropsychological test administration: Convergent and discriminant validity of the SAINT.* Unpublished manuscript.

Swiercinsky, D. (1983a, August). *A computer-patient system for neuropsychological assessment.* Paper presented at the annual meeting of the American Psychological Association, Anaheim, CA.

Swiercinsky, D. (1983b). *SAINT-II: System for the administration and interpretation of neuropsychological tests (user's manual).* Minneapolis: National Computer Systems.

Weaver, S. J. (Ed.). (1984). *Testing children: A reference guide for effective clinical and psychoeducational assessments.* Kansas City, MO: Test Corporation.

2

Differential Diagnosis of Anxiety and Depression

THOMAS REILLY, PH.D.

Controversy has arisen over whether anxiety and depression are different aspects of the same state, on the same continuum, or mutually exclusive states. Evidence that monoamines may be involved in both anxiety and depression has led to a unitary conception of affective disorders and in part to the notion of a masked depression in those patients who are anxious but lack clear evidence of being depressed. In outpatient settings, it is reported that the commonest form of affective disorder is the anxiety-depressed patient, and a high percentage of prescriptions are written for such patients (Roth & Mountjoy, 1982).

This chapter adopts the following working assumptions: 1) anxiety and depression are distinct affective states; 2) they can occur conjointly, sequentially, or separately; and 3) each state can be manifested somatically, cognitively, and in psychomotor activity. These assumptions are supported by empirical research (e.g., Izard, 1977).

The importance of making an accurate differential diagnosis stems from the kind of errors that follow from not doing so, such as in a failure to assess suicide risk or to prescribe an appropriate drug. Erroneously prescribed drugs can even aggravate a problem: administering anti-anxiety drugs, such as Valium, to an undiagnosed depressed patient may produce relatively common side effects of drowsiness, fatigue, confusion, and depression (Blum, 1984). Further, different psychotherapeutic interventions can be employed for the anxious patient (e.g., desensitization) versus the depressed patient (e.g., rational restructuring).

An accurate determination of the anxiety-depression issue does not necessarily constitute a diagnosis. Besides the anxiety disorders, the *Diagnostic and Statistical Manual of Mental Disorders* (DSM-III; American Psychiatric Association, 1980) recognizes the possible presence of anxiety in other disorders, such as somatoform disorders, ego-dystonic homosexuality, and adjustment disorders. Similarly, depression is not limited to the affective disorders. Anxiety and depression may constitute the diagnosis, be a component of the diagnosis, or be a part of the patient's reaction to his or her disorder.

10

PREDIAGNOSTIC SCREENING

How an assessor proceeds during this phase depends on the kind of setting, the mode of operation within the setting, the referral question, and the reason for the referral. A private practitioner will have to perform most or all of this initial information gathering, while within an institutional setting much might have been done before the patient arrives, such as compiling the medical, personal, and social history. In an institutional setting that tends to refer only the most difficult cases for assessment, there is probably perplexity or disagreement among the staff. The referral question(s) and the reason for referral are not always synonymous. The reason for the referral may be institutional policy, cautiousness, or diagnostic clarification. The referral question must be appropriate (e.g., presence/absence, severity, etiology, dynamic and interpersonal aspects, treatment implications, etc.), and consultation with the referral source may be in order to achieve this. Of course, the assessor can formulate appropriate assessment questions.

Prior to the administration of the tests, information must be collected regarding the patient's physical emotional, educational, occupational, and social functioning. Such data, considered as a whole, suggest probable diagnostic hypotheses and assist in the selection of the procedures employed. Thus, for instance, life changes that could indicate a perceived loss, especially if they correlate temporally with onset of symptoms, would tend to favor the presence of depression. Similarly, changes that imply a perceived anticipated threat or danger would tend to favor the probability of anxiety. The following sections indicate the kinds of information that should be collected and their possible diagnostic implications.

Physical

Physical changes resulting from illness, injury, or surgery that could involve a loss to or impairment of the body can trigger a depressive reaction. The appropriate baseline is the patient's subjective framework that defines a loss, and this may not correspond to a normative framework. Paradoxically, increased functioning also may be defined subjectively as a loss; for example, normal growth can be perceived as a loss by someone who does not want to accept normal adult responsibilities.

In the case of depression, the patient's construction of past events is of interest to the assessor. With regard to anxiety, the assessor is interested in the patient's anticipation of some event as a threat, however fanciful it might appear to others. Even what would be perceived ordinarily as desirable might be perceived as threatening; for example, a married man who learns he really does not have heart problems might be threatened by an expectation of increased sexual demands from his wife.

Finally, the clinician should obtain information about past or present medical treatments that could influence the patient's test results, such as medications or electroconvulsive therapy (ECT). Some research suggests residual and possibly permanent memory loss after ECT, and confusion may be a side effect of some drugs.

Emotional-Social

Information regarding the patient's social and emotional behavior, including time specifications of any changes, should be gathered both from the patient and from his or her relatives. In some cases, however, the patient and relatives will find it easier to report somatic symptoms. This is useful information, because different kinds of symptoms tend to occur with anxiety and depression. Tachycardia, flushing, increased blood pressure, sweating (including nocturnal), sighing, urinary frequency, trembling, and sudden attacks of diarrhea are suggestive of anxiety. Depression can be indicated by sleep disturbances (delayed onset, shallowness), boredom, loss of appetite, low energy, decreased libido, and weight loss.

Information about previous occurrences of such symptoms or clearly reported earlier anxiety or depression is relevant to the assessment of the patient's proneness toward depression or anxiety. In summary, the major affective state expected in the case of anxiety is fear, whether owned or disowned, specifiable or unspecifiable. In the case of depression, the major affective reactions involve sadness, guilt, unworthiness, and passivity, apathy, and/or withdrawal.

Educational-Occupational

For the client still in school, information should be gathered about past events perceivable as failures or disappointments and about anticipated events that could signify a threat. For those no longer in school, comparable data about occupational history and aspirations are collected.

In the prediagnostic screening, unless the results of previous IQ testing are available, one must revert to inferences about the patient's intellectual functioning based on data obtained in other areas, such as educational and occupational. If either anxiety or depression is present, diminished problem solving is expected and the magnitude of the decrement would index the severity of disruptive effects.

SELECTION OF TESTS AND PROCEDURES

In general, the kinds of data one needs to make the differential diagnosis relate to the patient's mood, cognitions, and psychomotor activity. The traditionally most common procedures ordinarily should suffice in this regard: clinical interview, Wechsler Adult Intelligence Scale-Revised (WAIS-R), Thematic Apperception Test (TAT), and Rorschach. These conventional procedures are those a clinical psychologist is expected to know, are most commonly in use (Piotrowski, Sherry, & Keller, 1985), and are comprehensive enough to permit a personality description.

If one merely wishes a screening measure of depression, the Beck Depression Inventory is appropriate. Mayer (1978) reviews a number of inventories, adjective checklists, interviewer rating scales, and behavioral techniques for assessing depression, but many of these measures are used primarily in research, not clinical practice, and some are of doubtful utility in differential diagnosis. For example, the Anxiety score on the Multiple Affect Adjective Check List correlates about .68 with clinical ratings of anxiety and .72 with clinical ratings of depression, and the Depression score correlates about .41 with clinical ratings of depression and about .34 with clinical ratings of anxiety. The Millon Clinical Multiaxial Inventory (MCMI) offers anxiety and depression scales plus a computerized interpretation and DSM-III diagnosis, but little research beyond Millon's in the original edition has been done to validate the interpretation program and Millon has not added any more in the second edition (Lanyon, 1984; Butcher & Keller, 1984).

A flexible plan is advised and tests can be added or dropped in the administration. For example, if the possibility of suicide arises in testing a depressed patient, it would be wiser to explore in a clinical interview the definiteness of any plan, the availability of means to execute the suicide plan, the lethality of the means, and the probable opportunities to intervene in a clinical interview, than to continue with a test.

A clinical interview should include personal and social history collection if this information is not already available. It is wise to check the patient's report with that provided by friends and relatives and to obtain friends' and relatives' impressions of the patient's behavior. The interview also provides an opportunity to assess suicide risk for a depressed patient and to observe nonverbal behaviors such as gait, posture, facial expressions, activity level, voice quality, restlessness, apathy, tremor, rigidity, and so on which may indicate anxiety or depression.

The WAIS-R offers a means of observing various aspects of the patient's thought processes. Attention or concentration problems can appear in subtest such as Arithmetic and Digit Span, or elsewhere in the form of intrusions into the thought process. Speed or slowness of response may be shown most prominently in the timed subtests, but also can appear elsewhere. The patient's verbal statements may indicate significant mood, cognitions, or themes suggestive of anxiety or depression. At times it will be possible to dispense with the WAIS-R, because it is not likely to be the best means to ascertain the nature of the threat (for anxious patients) or the kind of loss (for depressed patients). Thus, if previously administered procedures have determined the presence of anxiety or depression and the magnitude of their effect on the patient's conscious cognitive operations, the WAIS-R can be dropped.

The TAT may be the most useful test in this battery to collect information on mood and cognitions. One should select a variety of cards that can elicit a variety of emotional responses (positive, neutral, and negative) and contain a variety of human figures. The formal aspects of the stories (e.g., uniqueness of plot, coherence and logic, presence/absence of outcomes, problem-solving methods, past-present-future emphasis, language usage) can suggest the magnitude of experienced anxiety or depression together with the patient's level of ego functioning. The stories themselves may reflect significant material regarding: the patient's view of the world, the self, and/or others; mood; the nature of the threat or the loss; views of the past and future; and feelings of guilt, blame, unworthiness, vulnerability, inadequacy, etc. As such, the TAT may shed the most light on the etiology of anxiety or depression; therefore, the assessor should probe assiduously for completed stories and elaboration of details.

The Rorschach technique can contribute in several ways. The imagery and the patient's verbalizations may indicate moods and themes suggestive of anxiety or depression. Levels of psychomotor activity may appear in slowed reaction time, low productivity, or impoverished content. The degree to which the anxiety or depression is disabling the patient can be judged from the amount of discrepancy between the patient's actual performance and what would be expected given the patient's education, occupation, and so on, as well as by the frequency and degree of inefficiencies in the record (e.g., drop of form level). Personality features that might predispose the patient to be repeatedly anxious or depressed might be detected in the Rorschach. Finally, the potential strengths of the patient that are revealed may suggest prognosis and response to treatment.

At times, other tests can be of use. The Rosenzweig Picture-Frustration Study provides information about superego patterns and whether aggression is directed outwardly, inwardly, or impunitively. Such personality features are relevant to predispositions to depression. The Minnesota Multiphasic Personality Inventory (MMPI) is useful in assessing suicide risk and magnitude of anxiety or depression. The MMPI also can indicate somatization, rigidity, poor self-concept, passive orientation, and unacknowledged or unexpressed anger. It should be noted that the MMPI Depression scale has served as the validating criterion for many self-report measures of depression.

INTERPRETATION AND INTEGRATION OF RESULTS

Watsonian behaviorism espoused a philosophy that a scientific psychology could be built on invariant one-to-one relationships of stimulus and response. Knowing the stimulus, one could predict the response, and knowing the response one could identify the stimulus. This philosphy led to the sign approach to test interpretation; unfortunately, this simple notion is not valid in human responding. Everyday experience illustrates that the same response may arise from different causes—crying for joy, out of frustration, grief, relief, or from great laughter, not to mention from physiological and physical stimulation (dirt in the eye, tear gas, etc.). The early statement of the frustration-aggression hypothesis embodied the Watsonian notion and had to be revised.

The approach to interpretation advocated here is contextual; that is, any one behavior is interpreted within the context of other behaviors. Poverty of content in

TAT stories produced by a 35-year-old English professor does not suggest the same thing as when shown by a 19-year-old high school dropout; accordingly, no list of signs of anxiety and depression is offered. Instead, Table 1 indicates some basic distinguishing characteristics (cognitive, affective, and psychomotor) or anxiety and depression.

Ordinarily, the test stimuli per se are not adequate to cause anxiety or depression, though some TAT cards do tend to pull sad themes. Thus the clinician must attend to both inappropriate overreactions to test stimuli (e.g., a story of destruction in response to a tranquil landscape scene) and the patient's emotional involvement in the reponse. The frequency and intensity of such responding indicate the severity of anxiety or depression present and increase one's certainty in the judgment. How the patient deals with such reactions and his or her degree of success in returning to a more appropriate level of responding (i.e., recovery) indicate coping strategies and their effectiveness: they are aspects of ego strength.

The severity of the disorder is judged as a joint function of the intensity of the affect (anxiety, depression) and the effectiveness of coping. The intensity component can be judged from such factors as the ease and rapidity with which the affect is manifested, its frequency and pervasiveness, and the degree to which it is an overreaction. The effectiveness of coping can be judged from the degree of success the patient attains in performing the assessment task, especially at those points where anxiety or depression is manifested. On the Rorschach, the degree of success would be indicated by formal aspects such as response accuracy and definiteness, percent animal content, percent populars, percent originals of good form level, percent of whole responses, and organization/integration success. Formal aspects would also be used in the TAT, regarding coherence, logical plot development, successful story resolution, etc. In the WAIS-R, one can use quantitative aspects (2

TABLE 1

Characteristics of Anxiety and Depression

	ANXIETY	DEPRESSION
Time orientation	future emphasis	past emphasis (loss) future emphasis (no relief)
Self-cognitions	vulnerable, inadequate	unworthy, defective, guilty
World view	dangerous, hostile	burdensome, uncaring, thwarting, punitive
Affect	fear	sadness, guilt
Arousal	high (tense, restless, vigilant)	low (passivity, apathy, withdrawal)

points versus 1 or 0) and qualitative features such as brevity and accuracy of vocabulary definitions. Schafer (1954) provides an extended discussion of identifying defense mechanisms from Rorschach testing.

The assessor also should attempt to predict whether the condition is apt to recur. The patient's prior history offers the answer in most instances, especially when combined with a knowledge of the precipitating factors and their probable recurrence. Beyond this, however, one should address repetitive anxiety or depression reactions.

In the case of depression, a number of personality factors increase the probability of becoming depressed. Individuals who are markedly passive, especially if combined with an external locus-of-control orientation, are more apt to become depressed in response to events that are not sufficient stimuli for those who are more active or assertive. Other personality dimensions that favor the development of a depression include a marked dependent, succorant orientation to life, intropunitiveness and impunitiveness, and egocentricity.

In the case of anxiety, egocentricity can also be a predisposing factor, though there is a qualitative difference. Egocentricity in the depressed exists in terms of blame for misdeeds, while in anxiety the egocentricity is more apt to have a flavor of inadequacy to deal with a threat. Perfectionistic standards are an excellent means of stimulating anticipatory anxiety. Catastrophic thinking is a common companion to perfectionistic standards, and together they provide fertile grounds for fostering anxiety. Avoidance tendencies, as pointed out in learning theory analyses are reinforcing and self-perpetuating when acted upon: thus, repetitive anxiety reactions are predictable. From an intrapsychic orientation, one could say that because the underlying cause has not been confronted and resolved, recurrence of the reaction is expectable.

The assessor's conclusions regarding the presence of predisposing personality factors and their relative contributions to the development of anxiety or depression will significantly affect any recommendations concerning remediation. Therapeutic interventions that ignore such predisposing factors, when present, are apt to produce only temporary results and conceivably could be regarded as unprofessional.

Because it is all too easy to become rather exclusively pathologically oriented, it is important to remember not to overlook or minimize the patient's assets, which are of particular importance in formulating treatment recommendations. An extensive discussion is not feasible here, but some illustrations are offered. The possession of good abstract-thinking abilities suggest that the patient might be more accessible to verbally oriented modes of psychotherapy. A sense of humor, especially if it is nonhostile and facilitates self-objectification (Allport, 1961), can help the patient to develop new perspectives about him- or herself, the world, and the relative importance of chosen goals. Closely related to this ability would be the ability to perceive the world from another's viewpoint or to take the role of the other, which may help one to correct erroneous interpretations of others' intentions. This ability can be an extremely important means of preventing or detecting one's own projections, and it fosters an interest in reality testing by asking other people why they are doing what they are doing and what purpose they have.

COMMUNICATION OF RESULTS

Communicating to the Patient

What, if anything, should be communicated to the patient is determined by the circumstances under which the assessment occurs. If the assessor will not engage in further contact with the patient, and/or there is an established working relationship with the referring professional, the most appropriate choice may be to channel feedback through the established relationship. If such a relationship does not exist, or if there is a serious suicide threat, or if the assessor could enter into a therapy relationship with the patient, then imparting information directly to the patient would be appropriate.

In any case, the assessor's ultimate goal is to inform and to persuade, otherwise one would not formulate recommendations. Communicating directly with the patient emphasizes an obligation to be understandable and to be helpful. For individuals who are uncertain about what is happening to them (e.g., a patient who does not recognize he is depressed because the symptoms are mostly somatic), an important way to help may be to explain to them what the problem is. Informing a depressed patient that depressions tend to be time limited could offer him or her meaningful new information, perhaps instilling some hope that proves a useful therapeutically. Telling a depressed patient about the probably beneficial effects of actions, and attempting to mobilize him or her, can be extremely useful for current and future purposes.

Similarly, some patients will be unaware that they are anxious, because their symptoms are somatic; thus interpreting these symptoms as manifestations of anxiety can be quite useful. Anxious patients also may benefit from discussing that the anticipated dire effects of certain events might be grossly exaggerated. Helping the patient to examine the presumed catastrophic events can be very beneficial, especially if some suggestions can evolve about what one might do if such events would actually occur. Having a plan of action can be very anxiety diminishing. Discussing how short-term gains can compromise long-term resolution may promote some motivation to abandon short-term avoidance procedures that perpetuate or escalate the issue. Behaviorally oriented explanations of the self-perpetuating effects of avoidance tactics can be of use to some patients.

Communicating with the Family

At least two issues are central to communicating directly with the patient's family: knowledge of the patient's condition and discussion of the reciprocal effects between the patient and the family members. The results should include a statement of the patient's condition and perhaps what has caused it, though how much discussion is wise about precipitating factors depends on the role family members might have played in the development of the condition, and whether there is enough time to deal adequately with any negative reactions on the family's part.

Besides the possible exploration of the effect that family members may have had on the development of the patient's condition, there may be a need to explore the effects that the patient's depression or anxiety is having on the family members, together with effective/ineffective ways of responding to the patient. For example, there is a strong inclination first to try and cheer up a depressed person, and then when this is futile (as it probably will be), to go away, in order to avoid also becoming "down." Similarly, in the desire to help an anxious person, one might end up being under their control, as sometimes happens in agoraphobia.

Communicating with Professionals

Communications directed to other professionals are determined both by one's persuasive intent and by the other's theoretical orientation and sophistication in psychological assessment. The assessor must clearly indicate the probability levels of his or her conclusions in operationally defined terms (i.e., amount and quality of the supporting data). Extensively detailing the evidence for the conclusions may not be useful except to someone who is sophisticated about tests. Sometimes professional responsibility dictates recommending further evaluation, indicating what other kinds of information are needed to reach a more definite conclusion.

Diagnostic conclusions should be included and, if at all possible, the precipitating and maintaining factors should be indicated. These factors must be addressed and taken into account in any treatment recommendations offered. If more than one treatment approach is conceivable, than a rationale should be given for the choice advocated by the assessor.

REFERENCES

Allport, G. (1961). *Pattern and growth in personality.* Boston: Beacon.
American Psychological Association. (1980). *Diagnostic and statistical manual of mental disorders* (3rd ed.). Washington, DC: Author.
Blum, K. (1984). *Handbook of abusable drugs.* New York: Gardner.
Butcher, J. N., & Keller, L. S. (1984). Objective personality assessment. In G. Goldstein & M. Hersen (Eds.), *Handbook of psychological assessment* (pp. 307-331). New York: Pergamon.
Izard, C. (1977). *Human emotions.* New York: Plenum.
Lanyon, R. (1984). Personality assessment. *Annual Review of Psychology, 35,* 667-701.
Mayer, J. M. (1978). Assessment of depression. In P. McReynolds, (Ed.), *Advances in psychological assessment* (pp. 358-425). San Francisco: Jossey-Bass.
Piotrowski, C., Sherry, D., & Keller, J. W. (1985). Psychodiagnostic test usage: A survey of the Society for Personality Assesment. *Journal of Personality Assessment, 49,* 115-119.

Roth, M., & Mountjoy, C. Q. (1982). The distinction between anxiety states and depressive disorders. In E. S. Paykel (Ed.), *Handbook of affective disorders* (pp. 70-92). New York: Guilford.

Schafer, R. (1954). *Psychoanalytic interpretation in Rorschach testing.* New York: Grume & Stratton.

3

Assessment of Borderline Psychopathology

MELVIN BERG, PH.D.

The boundaries of mental illness have been extended vastly as psychological disorders not manifested by clearly defined symptoms nor attributable to bio-chemical deviations have been claimed as part of psychopathology's domain. The entire range of personality disorders has only in recent years come within the reach of mental health practitioners; patients previously regarded as nuisances, criminal menaces, or morally unfit are now the focus of study and therapeutic effort (Berg, 1982).

The use of outpatient services by increasing numbers of individuals with personality disorders has brought to light a variety of psychological difficulties that are severe and yet not of a psychotic degree. These illnesses defy the dichotomous categories of traditional taxonomy, demonstrating that a continuum of disorders spans the gap between the functional psychoses and the neurotic conditions. Also, recent advances in knowledge regarding the biological substrates of the major psychoses (affective illness and schizophrenia) have helped differentiate these conditions from the severe personality disorders, many of which have been desig-nated *borderline psychopathology* due to its midway position between psychosis and neurotic illness.

THE DIAGNOSTIC ISSUES

Since the 1950s a large body of literature has accumulated attempting to define the diverse manifestations of borderline psychopathology, which has been clothed in such numerous labels and diagnostic descriptions that skeptics have even questioned its identity and validity. Charges of diagnostic imposture have been leveled at the borderline concept whereby other more clearly defined pathological entities, such as schizophrenia or affective illness, masquerade their true identity. In the eyes of some, the borderline concept has served as a "wastebasket" category, bereft of content and clear definition. However, the varied abundance of diagnostic nomen-clature and description constitutes a convergent validation of the concept of borderline illness, for in fact the commonality among numerous clinical observers far outweighs the discrepancies implied by an overly meticulous attention to nonessential detail. Although borderline psychopathology can be manifested through a broad range of surface traits, an underlying unity emerges from the jumble, highlighting the validity and usefulness of this concept.

The Definition of Borderline Illness

Currently, borderline illness is designated by two overlapping definitions. The more narrow and concretely anchored category defined by the *Diagnostic and Statistical Manual of Mental Disorders* (DSM-III; American Psychiatric Association, 1980) refers to Borderline Personality Disorder and is manifested by eight clearly bounded symptoms: 1) impulsivity, 2) chaotic interpersonal relationships, 3) expressions of intense anger, 4) identity diffusion, 5) affective instability, 6) fear of intimacy, 7) propensity for self-destructive behavior, and 8) chronic feelings of emptiness and dissatisfaction. Alternatively, borderline is regarded as a level of *personality organization* or a *spectrum of several personality disorders* occupying the broad borderland between psychotic and neurotic conditions (Kernberg, 1976). From this perspective borderline illness can be manifested in a variety of apparently different personalities—infantile, antisocial, impulse ridden, narcissistic, paranoid, schizoid, inadequate, and hypomanic—in addition to the core borderline personality disorder described in DSM-III. However, the differences in surface traits conceal the underlying similarities that typify borderline illness: 1) impaired impulse control, 2) intolerance for anxiety, 3) limited capacity for productive work, 4) identity diffusion, 5) vulnerability to intermittant lapses in thought organization, and 6) failure to integrate highly discrepant aspects of the personality. This chapter focuses on the broader definition of borderline illness in order to illuminate its various forms. This conceptualization remains within the bounds of DSM-III guidelines, which acknowledges the many facets of the illness by permitting the diagnosis of borderline personality disorder to be combined with other personality disorders. The conceptual framework and clinical signs of borderline illness are surveyed by Kernberg (1976), Hartocollis (1980), and Stone (1980).

Typical Diagnostic Questions

Several diagnostic issues generally arise in the assessment of borderline patients. First, severely disturbed and disorganized borderline individuals are often referred for testing in order to establish whether they suffer from a psychotic illness. Generally, these patients demonstrate considerable disorder in most spheres of functioning; their interpersonal relationships are chaotic and productive accomplishments limited. Although such widely affected functioning suggests an illness of psychotic proportions, these borderline patients can also maintain islands of strength, including a capacity for vigorous involvement with others, as well as moorings to reality that generally preserve thought organization. The determination of whether the patient's illness falls within the borderline or psychotic range has a bearing on prognosis, need for medication, and potential for further regressive developments. The diagnostic task, beyond merely labeling the illness, must attempt to define the pattern of the patient's adaptive strengths and weaknesses to help prescribe a treatment strategy. A thorough evaluation based on testing can clarify whether the patient's psychological resources could sustain a reconstructive, therapeutic effort or one steering toward adjustment to the illness and the provision of support.

Higher functioning borderline individuals are often referred for testing when, in the course of diagnostic interviewing, strengths in the academic, vocational, or interpersonal spheres sharply contrast with subtle indications of ego weaknesses, such as odd beliefs, slips in thought organization, or lapses in judgment. These borderline individuals often instill a mild anxiety and unease in the clinician, who is perplexed and unable to determine the significance of the faint cracks in ego functioning. In other instances, interviewers may be puzzled by grossly discrepant aspects of the patient's personality, such as episodes of sexual promiscuity or drug abuse in an otherwise inhibited and moralistic individual, which hinder a consistent diagnostic formulation.

A third variety of assessment request arises when the referral source is unable to identify, express, or conceptualize clearly the nature of his or her concern regarding the patient, and consequently presents a vague, ambiguous, or even trite referral issue. Referrals that request mere taxonomic classification, measures of intelligence, or general descriptions of the patient's personality are frequently of this order and may be the product of the referring agent's anxiety in the face of a difficult clinical predicament with a borderline patient. Indeed, the affectively charged impact of these patients can interfere with the clear formulation of diagnostic questions. In such instances, the psychologist must help the referral source to articulate the underlying concern that provoked the testing request in the first place and thus reveal the important diagnostic issues. The examiner can serve then as a consultant who assists in a survey of the entire clinical situation, to shape the diagnostic questions and even evaluate whether testing is the proper course of action.

The assessment results should designate the nature and source of the patient's illness and its similarity to and differences from the typical clinical picture. Furthermore, in the course of elucidating the specific diagnostic issues, identified and established as the guiding frame of the assessment, the examiner attempts to construct a psychological model depicting the organizing principles and policies that structure the patient's life. This model then serves as the basis of the report, which will facilitate informed treatment decisions, including the circumstances under which treatment is most likely to be helpful. The model should render the previously perplexing discrepancies of borderline functioning predictable and even empathically comprehensible.

Diagnostic and Testing Procedures

The identification of borderline psychopathology and the elucidation of the organizing characteristics of the patient's functioning can be accomplished most confidently through the use of individually administered tests. The standard battery suggested here provides an overview of a wide range of functions, which must be evaluated in order to distinguish borderline illness and its idiosyncratic manifestation in the individual patient. Although symptom checklists have been developed that discriminate borderline individuals with a high level of reliability, these are best suited for research purposes because they do not provide data affording an individualized diagnostic picture. Despite the standardized procedures prescribed for each of these instruments, the literature on psychodiagnostic assessment has broadened the parameters of their use, such that through "testing the limits" the flexibility and diagnostic power of these instruments can be expanded geometrically (Berg, 1984). This flexibility is a boon in the assessment of borderline individuals, who typically confront the diagnostician with bewildering clinical riddles. Moreover, the precarious defensive equilibrium of these patients also necessitates examiner flexibility and willingness to offer a variety of supportive interventions to help them persist and complete the testing. Subsequently, the tests' standard administration must often be tailored to fit the individual's intolerance of stress, providing encouragement, advice, confrontation, or even recesses from the testing procedure to allow pressures to subside.

To some extent these instruments provide overlapping information. Their redundancy permits the examination of specific areas of functioning from various perspectives. Consequently, the inferences derived from these techniques can achieve a high level of validity when their findings converge toward the same conclusions.

Wechsler Adult Intelligence Scale (WAIS)

In borderline illness cognitive functions and reality testing remain largely intact, particularly in circumstances that lend themselves to objective problem solving and offer guidelines for conventional responses. The WAIS yields data demonstrating the patient's ability to adhere to logical and consensually accepted modes of thought, free from disruptions by idiosyncratic fantasies, emotional stirrings, or drive pressures. As has been noted often in the literature (Sugarman, 1980), borderline patients are able to manage the WAIS tasks in a relatively efficient manner in comparison to the gross disorganization noted in psychotic conditions. The preservation of functioning on the WAIS when coupled with indications of psychosis on the Rorschach is highly suggestive of borderline illness. Low functioning borderline individuals may temporarily lapse into fractured logic and loosely integrated thoughts on the WAIS; however, as distinct from psychotic conditions, these falterings are brief and usually recognized by the patient.

In addition to surveying the patient's capacity for efficient use of primary cognitive functions, the WAIS elicits other information that bears on treatment planning for the borderline patient. First, demonstrations of how affective arousal influences cognitive operations can reveal the extent to which the patient will require supportive treatment to prevent ill-controlled emotional storms or spurts of dangerous action. For example, dramatic displays of frustration or other affects accompanying inefficient test performance may point toward the disorganizing impact of emotional arousal. Second, the pattern of weakness and strength on the subtests can contribute toward an assessment of the patient's preferred cognitive style and defensive strategy, both of which are major coordinates of personality organization. For example, superior perceptual-motor performance relative to verbal operations is part of the personality configuration of action-prone individuals deficient in ideational controls and capacity for self-reflection. Such patients are apt to reject a highly expressive, uncovering form of treatment and may require external support to help them inhibit impulsive action during treatment. Finally, WAIS data can serve as an initial step in identifying minimal brain dysfunction, a frequent concomitant of borderline illness (Bellak, 1970), which can circumscribe prognostic expectations.

Rorschach Psychodiagnostic Test

The Rorschach complements the WAIS by enabling an evaluation of how cognitive functions and thought organization stand up under the pressure of affective arousal and when external structure is not available. In contrast to the WAIS, wherein the borderline patient can adhere to the structure of tasks requiring objective cognitive operations, in the course of the Rorschach the cognitive apparatus is not protected, by concrete task guidelines, from the buffeting of affective pressure. As external supports are withdrawn, the borderline patient's vulnerability to disorganized thought, affect-laden and fantasy-dominated ideas, and primitive defensive maneuvers come to the fore. Although the extent of thought disorder, fantasy intrusion, and affective discontrol approach that of psychotic patients, the moorings to reality remain relatively firm and serve as a crucial diagnostic boundary marker between borderline illness and psychosis.

Thematic Apperception Test (TAT)

The demands of the TAT generally do not tax the borderline patient's ability to maintain reality attunement and logical thought organization. Nevertheless, the TAT can strike a lode of data concerning the borderline patient's dynamic underground of wishes and fears that generate and guide their behavior. In addition, the cognitive schemata used to organize the perception and experience of self and others are dramatically illustrated by TAT productions.

INTERPRETATION AND INTEGRATION OF TEST DATA

The identification of borderline psychopathology through testing cannot be accomplished through the application of a simple linear formula. There is not an individual test sign that inevitably indicates borderline illness. Moreover, it is important to recognize that borderline pathology encompasses a *range* of illness between neurotic and psychotic conditions and that the boundaries at both ends of the continuum are vague. Thus, some low functioning borderline individuals are difficult to distinguish from psychotic patients; others, who are much less disturbed, approach the neurotic range of pathology. However, a gestalt of data patterns emerges that typically characterizes borderline individuals and highlights aspects of their functioning generally not discerned during interviews.

Ego Functioning

The ego functions, or coping mechanisms by which internal wishes, needs, and drives are controlled, channeled, and negotiated with the environment toward maintaining an adaptational equilibrium, are strikingly inconsistent in those who present borderline illness. It is this variability of ego functioning, hovering between a neurotic level of adjustment at one moment and abrupt lapses into psychotic disorganization at the next, that led to the apt description of "stable instability" (Schmideberg, 1959). Most facets of the borderline individual's coping mechanisms, including intellectual functioning, thought organization, reality testing, and defense mechanisms, are impaired to some extent and vary erratically as to the extent of their impairment. The quality of ego functioning in these areas is described below.

The severity of the patient's disturbance and its proximity to the psychotic level of illness can be gauged on psychological testing through an assessment of the extent of ruptures in ego functioning. The gravity of these breakdowns in ego functioning is determined by three criteria. First, the degree and frequency with which reality and logic are violated indicate the magnitude of ego dysfunction. The prevalence of strange ideas and impaired reasoning indicates severe illness. Second, the capacity to monitor and correct cognitive slippage points toward a resiliency and strength that distinguish borderline illness from psychosis. In this regard the patient's attitude toward the cognitive lapses and his or her capacity to become concerned about them ameliorates their otherwise foreboding significance. For example, a borderline patient may describe an odd Rorschach percept of a "Creature which is half man and, uh, half butterfly," and then qualify his percept by stating "I know it seems crazy and impossible." In contrast, a psychotic patient typically would fail to recognize and acknowledge the strange content of his thought. Third, ego failures resulting from the stressful impact of affective arousal distinguish the borderline level of illness from that of chronic psychotic conditions, in which ego failures occur even without the impingement of stress. The range of failures in ego functioning manifested on psychological testing is well described by Weiner (1966).

Intellectual operations: The performance of borderline patients on the WAIS generally does not reveal *gross* deficiencies. However, close scrutiny of the WAIS protocol, especially when the patient's verbalizations are recorded verbatim, reveals subtle though suggestive cognitive lapses in most borderline individuals. For example, a borderline man with paranoid features defined "matchless" as "no competition, nobody to *beat on you,*" revealing his violent preoccupations. Likewise, a dependent and infantile borderline woman defined "cushion" as "a soft pad to sit on," and then added as an aside "it comforts you." This syntactical error is suggestive of her vulnerability to disorganize when pressured by infantile longings. Performance across subtests is mildly to moderately erratic, reflecting either the disruptive impact of anxiety on various functions or an irregularity in maturation whereby specific skills failed to achieve adequate development. Moreover, performance varies within subtests as easy items are missed and more difficult ones passed, due to the sudden incursion of disturbing affects.

Except in those borderline individuals with an obsessive character structure, instances of impulsive behavior and thought commonly result from intolerance of the stress of struggling with the WAIS tasks. On the performance subtests, particularly Block Design and Object Assembly, the increasing difficulty of the tasks elicits haphazard, trial-and-error efforts, which are peppered with noticeable displays of impatience and frustration. This vulnerability to slide toward arbitrary problem solving is often noted on the Arithmetic subtest, especially when patients are asked to reveal the manner by which they arrived at an incorrect response. Similarly, on other verbal subtests subtle deviations from logical thought can become evident when the patient is asked to clarify vague or unusual verbalizations. Detection of such lapses relies on the clinician's sensitive inquiry into responses hinting at underlying disorder. Finally, the insufficient insulation of intellectual functions from the intrusion of affect can be observed in the connotations of the borderline patient's language, which is often too highly colored by personal concerns although remaining within the bounds of appropriate usage. For example, borderline individuals consumed with anger use language heavily spiced with metaphor advertising their internal turmoil. Thus, an explosive borderline individual defined "terminate" as "to murder, or kill someone, say for revenge."

Some of the impairments in intellectual functioning of borderline patients are also suggestive of organic cerebral dysfunction: arbitrary and haphazard reasoning, vulnerability to frustration, and disrupted concentration. However, borderline patients do not present other features typical of organic dysfunction: concreteness, perplexity, perceptual failures, psychomotor retardation, constriction, inflexibility, and oversimplification. Furthermore, organic patients generally present difficulties in memory and learning ability, which is not characteristic of borderline illness.

Thought organization: The minor lapses in the efficiency of intellectual functioning manifested on the WAIS expand into more flagrant demonstrations of disordered thought on the Rorschach. Instances of illogical combination and fabulized combination abound, as well as indications of autistic logic such as explaining a Rorschach percept looks like "female genitals because it's in the *middle of the blot, like the midsection.*" However, contaminations are rare and generally bode a schizophrenic illness. During the Rorschach inquiry especially, awkward word usage and mild misusage are common indicators of the borderline patient's liberal contortions of thought. Often, the borderline individual trips precipitously into a bog of loosely organized ideas during the inquiry when affect-laden concerns are touched on. In contrast, the TAT performance usually remains clear of serious failures in thought organization, although word misusage and subtle inconsistencies within the narrative are common.

Reality testing: The reality testing of borderline individuals remains largely intact. Rorschach form level hovers just below the average range and usually does not approach that which is typical of psychotic conditions. Nevertheless, the Rorschach is replete with formally weak responses, though not of grossly poor form level, suggesting a drift toward fantasy-dominated perception and impaired judgment. Instances of weak form level interspersed with many responses of acceptable and even highly articulated percepts attest to the near-psychotic deviations from reality to which these individuals are intermittently vulnerable. Even when Rorschach form level does not reveal distorted perceptions, the borderline individual is prone to overembellish responses with fantastic interpretations and inferences that the blot cannot possibly support. Percepts then become endowed with richly elaborated motives and narrations of action tending toward the incredible. For example, a borderline patient described the popular bat on Card V as "hungry looking, mean and straining in his flight to catch food. He doesn't get the insect."

Defensive structure: The borderline patient's defenses, or means by which unacceptable wishes and ideas are blocked from awareness, controlled, and integrated into the overall identity, are a patchwork of faltering and inconsistent maneuvers, leaving these individuals churning in a state of continuous upheaval. Immature and unreliable defensive operations predispose the individual to the earlier mentioned ruptures in thought organization, reality testing, and affect control. The sudden defensive shifts, collapses, and equally surprising moves toward reconstitution contribute to the stable pattern of instability, which can endure for a lifetime without deteriorating into psychotic fragmentation. For example, during the Rorschach, a patient flared up in irritation at the examiner, then calmed down and denied he had even been angry, saw an "atomic bomb blast" on Card IX, and at the end of the test described feeling depressed and inexplicably angry with himself, as though his anger were now being directed inward, the examiner surmised. Thus this patient in the course of a few minutes desperately attempted a series of defensive maneuvers to control his anger. Individuals within the borderline range vary with regard to their preferred defensive style, whether it be primarily paranoid, hysterical, or manic, yet all share a reliance on several particular defensive maneuvers.

Borderline psychopathology is predominantly characterized by the defensive measure of *splitting,* which theoretically results when the capacity to block, or repress, unacceptable ideas from awareness is developed inadequately (Kernberg, 1976). This presumed failure of repression gives rise to the coexistence of grossly discrepant wishes, attitudes, emotions, and perceptions of self and others, which can be readily observed in test data. Consequently, these polarized attitudes are "split off" from one another, maintain independent existence, and become dominant in an alternating manner. For example, rather than loving and angry feelings being tempered by each other and resolving into a realistic, continuous, and stable emotional amalgam, the borderline individual may shift between extremes of feeling such as adoration and hate. As the destructive feelings cannot be repressed, they are allowed into awareness, and the borderline individual attempts to neutralize or defend against them by suddenly shifting to emphasizing his or her loving feelings. The patient then flipflops in an inconsistent manner from one attitude and feeling to another. The whirl of conflicting attitudes contributes to the unstable adaptation of the borderline individual and the inconsistencies observed in the test data. Contradictory attitudes toward society and social convention are expressed in the Comprehension subtest of the WAIS. Rorschach percepts depicting polarized and extreme qualities, such as "devils" and "angels," follow each other in quick succession or are combined into illogical fabulized combinations such as "a devil with wings like an angel," where opposing values do not neutralize each other but exist side by side. Similarly, the TAT stories depict these needs, attitudes, and feeling states, as well as characters whose behavior is internally inconsistent.

In order to preserve equilibrium amid conflicting affect states, borderline individuals are prone toward massive obliteration of sectors of internal experience and external reality. As a result, facts that are disturbing are defensively obliterated or *denied.* The use of such denial may generate spasms of global constriction indicated by rejection of Rorschach and TAT cards or by failure to mention the use of a Rorschach determinant, such as color, when clearly it must have contributed toward the formation of a percept such as "fire" or "blood." Further violations of reality are suggested when percepts clearly emanating from negative affects of fear, depression, or loss are followed by percepts apparently contrived in order to deny the negative affect by means of their effusive optimism, such as "a glorious sunset." A readiness to deny external reality is indicated by gross disregard for the configuration of the inkblots, as in instances when the boundaries of percepts are arbitrarily drawn through the white space on the Rorschach cards. A cavalier attitude toward card configuration, whereby the patient freely ignores obvious aspects of the blot, suggests a willingness to deny major facets of reality.

Borderline individuals rely heavily on *projection* as unacceptable aspects of the self are disowned and attributed to others. In particular, aggressive impulses and moralistic self-accusations are externalized onto others. These paranoid maneuvers result in suspiciousness of the examiner's intent and an intense preoccupation with anticipations of criticism. The Rorschach and TAT productions are often inundated with depictions of malevolence, which attest to the borderline individual's experience of the environment as threatening. The potential for brief psychotic distortions of a paranoid nature frequently is revealed by ominous Rorschach representations of aggression aimed directly at the patient, as in the percept "a large monster who is coming at *me.*" In contrast to schizophrenics, the distortion of reality in such paranoid percepts of borderline patients is less severe and compelling.

Organization of Affect

The borderline patient's regulation of affect, impulse, and all motivational promptings is characterized by a primitive level of organization reminiscent of early childhood. Affective controls are generally coarse, inconsistent, and liable to slip and fail, whereby thought becomes temporarily obliterated by gales of emotional discharge.

Lability: Affective instability is manifested most obviously in overt behavior during the testing process as moods and feelings switch, often with little warning and after minor provocation. Shifting flurries of affect are reflected in the content of projective productions, which depict moods, attitudes, and feelings changing in a jarring and discontinuous manner. The formal correlates of this process are evident in Rorschach responses combining the usage of chromatic and achromatic tones. Certain WAIS Comprehension subtest items show that common sense and practical adaptive behaviors can give way to surges of feeling. The roller-coasterlike affective changes of these patients generally stir a sense of anticipation in the examiner, who is at a loss to know what to expect next.

Diffuse and intense discharge: Borderline psychopathology is marked by irregular and coarse affect modulation contributing toward diffuse and highly charged affect states. Ideational controls and considerations for logic, reality constraints, and the experience of others pale in the face of emotional arousal. Subsequently, the use of language throughout the testing is electrified by connotations and metaphors bristling with affective energy. On the Rorschach, color-dominated responses abound, or where form predominates, the level of perceptual accuracy deteriorates. Frequently color is avoided altogether except for color references, which are telltale traces of failure to bring ideational control to emotional arousal. Even in borderline individuals with obsessive, schizoid, or paranoid features, the affective controls are brittle, with inhibitory constraints intermittently giving way to sweeps of intense and ill-controlled emotion. This quality of diffuse, overpowering emotion is apt to typify the characters described in TAT stories. Likewise, human and animal percepts on the Rorschach are often enlivened with intense, emotional qualities. These peremptory affective promptings are frequently dramatized in the testing interaction itself as the patient displays swells of feeling that in turn trigger complementary reactions within the examiner, who is apt to feel drained or unnerved after such examinations.

Action potential: Borderline individuals often dissipate affective arousal by resorting to action, both to discharge tension and to avoid conscious awareness of inner stirrings that they can neither tolerate nor suspend. Their language is marked by action metaphors, and those who are not ideationally inclined usually demonstrate a concrete style of verbalization deficient in abstraction and elaborate conceptualization. However, this concreteness is not due to a deficit in the capacity for abstract thought, but an impulsive manner of conceptualization that simply bypasses higher level concepts requiring greater deliberation. Borderline individuals who manifest hysteroid, infantile, narcissistic, and antisocial features tend to excel on the WAIS performance subtests in contrast to their verbal functioning. Those skills requiring a readiness for action are more highly developed than verbally mediated thought, which requires a greater capacity for delay, impulse inhibition, and concentration on internal cognitive operations. WAIS response times are clipped as are those on the Rorschach, where movement responses portray vigorous activity, all of which point toward a potential for impulsive action. During the examination these individuals display a variety of extraneous nervous behaviors, showing the manner in which affective arousal overflows into impulsive motor discharge.

Primitive drive representations: Both sexual and aggressive drives in borderline individuals are marked by an arrest at infantile levels of development. Subsequently, oral, anal, and phallic-exhibitionistic wishes dominate those aimed at genital union, mutuality, and intimacy, as illustrated by Rorschach imagery and the behavior of TAT characters. In some instances the test material makes direct reference to perverse interests that permeate the sexual orientation of these individuals. Second, borderline aggression is untempered by social attachments and concern for others, giving rise to content representing raw forms of destructiveness. Rorschach records typically include responses depicting blood, explosions, or physical damage, and TAT stories describe violent behavior perpetrated without remorse. Third, sexual and aggressive wishes combine in odd or repulsive ways, as in TAT stories about rape, whereby a clear distinction between the two components is blurred. Fourth, a preoccupation with either sexual or aggressive themes on the Rorschach or TAT suggests the failure of these individuals to develop mature channels of expression that would transform these motives into productive aims.

Perception of Self and Others

The manner in which the self and other people are perceived and represented determines an individual's style of interpersonal relatedness. Social perceptions are organized by cognitive schemata, which serve as the road maps for interpersonal behavior. The borderline patient's experience of self and others manifests particular formal and substantive qualities that are shaped by the ego functions previously described and are readily observed in psychological test data.

Formal qualities of perceptions of self and others: In contrast to schizophrenic individuals, the borderline patient's investment in human relationships is made evident by a high percentage of human responses on the Rorschach. However, Hd responses greatly predominate over H due to an inability to perceive others as whole individuals. The borderline patient's propensity for percepts of hands, eyes, breasts, and various other body parts reflects a mode of relating to others that values isolated aspects of the other individual insofar as they provide egocentric gratification. Other people are not perceived as separate and whole individuals, made up of complex qualities and inner experience, with their own intrinsic value. Second, human representations on the Rorschach display contradictory qualities, due to the failure to achieve a smooth integration and consistency within the self-concept and the experience of others. Similarly, TAT characters portray this fragmentation and internal discontinuity. Third, the human percepts of the borderline patient are often based on weak form level, pointing to an impaired capacity for empathy with and objective perception of others. Fourth, representations of humans on both the Rorschach and the TAT are typically one-dimensional, appearing as caricatures composed of exaggerated qualities. These polarized representations suggest the idealizing and devaluing stance toward self and others, who are experienced without ambivalence as either all good or all bad. The tendency to experience self and others in these extreme terms can be enacted during the testing as the patient assumes grandiose or degraded postures vis-à-vis the examiner.

Content of human representations: The qualities attributed to human representations and the themes guiding interpersonal relationships in the test data illustrate the motivational forces shaping the patient's life, including the predominant wishes, needs, and fears. Borderline psychopathology is marked by a specific constellation of motivational concerns, which are abundantly manifested in test data. First, the pervading presence of anger as the primary affect is revealed by the proliferation of images of destruction and themes of aggression. Second, the anger of these individuals generally is derived from frustrated longings for infantile dependency. Consequently, the content of test productions reflects an absorption with oral gratification and yearning for caretaking and protection, which takes for granted the needs and autonomy of others. Accordingly, the Rorschach protocol often displays percepts illustrating symbiotic relationships, such as a "flea sucking an animal of some sort" or a fusion of two individuals as in "Siamese twins." Related to these images of mutual dependency are those denoting incipient forms of life, such as "a fetus," which reveal the patient's helplessness. Third, preoccupations with abandonment contribute toward images of deprivation on the Rorschach and themes of loss on the TAT, revealing the depressive experience at the heart of borderline illness. Fourth, the environment is experienced and depicted as inhospitable and perilous due to the externalization of aggressive impulses. Finally, test productions often reflect sexual preoccupations, with frequent percepts of sexual organs on the Rorschach and tales of promiscuous involvement on the TAT. The abundance of sexual ideation is generated by an infantile hunger for relatedness that masquerades as a facsimile of a more mature interest in genital sexuality and mutual interpersonal attachment. This infantile form of relatedness focuses on exploiting the other as a source of gratification rather than regarding the other as inherently valuable in his or her own right.

THE FEEDBACK PROCESS

Usually the examiner has tested the patient at the request of another professional from whom the patient has sought treatment or a consultation. The examiner should reach an agreement with the referral source regarding the extent of feedback to be provided to the patient. Those who refer patients for testing have various attitudes as to whether the responsibility for feedback is primarily their own or that of the examining psychologist.

Discussions with the borderline patient concerning diagnostic impressions should generally avoid traffic with diagnostic nomenclature. Often the borderline individual will pressure the examiner to render a judgment in the form of a diagnostic label; at such times it is most useful to explore with the patient the significance of the request, because the label itself is of little objective value to the patient. The concern with labels may be indicative of many underlying issues regarding how the patient views the illness. For example, such questions often reflect an anxious awareness of the severity of the illness, a fear that the illness will provoke censure even from treaters, or the frightening question of whether the situation is hopeless or remediable. These latent concerns should be uncovered and discussed, for they provoke the ostensibly reasonable question "What is my diagnosis?"

The feedback process with the borderline patient can be guided by the following considerations (Berg, 1985): 1) the examiner should use language and concepts that are within the patient's realm of experience; 2) the examiner should share those impressions and observations that can be made relevant to the patient and used in a therapeutic manner; 3) the examiner's conclusions will be most acceptable to the patient when they are illustrated by and refer back to the events of the testing; 4) the patient is most apt to understand, accept, and make use of the feedback when it begins with what the patient already knows about him- or herself and uses this as a basis for presenting inferences and ways of understanding the illness that are new to the patient; 5) the feedback should address those aspects of the illness or character organization that are likely to interfere with the acceptance of treatment (e.g., profound mistrust or a need to devalue those who have something valuable to offer)—obviously, if such issues are not adequately examined and understood by the patient, the feedback and treatment recommendation may be discounted and rejected; and 6) the examiner can often use the patient's behavior during the feedback process itself to illustrate the very issue being discussed. For example, when discussing the paranoid experience of others, the patient's suspicion and antagonism to the feedback may be pointed to as a manifestation of the paranoid stance. When the feedback adheres closely to the present and immediate experience of the patient as it unfolds in the interaction with the examiner, the patient will be most readily able to understand the conclusions being offered.

In communicating diagnostic impressions to the referral source the examiner should recognize that the variability of functioning and lack of identity integration in the borderline patient predispose professionals to discrepant views. The examiner should beware of the danger of competitively adhering to diagnostic views that may encompass only part of the clinical truth, and should strive for conceptualizations that synthesize the views of the various observers, including the data from the testing, social history, interviews, and behavioral observation.

REFERENCES

American Psychiatric Association. (1980). *Diagnostic and statistical manual of mental disorders* (3rd ed.). Washington, DC: Author.

Bellak, L. (1979). *Psychiatric aspects of minimal brain dysfunction in adults.* New York: Grune & Stratton.

Berg, M. (1982). Borderline psychopathology: On the frontiers of psychiatry. *Bulletin of the Menninger Clinic, 46,* 113-124.

Berg, M. (1984). Expanding the parameters of psychological testing. *Bulletin of the Menninger Clinic, 48,* 10-24.

Berg, M. (1985). The feedback process in psychological diagnostic testing. *Bulletin of the Menninger Clinic, 49,* 52-69.

Hartocollis, P. (Ed.). (1980). *Borderline personality disorders.* New York: International Universities Press.

Kernberg, O. (1976). *Object relations theory and clinical psychoanalysis.* New York: Aronson.

Schmideberg, M. (1959). The borderline patient. In S. Arieti (Ed.), *American handbook of psychiatry* (Vol. 1, pp. 398-416). New York: Basic Books.

Stone, M. (1980). *The borderline syndromes: Constitution, personality and adaptation.* New York: McGraw-Hill.

Sugarman, A. (1980). The borderline personality organization as manifested on psychological tests. In J. S. Kwawer, H. P. Lerner, P. M. Lerner, & A. Sugarman (Eds.), *Borderline phenomena and the Rorschach test* (pp. 39-58). New York: International Universities Press.

Weiner, I. (1966). *Psychodiagnosis in schizophrenia.* New York: John Wiley & Sons.

4

Assessing the Schizophrenic and Psychotic Patient

THOMAS REILLY, PH.D.

The term *psychotic* is defined as a "gross impairment in reality testing," specifically excluding minor distortions that involve matters of relative judgment (American Psychiatric Association, 1980). Categories of psychotic conditions include Pervasive Developmental Disorders, Schizophrenic and Paranoid Disorders, Psychotic Disorders Not Elsewhere Classified, some Organic Mental Disorders, and some Affective Disorders. Pervasive developmental disorders usually apply to children and will not be considered in this chapter. Discussion of organic psychotic disorders is excluded because neuropsychological, neurological, or medical procedures are involved in their assessment. This chapter focuses exclusively on functional psychotic conditions.

The considerations presented will emphasize the kinds of information needed for a diagnostic decision, tests and procedures that help provide this information, the interpretive process, and the communication of results. It is assumed that the goals of the assessment are to determine the presence or absence of psychotic processes, the types of conflicts involved in the disorder, and patient assets. Such issues would comprise appropriate referral questions, but others could include: 1) retesting after a time on antipsychotic medication to determine the presence of any residual psychotic thinking and whether any behavioral improvement is attributable more to the institution's structured environment or to patient's increased coping skills; 2) assessing progress in psychotherapy; 3) assessing suitability for psychotherapy; and 4) assessing legal competency.

PREDIAGNOSTIC SCREENING

The setting in which the assessor operates influences the initial screening process. In an institutional setting, the patient's social and psychiatric histories are

Comments by Tom Locke, Chris North, Tom Nowak, and Lynn Pace are gratefully acknowledged.

compiled prior to the referral for testing. The private practitioner usually collects this information him- or herself. In an institutional setting one might be referred only the most complicated or disputed cases, which may not be true in private practice. Referral questions are a function of the sophistication of the referring person. At times as initially presented they are unanswerable and must be reformulated (e.g., "What percentage of this patient's psychosis is organically determined and what percentage is psychogenic?"). Some referrals also presume to tell one how to answer the question (e.g., "Give this patient a Rorschach to determine the presence of thought disorder and send it to me."), and some consultation is in order.

Prior to seeing the patient the examiner must address the issue of whether the patient is taking any drugs. Consultation with a physician, or perhaps other professionals, is necessary to determine the possible effects of such drugs on test performance. An appropriately prescribed, effective antipsychotic drug can also "clear up" the test results; the clinician then must ponder the relative merits of testing performed while the patient is on versus off the medication. Another issue can arise with the administration of neuroleptic (antipsychotic) drugs. Antipsychotic drugs can cause psychomotor effects that mimic neurological disease and confuse the clinical picture. Further, other drugs such as amphetamines can produce psychotic symptoms, such as delusions, auditory hallucinations, and suspiciousness. (Blum [1984] is a useful resource in this regard.) Thus, drugs can increase the difficulty of the assessment either by reducing psychotic functioning or by inducing a toxic psychosis with apparently neurological symptoms.

The importance of knowing *exactly* what question(s) one is setting out to answer cannot be overemphasized. The assessor must clarify with the referring source what he or she wants to know, as some questions may be unanswerable. Examples of such questions are those that seek specific behavioral predictions (e.g., "Will this patient kill someone?") rather than more general predictions (e.g., "How will this patient deal with his anger?"); those that seek numerical probability percentages rather than a general statement of probability; and those that seek predictions when the assessor cannot know what kinds of environmental forces will confront the patient (e.g., "Will this patient have another psychotic break?"). In such instances, a reformulation of the referral question is necessary or the assessor must state predictions in combination with different environmental conditions (e.g., "If the patient's social support network remains intact he is not likely to have another psychotic break, but if his social support system becomes inoperative, then he will not easily compose another support system and will be at great risk of another psychotic break").

The assessor should also consider the costs and benefits of the clinical time that is consumed and how it is used. Psychological assessments are costly in terms of time, effort, and money, and they should be used judiciously. In some instances, the question "Is this patient psychotic?" may be answered adequately and appropriately by a quickly administered and scored screening device; in others, there is a need to devote more time because of the actions that would ensue from the diagnosis of psychosis (e.g., being declared legally incompetent to manage one's estate). In some circumstances, a clinical interview can suffice, especially if it elicits strong indicators such as the stare that seems focused on some point behind the examiner's head, with no eye contact felt. On the other hand, certain questions are more complicated and may be necessary to address without any assurance of arriving at a valid answer. An example might be the man who, having killed a Stanford University professor with a hammer (presumably because of delusional thinking, judging from newspaper accounts), is now eligible for parole and refuses to accept being barred from the vicinity of the university.

The assessor must become aware of any physical conditions that can affect test administration or the interpretation of results. Motor impairments can affect the patient's performance on the WAIS-R Performance scale. Sensory impairments (e.g., hearing loss, visual acuity loss, color blindness) can restrict the patient's ability to respond adequately and can lead to erroneous interpretations. Knowledge of medical examinations and whether the results indicate possible organic involvement is essential because the need for alternative procedures can thus become apparent. Familiarity with the patient's prior intellectual, educational, and employment achievements provides a baseline for interpreting current test results. Social and emotional factors are relevant to the presumed etiology of functional psychoses and perhaps to the prognosis for improvement. For example, some family therapists feel that certain families seem to require someone to be psychotic, and Laing and Esterson (1970) report that supposedly delusional material from female schizophrenics did not seem delusional when the families were interviewed.

In summary, the assessor must have clear and answerable referral questions, must judge the appropriateness of the tests and procedures for the particular patient, must become aware of conditions (such as drugs) that may affect the test results, and must have information that permits the setting of a baseline against which the results can be evaluated.

SELECTION OF TESTS AND PROCEDURES

Though it is advocated that one plan in advance what tests and procedures to employ the prudent clinician is prepared to change during the assessment process. There are several reasons for this strategy. A test may fail to elicit useful data, such as only card-descriptive responses on the TAT, or a large number of unanswered items on the MMPI, or a large number of rejections on the Rorschach. Two alternatives can be considered: 1) drop the test and substitute another procedure, or 2) attempt a new administration after some discussion with the patient about noncompliance with the test instructions and, in some instances, about the possibly unfavorable consequences of continued noncompliance (e.g., "This behavior will not do much to convince the staff that you are ready for discharge"). Sometimes the battery can be terminated early, when the assessor believes there is enough information to answer the referral question with certainty.

New questions or issues can arise during the testing for which other tests or procedures should be added. For example, if it became evident early on that a patient exhibited paranoid thinking that had crystallized on one person as the source of all the patient's problems, it would be important to test out how rigidly the patient embraced such thinking. In such a case, switching to some measures such as Guilford's tests of divergent thinking (e.g., "How many different ways can one use a brick?") would be sensible. Or one could use this kind of approach with the proposed battery in a sort of testing the limits procedure (e.g., "Can you think of other ways that this person might be feeling (thinking)?" for a character in a TAT story). In addition, one can propose alternative TAT stories and Rorschach responses to the patient to see if he or she accepts them as plausible.

Various criteria can be used for selecting tests and procedures. The specificity versus comprehensiveness of the referral question influences the choice and variety of procedures. Reality considerations such as the time available or the potential consequences of a bad decision affect what bandwidth-fidelity choices are made (Cronbach & Gleser, 1957). This discussion will focus on the most widely used tests and procedures and will indicate how each one might provide relevant data in the assessment of psychosis. The recommended battery includes: the clinical interview, the Minnesota Multiphasic Personality Inventory (MMPI), the Rorschach, the Thematic Apperception Test (TAT), and the Wechsler Adult Intelligence Scale-Revised (WAIS-R). This battery is chosen to cover a variety of tasks embedded within varying degrees of structure, to shed light on the patient's cognitive, intrapsychic, and interpersonal functioning. These measures are employed very commonly in clinical practice and much information is available on them to assist the assessor.

A clinical interview offers information about the patient's affective output in addition to the content. The amount and variety of affect expressed, its appropriateness/inappropriateness, and so on are important to note. The patient's language is significant in terms of rate of speech, coherence/incoherence, neologisms, peculiarities of expression, etc. Delusional content, hallucinations, and the patient's insight or lack thereof are usually apparent in the interview. The patient's motoric behavior should be monitored for such aspects as stereotypic movements, excitement, rigidity, stupor, apathy, or restlessness.

An individual intelligence test, such as the WAIS-R, provides multiple opportunities to evaluate the patient's thought processes in a relatively structured context. Loosening of associations, clang associations, illogical leaps, intrusions into the flow of thought and diminished ability to maintain a mental set, absurd responses, inappropriate affects, and so on may be manifested.

The MMPI can indicate psychotic functioning, confusion, disorientation, possible somatic delusions, attitudes of succumbing to or combating the illness, and possibly whether the condition is chronic or acute. The Rorschach may provide data on reality testing, deviant verbalizations, perceptual instability, blatant (crude or gory) sexual and aggressive content, etc. Special care should be given to the inquiry for the Rorschach; frequently it is in the inquiry that the manifestation of psychosis occurs most clearly. The TAT offers opportunities for the manifestation of perceptual distortions, idiosyncratic or bizarre plots, inappropriate affect expression, illogical or magical thinking, grandiosity, and themes of destruction, annihilation, deterioration, and decay.

This battery is usually comprehensive enough to provide the data needed for a diagnostic decision. Inclusion of the less structured tests follows Rapaport's (1951) suggestion: "The more general the task, the more clearly does it reveal the pathology" (p. 590). The more specific and structured measures, such as the WAIS-R, can assess better than the projectives how the patient responds on an everyday reality basis. As mentioned previously, in some instances the battery could be shortened (e.g., in the case of a floridly psychotic individual); in others, additional procedures could be considered. For example, Holt's primary process scoring for the Rorschach could be used (Holt & Havel, 1960), as could a more explicit tabulation of Rapaport's deviant verbalizations (Rapaport, Schafer, & Gill, 1946, pp. 331-366 and Appendix II); critical items from the MMPI could be explored in an interview (Dahlstrom & Welsh, 1960, Appendix G); Harris and Lingoes' subscales for MMPI Scales 2, 6, 8, and 9 could be scored (Dahlstrom, Welsh, and Dahlstrom, 1970); or Schafer (1954) could be used to identify psychoanalytic defenses.

Because the patient's ability to exercise control over thought processes is an important criterion in the determination of psychosis, the assessor can modify test administration by instructing the patient to exercise more control. The rationale is similar to a testing the limits period in a Rorschach—what will the patient do with an increased amount of structuring? Possible choices include rejecting a poor form level response on the Rorschach and asking perhaps for a popular, demanding other responses instead of a perseveration, and perhaps asking the patient to respond as most others would respond.

INTERPRETATION AND INTEGRATION OF FINDINGS

Goals of the Interpretation

At this stage, the assessor may formulate different goals, varying in scope. Perhaps the most narrow goal would be to answer the question of whether or not psychosis is present. Another, more intermediate goal could be the assignment of a DSM-III diagnosis. Perhaps the broadest goal would be a comprehensive personality assessment including the types of conflicts, intensity of conflicts, areas of strength, defense mechanisms, and the effectiveness of coping. The assessor's theoretical framework influences what is deemed important, what relationships between variables are presumed, and what constitutes a comprehensive formulation; neither data collection nor interpretation is theory neutral. It should be noted that specific DSM-III diagnoses cannot always be made from the tests alone, as the criteria may include time periods (e.g., age at onset, duration of symptoms) or the impairment of the routines of daily functioning.

Psychotic Indicators

Table 1 lists a variety of ways in which psychosis can be manifested in the assessment data and where in the tests and procedures each indicator may be shown. Brief definitions of some terms are given. Rapaport et al. (1946) offer more extensive examples than it is possible to provide here. The categorization in Table 1 is somewhat arbitrary, because some traditionally defined thought disorders are not explicitly listed (e.g., neologisms, which has been subsumed under incoherence of speech) and some thought disorders have been grouped under other headings (e.g., contaminations). Although thought disorders are not unique to psychosis (Rapaport, 1951), and though DSM-III abandoned formal thought disorder as a criterion pathognomic of psychosis, some types of thought disorder still appear as diagnostic criteria (e.g., incoherence of speech, markedly illogical thoughts, neologisms); thus the condition is retained here on the grounds that some types of thought disorder are more apt to appear in psychosis.

The Contextual Approach

Table 1 should not be regarded as a list of signs that clearly and definitely, in isolation from other considerations, determines the presence of a psychosis. The context of the behavior must be taken into account before it is counted as a sign of psychosis. For example, the patient whose behavior clearly suggests a playful attitude toward the Rorschach, as if it were a game, may produce psychoticlike responses that must be distinguished from one who invests the blot with reality and gives a position response or a contamination. Beck (1949) reports the Rorschach of a nationally known psychiatrist about three-quarters through his analysis, who gave 11 form minus responses, 1 pure color, and an irregular sequence of W D Dd in the 52 responses. The conclusion would be that the analysis had increased affect expression and decreased rigidity.

Characteristics of Psychotic Process

The assessor should delineate the psychological processes demonstrated in the patient's responses. The nature of the process permits the judgment that psychosis is or is not present. For example, a contamination response in the Rorschach means that the patient has not kept separate two responses to the same area and has presented a single fused response (e.g., three dancing girls to the middle part of Card I). As such, the response indicates a weakened control.

An important aspect of psychotic responding is the issue of voluntary control.

TABLE 1

Behaviors Suggestive of Psychosis

Misperception of reality

perceptual distortion (R, T, W)
confabulation (I, R, T, W)—extensive, arbitrary associative elaboration
without objective support
contamination (R)—two interpretations fused into one
perseveration, esp. thematic perseveration (I, R, T, W)

Thought disorder

autistic logic (I, R, T, W)—faulty attempt to derive response "logically"
blocking (I, R, T, W)
flight of ideas (I, M, R, T, W)
incoherence (I, R, T, W)

Self/world conceptions

deterioration (I, R, T, W)
decay (I, R, T, W)
decomposition (I, R, T, W)
grandiosity (I, M, R, T, W)
ideas of reference (I, M, R, T, W)

Affective behaviors

blunted (I, M, R, T, W)
bland (I, M, R, T, W)
incongruent (I, R, T, W)
euphoria (I, M, R, T, W)
silly (I, M, R, T, W)
hostile (I, M, R, T, W)

Motoric behavior

stupor (I)
retardation (I, M, R, T, W)
restlessness (I, M, R, T, W)
excitement (I, M, R, T, W)
stereotypic (I)

Attitudes

vigilance (I, M, R, T, W)
transductive reasoning (I, R, T, W)—reasoning moves from part to part
with assumption it holds for the whole
invests stimuli with reality (R, T)

Key: I—clinical interview; M—MMPI; R—Rorschach; T—TAT; W—WAIS-R

The contamination response just mentioned illustrates an impaired control. Earlier it was advised to test out the patient's ability to control by such methods as rejecting perseverations. Another way to evaluate a patient's ability to exercise control is to attend to recovery (i.e., increase of functioning after a decrease). The speed, degree, and frequency of recoveries are important. If a patient first gave an F minus response to Card III in the Rorschach and then gave a whole response, successfully integrating form and color for both of the red areas and organizing a popular in the black with a popular in the center red, that would be a very great increase in functioning. It should be noted that spontaneous recovery implies some degree of insight and intact reality testing on the part of the patient.

The significance of any one indicator will be a function of such intratest analysis. Beyond such immediate locale considerations, the assessor must shift subsequently to the perspective of an entire test and then to the entire battery, including both test and nontest behaviors. This procedure permits a determination of the pervasiveness of deterioration and any residual areas of intact functioning. Thus, a patient functioning at a borderline psychotic level may show more normal functioning on tests, or parts of tests, where there are clearer cues as to what is expected (i.e., more structured, less ambiguous stimuli).

Though clear verbalizations of delusions or hallucinations may appear in the interview or other procedures, the assessor must be alert to more subtle cues that could indicate their presence. For example, blocking can be the consequence of auditory hallucinations. Hypervigilance, especially to apparently innocuous details, may signal the presence of persecutory delusions. Ideas of reference, disruptions in the flow of speech, episodes of excitement, or mutism can indicate hallucinations or delusions.

The Interpretive Process

The interpretive process will first be described and then illustrated. The example is incomplete as it does not address all the data (case history material, test and nontest behaviors) that should be considered. The process advocated is recursive, probabilistic, and involves a search for antecedent causes to account for the test responses and patient's behavior. That is to say, it is a process of reasoning backward from known effects (e.g., a response) to causes (e.g., a psychological process). Because more than one thing could have caused the patient's behavior, one judges the relative probability of each conceivable event causing the response. The probabilities are estimated from the amount and quality of evidence, pro and con, that appears in the entire body of data. The process is recursive, because while proceeding through the material one must keep returning to reexamine past decisions in terms of later data. It is a repetitive hypothesize-and-test procedure, analogous to the hypothetical-deductive method: 1) invent multiple hypothesized causes of the same behavior; 2) test out these hypotheses by checking out whether their implications are supported in the data; and 3) accept, modify, and reject hypotheses until one attains a formulation that explains all of the data. The goal is a conceptualization of the patient that integrates all the components (e.g., traits, instinctual drives, etc.) into an organized pattern of relationships, accounting for both consistencies and inconsistencies in the patient's behavior. The conceptualization is analogous to a theory, so that one evaluates it much as one evaluates a theory, namely: comprehensiveness (how much of the data is accounted for?); parsimony (is a simpler version workable?); utility (can one predict from the conceptualization?); the amount of empirical support; and internal consistency (does it hang together?). If not, then one reworks it and the process, which is somewhat self-correcting, continues.

The internal consistency criterion does not mean that the patient always behaves exactly the same way. Indeed, in psychotic individuals considerable variability is typical. The presumed consistency of behavior relates to situations that the patient subjectively defines as similar or the same. The assessor strives to define the conditions under which the target behavior will occur, much like a dispositional concept—a rubber band's elasticity will be revealed only if force is applied to it. A paranoid patient may be hypervigilant, but perhaps not consistently; therefore, one must attempt to refine the hypervigilance to perhaps only those situations construed as a threat to the patient's sexual identity (i.e., a perceived homosexual overture).

The decision that the patient is psychotic is not simply quantitative, but also qualitative. The degree of recovery mentioned earlier is an example that influences judgments of severity, insight, prognosis, and treatment potential. Other qualitative aspects include the extremity of an indicator and its specificity to psychotic functioning. For example, perseverations can also occur in persons who are organically impaired but not psychotic. In the psychotic patient, perseverations tend not to involve the repetition of a specific percept, but rather the perseveration of a theme (often those of decay, rottenness, deterioration, etc.).

Another important qualitative aspect is the presence/absence of subjective distress in the patient, which can suggest the presence or absence of insight and whether the patient is succumbing to or combating the illness. For example, a patient who fidgets, coughs, and somewhat hesitantly gives the Rorschach response, "This is weird, but it could look something like my girl's vagina. Did anyone else ever see that?" is in much better shape than the patient who says, "This is clearly my girl's cunt. When did you see her?" The subjective distress expressed in the first response indicates some awareness of and hesitancy about the appropriateness of the response; thus, the patient has not succumbed completely to a psychotic process. The second response is a crude, blatant sex response that is bad form (both socially and perceptually), as the patient has moved from interpreting the blot to treating it as real: *This is clearly . . .* (emphasis added). So real, indeed, that the examiner must have seen her! Evidence of subjective distress can be seen in other tests as well. In the MMPI, if Scale 7 is close to or higher than Scale 8, the same interpretation of subjective distress and not succumbing can be made, especially if Scale 2 is also elevated. The more evidence supporting that the patient has succumbed, the more likely it is that the patient is chronic; the inverse is true for judging the condition acute.

A major problem in deciding from test data that a person is psychotic is the fact that there is not a perfect positive correlation between test performance and everyday functioning. It is quite possible for a patient's test data to suggest more pathology than would his or her everyday functioning. Tests that easily stimulate fantasy material, such as the TAT and Rorschach, are prime candidates for emphasizing pathology, and being pathology-oriented aggravates the situation. Remedial measures include the contextual approach, attending to residual areas of strength, and the inclusion of more structured tests such as the WAIS-R. If the patient's WAIS-R performance is superior to that on the projectives, it is likely that he or she is compensating with some success on an everyday basis.

An Example

Table 2 contains a fabricated, partial Rorschach to illustrate the interpretive process. The patient is a 35-year-old white single male, who is a graduate student in experimental psychology. The background data suggest above average intelligence, good language skills, and above average abstracting, conceptualizing, analytical abilities, and logical thinking.

The first response comes after some card turning and delay. At least two hypotheses are possible: 1) he's taking his time (i.e., a disposition of slow tempo), or 2) he's being cautious (guardedness? anxiety?). The dispositional hypothesis would be checked against other data, such as speed of speech and movements, speed in responding to other tests, use of any medications or drugs, case history data, and so on. Assuming that such checks fail to confirm the hypothesis, which is consistent with three more rapid Rorschach responses, one proceeds to the guardedness hypothesis, which would be rechecked against information from others and against his behavior on other tests (assuming the Rorschach is not the first test given). Assume that on the WAIS-R the patient made no comments nor asked any questions about the purpose of the test, and seemed to answer quickly and directly. At first this style of responding seems to negate the guardedness notion, but remembering that he is a psychology graduate student raises the possibility that he might know what an intelligence test and the Rorschach are used for and that the Rorschach is reputedly not transparent. If these assumptions checked out, one might revise the guardedness notion to include anxiety and control. The patient gets anxious when he has less control and he reacts more slowly, which implies an internal locus-of-control orientation. The revised hypothesis implies some possible behaviors that would then be checked out; for example, he might be more inquisitive and critical of projectives than of the WAIS-R (he does this several times later in the protocol), he might become more angry at the examiner during projective testing, he might become less cooperative during projective testing, etc.

Assume that there are enough supporting data to retain the guardedness-

TABLE 2

Fabricated Rorschach Protocol

FREE ASSOCIATION	INQUIRY
I ∧v∧ 45″ 1. Jaws Two animal . . . swallowed 2 evil witches (anything else?) That's the only thing it could be. *W FM−C'Ad,(H) contamination tendency*	(?) all of it, here's great, big teeth (inner S) witches on broomsticks (side D) (evil?) black means evil and animal's happy to eat them—see the grin?
II ∧ 10″ 2. This red down here must be symbolic of women. Black part is too blurry to know what it is . . . they're not well constructed. (anything else?) I told you, no! *D CF,m blood, Abst fabulation*	(?) (1.ctr.red) (?) red suggests blood involved in giving birth to new life, see it flowing down? You botched up these cards.
III < > v∧ 50″ 3. two peculiar males, unsure of themselves, standing rigid, eyeing each other *D M H,Obj P fabulation*	(?) (side D) (unsure?) obviously they don't know who they are (?) they're cooking stew in this pot—they're the same so they must like each other. . . . It's an ugly scene.
IV ∧ 40″ 4. this is an animal's skull, the rest is a mess *D F At*	(?) (1.ctr.D) (skull?) ragged, boney edges, teeth or tusks sticking out
V v 15″ 5. butterfly plunging down to to earth, Kaput. *W FM A P fabulation*	(?) (W) (?) the weak perish
VI rejected	
VII v 10″ 6. Napoleon *S M H,Cltg.*	(?) (S) he's got one of those hats on

anxiety-control hypothesis and proceed. The first response is arresting in that: 1) it is aggressive; 2) evil is destroyed (the witches, presumably female); and 3) there is a peculiar combination of vagueness and definiteness in "Jaws Two animal" (i.e., it's not the original Jaws, but it's an animal, not a shark). Point 3 suggests an emotionally based inefficiency in the quality one would expect from him (cf. background data). The inquiry supports the judgment of inefficiency in that identifying all four white spaces as teeth is poor form and indicating that the witches on broomsticks inside the mouth are still visible is bad form, not to mention the even worse possibility that the animal is treated as if it is transparent. The aggressive content offers the possibility of being connected to the form accuracy decrease, but the happiness at destroying evil belies that notion. Instead of suggesting fear or guilt over expressing aggression, it seems more like this is socially sanctioned aggression in the service of society—they got what they deserved—which suggests the externalization of blame. Also implied, if the witches are female (which used to be predominantly true), is a hostility to women symbolically expressed without guilt.

But, why the inefficiency? Two added elements offer some possible light. One aspect is the suggestion of projection operating in "the witches are evil and get what they deserve," plus the process of very rapid, rigid attribution of a single meaning on very little evidence (black means evil, "That's the only thing it could be"). The other element is that which is avoided: the popular bat or butterfly and the female form in the center. Missing the populars suggest that the response given has more emotional significance. The center female form often has sexual overtones because of the transparent dress aspect.

The following hypothesized components have thus evolved (which one must continue to test and attempt to integrate): 1) anxiety over sexuality; 2) use of projection; 3) guardedness; 4) need to control; 5) free expression of aggression, and hostility perceived as socially sanctioned; and 6) rapid and rigid attribution of meaning.

The subject's second response is quicker, uses only the center red, does not integrate form and color, offers a vaguely based intellectual rationale for the response, is clearly sexually triggered, and involves forces outside of his control (m-gravity). In addition, criticism and anger are overtly directed at the male examiner, the heavily shaded black areas are firmly excluded, and there is a quest for the single meaning of a blot area, what it must be. After the first response, one can now say sexuality is more openly expressed, a freer affective response occurs with more tension (CF,m), and control declines. (The scoring CF rather than C could be debated.) Exclusion of the heavily shaded areas would be interpreted as avoidance of affectional need recognition.

Summarizing, the following is retained: 1) easily manifested hostility without guilt or anxiety, but with the expectation that it is justified and perhaps more readily expressed to males; 2) disturbed sexuality; 3) difficulty in accepting affectional needs; 4) anger in response to anxiety; and 5) use of intellectual assets to ascertain meanings and intentions, and which fairly rapidly becomes crystallized into one, indubitable choice. These notions are not inconsistent, but make good clinical sense—they suggest paranoid ideation.

Detailed discussion of the remaining responses will not be offered, but noteworthy aspects will be briefly listed. The form level is good and they are common or popular responses. It is the affective overelaboration, not readily supportable by the blot, that is striking. The more heavily shaded cards are not handled well (the subject responds to only part of Card IV and the shading is denied; Card VI is rejected). Areas are avoided where sexual responses are expectable (Cards VI and VII). The patient seems confident about the good quality of his responses; there is no subjective distress. None of this is inconsistent with the prior formulation, so the tentative diagnosis from the Rorschach would be paranoid schizophrenia, chronic but not very deteriorated, and the process would continue.

COMMUNICATION OF RESULTS

To the Patient

What the assessor communicates to the patient can vary from little or nothing to a diagnostic statement and treatment recommendations. The major factors determining what is said are the circumstances under which the assessment occurs, the presence or absence of an ongoing therapy relationship, the degree of insight evidenced by the patient, and the nature of the findings. At times the wisest course may be to channel recommendations through the referral source. For example, if there is a therapist in place, he or she might gradually integrate the findings into the therapy at appropriate times. If the patient is neither in treatment nor in a controlled environment, lacks insight into his or her condition, and is possibly violent, communicating these conclusions to him or her would be foolish. Instead, one should communicate with the relatives and encourage them to take appropriate action. The usual ethical restraints of confidentiality should in that instance recede in comparison to the protection of life.

If the assessor does communicate directly with the patient, the paramount goal should be to help. At times, it can be beneficial for the patient to know what is wrong, as it can reduce the anxiety of not knowing and/or confusion. This is especially true if some hope can be offered and the possible stigma of mental illness counteracted. A basis for hope might be built on the positive effects of treatment and by pointing to the patient's strengths and assets. In any event, communications should be free of technical jargon and should be presented in simple, comprehensible language.

With the Family

Whether the assessor communicates with the family is in part a function of the factors previously mentioned plus issues of confidentiality. In the case of adults, frequently there will be no communication at all. If the assessor does communicate with the family, several common reactions to a diagnosis of psychosis can be anticipated; one must be prepared to uncover these emotional reactions and to deal with them. One such reaction is that the patient is tainted forever. Other common concerns are violence toward the family, anger or strained bonds to the patient if involuntary commitment occurs, and fear or despair among the patient's children that they also are destined to become psychotic. There may be a desire, or an attempt, to extrude the patient from the family. It may be useful to discuss with the family how they behave toward the psychotic member, explaining which behaviors would be effective and which would be useless or harmful. Family members might not know how to be emotionally supportive while not reinforcing psychotic behavior.

With other Professionals

Several kinds of professionals, with diverse training and theoretical orientations, can be the recipients of assessment feedback. The assessor's purpose will help to determine what is communicated. If the other professional is drawn in for further assessment procedures, one communicates what the question is and what suggests it. When communicating with a therapist, the results should be accompanied by implications for therapy, expectable therapy issues or problems, an opinion of patient's accessibility to treatment, and, at times, recommendations for a specific form of therapy. All such communications must be comprehensible in order to be persuasive, so using test jargon is unwise as a rule, but employing the recipient's theoretical framework is useful if it is known.

REFERENCES

American Psychiatric Association. (1980). *Diagnostic and statistical manual of mental disorders* (3rd ed.). Washington, DC: Author.

Beck, S. J. (1949). *Rorschach's test: II. A variety of personality pictures.* New York: Grune & Stratton.

Blum, K. (1984). *Handbook of abusable drugs.* New York: Gardner Press.

Cronbach, L. J., & Gleser, G. (1957). *Psychological tests and personnel decisions.* Urbana, IL: University of Illinois Press.

Dahlstrom, W. G., & Welsh, G. S. (1960). *An MMPI handbook.* Minneapolis: University of Minnesota Press.

Dahlstrom, W. G., Welsh, G. S., & Dahlstrom, L. E. (1970). *An MMPI handbook* (Vol. 1). Minneapolis: University of Minnesota Press.

Holt, R. R., & Havel, J. (1960). A method for scoring primary and secondary process in the Rorschach. In M. Rickers-Ovsiankina (Ed.), *Rorschach psychology* (pp. 263-315). New York: John Wiley & Sons.

Laing, R. D., & Esterson, A. (1970). *Sanity, madness and the family.* Baltimore: Penguin Books.

Rapaport, D. (Ed.). (1951). *Organization and pathology of thought.* New York: Columbia University Press.

Rapaport, D., Schafer, R., & Gill, M. (1946). *Diagnostic psychological testing.* (Vol. II). Chicago: Year Book Publishers.

Schafer, R. (1954). *Psychoanalytic interpretation in Rorschach testing.* New York: Grune & Stratton.

5

Differentiation of Hysterical Conversion/ Psychosomatic Disorder and Physical Disease

MARY ANN STRIDER, PH.D., FRED D. STRIDER, PH.D.

The evaluation of persons referred with questions regarding the extent to which psychological factors complicate their physical or psychiatric illness can be a challenge for several reasons. Physicians are often confused and/or frustrated in their attempts to treat such patients, there are frequently several health care professionals involved, and a need arises for a multidisciplinary data base. In addition, there is not a clearly agreed upon diagnostic system for differentiation between these physical and/or mental disorders.

The responsibility or role of the mental health clinician in diagnosis may range from providing a description of intellectual or personality functioning to assist the referral source in developing a better understanding of the patient and his/her abilities to rendering a diagnosis that the psychologist feels is the best categorization of the patient's psychological problems. In many settings, most of the referring sources are physicians and they do expect a diagnosis. However, in order to formulate a diagnostic impression, the psychologist is dependent on the medical professional's test findings and medical diagnosis. Psychologists are not trained or authorized to order medical procedures. They may use, and many times require, the results of medical tests and procedures to reach their own diagnostic formulation. Sometimes it is possible for the psychologist to describe the psychological test results in such a way as to give the physician all he or she needs to make a differential diagnosis, particularly when the referring physician is a psychiatrist. However, especially with regard to the physical illnesses described in this chapter, most general practitioners, internists, oncologists, surgeons, and other medical specialists are not trained in psychiatric diagnosis, and many are not willing to make psychiatric diagnoses or take responsibility for doing so. It is therefore necessary if one is to function as a medical psychologist to have an understanding of the meaning of medical disorders and their emotional and psychological concomitants and effects on the individual's intellectual and personality functioning.

The general concept of psychosomatic disorder has evolved from Freudian theory. Freud observed repressed conflicts and needs reflected in physical symptoms that did not respond to medical treatment and he regarded such symptoms as entirely "functional" or psychological. Subsequent researchers have emphasized more psychophysical responses to environmental stimuli and have included psychosocial aspects in a broader conceptualization of psychosomatic disorders. It is generally accepted in clinical practice today that physical and psychological factors are intertwined and "illness" is seen as multiply determined by the interaction of social, psychological, and biological factors. Such a biopsychosocial model is assumed in this chapter. A workable clinical approach considers health and illness as a continuum that is affected by biopsychosocial components. The ratio of each component may vary and, on that basis, a differential diagnosis may be approached, if not completely attained.

It is helpful to conceptualize "psychosomatic" disorders as falling into one of five classes:

1. *Physical symptoms created by an interaction of psychological and physical factors.* In this category are physical disorders that are precipitated, exacerbated, or perpetuated by emotional or stressful events in the individual's life. There is ample evidence that a primary causative factor in the development of these disorders may be a biological predisposition or physical vulnerability to stress. Commonly seen disorders in this category, which have stress as one significant factor in their etiology, are asthma, peptic ulcers, eczema, certain menstrual disturbances, and certain idiopathic epilepsies. The most common diagnosis in these situations is usually "psychological factors affecting physical condition." The current edition of the *Diagnostic and Statistical Manual of Mental Disorders* (DSM-III; American Psychiatric Association, 1980) requires that there be evidence of a temporal relationship between the environmental stimuli (and the meaning ascribed to them) and the initiation or exacerbation of the clinical condition. An example would be vomiting that occurs whenever family arguments develop. In assessment, one must obtain two crucial pieces of information to substantiate a diagnosis in this category: 1) the person ascribes to the environmental stimuli some meaning that carries a high negative emotional loading and 2) the environmental event directly precedes the demonstration of symptoms. These disorders of psychological factors affecting physical condition will be seen to differ from conversion disorders by the type of organ system involved and by the absence of psychological gains.

2. *Physical symptoms created primarily by psychological factors.* In these conditions, the psychological symptoms presented are seen to overlap with the possibility of many physical disorders. Frequently involved are the physiological symptoms of depression (as manifested in fatigue, weakness, weight loss, and insomnia) and of anxiety (palpitations, dizziness, pain related to back or head areas, numbness, and parasthesias) as well as tremors and changes in motor activity (psychomotor retardation or hyperactivity.) Usually, physical treatment alone does

not reduce these symptoms. Frequently, such physical symptoms mask an underlying depressive disorder and do not diminish until the basic depressive process is effectively treated.

Symptoms that involve three or more organ systems automatically raise the question of underlying psychological causes. The majority of disorders falling under this category merit a diagnosis of a somatization or conversion disorder. In both of these the patient presents physical symptoms that have neither a known physical cause nor a suspected underlying physiological mechanism, and evidence exists that psychological factors are involved. In this classification the symptoms also must fall under the control of the autonomic nervous system; the patient does not feel that these symptoms are under his or her control.

3. *Psychological symptoms indirectly caused by physical illness.* The sequelae of physical disease, such as fatigue, deformity, loss of independence and mobility, and fear of dying from the disorder, fall under this classification. The disorder itself does not cause the psychological or psychiatric symptoms; it is the patient's response to and subjective experience of the disease that give rise to the symptoms. Examples can be seen in the adjustments required in chronic disorders, such as diabetes, epilepsy, hemophilia, and congenital heart defects, or in the diagnosis of carcinoma. Usually, assuming adequate prior functioning, the most common diagnosis is adjustment reaction. Depression and anxiety frequently occur after the onset of physical illness. For example, a fear of needles may develop during chemotherapy for carcinoma. A more common example is the elevation of blood pressure in a nonhypertensive person whenever blood pressure is measured by the physician. Early awareness and monitoring of newly diagnosed patients with physical disorders are most important in the prevention of more serious psychological consequences. Crisis intervention usually can prevent significant maladaptive reactions and long-term disorders.

4. *Psychological problems created directly by physical illness.* Many physical illnesses may be associated with psychiatric symptoms, and effective treatment of the primary physical disorder alleviates or reduces such symptoms. Medical treatment, in combination with patient education regarding the reasons for subjective experiences of psychological difficulty, should manage the psychological factors involved. However, there is still the possibility of the patient's reaction or response to the medical diagnosis and treatment causing difficulties that may fall into category 1 or 3, noted previously.

5. *Psychological problems and psychiatric symptoms caused by environmental events and/or medical treatment.* The relationship between the presenting symptoms and psychosocial events is usually clear in these instances. Into this category fall the stress reactions, such as post-traumatic stress disorder, job burnout, and muscle tension headaches. In these instances, the cumulative effects of change or precipitous demands for adjustment are usually clearly present in the patient's history of the current illness. This category also includes the reactions of

elderly patients with diminished sensory perception who are moved to new environments and quickly develop anxiety, paranoia, or aggressive behavior.

Also included in this category are iatrogenic conditions, such as the side effects of steroid, antihypertensive, and antiparkinsonian medications. In addition, some cardiac medications (e.g., digitalis and lidocaine) and epinephrine compounds are associated with psychological and behavioral changes. Side effects of medications must always be considered in the assessment of any patient, whatever the referral question.

The focus of this chapter is primarily on categories 2, 3, and 4 and their differential diagnostic considerations.

PREASSESSMENT CONSIDERATIONS

Obviously, it is not possible for a clinician to make a diagnosis that he or she does not think of; knowledge of physical disorders that can cause psychiatric-like symptoms is essential. A brief review of relevant physical disorders by organ systems is presented here; a more complete review can be found in Ariel and Strider (1983) and in Lishman (1978). Martin (1979) and Ouslander (1983) are also excellent resources for information about physical illnesses manifesting as psychiatric disorders.

Metabolic disorders. Illnesses such as Wilson's disease, pernicious anemia, or acute porphyria may mimic psychiatric disorders. A person with Wilson's disease may show mood swings, aggressive behavior, and intellectual impairment, usually with an onset in adolescence. The disease may be misdiagnosed as an adjustment reaction of adolescence until clearer symptoms of hepatic failure and movement disorders appear. Pernicious anemia may present with depression, lethargy, and fatigue, and in the early stages may be confused with depression. Acute porphyria patients may show a sudden onset of anxiety and marked emotional lability; until they present symptoms of abdominal pain, their condition may be misdiagnosed as a conversion reaction or anxiety state. Even more general metabolic disorders, such as fever, dehydration, acid base disturbances, and hypoxia, may often appear clinically as delerium, especially in older patients.

Endocrine disorders. Thyroid and parathyroid disorders, hypoglycemia, Cushing's disease, and Addison's disease may produce psychiatric symptoms. Hypothyroidism causes a lowering of the body's rate of metabolism and the person will appear lethargic and may complain of slowed cognitive functioning. One may also see mental confusion, psychosis, paranoia, auditory hallucinations, and even delerium in this disorder. Hyperthyroidism is a state of accelerated metabolism and the patient may appear nervous and irritable, overactive, and, possibly, paranoid. This disorder may be confused with a manic condition.

Hyperparathyroidism causes a defect in calcium metabolism and may produce symptoms of irritability and hyperactivity. Social withdrawal, apathy, and depressed mood may also be present in this condition. Hypoparathyroidism is associated with anxiety, depression, and irritability. In either of the parathyroid disorders, a toxic condition may develop and psychotic behavior may result.

Hypoglycemia can produce anxiety, tremors, fatigue, sweating, anger and irritability, and cognitive inefficiency.

Cushing's disease is the result of an excess of cortisol, producing high blood pressure and elevated blood glucose levels. These patients may describe personality changes and complain of fatigue and wakefulness; females may report menstrual irregularity. Depression is frequently associated with the disorder and a small percentage of these patients may appear psychotic.

Addison's disease entails underactivity of the adrenal glands, low blood sugar, and a vulnerability to infections. The patient may exhibit psychomotor retardation, may become quiet, seclusive, and apathetic, and paranoid delusions, agitation, and hallucinations may be present.

Cardiovascular disorders. Congestive heart failure and myocardial infarction may be associated with memory problems, cognitive impairment, and signs of anxiety; fatigue and depression are common. Some medications for cardiovascular disorders may produce fatigue and delerium.

Infections. Viral pneumonia, encephalitis, meningitis, bacterial pneumonia, endocarditis, and, more rarely encountered, neurosyphyllis or tuberculosis may be associated with symptoms of psychosis, delerium, agitation, and cognitive impairment.

Gastrointestinal disorders. Malabsorption syndromes, hepatitis, and vitamin and nutritional deficiencies may be associated with significant psychiatric symptoms, even to the extent of psychosis and delerium. The fatigue, sleep difficulties, confusional states, loss of energy, apathy, and anhedonia accompanying gastrointestinal illnesses may be confused with a depressive disorder.

Genitourinary disorders. Severe psychological and neuropsychological complications may arise from uremic poisoning and toxic conditions. Anorexic conditions, sleeplessness, depression, and complaints of "slowed thinking" are associated symptoms in these disorders.

Musculoskeletal disorders. Degenerative arthritis and rheumatoid disorders often involve pain and depressive symptoms.

Neurological disorders. Disorders that affect the brain's vascular system, including strokes, transient ischemic attacks, and neoplastic conditions, may result in personality change and memory, cognitive, and perceptual problems, along with a full range of emotional reactions. These may include anxiety, irritability, emotional lability, depression, rage reactions, apathy, paranoia, and sleep difficulties. Multiple sclerosis, Parkinson's disease, and seizure disorders may all have significant psychological sequelae, especially in the early stages of the disorder when these underlying conditions have not been fully identified or manifested in diagnostic symptomatology.

Chronic obstructive pulmonary disease. Lung disorders may be associated with fatigue, depression, and irritability. Medications given for bronchitis, emphysema, and asthma frequently contain epinephrine, which may produce irritability, restlessness, anxiety, and sleep disturbances.

Systemic disorders and connective tissue diseases. Disorders of hemolitic blood deficiencies, such as anemia and immune disorders, may be associated with cognitive, personality, or emotional changes. Fatigue and depression are also common reactions to these disorders. Lupus erythematosus may first appear with psychotic-like symptoms.

It is obvious that many physical disorders have associated psychological and psychiatric symptoms. In order for the clinician to determine whether psychological evaluation is appropriate, the referral question should be clearly understood by both the clinician and the referral source. Before seeing the patient, a review of the medical record is essential to determine whether a medical disorder has been considered. It is not always fruitful to plan an assessment before this information is available. When this is not possible, one should make it clear to both the referral source and the patient that more than one assessment session may be necessary. Without a thorough medical history, the clinician risks drawing an erroneous conclusion about underlying pathology and recommending treatment that not only is ineffective but that postpones appropriate treatment until too late in the disease process for effective results. One cannot assume that, because the patient is referred by the family physician or a medical specialist, adequate studies have been done automatically. The psychologist should also be aware that routine intake physical examinations will not reveal all relevant disorders. Medical referral questions must be targeted, as do psychological ones, for evaluation procedures to be useful and effective.

History is the cornerstone of diagnosis, particularly when dealing with psychosomatic conditions. A thorough review of health history is crucial. If the clinician can determine from the preassessment information provided that the symptoms are quite circumscribed, some areas of assessment may be covered on a screening level (e.g., surveys of intellectual and cognitive functions). When the presenting problems do not include memory or cognitive impairments, one may focus more on social, personality, and physical health issues. It is helpful to know, before seeing the patient, whether the situation is an acute or chronic one. Chronic conditions are likely to have more pervasive effects because they encompass the original problem and its effects as well as the patient's adaptation and reaction to the symptoms.

The age of the patient determines not only what instruments are applied but also what sources of information may be useful. For example, school performance and school records may provide valuable information for the assessment of a young adult, but would generally be of no use in the evaluation of an 80-year-old with no cognitive disturbances. Knowing the number of physicians or health specialists involved in the case and the extent and nature of emergency-room visits may be quite useful in the differential diagnosis of some patients. Sometimes there is no coordinating health-care provider managing these cases; thus, misdiagnoses and contradictory or dangerous combinations of medications and treatment may be important considerations in the patient's current difficulties. Some personality evaluation, both through history gathering and psychological testing, is usually necessary, and an assessment of the person's health concerns (knowledge about and reaction to symptoms) is useful. With a clear referral question and a review of medical information, one can plan the specifics of the assessment. Occasionally, of course, one needs to change those plans on the basis of new information or observations during the initial interview.

Assessment Procedures

The intake interview offers the most efficient manner of covering the relevant dimensions of the patient's history from the patient's point of view. The patient should describe the symptoms in his or her own words and discuss in detail any recurring patterns of symptoms. Important questions for the clinician are: Was the onset of the symptoms sudden or insidious? How long has the patient been aware of the problem(s)? What interventions have been tried and what was the response of the patient to them? What appeared first in the symptom constellation, the physical or the psychological aspects? What was going on in the patient's life at the time of onset? If any physical disease has been found, what has the patient been told about the nature of the disorder? How pervasive and influential have the symptoms been on the individual's functioning? To determine to what extent the symptoms have limited the patient's functioning, the clinician should ask "What have you stopped doing because of these symptoms?" It is often useful to ask the patient what he or she thinks is wrong with them and what would make the situation better.

How concerned and distressed does the patient appear regarding the presenting difficulties? The patient's communication style and demeanor during the interview can reveal useful personality aspects. Is the history presented in a dramatic fashion or is the patient inclined to understate and minimize distressing experiences? What, if any, precipitating events can be determined, whether real or perceived? Are these conditions internal or external to the patient? One should ask about family members, their role in the patient's life, and their reaction to the patient's illness. Has anyone in the patient's family or circle of acquaintances had similar problems? Is there evidence of secondary gain (i.e., components of financial or psychological advantage to the perpetuation of the symptoms)? Are there legal issues involved, either criminal charges or litigations involving injury? Direct questions about the use of alcohol and medications, including prescribed, over-the-counter, and street drugs, are most effective. Questions regarding diet, exercise, and other health-care beliefs and practices may also prove useful. The Illness Behavior Questionnaire is a 62-item self-report instrument that might help delineate the patient's attitudes, affects, and attributions in relation to illness (Pilowsky, Spence, Cobb, & Katsikitis, 1984).

Intelligence Tests

The use of intelligence tests in the differentiation of psychosomatic conditions may reveal cognitive deterioration and indirect evidence of anxiety and thus provide a survey of the patient's intellectual resources for participating in psychotherapy. A screening measure such as the Shipley Institute of Living Scale (SILS) has the advantage of taking only 20 minutes to administer and it can be quickly scored. The disadvantage of this approach lies in its inaccuracy at the extreme ends of the intellectual continuum. The SILS requires good vision and the ability to read and is a power test, allowing only 10 minutes for a list of vocabulary words and another 10 minutes for completing patterns of symbolic relationships. In addition, many brain-impaired patients will not be accurately diagnosed and the effect of anxiety and depression may greatly distort the patient's performance.

The best estimate of intellectual functioning is the Wechsler Adult Intelligence Scale-Revised (WAIS-R). It should be noted that outside of significant depression, anxiety, or brain impairment, most persons experiencing somatic symptoms due to psychological problems will not necessarily have significant cognitive deterioration. Qualitative observations may be very helpful in certain cases, but there is no consistent pattern of intellectual impairment associated with conversion reactions, somatization, or hypochondriasis.

Acute anxiety may be manifested predominantly on those WAIS-R subtests that rely heavily on attention and concentration, and indirectly on those that are timed. Low performance due to anxiety may be seen mainly on Digit Span, Arithmetic, and the Digit Symbol subtests. Anxiety may also interfere with planning and sequencing behavior, so that one also may see some distractibility, fumbling, or an aimless approach to all the performance subtests of the Wechsler (e.g., erratic failures on Picture Completion, clumsiness or fumbling on Block Design, and poor planning on Picture Arrangement and Object Assembly). Chronic anxiety may interfere with all processing and have a more pervasive effect on learning ability and performance.

Significant depression that results in motor slowing will lower the scores on all timed WAIS-R subtests. It is useful to employ a testing-the-limits approach on these tasks, for example by seeing if the individual can perform the arithmetic problems using pencil and paper or can tell the examiner the story for picture arrangement items. In these instances, one can see that the patient understands the tasks and is failing them due to slowed mental processing or other symptoms of depression.

Wechsler's "hold/don't hold" tests have not been substantiated in the research literature. Intellectual deterioration may be documented most validly by the use of history, a neuropsychological evaluation, and the testing-the-limits approach discussed previously. Both intellectual and personality functioning must be assessed to arrive at valid conclusions about deteriorating disorders. In some instances deterioration is best established by repeated administrations of the Wechsler scales. Anxiety variables alone ordinarily do not produce consistent patterns of failure within WAIS-R subtests.

In the somatization and conversion disorders, depression tends to be more masked. The classic vegetative signs are seldom described by the patient and one generally does not see the usual symptom of motor slowing. Occasionally, the constrictive effects of anxiety may be present. Because of the nature of these disorders, which serve to avoid psychological conflicts, such patients usually have a need to be seen as intact, functional, and intelligent, but physically ill.

When intelligence testing reveals evidence of cognitive deterioration, one must determine if this is the result of significant depression and anxiety. The other hypothesis that must be ruled out is the presence of brain impairment or dementia. In these cases, a complete neuropsychological evaluation is necessary.

Personality Tests

The component that, along with the patient history, is essential in the differential diagnosis between these conditions is the personality evaluation. The Minnesota Multiphasic Personality Inventory (MMPI) is perhaps the most useful in making these distinctions. The patients under discussion here usually have significant elevations on the Hypochondriasis, Depression, Hysteria, and Psychopathic Deviate Scales, now referred to as Scales 1, 2, 3, and 4, respectively. Worry and rumination are frequently reflected in minor elevations on Scales 7 (Psychasthenia) and 8 (Schizophrenia). The following patterns of scale scores are most reliable in making distinctions between conversion hysteria, somatoform, hypochondriasis, factitious disorder, and psychological factors affecting physical disease:

Conversion reactions. The hallmark of the diagnosis of a conversion reaction remains the familiar elevations on Scales 1 and 3 of the MMPI with a distinctive low score on Scale 2: the familiar "conversion V." The relative depth of the Depression score depends on the degree to which the patient's conversion symptoms are effective in defending against depressive symptoms and experiences. As the use of physical symptoms and complaints fails either to evoke a response from others or to control the conflicts involved, clearer signs of depression develop, reflected in more pronounced vegetative signs, in patient reports of hopelessness, guilt, and helplessness, and in episodes of sadness and crying.

Since the conversion disorder serves to keep a conflict out of awareness, the MMPI profile is unlikely to show significant elevations on either depression or anxiety scales. There is a greater probability of a high L (Lie) and K (Defensiveness) with a low F (tendency to fake good) on the validity scales, consistent with the conversion patient's need to see him- or herself as psychologically intact and physically ill. Conversion disorders occur more frequently in persons who have a histrionic personality style, although this is not always the case. The histrionic components of a woman's personality disorder are revealed in elevations of Scales 3 and 4 with a low 5 (Masculinity-Femininity). The histrionic components of a man's personality may create either an extremely low or an extremely high 5 along with an elevation on Scale 3.

Some patients describe single-organ-system complaints, with dramatic presentations of symptoms and clear convictions about both the uniqueness of their problems and its role in physicians' failure to diagnose their difficulties in previous evaluations. The more likely diagnosis in these cases is a narcissistic personality disorder. These persons will not meet the criteria for any of the psychosomatic disorders, although they may consistently present themselves to a series of physicians because of their need for attention. Unlike conversion or somatization disorder patients, these individuals usually are not willing to undergo painful or drastic medical and surgical procedures.

Many persons showing conversion Vs will not necessarily have elevations on any scales other than 1 and 3. In fact, the personality style that appears to be second-most vulnerable to conversion disorders is the obsessive-compulsive individual with a history of conscientiousness and achievement with work and family. These patients are seen by others as "in control" and well able to handle family and work obligations; in fact, family members and work associates may report that the patient is the one person they consult for assistance with their own problems. Obsessive-compulsive people tend to develop conversion disorders for secondary gain, more so than as a result of internal conflicts, when their obligations or roles become overpowering for them and the perception of their own psychological problems or weaknesses is intolerable.

Somatization disorders. The validity scales for these profiles are usually within the normal ranges of variability. These individuals are usually not defensive, though they may show a relative elevation on the F Scale, which seems to denote a need to exaggerate; seldom does this elevation exceed 75. The somatization disorder will likely show elevations on Scales 1, 2 and 3 in some combinations not producing the conversion V noted previously. There may be no other elevations on the profile. When one sees Scales 8 (Schizophrenia) and/or 9 (Hypomania) also elevated, the presence of systemic disease or multiple sclerosis becomes a greater possibility, as the somatoform disorders do not as a rule report a considerable number of unusual experiences. The elevations on Scales 8 and 9 relate to the sensory and perceptual disturbances resulting from physical illnesses. One should clarify by interview the nature of any hallucinations that the somatoform patient may be endorsing on the MMPI. These "hallucinations" are more likely to consist of hearing one's name called or hearing a particular word or phrase, lacking the bizarre quality and external location of the voice that schizophrenic patients describe. Although, in a sense, somatoform patients have unrealistic ideas about their health, their descriptions and explanations of symptoms differ significantly from the more delusional quality of the schizophrenic. The schizophrenic patient presents not only physical symptoms but also a strongly held though untenable or bizarre explanation for their development. Scale 7 (Psychasthenia) may be relatively elevated in somatization disorder, as may Scale 4 (Psychopathic Deviate) if the person has a history of borderline personality. Rarely does an individual with a classic antisocial personality disorder fully qualify for the somatization disorder, although he or she would certainly be a candidate for one of the malingering disorders.

Hypochondriasis. The distinguishing feature of this patient is the degree to which he or she devotes significant amounts of time and psychological investment to fears of physical illness, physical symptoms, and the possibility of contracting disease. Such patients usually have acceptable MMPI validity scales, extremely high scores on Scale 1, and other elevations reflecting accompanying qualities of anxiety, depression, and obsessive-compulsive characteristics. Elaborate health precautions, odd preventive measures, unusual ideas about diet and cleanliness, and even magical ideas about how illnesses are caused and transmitted are not uncommon. These patients usually devote great amounts of time to health fads, and their MMPI profiles do not reveal elevations on the "impulsive" scales 3, 4, and 6.

Psychological factors affecting physical conditions. Stress figures prominently in these conditions when precipitating factors are involved. When symptoms of anxiety and depression are not prominent, these patients' MMPI profiles may fall within the normal range of variability.

When the patient is neither aware of nor able to report (in the history or on the MMPI) the depressive and anxious components of his or her situation, the Rorschach can offer a means of assessing these aspects. If one sees the presence of shading determinants beyond the normal range, depressive content, or an absence of color, even in a record of average or above average length, there is evidence for repression, depression, and/or anxiety. Patients with psychological factors affecting physical conditions as a rule do not reveal any significant reality distortions on the Rorschach and usually show available resources for both thinking through problems and contacting their emotions. Persons with a conversion reaction will show the immaturity, emotionality, global impressionability, and other signs of a hysteroid personality. In instances in which the conversion appears in an obsessive-compulsive personality constellation, the Rorschach indices will show over-control (as in high lambdas), low color, long reaction times, elevated Dd scores, and other obsessive-compulsive characteristics.

Classic conversion patterns of paralysis, blindness, or deafness seem much less prevalent, or at least are diagnosed less frequently, in current psychiatric practice than 20 or more years ago. Apparently as people become more educated and sophisticated, more subtle manifestations of this disorder are seen. It is still possible, particularly with children, for persons from more rural or remote settings or those who have been raised in sequestered and sheltered environments to develop the classic conversion disorders, but this is probably rare. Clinicians are more apt to see individuals whose physical symptoms contain components of the conversion process.

A variety of symptom checklists, questionnaires, and personality inventories (e.g., the 16PF, the Eysenck Personality Inventory, the Illness Behavior Questionnaire, and the Somatic Symptom Checklist) may give some evidence of physical concerns and may be useful in augmenting the assessment process. More recently, clinicians who have expertise in biofeedback and stress evaluation have found certain medical procedures useful (e.g., the electromyograph may be used in determining whether "tension headache" is, in fact, associated with the expected amounts of frontalis muscle tension). Detailed information about these methods is beyond the scope of this chapter; however, a clinical psychologist should be aware, for instance, of the advantages of the specialized EEG with nasopharyngeal leads and of some of the pharmacological activation techniques that enable a physician to discriminate between epileptic and hysterical seizures in the same patient, as well as of the audiologist's capability with the Lombard response to determine cases of hysterical aphonia. Such procedures are far more precise, definitive, and cost-effective than would be the usual psychological evaluation.

The Millon Clinical Multiaxial Inventory (MCMI), due to its development using psychiatric and mental health clients, may be inappropriate for use with medical patients. Millon suggests that clinicians working with medical patients or rehabilitation patients use the Millon Behavioral Health Inventory (MBHI).

INTEGRATION OF FINDINGS

When one encounters a documented physical condition that is associated with psychological symptoms, there are two major possibilities: 1) the diagnosis of psychological factors affecting the physical condition or 2) the diagnosis of a conversion reaction in a person who also has a physical illness. The most common psychological factor affecting a physical condition is anxiety. Also common is the situation in which a person develops a reactive depression in response to a physical illness or its implications for living. Both conditions share a sudden onset of symptoms. The psychological factors diagnosis requires a temporal relationship between a psychologically meaningful event and the emergence or exacerbation of the physical condition. In a thorough interview, it is possible to discover the precipitating event, and usually these individuals are more aware and more accepting of the possibility of a psychological explanation than are somatoform disorder patients. When one can clearly establish this link and the person does not qualify for any of the other disorders discussed, this would be an appropriate classification.

A more difficult case is one in which the patient shows a clear conversion component on psychological testing but also has a well-established physical disorder. For example, an epileptic individual may have seizures precipitated both by abnormal brain activity and by psychologically provocative episodes in daily living. Treatment in such a case requires both medication for the seizure disorder and psychotherapy for the conversion component.

The remaining diagnostic categories in this discussion require that no physical disorder has been found or is suspected.

Factitious Disorders

The identifying characteristic of factitious disorders is that they are produced by the individual and are under voluntary control. This person's goal is to assume the "patient role," many times to a desperate or dangerous extent. These disorders contain elements of both masochism and inadequacy. In the factitious disorder, the patient causes, in an active and compulsive manner, his or her physical or psychological symptoms. There is no evidence for other gains, either financial or psychological, and psychological testing will usually reveal a severe personality disorder in which striving for the patient role meets a variety of desperate needs for dependency, security, and attention. In contrast, the "malingering" patient seeks some financial or psychological gain.

Somatization Disorders

The hallmark of the somatization disorder is a long history of recurrent and multiple somatic complaints that wax and wane in severity, usually beginning in adolescence but before the age of 30. Multiple organ systems are usually involved. DSM-III requires that from a list of 37 possible symptoms at least 14 are present in a female patient or 12 in a male. In addition, these symptoms must have caused the person to take some medication (with the exception of aspirin) or to alter their life pattern or to see a physician. The symptoms cannot be explained by a physical disorder or injury and are not the side effects of drugs or alcohol. In interview, these patients will often present their medical history in an exaggerated and dramatic way, though the description of their symptoms is vague and ambiguous. Typically, they have sought multiple consultations with a wide variety of health care providers and have had some intervention or complaint within each 9- to 12-month period. These individuals are prone to substance use disorders because of their extensive contacts with medications but do not seem to self-prescribe, preferring a physician's order instead. They usually do not present with the pain or anxiety symptoms seen in alcoholics and addicts. The somatization disorder patient differs from the factitious disorder in presenting such a variety of symptoms. The most difficult differential may be in ruling out physical disorders that mimic the vague systemic and confusing pattern of multiple symptoms, such as multiple sclerosis and systemic lupus erythematosus.

Conversion Disorders

The symptom picture in conversion reactions remains one in which the symptoms are limited to one organ system per episode. Integration of assessment data requires documenting the primary and secondary gain that the symptoms provide. In the interview, the clinician must look for the necessary temporal relationship to show a psychological conflict or need exists that triggers symptom development. Classic cases are ones of blindness or deafness serving to deny an extremely emotional event (such as having witnessed one parent kill the other). The alternative mechanism is one of secondary gain, which entails a more indirect relationship between symptom production and either avoiding some negative activity or experience or obtaining affection, attention, psychological resources, or support from persons who would otherwise withhold it. The clinician must identify, from interview or other sources, the psychological stress evoking one of these mechanisms. Conversion reactions tend to appear in either early adolescence or early adulthood; however, one may also see middle-aged people experiencing multiple stresses and developing conversion reactions. The older person developing these symptoms is more apt to be experiencing sudden, significant external stresses, the psychological import of which is devastating. Where real neurological disorders exist, it is apparent that primary and/or secondary gain is either absent or difficult to substantiate, and personality testing does not reveal evidence of a conversion disorder. It may be crucial for the clinician to determine whether a source of symptom modeling exists in the patient history, such as a similar symptom constellation in a parent, sibling, or close relative.

As noted previously, classic conversion reactions probably are seen rarely today because of the increased sophistication in American society. The medical setting in which these authors practice produces a moderate proportion of referrals from neurology and more frequently from internal medicine of persons showing a conversion pattern who are facing unmanageable external stresses. The more classic symptoms are apt to appear in persons with internal conflicts. Patients presenting with primary symptoms of pain or sexual dysfunction are not eligible for a diagnosis of conversion reaction under current diagnostic systems.

Hypochondriasis

Hypochondriacal patients differ from the previous categories in that, because of their characteristic fear of disease, they neither evidence the wide variety of symptom patterns nor have undergone the number of surgeries and dramatic medical procedures that are characteristic of the somatization disorder. Clinically, they appear more phobic and less definite in the symptom constellations they describe. When their physician refers them for a psychological or psychiatric evaluation, these patients are apt to change physicians and to resist medical evidence and reassurance that the fear of disease is unfounded.

COMMUNICATION OF RESULTS

Referral sources usually want a diagnostic impression and recommendations for intervention and treatment. This can become an issue because psychological explanations of their symptoms may be strongly resisted by these patients. It is important to assist the physician in continuing to provide appropriate medical care and to present the role psychological factors play in determining the patient's symptoms. For many physicians it is reasonable to believe that they will remain open to the possibility that physical factors are involved in the patient's problems while accepting that at the present time effective treatment requires attention to psychological factors. Occasionally the psychological assessment will show no evidence of psychosomatic involvement when the physician is convinced that such factors are primary in the patient's difficulties. Diplomacy may be required to persuade the physician to look further for possible physical pathology. If appropriate, the report of findings should note the patient's vulnerability to abuse of or addiction to prescribed medication. Although suicide risk tends to be low in these patients, in instances in which depression is prominent such factors need to be carefully addressed in the evaluation and feedback.

Patients in these categories not only lack psychological insight but are resistant to it as well. They also tend to be passive, unassertive, and have difficulty in experiencing and appropriately expressing anger. One can facilitate the presentation of findings to these patients by educating them in how psychological factors affect physical functioning, by using paradigms common to stress management, and by presenting the information in ways that preserve the patient's self-esteem, avoid the possibility of traumatic insight, and stress the need to devise treatment programs addressing holistic goals.

REFERENCES

American Psychiatric Association. (1980). *Diagnostic and statistical manual of mental disorders* (3rd ed.). Washington, DC: Author.

Ariel, R., & Strider, M. A. (1983). Neurological effects of general medical disorders. In C. J. Golden & P. J. Vicente (Eds.), *Foundations of clinical neuropsychology* (pp. 273-308). New York: Plenum Press.

Lishman, W. A. (1978). *Organic psychiatry: The psychological consequences of cerebral disorder.* Oxford: Blackwell Scientific.

Martin, M. J. (1979). Physical disease manifesting as psychiatric disorders. In G. Usdin & J. M. Lewis (Eds.), *Psychiatry in general medical practice* (pp. 337-351). New York: McGraw-Hill.

Ouslander, J. G. (1983). Psychiatric manifestations of physical illness in the elderly. *Psychiatric Medicine, 1, 4,* 363-388.

Pilowsky, I., Spence, N., Cobb, J., & Katsikitis, M. (1984). The Illness Behavior Questionnaire as an aid to clinical assessment. *General Hospital Psychiatry, 6*(2), 123-130.

6

Evaluation in Medical Psychological Settings

LAWRENCE C. HARTLAGE, PH.D.

Psychologists practicing in medical settings must be prepared for diverse evaluation requests, with the requests initiated by professionals who may approach assessment issues from perspectives quite different from those of psychologists. Perhaps the most common tendency of psychologists who find themselves in such an unfamiliar context is to revert to the canons of scientific conservatism learned in graduate training, whereby they are inclined to either "hedge" their findings in psychological jargon involving "confidence intervals" or "standard errors of measurement," labor over minor points of phraseology or interpretation, or retreat to literature searches to help buttress their conclusions. Whereas the psychologist may perceive his or her role as providing accurate *description,* the medical specialist generally requests psychological consultation as an aid to the formulation of a *decision.* The psychologist who can recognize and act on this disparity of perception is much more likely to make meaningful contributions in medical settings.

Preparation for work in medical psychological settings is in many ways similar to that appropriate for work in other settings; that is, developing a repertoire of assessment skills that includes a variety of instruments with which one is comfortable and proficient. To be uniquely effective in specific medical specialty areas, however, this preparation must be augmented with some knowledge of the diseases one is likely to encounter, along with their clinical features, terminology, and possible psychological implications. One means by which psychologists without such prior knowledge or access to teaching rounds dealing with specific diseases may acquire this second level of proficiency is to review the "primer" booklets covering relevant medical specialty areas, which are designed for use by medical students during their rotations through the various specialty areas.

Conversely, education should not be unidirectional: the psychologist must take some responsibility for helping the medical specialist understand both the potential and the limitation of psychological assessment. It is typically through such a mutual education process that a system evolves that enables the psychologist to make maximum contributions to patient care. One procedure for helping to educate one's medical colleagues about psychological assessment involves attaching a relevant reprint to a psychological report. This allows the referring physician to review the contents at his or her leisure and may open the way for future meaningful dialogue about other aspects of psychological assessment.

PREASSESSMENT CONSIDERATIONS

There are a number of factors for the clinician to bear in mind when approaching assessment in medical psychological applications. One involves the likelihood, in a medical patient population, of a very high incidence of medical disorders that can affect the results of standard psychological assessment procedures. Obvious examples include patients with motor problems such as cerebral palsy, arthritis, or orthopedic injuries, which impair performance on some performance IQ measures, or sensory problems affecting vision or hearing, which can influence performance on tests involving these faculties. Perhaps less obvious are conditions such as chronic pain, which can present as depression, hypochondriasis, or diminished concentration, causing one to base potentially erroneous diagnostic conclusions on findings from psychological assessment measures that were standardized and validated on populations relatively free of these problems. Because a variety of medical problems are known to have fairly predictable psychological manifestations, greater attention will be addressed to such problems in this chapter.

Another factor in approaching medical psychological evaluations concerns the nature of the referral questions. Encountered to a much lesser degree in fairly standardized evaluations of mental status, academic problems, or other questions frequently asked of psychologists, the findings in a medical psychological assessment may need to be individualized to answer very discrete referral questions. Examples might include such specific issues as "Is this patient psychologically capable of being responsible for taking medications without supervision?", "Is this patient suffering toxic behavioral effects from this drug?", or "Are these complaints likely of functional vs. organic etiology?" Less explicit referral questions might entail a request such as "Forty-nine-year-old white female with history of uncontrolled diabetes, without any organ damage. Please evaluate." or "Patient diagnosed as generalized tonic-clonic seizure activity. Please do psychological assessment." In such cases, a conversation with the physician who initiated the consultation may be necessary to determine what question(s) he or she had in mind when requesting the psychological evaluation. In the case of the female diabetic, for example, the underlying question may concern the presence of significant depression, whether some mental impairment exists, or whether in the psychologist's opinion the patient has been faithful about adherence to prescribed medication and diet regimens. For an epileptic patient, the question might involve assessing mental status, possible lateralizing signs, extent (if any) of cognitive impairment, or drug toxicity.

Obviously, in order to choose psychological assessment procedures that will provide information relevant to the referral question, the referral question must be understood. Additionally, in cases wherein the psychologist does not have a good understanding of how the physician will apply the assessment findings, both in an immediate and long-term sense, it is important to clarify these issues as well before deciding what tests will be most relevant. The physician may intend, for example, to compare current findings with patient status at some future date; for such an application, the psychologist should consider using tests that could be replicated and would yield objective and sensitive measures of the behaviors in question.

MEDICAL DISORDERS AND SELECTING ASSESSMENT PROCEDURES

Because medical disorders and the side effects of their treatment must be taken into account when interpreting psychological tests in medical settings, the psychologist who practices in such a context must have a working knowledge of these issues in order to select an appropriate test or battery. In many cases, it may be possible to choose a test or battery that will not be influenced substantially by such factors. When no such alternative is available, it may be possible to use an additional measure or measures to help tease out the effects of the disease or its treatment on a given test. In the case of a drowsy or sedated patient who performs poorly on the Wechsler Adult Intelligence Scale-Revised (WAIS-R) Block Design, for example, one may be able to determine whether the poor performance was due to slowed motoric execution as opposed to altered perception by adding a measure involving recognition of test stimuli without a motor component, such as with the Motor Free Block Design Test (Levitt & Hartlage, 1984).

There are two major conceptual approaches to considering the possible effects of given diseases or their treatment on psychological test performance. One approach focuses on studying the signs or symptoms of a variety of common diseases or the psychological treatments for these diseases, which can influence test results, and obtaining medical consultative support for confirming the suspected medical or therapeutic etiology. Symptoms such as anxiety, for example, which clearly can influence (as well as be the subject of) psychological examination, may be attributable to a wide variety of nonpsychological factors (e.g., Giannini, Black, & Goeltsche, 1978), along with such common presenting complaints as depression. In cases of depression, it is especially relevant in medical psychological practice to differentiate between endogenous depression and that which is secondary to concern over a medical illness (e.g., Cassem, 1978). Similarly, presenting complaints such as fatigue may have a variety of medical bases (e.g., Hart, 1979), and even apparently psychological symptoms such as hallucinations can be caused from neurological disorders (e.g., Lowe, 1973), or from chemical substances used in the treatment of certain disorders (e.g., Goodwin, Alderson, & Rosenthal, 1971).

Though a broad knowledge of symptoms and their possible medical or therapeutic etiologies may be necessary for the psychologist who regularly sees an unselected patient population, such as in a health center or family practice clinic, the majority of medical psychologists function in more discrete specialty areas, such as neurology, cardiology, or the like. For those medical psychologists who practice in more generalized medical settings, a reference source such as *Neuropsychiatric Features of Medical Disorders* (Jefferson & Marshall, 1981) may be of considerable value.

Cardiovascular Disorders

Because the majority of nonpsychiatric health problems tend to involve the specialty of internal medicine, it is appropriate to start a discussion of psychological assessment problems in medical specialty areas with a sample of medical problems commonly seen in such practice. Prototypical of the diseases encountered in an internal medical practice is heart disease, which for a number of years has been the leading cause of death in this country. Although clearly a medical disease, psychological factors such as the Type A behavior pattern have been identified as independent risk factors that can double the rate of incidence. More recently, research has found that hostility in a Type A personality may be an important addition to the prediction of coronary disease in younger individuals (Chesney, 1984); thus, where coronary disease may be a factor, the psychologist may wish to include some assessment of hostility, as found in tests like the Multiple Affect Adjective Check List (MAACL). The MAACL can be administered with little investment of either patient or examiner time and can provide valuable baseline data against which to evaluate possible indicators of risk for coronary disease. Clinical features of certain cardiovascular disorders such as heart failure may present as apparently psychological in nature, including such complaints as poor appetite, lack of energy, decreasing sexual activity, or insomnia. For assessment purposes, standardized instruments such as the Minnesota Multiphasic Personality Inventory (MMPI) may be of value in determining the extent to which the underlying medical disease may be of primary etiology. Presuming that MMPI scales such as Depression and possibly Anxiety do not show elevations, these impairments of psychological functions may be merely sequelae of the underlying circulatory problem.

Another disorder of relevance to psychologists involved with internal medicine consultation is mitral valve prolapse syndrome (Barlow's syndrome), which it has been suggested occurs in up to 20% of otherwise healthy people (Jefferson & Marshall, 1981). This disorder may present with symptoms of hyperventilation, migraine, psychoneurosis, or psychosis. A number of researchers have reported many similarities between the psychological symptoms of Barlow's syndrome, anxiety neuroses, and panic states (e.g., Pariser, Pinto, & Jones, 1975; Wooley, 1976). Indeed, the relationship between symptoms of anxiety neurosis and Barlow's syndrome is so strong that a study of patients diagnosed as anxiety neurosis found that nearly 40% of them suffered from mitral valve prolapse (Venkatesh, Pauls, & Crowe, 1978). As the manifestations of psychological symptoms associated with

Barlow's syndrome tend to be episodic, repeated evaluation with such objective measures as the MMPI or MAACL or with projective measures such as the Rorschach or Holtzman Inkblot Technique, which are sensitive to anxiety, may help clarify the periodicity of symptoms as opposed to a more chronic anxiety state.

The drugs used to treat cardiovascular disease also can precipitate some psychological problems. Digitalis, for example, has been reported to cause such symptoms as apathy, aphasia, combativeness, confusion, delusions, disorientation, depression, euphoria, memory problems, and personality changes (Greenblatt & Shader, 1972). Before proceeding with the psychological testing of cardiological patients known to be receiving drug therapy, the psychologist should take a careful history, examining the onset of symptoms in relation to the initiation of digitalis therapy, in order to have a conceptual framework into which to integrate test findings. Other drugs used with cardiovascular disease include quinidine and lidocaine (sometimes used for treating arrhythmic conditions), which have been known to cause apprehension, confusion, or disorientation (Gilbert, 1977; Moe & Abildskou, 1975). Antihypertensive drugs need the psychologist's special attention because they may be used with patients who have no other specific cardiovascular disease. Examples of these agents include hydralazine, reported to cause anxiety, depression, and disorientation, and methyldopa, which may result in depression, forgetfulness, hallucinations, and impaired mental activity (Adler, 1974; Kutz, 1978). In addition, decrease in sexual potency is a fairly common problem with a variety of antihypertensive drugs. Thus the psychologist must consider a number of factors in the interpretation of test data for patients undergoing this type of drug regimen.

Neurological Disorders

Neurological disorders present with a wide variety of symptoms and problems that may appear to be psychological in origin. Especially confounding is the fact that a number of "psychological" disorders such as autism and schizophrenia have, in at least some cases, specific neurological substrates, so that the differential diagnosis of "psychological" versus "neurological" etiologies presents special challenges for the psychologist working with such patients.

Epilepsy, estimated as affecting from 1-4% of the population, is not diagnosed easily and is an unusual disorder in that most of the time the symptom is not present (Hartlage & Telzrow, 1984). Many psychologists have heard of the episodic bizarre or unusual behaviors manifested in partial complex or temporal lobe epilepsy, following which the patient has no recollection of his or her behavior. This condition presents a difficult diagnostic task in differentiation from amnestic or fugue states, and may have occasional legal implications in cases in which the patient has no memory of illegal activities. Though no specific psychological tests exist to diagnose this condition, neuropsychological evaluation of the functions of given brain areas may reveal impairment of a temporal area, which may be related to the symptoms. Neuropsychological batteries such as the Halstead-Reitan or the Luria-Nebraska may help clarify the diagnostic issue, but negative findings on either of these batteries do not necessarily rule out the condition. This disorder, along with generalized tonic-clonic or grand mal epilepsy and absence or petit mal epilepsy, though generally diagnosed by combined behavioral and electroencephalographic data, represents a common referral problem presented to medical psychologists. Typical questions involve issues such as the patient's general psychological status, which often can be addressed with objective personality inventories, such as the MMPI or California Psychological Inventory, and perhaps augmented with appropriate projective measures, such as the Rorschach or the Thematic Apperception Test.

Because epilepsy represents such a heterogenous set of conditions, there is no typical profile or constellation of personality traits common to all affected patients. In most referral cases, whether the question be direct or implied, the patient's current level of functioning on psychometric measures, for purposes of comparison with future measures, is of interest. For this purpose, an age-appropriate Wechsler scale is useful. If the epileptic patient is being seen in a comprehensive rehabilitation program, vocational measures involving aptitude and interest, such as the Kuder Personal Preference Record or the U.S. Employment Service Interest Inventory will help identify areas for vocational development, which can be augmented by vocationally relevant broad spectrum ability measures such as the General Aptitude Test Battery. If psychosocial issues are involved, the Washington Psychosocial Seizure Inventory provides a fairly comprehensive profile, which can be used to complete the overall diagnostic picture.

Mental assessment in epilepsy is made somewhat more difficult than that encountered with other neurological conditions because epilepsy is not a unitary disease entity and may be a symptom of brain tumor, ingestion or inhalation of a toxic substance, anoxia, head injury, or an idiopathic, chronic condition. Depending on whether several brain areas, a discrete focus, or a more generalized abnormality is etiologic in the seizures, the psychometric profile will differ. Further, psychological assessment during the period following a seizure when there is some post-ictal confusion may produce findings that are lower than would be obtained one or two days later. Special impairments on performance IQ abilities may occur during the post-ictal phase, to a greater extent than on verbal IQ tasks. A number of studies have found that the ratio of ability to achievement is somewhat lower for epileptics than for the general population, with persons having epilepsy typically achieving both academically and vocationally at levels below what might be indicated by their intellectual levels (Green & Hartlage, 1971). The actual type of epilepsy appears to be a factor in this discrepancy, in that individuals with idiopathic epilepsy tend to have somewhat higher IQs than those for whom specific etiologies have been discovered, but with comparatively lower achievement levels than for those with known causes (Dodrill, Batzel, Queisser, & Tenkin, 1980; Green & Hartlage, 1971).

To an extent perhaps greater in neurological disorders than in any other medical specialty, the effects of medications used for symptom control can represent a major referral question for the medical psychologist. Each of the medications used to control or reduce the frequency of seizures is likely to have some effect on mental processes because each is intended to affect some aspect of brain function. Phenobarbital, the most venerable of anticonvulsant medications in widespread use, causes significant psychomotor slowing, and thus may affect performance on any test that depends on psychomotor efficiency. As optimum drug therapy in epilepsy maintains a balance between controlling seizures and minimizing behavioral side effects, psychological evaluation for drug effects can be an important ongoing aspect of patient management, with important implications for both types and levels of anticonvulsant medication. For such assessment purposes, the tests found most sensitive to anticonvulsant medication side effects include the Wechsler Coding, Digit Symbol, and Digit Span subtests; the Symbol Digit Modalities Test; rate of rapid finger oscillation; and the Minnesota Rate of Manipulation Test (Hartlage, 1981). As these measures all involve elements of motor speed and/or attention and are differentially sensitive to specific anticonvulsant medications, other comparable measures, such as the Purdue Pegboard Test, the Revised Minnesota Paper Form Board, or the Lincoln-Oseretsky Motor Development Scale, may be substituted by the psychologist concerned with the behavioral toxicity of drugs. For some patients with epilepsy that has been chronically intractible to drug therapy, surgical resection of the epileptogenic brain areas may be performed. In such cases, pre- and post-operative assessment of personality, intellectual, and psychomotor functions, using the same tests as in the evaluation of nonsurgical epilepsy patients, is valuable (Hartlage & Flanigan, 1982).

A special problem that has gained recognition in recent years involves the assessment of mental function in Alzheimer's disease. Although the definitive diagnosis of Alzheimer's disease may depend on postmortem examination, the putative diagnosis often is made on the basis of exclusionary medical and neurological criteria combined with deterioration in mental function. As the progress and course of this disease tend to vary among individuals, there is no uniquely relevant test or battery. Rather, measures of mental function that are appropriate to the individual's mental functional level and that cover a range of abilities including memory, concentration, and attention usually are selected to measure the rate of deterioration or decline for these patients. As memory deterioration represents a major clinical feature of Alzheimer's disease, measures of short-term and working memory may yield especially helpful information (Baddeley, Della Salla, Logie, & Spinnler, 1985; Becker, Boller, Saxton, & McGonigle, 1985). When compared with baseline measures of intellectual function, such data can both document the nature and extent of memory impairment and in turn serve as a baseline for subsequent measures.

In adult medical psychology settings, there are of course a variety of other medical specialties that may produce psychological consultation requests. It is hoped that, by presenting simple medical and neurological specialties, a model for consideration in other specialties can be developed by the medical psychologist, unique to his or her setting and accordingly sensitive to the specific issues that may be encountered.

INTEGRATING FINDINGS AND COMMUNICATING RESULTS

An element of medical psychological assessment that differs from traditional mental health, counseling, or educational evaluations involves the mechanics of preparing and disseminating test findings. Typically, in medical psychology settings a considerably greater emphasis is focused on conclusions as opposed to findings. Conferring mental health professionals, for example, may appreciate a discussion of responses to given projective test items, and those from educational settings may be interested in subtest scatter and other relevant details. The medical psychologist, however, must keep in mind that psychometric entities such as "confidence intervals," or personality assessment concepts such as Rorschach "human movement" or MMPI "4-9 profile type," typically will fall outside both the ken and the interest of most nonpsychiatric physicians. These physicians usually look to the psychologist for his or her conclusions, to a much greater extent than is appreciated by psychologists who have not spent time in medical settings. It is not at all uncommon for physicians to scan a psychological report in search of a section captioned "Conclusions" or "Impression."

With respect to the dissemination of psychological test findings, there is a real need for promptness in medical settings. It is common for a consultation request both to be assessed *and answered in writing* on the day of the request, or at least within 24 hours. A number of very practical reasons for this exist. With hospitalized patients, for example, a drug regimen or surgical procedure may be deferred pending the completion of a baseline psychological assessment for comparison with posttreatment status. Delay in processing consultation requests can prolong the patient's hospital stay, which incurs needless additional cost to the patient (or, with the advent of Diagnostic Related Groupings as a reimbursement mechanism, extra costs to the hospital), can tie up hospital beds that are needed for new admissions, and can postpone the initiation of vital therapy. With outpatients, especially those who may have had to take time away from work, delays can cause needless additional missed work and disruptions in the scheduling of baby sitters, transportation to the hospital, etc. For patients who must travel some distance to the hospital or clinic, failure by the psychologist to see them in conjunction with the clinic visit that precipitated the psychological consultation request may necessitate another visit, with attendant loss of travel and work time, plus extra transportation costs.

Thus medical psychologists must maintain considerable flexibility in assessment approaches, as insistence on performing a standard test battery that is relatively independent of the referral question may involve more time than is either available or necessary. Nonpsychiatric physicians, who see 20 or more patients a day in clinics, often have difficulty understanding why a psychologist is unable to test (and summarize test findings for) a single patient in a day or significant portion of a day, even if the testing was unscheduled and unanticipated. While communication concerning the unique features of psychological testing may help overcome this lack of understanding, it is a poor substitute for a prompt response to consultation requests.

It is this emphasis on prompt responses that enhances the importance of a medical psychologist's knowledge of a wide variety of test instruments, with differing time durations and sensitivities to diverse referral issues. Within a given week, the medical psychologist may be asked to evaluate patients with an assortment of referral questions; in a medical setting one can ill afford to have to choose or learn a new test for someone in the outpatient waiting room or in a hospital bed awaiting the initiation of necessary treatment.

Medical psychology has made important progress within the past decade (e.g., Prokop & Bradley, 1981), and shows promise for future growth and specialization. The psychologist who is well versed in psychological assessment and willing to translate psychological findings into terms relevant to enhancing medical intervention programs can make important and valued contributions to the alleviation or amelioration of a variety of human problems, both medical and psychological.

REFERENCES

Adler, S. (1974). Methyldopa induceal decrease in mental activity. *Journal of the American Medical Association, 230,* 1428-1429.

Baddeley, A., Della Salla, S., Logie, R., & Spinnler, H. (1985). Working memory and dementia. *Journal of Clinical and Experimental Neuropsychology, 7*(2), 139 (abstract).

Becker, J. T., Boller, F., Saxton, J., & McGonigle, K. (1985). Short-term memory in Alzheimer's disease. *Journal of Clinical and Experimental Neuropsychology, 7*(2), 140 (abstract).

Cassem, N. H. (1978). Depression. In T. R. Hackett & N. H. Cassem (Eds.), *Massachusetts General Hospital handbook of general hospital psychiatry* (pp. 209-225). St. Louis: C. V. Mosby Co.

Chesney, M. A. (1984, August). *Behavioral factors in coronary heart disease: Separating benign from malignent.* Paper presented at the annual meeting of the American Psychological Association, Toronto.

Dodrill, C. B., Batzel, L. W., Queisser, H. R., & Tenkin, N. R. (1980). An objective method for the assessment of psychological and social problems among epileptics. *Epilepsia, 21,* 123-135.

Giannini, A. J., Black, H. R., & Goeltsche, R. L. (1978). *Psychiatric, psychogenic and somalopsychic disorders handbook.* New York: Medical Examination Publishing Company.

Gilbert, J. J. (1977). Quinidine denertica. *Journal of the American Medical Association, 237,* 2093-2094.

Goodwin, D. W., Alderson P., & Rosenthal, R. (1971). Clinical significance of hallucinations in psychiatric disorders. *Archives of General Psychiatry, 24,* 76-80.

Green, J. G., & Hartlage, L. C. (1971). Comparative performance of epileptic and nonepileptic children and adolescents. *Diseases of the Nervous System, 32,* 418-421.

Greenblatt, D. J., & Shader, R. I. (1972). Digitalis toxicity. In R. I. Shader (Ed.), *Psychiatric complications of medical drugs* (pp. 25-47). New York: Raven Press.

Hart, F. D. (1979). Fatigue. In F. D. Hart (Ed.), *French's index of differential diagnosis* (p. 285). Bristol, England: John R. Wright.

Hartlage, L. C. (1981). Neuropsychological assessment of anticonvulsant drug toxicity. *Clinical Neuropsychology, 3*(1), 20-22.

Hartlage, L. C., & Flanigan, H. (1982). Neuropsychological aspects of temporal lobe resection in epilepsy. *Clinical Neuropsychology, 4,* 89-90.

Hartlage, L. C., & Telzrow, C. F. (1984). Neuropsychological aspects of childhood epilepsy. In R. E. Tarter & G. Goldstein (Eds.), *Advances in clinical neuropsychology* (pp. 159-179). New York: Plenum Press.

Jefferson, J. W., & Marshall, J. R. (1981). *Neuropsychiatric features of medical disorders. New York: Plenum Press.*

Kutz, J. B. (1976). Methyldopin and forgetfulness. *Lancet, 1,* 202-203.

Levitt, R. A., & Hartlage, L. C. (1984, February). *Clinical utility of a multiple choice block design test.* Paper presented at the meeting of the International Neuropsychological Society, Houston.

Lowe, G. R. (1973). The phenomenology of hallucinations as an aid to differential diagnosis. *British Journal of Psychiatry, 123,* 621-633.

Moe, G. K., & Abildskou, J. A. (1975). Antiarrythmic drugs. In L. S. Goodman & A. Gilman (Eds.), *The pharmacological basis of therapeutics* (pp. 683-704). New York: Macmillan Publishing Co.

Pariser, S. F., Pinto, E. R., & Jones, B. A. (1978). Mitral valve prolapse syndrome and anxiety neurosis/panic disorder. *American Journal of Psychiatry, 135,* 246-247.

Prokop, C. K., & Bradley, L. A. (1981). *Medical psychology.* New York: Academic Press.

Venkatesh, A., Pauls, D. L., & Crowe, R. (1978). Mitral valve prolapse in anxiety neurosis. *Clinical Research, 26,* 656.

Wooley, C. F. (1976). Where are the diseases of yesteryear? *Circulation, 53,* 749-751.

7

Neuropsychological Testing: Essentials of Differential Diagnosis

WILLIAM J. LYNCH, PH.D.

In the assessment of adults, particularly older adults, the clinician must remain alert to the possible presence of brain impairment. Beginning with the pioneering work of Luria (1966) and Halstead (1947), and later through Reitan (1966) and Christensen (1979), clinical neuropsychology (the study of the effects of brain disorders on behavior) has developed into a complex and significant specialty. However, those who through a combination of specialized education, supervised training, and experience have attained the status of specialists in this area represent a minority among the many clinicians called on to perform these assessments. The majority of clinicians faced with the problem of recognizing and accurately categorizing the signs and symptoms of neurological impairment have not had such training and therefore must strive to attain some proficiency in screening patients for possible referral to a specialist in clinical neuropsychology.

This chapter provides information relevant both to experienced general clinicians as well as to those who have attained some level of expertise in clinical neuropsychology. This does not imply, however, that someone with inadequate training and experience in neuropsychological assessment should expect to become proficient merely by reading this chapter. While a certain amount of what the clinician needs to learn is of a technical or *quantitative* nature (i.e., techniques of administration or scoring), the critical element of competent neuropsychological assessment is more *qualitative* and *observational,* requiring considerable firsthand experience with a variety of patients.

From time to time clinicians are asked to evaluate patients with the common "functional" complaints of confusion, memory loss, fatigue, or depression—any of which can also represent the early onset of a neurological disorder such as Alzheimer's disease. The psychologist's task is to determine when to administer certain additional tests and, more importantly, when to consult with or refer to a neuropsychological specialist for a more definitive evaluation.

Evaluations typically are requested by other professionals (e.g., psychologists, physicians, speech pathologists), school or employment personnel, or attorneys representing the patient in a lawsuit. The information sought may involve determining the presence, severity, location, type, progression, and/or behavioral/emotional consequences of brain dysfunction. Any of these alone is a substantial undertaking, and thus to deal with two or more of these issues requires considerable skill, patience, and effort. Despite what one might read, there is no "quick and easy" way to evaluate complex human abilities comprehensively, and this is particularly true of neuropsychological abilities. The issue of differential diagnosis is a complex one, requiring a high degree of intuitive skill and flexibility. Clinicians involved with a neuropsychological assessment must concern themselves both with failing to detect an existing cerebral dysfunction and with the equally distressing problem of false detection. Both forms of error have tremendous implications for the patient's health and welfare, but it seems that the general clinician is more apt to consult with colleagues only when suspected impairment is not found. Neuropsychological deficits are more often overdiagnosed or misdiagnosed than missed altogether. The discussion that follows is intended to provide a framework for reducing the frequency of these errors by suggesting ways to enhance diagnostic testing skills.

PREDIAGNOSTIC STAFFING:
APPRECIATING THE COMPLEXITIES OF THE PROBLEM

Nature of the Problem

In psychological assessment there are very few "always" and almost no "nevers." Thus, no behavior observation or test finding, in isolation, can confirm or deny reliably the presence of organic brain impairment or can attribute a behavioral abnormality to a specific neurological cause. The difficulty in the differential diagnosis of neuropsychological problems lies in the tremendous variety of both presenting problems and the forms they take. The nature of the patient's symptoms and complaints depends on the type, location, rate of progression, and chronicity of the lesion or brain disease process. In addition, the age, intellectual level, stress tolerance, and general health of the patient significantly affect his or her response to the impairment. Such complex influences call for complex assessment strategies.

Any complex behavior is multidetermined, and there are many possible causes for symptoms of psychological distress. The clinician must make every effort to discover the exact etiology of these symptoms so that appropriate treatment can be instituted. For example, many causes of the dementia symptom complex are treatable and reversible, and thus it is critical to make the differential diagnosis as quickly as possible so that treatment can commence. Some neurological conditions may masquerade as (i.e., be mistaken for) psychogenic disorders, such as complex partial seizures (formerly termed "temporal lobe epilepsy") and Tourette's syndrome (featuring facial tics and unusual vocalizations).

Symptoms and Signs

As noted, virtually any symptom or sign presented by a patient could be the result of a neurological disorder or a functional psychological disturbance. The common symptoms of a major depressive disorder—psychomotor slowing, fatigue, memory impairment, and sleep disturbance—are often observed in early dementia. Similarly, the list of possible symptoms associated with complex partial seizures includes hallucinations (especially of a visual, olfactory, or gustatory nature), delusions, feelings of unreality, decreased anger control, excessive writing, and periodic episodes of automatic movements and/or verbalizations.

Whereas a complex pattern of behavioral signs and neurological or psychological symptoms must be considered in differentiating disturbance etiology, some relatively isolated symptoms that demand immediate clarification include the following:

Sudden, severe headaches: These are often described as "explosive" in character and termed "the worst headache in my life." This symptom may point toward intracranial bleeding from an aneurism or arteriovenous malformation, as well as toward the possibility of an inflammatory process such as meningitis.

Substantial and intensifying impairment of memory or orientation: Few functional psychological disorders feature substantial memory problems or impaired orientation regarding time, place, and/or person. While depressed persons may report some mild "memory problems," they do not lose track of the date, their location, or who they are. The conditions that could give rise to these problems include degenerative dementia (Alzheimer's or Pick's disease, for instance), infectious processes, or toxic states (from alcohol, solvents, heavy metals, or liver disease).

Gradual or rapid impairment in language functions: The patient who reports more-or-less sudden difficulty in naming, word finding, writing, reading, or verbal comprehension should be examined carefully for aphasia. There are few nonorganic conditions that produce serious language disorders, and thus one should suspect an organic etiology until proven otherwise. The conditions that commonly produce such clear-cut aphasia include stroke, brain tumors, and focal brain infections (cysts).

Loss of motor and/or sensory functions: The person presenting with either gradual or rapid loss of motor or sensory functions, especially if the pattern extends to an entire side of the body, should be referred immediately for neurological evaluation. The incidence of functional paralysis or anesthesia is rare enough, and the consequences of failing to correctly diagnose the problem dire enough, to presume an organic basis for these symptoms whenever they occur. Less common, but no less significant, is the symptom of visual field loss (quarter- or half-field loss in each eye). When present, such a defect is not only significant but also points directly to the location of the offending brain lesion. Possible causes of sensorimotor losses are stroke, brain tumor, or focal brain infections.

Complaints of unusual or noxious tastes or smells: The individual who reports the constant or occasional experience of a bad taste or smell should be evaluated for the presence of temporal lobe dysfunction. This is particularly true if these experiences precede any recurring behaviors such as seizures. In certain traumatic brain lesions, there may be a loss of sense of smell due to damage to the olfactory nerve(s) beneath the frontal lobes.

Other critical symptoms or signs include changes in gait, slurred speech, and persistent nausea/vomiting. Any of these could be the result of a stroke or brain tumor and should be considered ominous signs.

Formulation of Assessment/Diagnostic Strategy

Though a thorough history is an important element of any assessment, it is absolutely essential in neuropsychological evaluation. The history provides a dynamic and chronological picture of the onset, progression, and course of the patient's symptoms. The history is the first and most important step in the diagnosis of neuropsychological disorders because most conditions have a characteristic pattern in terms of rapidity of onset, rate of progression, and type of course. For example, most strokes have a sudden or fairly rapid onset (from seconds or minutes up to hours or days), while brain tumors generally have onsets of months or years. With regard to progression, strokes tend to progress fairly rapidly, while tumors do so more slowly. These conditions also vary in course, with strokes having a characteristic pattern of rapid deficit followed by steady or stepwise improvement; tumors, on the other hand, tend to result in steadily increasing neurological deficit over time. The history may also reveal the presence of certain familial conditions such as Huntington's disease or progressive degenerative dementia (Alzheimer's disease), as well as past surgery or medical treatment, which could relate to the patient's current symptoms.

The format of the history should be both structured and flexible, containing a standard data base and additional information such as the patient's subjective experiences of the illness. A simple topical outline of a neuropsychological history would be as follows:

1. Personal/demographic information—include name, address, phone number, age, birthdate, level of education, etc.

2. Reason for referral—from the perspective of both patient and referral source; note who referred patient and identify current treating professionals.

3. Current complaints/symptoms—note symptoms/signs and their onset, progression, course; determine what aggravates the symptoms as well as what alleviates them, and what the patient can and cannot do because of them.

4. Work background—note current and significant past jobs, how long held, why patient left; obtain a description of actual job duties.

5. Family background—note age and health status of all parents and siblings; in case of deaths or serious illnesses, determine the diseases and/or causes of death.

6. Marriage history—include dates of all marriages and divorces, and reasons for the latter, plus number, age, and health status of all children.

7. Health history—note dates, diagnoses, and outcomes of any major surgical procedures and illnesses; determine any history of seizures, head injury, brain tumor, stroke, or CNS infections; inquire about current or past problems with stress-related somatic complaints, such as ulcers, hypertension, headaches, and any sleep, sexual, or eating disorders.

8. Medications history—include current and previous medications, their dosages, time period over which taken, reasons for taking, and side effects; also include use of recreational or "street" drugs as well as alcohol and cigarettes.

9. Mental health history—note dates, diagnoses, treatments, and outcomes relating to any formal mental health contacts.

10. School history—include grades obtained, best/worst subjects, and scores on any standardized tests, such as achievement tests, SAT, ACT, or GRE.

11. Current level of independence—determine the patient's actual performance and premorbid level of performance on activities of daily living, such as dressing, eating, ambulation, toilet activities, bathing, work, socialization, and communication skills; consult with family and/or friends whenever possible to obtain an objective view of patient's abilities.

The clinician should be willing to solicit information from many sources (with the patient's permission, of course), including family, workplace, school/college, and friends. If the patient is in the hospital, the observations of nursing staff as well as occupational, speech, or physical therapists should be consulted. A valid and comprehensive picture of the patient is not likely to emerge from a self-description alone.

SELECTION AND ADMINISTRATION OF TESTS AND PROCEDURES

The formal assessment should then continue with the selection and administration of neuropsychological tests. The choice of measures depends on the differential diagnostic question being considered, the commonest of which is dementia versus "pseudodementia" (i.e., between an organic and functional mental deterioration). The typical referral will describe the patient as being mildly confused, distractible, sad, and forgetful. Today many such patients are referred for CT (computerized tomography) scans of the head, the results of which are usually either negative or only slightly out of the ordinary. The clinician's task, therefore, is to determine whether the patient's complaints are due to organic brain dysfunction or to a mental disorder such as major depression.

Neuropsychological assessment for differential diagnosis should be both general and specific in scope. Because the clinician is usually unaware of the exact problem early in the assessment, it is important to evaluate a reasonably broad range of abilities so that the chances of detecting a particular deficit are enhanced. Similarly, once the clinician becomes aware of some possible deficits, specific and more in-depth assessment is required to characterize properly the nature and severity of deficits present. Though certain isolated deficits such as spatial disorientation may not be fully appreciated by the patient, he or she may be aware that "something is wrong with me." This may result in depression.

There are certain measures or assessment strategies that should be utilized for virtually all neuropsychological evaluations. Some examples of these essential tools are measures of mental status, psychometric intelligence, and memory. (Specific tests in these areas will be discussed.) Additional measurement areas that are generally useful are communicative abilities (speaking, understanding, reading, writing, and gesturing) and academic achievement (e.g., reading, spelling, and arithmetic). If the diagnostic question concerns focal (i.e., localized) versus diffuse or generalized brain impairment, the clinician will want to sample such areas as sensory, motor, auditory, spatial, and abstract reasoning abilities, especially if these are noted cursorily as deficits during intelligence testing. Particular attention should be paid to the patient's performance on tasks that assess the two sides of the body, such as sensory-perceptual and motor skills tests. Focal brain lesions or disorders do not usually affect the ipsilateral (same) side of the body to the same extent that they affect the contralateral (opposite) side.

In summary, it is critical that the clinician evaluate a wide variety of cognitive and perceptual-motor abilities at some level. Certain ability areas, such as memory, should be evaluated broadly, using different content (verbal or nonverbal), different modes of presentation (oral or written), different time intervals between presentation and recall (immediate, 3 minutes, 20 minutes, or 1 hour), and different techniques of recall (free, prompted, or multiple choice). If there is a question concerning differential diagnosis between an organic condition and depression, some personality assessment will be required. In addition to the standard measures, specialized instruments or specific depression rating scales may be of value.

The clinician's choice of tests should depend on a number of factors. Of primary importance is the relevance of the test to the situation; that is, is it the best available measure of what one needs to measure? An additional consideration is the clinician's degree of expertise in administering, scoring, and interpreting that test. Another factor is whether the patient's current physical and mental state will allow him or her to perform validly on the measure(s) in question. Finally, the clinician must decide whether the time alotted for the assessment justifies employing a given test (i.e., whether the informational payoff is proportional to the expenditure of time required for administration).

The following sections present a selection of specific tests that many neuropsychologists find useful when faced with the problem of differential diagnosis.

Measures of Mental Status

The mental status examination (MSE) is classically a rather lengthy and detailed procedure. Although a recent text was devoted to this (Strub & Black, 1977), most clinicians employ a shorter form of the MSE when the procedure is warranted. Descriptions of some of the briefer MSEs follow:

The Short Portable Mental Status Questionnaire (SPMSQ) is a 10-item questionnaire that is widely used as a quick-screening device or as a serial measure of mental status for inpatients. The items on the SPMSQ deal with orientation to time and place, personal information, and mental control. Each item is scored as right or wrong, with the total indicating the overall level of impairment. Like many ultrabrief cognitive measures, the SPMSQ may lead to excessive false negative diagnoses (Lezak, 1983), but is less likely to lead to false positive diagnoses because the items are quite simple and are failed by very few nonimpaired persons. The main advantages of the SPMSQ are its brevity, simplicity, and oral format (i.e., the patient does not have to be able to write, draw, or manipulate objects). It is most useful for rough screening and where time is of the essence. Because of its simple format, the SPMSQ is generally well tolerated by disabled patients. It should not be used in instances in which a careful assessment of mental status is required, such as in competency or litigation cases or when evaluating for dementia.

The Mini-Mental State Examination (MMSE) is a somewhat more comprehensive mental status measure that appeared in the mid-1970s. This instrument has been used in numerous research studies and is well known among psychiatric investigators. The MMSE consists of the following sections: 1) Orientation: Time (5 items); 2) Orientation: Place (5 items); 3) Memory (3 words; no delay); 4) Attention/Calculation (serial 7s; 5 subtractions); 5) Recall (3 words from memory section with 2 minute delay); and 6) Language (confrontation naming; repetition; following three-step verbal command; following simple printed command; writing sentence; copying intersecting pentagons).

The MMSE is scored by awarding a point for each item that is performed correctly, to a maximum of 30 points. Norms are presented for various groups: normals, demented patients, and a variety of mental disorders such as depression and schizophrenia. A sample form of the MMSE is presented in Lezak's (1983) text, although the clinician can devise one by referring to the original article (Folstein, Folstein, & McHugh, 1975) for details of the MMSE items.

Measures of Intellectual Functions

The centerpiece of any comprehensive neuropsychological assessment is the measure of psychometric intelligence. For adults, the Wechsler Adult Intelligence Scale-Revised (WAIS-R) is the best normed and standardized individual measure of intelligence available, yielding individual subtest scaled scores as well as a Verbal, Performance, and Full Scale IQs. Because of the number and variety of WAIS-R subtests, the clinician is provided with a rich assortment of qualitative and quantitative data for analysis. In differential diagnosis, it is helpful to have such a variety of observations of the patient's performances.

Other appropriate tests for determining IQ include Raven's Progressive Matrices (Advanced, Coloured, Standard) and the Shipley Institute of Living Scale; these can be used to estimate WAIS-R intelligence levels. However, it is *not* recommended that such measures be employed for a differential diagnosis of neuropsychological deficit, as they are neither sufficiently normed nor sufficiently multidimensional to provide useful diagnostic information.

Measures of Memory

The selection of memory measures is determined by the diagnostic question. As noted previously, *some* memory measure is indicated in virtually all neuropsychological assessments; however, it is critical to tailor the measure (or style of measure) to the specific needs of the case. For example, if the evaluation calls for an assessment of language abilities or perceptual-motor skills, the need for detailed memory testing is less pronounced than if the evaluation calls for determining the presence, extent, and type(s) of memory dysfunction.

When a general assessment of memory is desired, the most frequently used test is the Wechsler Memory Scale (WMS). The popularity of the WMS is due more to its longevity and lack of serious competition than to its inherent qualities as a comprehensive measure of memory (see, for example, Prigatano, 1977). The WMS comes in two forms (I and II), which facilitates serial testing, and yields raw scores for each subtest, all of which are summed to arrive at a total score for the entire test. One then adds an age weight to arrive at the total raw score, which then yields a final "Memory Quotient" or MQ. The WMS measures only immediate memory, does not include any interference trials, and utilizes only free recall.

As a result of weaknesses in the WMS, clinicians have developed various modifications (e.g., Russell, 1975). These modified versions of the WMS typically include delayed recall trials for the Logical Memory (stories) and Visual Reproduction (designs) subtests. Edith Kaplan (n.d.) at the Boston Veterans Administration Hospital has developed an extended WMS that in addition to delayed recall includes interference, prompting, and recognition memory trials for the Logical Memory and Visual Reproduction subtests. Kaplan's unpublished version also provides for more extensive qualitative observations than does the WMS.

Another memory measure that has become popular in recent years is the Rey Auditory Verbal Learning Test (RAVLT), which consists of three lists of 15 semantically different words. The first list is presented five times, with the instruction to recall as many words as possible each time, *including words recalled on previous trials* and in *any* order. The examiner records the patient's responses in the order in which they are given so that patterns or strategies of recall can be examined. Following the initial five trials a new list of 15 words is presented for recall, which functions as an interference trial. After recording the patient's responses, the examiner then asks the patient to recall as many words as possible from the *first* list (this is considered Trial VI). Finally, a recognition memory trial is presented, consisting of a brief story containing all the words in the original list. The patient is required to indicate which words in the story belong to the original list. Lezak (1983) presents a set of norms for the RAVLT, including norms for the performance of patients and normals on Trials V and VI.

There are a number of visual memory tests available. The Rey-Osterreith Complex Figure consists of numerous simple elements (squares, rectangles, lines, and triangles) combined into a complex design. The patient is required to copy the design, then to reproduce it from memory after a delay (15 to 45 minutes). Scoring includes timing, accuracy, and sequence of approach measures.

The Benton Revised Visual Retention Test is available in two formats. The standard version consists of three parallel forms (C, D, and E) that are sets of 10 designs, eight of which contain two or more designs on each card. There are four "standard" administrations: A (10-second exposure, immediate drawing); B (5-second exposure, immediate drawing); C (direct copy); and D (10-second exposure, 15-second delay before drawing). The test is administered by presenting the items (in booklets) for the prescribed time limits, with the patient drawing each design on separate 5″ x 8″ sheets of paper. The multiple-choice version, the Visual Form Discrimination Test, is easier to administer and less affected by the patient's motor difficulties. The set of designs is presented on a page of the test booklet; this is then flipped over, revealing four choices, one of which is correct. The three "foils" (wrong choices) are quite close to the correct choice, with one main error (e.g., peripheral figure rotated; central large figures reversed). The examiner can identify easily the type of error made by referring to the answer form.

Measures of Language Disturbance

It is common for brain disorders to cause disruptions in some aspects of language. The precise assessment of language abilities requires the expertise of a speech/language pathologist; however, a psychologist can effectively *screen* patients in order to identify those in need of further assessment. In differential diagnosis, the clinician is often called on to assess many facets of language, including speaking, reading, writing, and listening abilities. Systematic screening for problems in one or more of these areas typically includes a review of language performances in the interview and history, and test responses on IQ and memory measures and formal measures of language efficiency.

The clinician who has had sufficient training and experience can employ one of the standard comprehensive language examinations, such as the Boston Diagnostic Aphasia Examination (BDAE), the Minnesota Test for the Differential Diagnosis of Aphasia, or the Porch Index of Communicative Ability (PICA). The BDAE is probably the most commonly employed by clinicians across disciplines because it is flexible and lends itself to selecting one or two subtests for the assessment of a particular problem. The PICA is unique in that it employs a complex multidimensional scoring system that quantifies wide varieties of communicative performance.

The most common brief measures of language abilities are the Aphasia Screening Test (AST) and the Token Test. The AST, part of the Halstead-Reitan Neuropsychological Test Battery, is intended to assess quickly a variety of abilities related to language in addition to a number of other abilities such as drawing and right-left orientation. The AST is brief (32 items) and requires only a small test booklet for administration (along with paper and pen). While the AST is helpful in making rough determinations regarding the presence of organic pathology or the side of the brain that is most affected, it is *not* an adequate measure of language abilities nor should it be used to diagnose the type of aphasia if present. The Token Test consists of a set of 20 plastic pieces that differ in shape (squares or circles), size (large or small), and color (red, blue, yellow, green, and white). The instructions vary from simple ("touch the large red square") to complex ("after picking up the small red circle, touch the small blue square"). The test is intended to measure a broad range of verbal comprehension abilities and is especially helpful in discriminating receptive versus expressive language problems because it places minimal demands on the patient's motor system.

Evaluating Educational Deficits

The determination of educational deficit requires a combination of information. The first step is to ask the patient how far he or she went in school, what degree(s) were awarded, and when. It is important to ascertain actual school grades in significant academic subject areas such as English, math, and science. The clinician must try to determine a trend in the patient's school performance, if any, as this would have a bearing on his or her current level of ability. Whenever possible, one should corroborate the patient's recollections with independent information from relatives and/or school records. Performance on standardized tests (such as the Scholastic Aptitude Test) is easier to evaluate than school grades, because the latter are highly variable in meaning from one school to another.

In addition to grades, certain tests may be administered to obtain grade equivalents, standard scores, or percentiles for particular academic subject areas. For example, the Wide Range Achievement Test-Revised (WRAT-R) yields standard scores (deviation IQs and T-scores), percentiles, and grade equivalents for persons from ages 5 through 74.

Educational assessment is particularly helpful in the diagnosis of conditions such as "attention deficit disorder" or "specific developmental disorders," which may involve reading, arithmetic, language, or articulation. In adults, the presence of spelling errors on aphasia testing is considered more ominous when achievement testing indicates normal spelling ability. Some clinicians may wish to consider administering entire neuropsychological batteries rather than selected tests. The three principal systems used in the United States are the Halstead-Reitan Neuropsychological Test Battery, Luria's Neuropsychological Investigation, and the Luria-Nebraska Neuropsychological Battery. A detailed description of these approaches is beyond the scope of this chapter, but it should be made clear that such procedures are complex and require considerable expertise for proper administration and interpretation.

Evaluating Emotional Status

If the diagnostic question concerns differentiating between a major mental disorder (such as schizophrenia or depression) and organic pathology, the clinician must consider employing some type of personality test. Generally, assessment procedures such as the Rorschach technique or the Thematic Apperception Test (TAT) are not helpful in this regard. As a rule, a careful diagnostic interview along with one or more structured personality tests will be sufficient. In the area of depression, several brief questionnaires are available, such as the Beck Depression Inventory and Zung's Self-Rating Depression Scale (1965). The Minnesota Multiphasic Personality Inventory (MMPI) is often helpful in identifying affective or thought disorders, and in addition to the standard form (with 566 items) there are shorter versions available, such as the MMPI-168 (Overall & Gomez-Mont, 1974) or the OBD-168 (Sbordone & Caldwell, 1979), which require much less of the patient's time and yet yield helpful personality data. One of the drawbacks to questionnaires is the obvious fact that they should not be given to aphasic patients or patients with visual-perceptual deficits.

INTERPRETATION AND INTEGRATION OF FINDINGS

Neuropsychological tests must be interpreted in several ways simultaneously to be most effective in differential diagnosis (see Golden, 1983; Filskov & Leli, 1981). These methods include level of performance, patterns of performance, comparison of the performance of the two sides of the body, and pathognomonic signs.

Level of Performance

The most common interpretive procedure is simply to determine how well the patient performed by comparing his or her score to an appropriate norm group, revealing whether the score is abnormal. Tests such as the WAIS-R, the Wechsler Memory Scale, and most achievement tests have means of 100 and standard deviations of 15. Scores below 90 are considered "below average" and scores above 109 are "above average." Other instruments have cutoff scores to separate normal from abnormal performance; performances are considered normal unless they reach or exceed a certain critical level. The Halstead-Reitan battery uses this approach. It is useful to convert the patient's performances to standard scores such as T-scores, which have a mean of 50 and a standard deviation of 10, because this helps greatly in the intertest comparison of performance levels. T-scores can be plotted on profiles and averaged as a general measure of test performance (Kiernan & Matthews, 1976).

There are certain cautions to consider in relying on level of performance alone in neuropsychological assessment. The clinician must be certain that the norms on which the cutoff scores are based are appropriate for the patient being evaluated. It is rare, for example, to find tests with different cutoff points for more than one or two age groups. It is well known that tests with significant memory and/or perceptual-motor speed components must have adjusted cutoff scores for older patients. Another consideration when employing level of performance as a criterion is the fact that certain nonorganic mental disorders (e.g., depression, schizophrenia, manic disorder) can cause significant declines in cognitive efficiency and therefore test performances may fall spuriously in the "organic" range.

Patterns of Performance

By taking note of the relative strengths and weaknesses exhibited by the patient, the clinician can glean a great deal of diagnostic information. For example, does the patient perform poorly on motor tasks but not on tasks that are sensory in nature? Is receptive language more affected than expressive language? Are language abilities better preserved than visual-spatial abilities? Is verbal memory more impaired than nonverbal memory? By analyzing such patterns, the clinician often can determine the presence and general location (i.e., anterior vs. posterior, left vs. right hemisphere) of a brain lesion. By searching for consistencies (and inconsistencies) in the test data it is often possible to differentiate organic from nonorganic patterns. As an example, the patient who can recall only three digits forward but can recall seven words from a word list (such as the Rey AVLT) is not apt to have an organic memory disorder. Likewise, the patient who has normal Digit Span and Arithmetic scores on the WAIS-R yet who claims to remember no details from the Wechsler Memory Scale stories (Logical Memory) is more likely lacking in effort and motivation than in innate memory ability.

The most frequent test pattern used by the average clinician is the Verbal-Performance IQ difference on the WAIS-R. While differences of 10 or more points are rare statistically (Wechsler, 1981, p. 35), differences of this magnitude seem to occur with some frequency among a variety of patient groups. It is safer, in the opinion of this author, to adopt a more conservative criterion of 13-15 points, especially if the IQ scores are outside of the "average" range (90-109). The rule of thumb is that in right-handed persons, a significant Verbal deficit *may* imply left-hemisphere impairment, and a significant Performance deficit suggests right-hemisphere impairment. However, this interpretation should be made with caution and *not* to the exclusion of other testing.

The clinician should take note of differences in performance that occur as a result of changes in modality with the task content held relatively constant. For instance, the patient who can point to a picture of a pen on command but cannot say the name aloud may have an expressive speech problem. By systematically varying the stimulus and response characteristics of tasks, it is often possible to isolate the limiting factor(s) responsible for failure. Such an approach was promulgated by Luria and is central to his diagnostic approach (Christensen, 1979).

Right-Left Differences

The three principal neuropsychological assessment systems mentioned previously (the Halstead-Reitan, Luria's Neuropsychological Investigation, and the Luria-Nebraska) all evaluate the relative performance of the two sides of the body on certain motor and sensory tasks. The Halstead-Reitan in its present form, for example, measures the following: *Motor*—grip strength, finger tapping, foot tapping, and fine manipulative dexterity (via a pegboard task); *Sensory*—hand touch, hand-face touch, fingertip number perception, finger localization, tactile form/object recognition, auditory perception, and visual perception (including visual fields). Since motor and sensory pathways are largely crossed there is primarily unilateral cortical representation of these functions for each side of the body. Thus, deficits in motor or sensory performance can be assumed to implicate the side of the brain opposite to the side of the body that is affected, *providing that peripheral motor or sensory dysfunction has been ruled out.* Patients with weakness (paresis) or paralysis on one side of the body should show a consistent pattern of greater motor and sensory impairment on that side of the body compared to the nonaffected side.

Pathognomonic Signs

These are behaviors or test performances that never (or very rarely) occur in normals, to the extent that their presence is virtually indicative of organic pathology. Examples of pathognomonic signs are the presence of aphasia, failure to perceive stimuli under bilateral simultaneous stimulation conditions, omission of a significant portion of a copied figure (such as a cross or clock face), and the presence of seizures (confirmed by EEG). The clinician must keep in mind that pathognomonic signs are by nature rare, and therefore by no means are present in all cases. However, the absence of pathognomonic signs is *not* evidence of the absence of organic pathology.

The clinician must seek to integrate data from all available sources when making a differential diagnosis: history, information from family/relatives/friends, interview, behavioral observations, and test data. Experienced clinicians place considerable emphasis on the qualitative features of an evaluation, such as approach to the tasks, response to failure, effect of feedback, rate of learning, and response to simplification of tasks. Though it is important to determine the patient's level of performance (i.e., "quantity"), it is equally important to note stylistic and behavioral features (i.e., "quality").

The evaluation should proceed from the general to the specific. That is, the determination of the presence or absence of organic pathology should precede any attempt to localize the pathology to a hemisphere or to a specific brain region. In general, the data derived from level of performance and pathognomonic signs are most helpful in determining the former, while pattern and right versus left side of the body data aid in the latter. On many occasions the question of differential diagnosis has been resolved, and the clinician is called on to assess the *consequences* of brain impairment. The quantity and quality of impairment are of critical importance to the patient, the family, and to those involved in treatment. The patient's current and predicted level of independence, potential for improvement in speaking or writing, and the extent of cognitive impairment are just some of the areas that can be assessed through neuropsychological assessment.

COMMUNICATION OF RESULTS

To Other Professionals

Reports of results may be either oral or written, and often both are required. It is advisable to develop the habit of communicating orally as soon as the results are available so that the referral source can benefit from the findings at the earliest possible moment. An additional advantage to this approach is that the referral source can advise the psychologist regarding specific information to include (or delete) from the final written report. The report should be as brief as possible, providing it answers all the referral questions. Many clinicians seem to equate verbosity with diagnostic skill, resulting in unnecessarily lengthy reports that tend to obscure rather than illuminate the diagnostic issue. It is helpful to organize a written report under various topical headings, such as: Referral, History of Problem, Tests Administered, Test Behavior, Test Results (Mental Status, Memory, Intellectual Functions, Academic Achievement, Neuropsychological Measures: motor, sensory, visual-motor, language, and problem-solving abilities), Conclusions, and Recommendations. Such headings assist the writer in maintaining an organized approach and they greatly aid the reader in locating areas of special interest. When writing for another professional, it is also helpful to provide certain key test scores (such as IQ and achievement scores) in the body of the report for current and future reference. Certain graphic aids are informative and should be considered as additions or attachments. Standard score profiles or graphs are not difficult to generate with available microcomputer software and are preferable to hand-drawn or improvised charts or graphs.

To Patients and Families

Often the patient or family will request an informal or formal report of the evaluation, separate from that provided to the referral source. It is essential to present a different style of report to a nonprofessional reader or listener. The clinician should make every effort to communicate clearly and in easily comprehended terminology. For this purpose it helps to provide descriptive analogies or actual examples of whatever deficits are being described in the report. In addition, selected charts or graphs will further clarify the narrative for the patient and family. The clinician must take care to balance the report with assets as well as liabilities (if assets are present) to avoid painting an overly pessimistic portrait of the patient. In many instances, it is advisable to provide the patient and family with a copy of the formal report for future reference. A hallmark of the fully matured professional is the ability to communicate, sensitively and appropriately, the results of a neuropsychological examination to a patient and his or her family.

REFERENCES

Christensen, A. L. (1979). *Luria's neuropsychological investigation: Text* (2nd ed.). Copenhagen: Munksgaard.

Filskov, S., & Leli, D. (1981). Assessment of the individual in neuropsychological practice. In S. Filskov & T. Boll (Eds.), *Handbook of clinical neuropsychology* (pp. 545-576). New York: John Wiley & Sons.

Folstein, M., Folstein, S., & McHugh, P. (1975). Mini-Mental State. *Journal of Psychiatric Research, 12,* 189-198.

Golden, C. (1983). The neuropsychologist in neurological and psychiatric populations. In C. Golden & P. Vicente (Eds.), *Foundations of clinical neuropsychology* (pp. 163-187). New York: Plenum Press.

Halstead, W. (1947). *Brain and intelligence.* Chicago: University of Chicago Press.

Kiernan, R., & Matthews, C. (1976). Impairment index versus T-score averaging in neuropsychological assessment. *Journal of Consulting and Clinical Psychology, 44,* 951-957. 951-957.

Lezak, M. (1983). *Neuropsychological assessment* (2nd ed.). New York: Oxford University Press.

Luria, A. R. (1966). *Higher cortical functions in man.* New York: Basic Books.

Overall, J., & Gomez-Mont, F. (1974). The MMPI-168 for psychiatric screening. *Educational and Psychological Measurement, 34,* 315-319.

Prigatano, G. (1977). Wechsler Memory Scale is a poor screening test for brain dysfunction. *Journal of Clinical Psychology, 33,* 772-777.

Reitan, R. (1966). A research program on the psychological effects of brain lesions in human beings. In N. R. Ellis (Ed.), *International review of research in mental retardation* (Vol. 1, pp. 153-218). New York: Academic Press.

Russell, E. (1975). A multiple scoring method for the assessment of complex memory functions. *Journal of Consulting and Clinical Psychology, 43,* 800-809.

Sbordone, R., & Caldwell, A. (1979). The "OBD-168": Assessing the emotional adjustment to cognitive impairment and organic brain damage. *Clinical Neuropsychology, 1*(4), 36-41.

Strub, R., & Black, F. (1977). *The mental status examination in neurology.* Philadelphia: F. A. Davis.

Wechsler, D. (1981). *WAIS-R manual.* Cleveland: The Psychological Corporation.

8

Considerations in Cases of Visual, Auditory, or Motor Impairment

CHARLES J. GOLDEN, PH.D., DOUGLAS E. ROBBINS, PH.D.

The impact of a peripheral physical handicap, though influenced by a number of specific variables, is likely to penetrate nearly every aspect of an individual's life. Perpipheral disorders by definition involve both sensory and motor functions, but are not attributable to a disruption of the functioning of the cerebral cortex. Although there is not a common psychological profile per se of a disabled subject, the person's reaction to the disability can follow a pattern also seen in individuals experiencing post-traumatic stress disorder. The purpose of this chapter is to provide some insight into the assessment of individuals with visual, hearing, and motor or orthopedic impairments.

Although individuals with peripheral disorders comprise unique populations, few clinicians receive specific training for working with such patients. This is significant, as the assessment of these individuals requires not only an understanding of the physical handicap itself but an understanding of how such disorders can influence development and perception of the environment. An individual with a peripheral disorder is compromised not only in that they are disabled, as with a visual handicap, but perhaps also in areas not generally associated with the specific disability. For example, although blind children typically do not appear significantly delayed in language development in the first 8 to 10 months of life, they generally are delayed in acquiring concepts of concrete objects (Reynell, 1978). And, contrary to belief, the blind do not necessarily possess a true superiority in other sense modalities because of their blindness. For example, Cobb, Lawrence, and Nelson (1979) report that accuracy of memory for material presented by tactile and auditory stimulation is no better for a blind subject than for a sighted one, though the blind subject is able to retain more tactile sensory information. Differentiating between a subject's inability to perform a specific task because of the peripheral deficit versus a general inability to perform the task is the major challenge to the clinician.

Psychological evaluation of subjects with peripheral disorders is complicated by the fact that comparatively little progress has been made in the development of psychometric instruments for them. The apparent reason for this is twofold. First, these individuals comprise a significantly small percentage of the patients seen by the typical clinician. It has been therefore somewhat common for clinicians simply to modify traditional psychometric instruments for use with these special populations. Second, the development and standardization of tests for these populations pose challenges not experienced with nondisabled subjects. For example, when developing a test for the blind, what criteria are used for group inclusion? "Blindness" ranges from a total visual deficit to what has been termed "legally blind" (20/200 best corrected vision). Similarly, are subjects included if their blindness was congenital versus acquired?

Prior to initiating any assessment procedures the clinician must determine the exact purpose of the evaluation. For example, is the object of the assessment to measure the subject's learning level and learning style or is it to ascertain the extent of the handicapping condition? The answer to this question will dictate in part the kind of test instrument that should be employed. If, for example, the purpose of testing is to compare the disabled client to unimpaired subjects, the clinician may choose test procedures that have been standardized on a normal population. Clearly, the individual with a peripheral disorder would be at a distinct disadvantage in such a comparison. Adapting a test to compensate for a client's disability, as noted earlier, is a fairly common practice, but the meaning of such evaluations is not entirely clear in terms of their reliability or validity. A final approach would entail utilizing tests that were normed on subjects who also demonstrated the particular peripheral disorder, which would allow the clinician to avoid measuring the disability per se. This strategy suffers from the fact that it requires the clinician to learn a new testing procedure that may have only limited utility. In addition, few tests have been developed for such subjects that demonstrate acceptable psychometric properties. Those that are available typically have poor or unreplicated norms derived from a population that itself may be small, biased, or very heterogeneous. For subjects with multiple peripheral disorders (e.g., deaf and blind) the situation is even more difficult in that there are no normed or standardized tests known to these authors that permit, for example, the measurement of intellectual ability.

In summary, given these problems of availability and appropriate standardization, the examiner must augment testing with observation, interviews, case history, and clinical judgment. Situational observations, retesting, and careful attention to the quality and speed of response, all in the context of what is known of the subject's background, will help the examiner in the evaluation of individuals with peripheral disorders.

EVALUATION OF THE BLIND AND VISUALLY IMPAIRED

In the assessment of the visually impaired adult certain information is crucial to the formulation of a clinical opinion: 1) the subject's degree of disability (i.e., absolute blindness, no light perception; light perception and projection only; motion perception; form perception; restricted fields); 2) the etiology of the impairment (e.g., insidious vs. traumatic onsets); 3) the age of the subject at onset of the impairment (i.e., congenital vs. acquired); 4) whether the subject has received any special remediation or treatment for the impairment; and 5) how the subject's family or significant others respond to the impairment. It is important to recognize that the subject's disability may have an impact on how he or she is perceived and reacted to by others. The subject's own perception of the disability is also likely to affect social or psychological interaction.

In evaluating the individual's adaptation to the handicap it is important to ascertain whether the subject has received any remedial help for the disability. For example, has the person been to a special school or attended classes where the use of braille for reading and writing and the abacus for arithmetic are taught? Or has the subect learned in a vicarious fashion to utilize haptic cues and skills without "formal training"?

The second step is to determine if the subject has residual vision and how it is used. For example, can he or she read? What size print is needed? How long can the subject attend to a visual task? At what angle and at what distance are reading materials held? Can the subject discriminate between colors? How do variable lighting conditions affect vision? And finally, is the subject taking any medications that might affect his or her vision? It is important that the examiner be cognizant of any observable abnormalities and unusual behaviors. For example, are the patient's eyes red or watery? Does the patient rub his or her eyes frequently? Does the patient turn his or her head to favor one eye, or move the head rather than the eyes when reading? Such information is important as it helps the examiner better to define the parameters of the patient's disability. These observations also may have important implications in terms of recommendations for treatment.

Test Selection and Administration

In testing the visually impaired subject, the examiner first may wish to initiate some type of physical contact, such as by taking the patient's arm. Comments that offer the patient some orientation, such as mentioning the location of the table or position of the testing materials, are also helpful. Besides aiding in building rapport, friendly conversation provides time for the subject to become oriented to the sounds both within and outside the room. The examiner may even wish to describe the testing room as a means of making the individual more comfortable with the surroundings. The examiner thus should attempt to ensure that the subject is completely oriented to the testing situation.

Unlike the sighted subject, the visually impaired person will not have had the opportunity to "study" the test materials and so on prior to testing. The examiner thus should describe the nature of the test materials and even allow the subject to manipulate the objects before the testing begins. It is important that the nature of the task is clear to the subject to avoid the possibility of evaluating the subject's ability to function in "new" situations rather than the ability the test is designed to measure. The examiner also should speak in a normal tone of voice and should not feel uncomfortable using sight-oriented words such as "look" and "see." Tactile and verbal reinforcements should be used frequently. Finally, in the assessment of individuals with residual vision careful consideration should be given to the kind of lighting in the room and the type of paper utilized (as different papers show different propensities for reflecting light). The examiner may need to experiment with natural and artificial light in order to optimize the setting for the patient. A tensor desk lamp is often helpful. To minimize and control glare, lighting should come from behind or over the shoulder of the patient.

Test administration may be conducted via several formats. Items may be read aloud by the examiner, may be presented in braille (if materials are available in this medium), or may be presented on recorded tapes. The subject's intact abilities will be the best guide to format selection. For example, subjects who are not proficient in the use of braille are placed at a disadvantage if this medium is chosen. Even when braille is employed appropriately it is important to remember that reading speed is generally much slower than that of sighted individuals. Many tests that are verbal in nature may be read aloud to the subject. A number of measures, including performance items, may be used without modification with subjects who make good use of residual vision, and may even be adaptable for those classified as "blind" if sufficient time is allowed for orientation to the materials.

As noted earlier, the primary means of evaluating the performance of a subject with a peripheral disorder is to either compare their relative performance to other individuals with the same disorder, or to adapt existing tests for subjects with peripheral disorders. One of the earliest attempts at such adaptation was the Interim Hayes-Binet Intelligence Test. This modification of the Stanford-Binet has been superseded by others, as its norms are quite dated. The most recent adaptation, the Perkins-Binet, attempts to measure learning ability and is standardized on a legally blind sample. There are two forms of this test: Form N for subjects with no usable vision and Form U for those with usable vision.

The Blind Learning Aptitude Test (BLAT) is an example of a test that was specifically developed and normed on a blind population. The BLAT was developed to measure the learning potential of blind subjects ages 6 to 20 and consists of a verbal-touch test of tactile discrimination not employing braille stimuli.

The Haptic Intelligence Scale (HIS) represents an attempt to translate the performance section of the Wechsler Adult Intelligence Scale (WAIS) into test material that can be used with the blind. Four WAIS subtests (Digit Symbol, Object Assembly, Block Design, and Picture Completion) were modified to a tactual and kinesthetic presentation. In addition, two new tests were included—Pattern Board (copying pegboard arrangements) and Bead Arithmetic (a modification of the abacus). The HIS appears to assess an individual's ability to use touch and kinesis without visual clues and may reveal how a subject has compensated for the loss of sight. Although some researchers have proposed that the HIS and the performance subscales of the WAIS are essentially equivalent in that they assess comparable areas of functioning, this point appears debatable (Jordan, 1978).

Although a number of tests have either been adapted or developed for use with the blind, psychologists tend to employ the WAIS verbal scales more than any other instrument (Bauman, 1979). Regardless of the type of test utilized to assess intelligence with this population, the clinician should augment his or her test findings with observations, social history, and so on to counter the potential unfairness of quantified intellectual assessments.

Personality evaluations of subjects with peripheral disorders obviously are limited to procedures that are not dependent on vision, hearing, or whatever the subject's specific handicap. Blindness eliminates many traditional projective techniques such as the Rorschach and the standard administration of the Thematic Apperception Test. Tests such as the Rotter Incomplete Sentences Blank can be administered as with any other population, while a measure such as the Minnesota Multiphasic Personality Inventory (MMPI) can be adapted by presenting the questions on tape or in braille, or by reading them aloud to the subject.

Special consideration should be given to the interpretation of the MMPI, or of any other personality inventory, when such tests are administered to the blind. For example, the blind subject's responses to such statements as "The only interesting part of the newspaper is the funnies" or "In walking, I am very careful to step over sidewalk cracks" may be interpreted inappropriately as contributing to a specific personality trait instead of reflecting a physical disability. A similar problem occurs on tests that assess abstract thinking via the interpretation of proverbs. For example, the saying "A bird in the hand is worth two in the bush" means something totally different to a blind person versus a sighted one, especially if the blindness is congenital. Similarly, for the hearing-impaired patient, the meanings of such conceptualizations are typically lost. The use of an interpreter in such situations would prove of limited utility because signing a proverb entails interpreting it concretely in order to sign it. Some researchers have suggested that to control for this problem tests should be screened to determine "false-blind" items in advance.

A second major problem in utilizing tests such as the MMPI with a blind population concerns an issue that has been reiterated several times in this chapter—the MMPI was not standardized with a blind sample. Adrian, Miller, & De L'aune (1982), in a study of 128 visually impaired subjects (either blind or partially sighted from birth), found significant differences in comparison to the reference group on nine of the MMPI clinical scales and two of the validity scales for women; males were found to differ significantly on nine of the clinical scales and one of the validity scales. These differences between the visually impaired subjects and the reference group were interpreted as not necessarily reflecting psychopathology, but rather was a possible indicator of the unique adaptive processes of individuals who experienced early visual impairment. The patient with a peripheral disorder therefore differs from the unimpaired subject not only in possessing a physical handicap, but also in that his or her *experience of the world* is very different from that of the unimpaired subject because of the physical disability.

Table 1 provides a synopsis of the tests that are commonly used in the assessment of the blind and visually impaired. (See Sweetland & Keyser [1983] and Scholl & Schnur [1976] for a more extensive listing of tests that have been modified for use with this population.)

TABLE 1

Assessment Procedures for the Blind and Visually Impaired

Adjective Check List

Anxiety Scale for the Blind

Auditory Projective Test*

Binet Adaptations (Irwin-Binet, Hayes-Binet, Interim Hayes-Binet, Perkins-Binet)

Blind Learning Aptitude Test

Haptic Intelligence Scale

Kahn Intelligence Test: A Culture-Minimized Experience

Minnesota Multiphasic Personality Inventory

Peabody Picture Vocabulary Test

Raven Progressive Matrices for Presentation to the Blind
   (Tactual Progressive Matrices)

Rotter Incomplete Sentences Blank

Slosson Intelligence Test for Children and Adults

Stanford-Ohwaki-Kohs Block Design Intelligence Test for the Blind: American
   Revision*

Wechsler Adult Intelligence Scale

Wide Range Achievement Test

---

*in-print status uncertain

ASSESSMENT OF THE DEAF AND HEARING IMPAIRED

A basic element of any evaluation entails the ability to communicate with the person being assessed. If the subject demonstrates a hearing impairment, then oral/aural communication is compromised with that patient. As a prelude to assessing the patient the examiner must ascertain as much information as possible regarding the nature and degree of hearing loss and how the patient compensates for the loss (i.e., lip reading, amplification, signing, or writing).

In the case of subjects with relatively little hearing loss and satisfactory language skills, only general precautions are necessary. For example, testing should be conducted in quiet surroundings, with good visibility, and the examiner should speak slowly and clearly while avoiding exaggerated speech.

If the subject suffers from a high-frequency loss, special considerations in testing are necessary. For example, the patient suffering from a high-frequency loss might communicate better with a male examiner, whose speech sounds are in a lower register. Because of the possibility of sound distortions or even omissions, the clinician must ensure that the client comprehends what is being communicated to him or her.

Communication with the hearing-impaired subject can be enhanced if the examiner is well versed in signing and the subject is familiar with the specific technique used by the examiner. If signing is not possible, but the subject can read and write, then communication via a written medium may be possible.

An alternative means of communication would entail the services of an interpreter. If such an approach is utilized, special care must be taken to ensure that the interpreter is trained to communicate information in a neutral and precise manner. Even when signing is employed, test administration may be difficult because concepts that are expressed easily in English may make little sense or be impossible to communicate in sign language. On one occasion, for example, these authors were testing the spelling ability of a deaf adult with the aid of an interpreter. When more abstract and difficult words were involved, frequently no appropriate signs existed, so the interpreter began to ask "How do you spell H-E-M-O-P-O-E-S-I-S?" in sign, a procedure that clearly invalidated the test. This little example also illustrates the nature of problems one can encounter when using an interpreter.

Some hearing-impaired subjects, perhaps showing evidence of partial hearing, are sufficiently skilled at lip reading to allow an oral administration of test instructions, items, and so on. Given this situation, the examiner must be cognizant of always facing the client so that a full view of the examiner's lips is possible. The examiner must take care not to speak so slowly or with exaggerated lip movements as to confuse the patient.

Test Selection and Administration

As is true in all testing situations, the kind of test instrument employed with the hearing impaired is a function of the purpose for the evaluation. If the referral question is to assess the patient's intellectual abilities compared to a normal reference group, then any generally accepted test of intelligence should suffice. If, however, the purpose of the assessment is to measure intellectual ability separate from verbal and language facility, only certain tests will be appropriate. Similarly, if one wishes to assess intellectual ability as compared only to others who are deaf, tests normed on a deaf sample will be appropriate.

It is not uncommon to see deficits in linguistic development in the hearing impaired when compared to hearing individuals. This may be solely the result of a paucity of language contact, or it may represent differences occuring in brain developmental patterns when auditory channels are absent. The fact that sign language does not offer the same language structures as oral language is certainly a determinant. Because of this, these subjects are handicapped on verbal tasks, even when the verbal content is presented visually. The most commonly employed test instrument with this population has been the WAIS or some adaptation thereof. For example, some researchers have suggested that only the WAIS performance items should be administered to the hearing impaired, while others have indicated that the verbal subtests can be administered if the oral questions are typed on cards. Numerous procedures for communicating the instructions for the performance subtests have also been established (see Sattler, 1974, pp. 170-172). As noted earlier, the difficulty with employing such adaptations is that one cannot assume that validity, reliability, and norms remain unchanged. As the WAIS was normed on hearing subjects, if one chooses to employ the scales with a deaf examinee one should be aware of this limitation.

The most noted attempt to derive a test standardized on a significantly large sample of deaf and hearing-impaired subjects is the Hiskey-Nebraska Test of Learning Aptitude. This test can be administered entirely via pantomimed instructions and requires no verbal response from the subject. Overall, the Hiskey-Nebraska has experienced moderate popularity among psychological examiners of the deaf, ranking behind the Wechsler scales in general use. The greatest limitation of this instrument is that its normative data are somewhat dated and its age range (21½-18½ years) presents limited utility for adults. Correlations of .78 to .86 have been reported between the Hiskey-Nebraska and the Stanford-Binet and the Wechsler scale IQs.

Given an average reading ability, most objective personality tests are applicable for the hearing-impaired subject. As with the visually impaired, however, precautions are necessary in interpreting tests such as the MMPI, which might contain questions that are "loaded" for the hearing-impaired subject (e.g., "I find it hard to make talk when I meet new people"). Contingent on the client's expressive and receptive abilities, projective techniques such as the Rorschach, the Thematic Apperception Test, the Rotter Incomplete Sentences Blank, and the Draw-A-Person are possible.

Table 2 provides a synopsis of the tests that are commonly employed in the assessment of deaf and hearing-impaired persons.

In using any of the cited tests, however, caution must be exercised in that deaf individuals may show deficits unrelated to personality function caused by expressive language deficits, whether the material is expressed orally, in written form, or through signing. This requires very cautious interpretation, and suggests that normative data such as frequency of a given Rorschach response may be meaningless. In all such cases, interpretations should be geared toward generating

TABLE 2

Assessment Procedures for the Deaf and Hearing Impaired

Adjective Check List

Advanced Progressive Matrices

Arthur Point Scale of Performance Test, Form I

Hiskey-Nebraska Test of Learning Aptitude

Kahn Intelligence Test: A Culture-Minimized Experience

Kohs Block Design Test

Leiter International Performance Scale

Minnesota Multiphasic Personality Inventory

Non-Language Multi-Mental Test

Porteus Mazes

Rotter Incomplete Sentences Blank

Sixteen Personality Factor Questionnaire

Standard Progressive Matrices

Test of Nonverbal Intelligence

Wechsler Adult Intelligence Scale

hypotheses rather than forming conclusions reached from research on normal hearing clients.

ASSESSMENT OF THE ORTHOPEDICALLY OR MOTOR HANDICAPPED

Subjects with severe motor disorders may be unable to respond in either an oral or written modality and the manipulation of test materials may be impossible for them. Requiring such individuals to adhere to standard time limits may only exacerbate their motor difficulties and, as is true for physically disabled patients in general, the clinician needs to be especially sensitive to the possibility of patient fatigue.

An orthopedic disorder may have relatively little effect on the overall psychological assessment procedure except for the general effect caused by all chronic medical disorders (i.e., fatigue, depression, impaired ability to concentrate, etc.). For example, impairment to the lower limbs would affect the administration of few psychological tests. Similarly, impairment to the arms interferes only with tests that have a heavy motor component, and even these tests are inaccurate insofar as they suggest fine or gross motor impairment. As a result of this, working with this population is quite a bit easier than working with sensory-impaired clients.

Obviously, in cases of upper limb disorders measures such as the WAIS performance tests or the Tactual Performance Test do not gauge cognitive-motor ability but only motor skills. Tests like the WAIS verbal scales are unaffected by such injuries. The Peabody Picture Vocabulary Test, for example, can be adapted for this population by having the patient give a spoken response rather than pointing to a specific picture. Such modifications are possible without compromising the validity of the test. Similarly, tests like the MMPI can be answered aloud (although the appropriateness of some items may be questionable, as was the case with sensory impairments).

Some motor handicaps, however, do present special problems. In cases of violent limb movement rather than paralysis, the disorder may interfere seriously with the patient's attention and concentration. In such situations the examiner may attempt to "fit testing in as best as possible," making results questionable in terms of idealized concepts such as "intelligence" but still useful as measures of actual performance.

More serious are the motor disorders that also impair expressive speech, as occurs with certain high spinal cord injuries. In these cases, in which the patient cannot make verbal responses, it is often useful to substitute alternative responses (e.g., eye blinks for yes/no) allowing some communication, although tests that require detailed answers are clearly out of the question. Some communication also may be achieved in these situations through language boards, on which the patient may point to letters or terms (obviously this will work only when paralysis is just partial). For the worst cases, in which no motor behavior is possible but the patient is still alert (the "locked in" syndrome), there is ongoing research on the use of direct monitoring of EEG response (such as alpha rhythm), which can be controlled voluntarily and thus can act as a form of communication.

While tests may be used in this manner, one again must be cautious about their interpretation, particularly (as with the sensory handicaps) when personality tests are involved. Patients with motor disorders also may be impaired in their ability to interact with and experience the world, and thus many items on both objective and projective tests may have quite different significance to this population in ways largely unexplored by researchers to date.

A limited number of tests or test adaptations are available specifically for working with this population. Adaptations of both the Leiter International Performance Scale and the Porteus Mazes have been developed in which the examiner manipulates the test materials while the subject responds by appropriate head movements. The Peabody Picture Vocabulary Test (PPVT) represents another type of test requiring a simple pointing response. This test consists of a series of 150 plates, each containing four pictures. The subject must point to the picture on the plate that best illustrates the meaning of the stimulus word. Table 3 provides a synopsis of those tests typically employed in assessing the orthopedically or motorically handicapped.

TABLE 3

Assessment Procedures for the Orthopedically Handicapped

Adjective Check List
Advanced Progressive Matrices
Full Range Picture Vocabulary Test
Peabody Picture Vocabulary Test
Rotter Incomplete Sentences Blank
Thematic Apperception Test
Wechsler Adult Intelligence Scale

INTEGRATING FINDINGS AND COMMUNICATING RESULTS

Working with a blind, deaf, or motor-impaired client is a difficult task for the clinician who does not routinely assess such populations. In all cases of testing, one must take care to consider conclusions only as hypotheses and to examine procedures and interpretations for problems that may not be immediately obvious. Conclusions when reached should be checked carefully against history and actual behavior, and the report should clearly indicate to what groups the client is being compared. Interpretive rules and guidelines derived from research based on normal populations are not directly applicable to impaired populations. Failure to recognize this factor will likely result in significant interpretive errors. The clinician also must be cautious and aware of his or her own prejudices and assumptions, which can color an evaluation. In addition, one must readily admit when there is not adequate information to reach a given conclusion.

Because of the inherent difficulties, such as the lack of standardized tests, in assessing patients with peripheral disorders, care must be taken in the communication of results to the referral source, the patient, and others. The decision of whether to report an IQ score, for example, will depend on who the referral source is and the nature of the referral question. In most situations, the examiner should rely on straightforward narrative statements as a means of reporting the results of the psychological testing. In those situations in which IQ scores are deemed necessary, the psychologist should accompany these findings with a discussion of the client's relative strengths and weaknesses as compared to other subjects with the same peripheral disorder. Of equal importance to the referral source will be the qualitative data obtained during the evaluation, as well as any information gathered by testing-the-limits procedures.

Whenever possible, the patient should be given direct feedback regarding the findings. Such feedback serves to allay the patient's concerns about his or her performance, reinforces the usefulness of such evaluations, and hopefully facilitates in securing the patient's cooperation for future evaluations. These "feedback sessions" should be geared toward answering any questions that the patient might have about the results of the evaluation, as well as addressing why the testing was requested initially. Psychological jargon should be avoided in communicating this information.

Psychological evaluations provide not only a measure of the patient's current level of functioning, but also a baseline from which future performance can be compared. It is this aspect of the psychological evaluation that is of special importance in working with the peripherally impaired patient. Such assessments help monitor changes that might be masked by the physical disability (i.e., changes in the intellectual or psychological functioning) and also may be utilized as a means of evaluating the effectiveness of a specific treatment or program.

REFERENCES

Adrian, R. J., Miller, L. R., & De L'aune, W. R. (1982, May). Personality assessment of early visually impaired persons using the CPI and the MMPI. *Visual Impairment and Blindness*, pp. 172-178.
Bauman, M., & Kropf, C. (1979). Psychological tests used with blind and visually handicapped persons. *School Psychology Review*, 8(3), 257-270.
Cobb, N. J., Lawrence, D. M., & Nelson, N. D. (1979). Report on blind subjects' tactile and auditory recognition for environmental stimulus. *Perceptual and Motor Skills*, 48(2), 363-366.
Jordan, S. (1978). Haptic Intelligence Scale for adult blind. *Perceptual and Motor Skills*, 47(1), 203-222.
Reynell, J. K. (1978). Developmental patterns of visually handicapped children. *Child: Care, Health and Development*, 4, 291-303.
Sattler, J. M. (1974). *Assessment of children's intelligence*. Philadelphia: W. B. Saunders.
Scholl, G., & Schnur, R. (1976). *Measures of psychological, vocational, and educational functioning in the blind and visually handicapped*. New York: American Foundation for the Blind.
Sweetland, R. C., & Keyser, D. J. (Eds.) (1983). *Tests: A comprehensive reference for assessments in psychology, education and business*. Kansas City, MO: Test Corporation.

9

Determining Post-Traumatic Stress Disorder

TOM W. PATTERSON, PH.D., ANDREW H. SCHAUER, PH.D.,
CARROLL D. OHLDE, PH.D., NANCY J. GARFIELD, PH.D.

Although Post-Traumatic Stress Disorder (PTSD) is a relatively recent diagnostic category, the symptoms have been seen in patients for many years. PTSD may develop following a physically or psychologically traumatic event, the nature of which would evoke significant symptoms of distress in most people. The most frequently mentioned stressors include military combat, natural or man-made disasters, rape or assault, and serious accidents. Assessment may be requested as part of a clinical workup to enhance treatment, for legal reasons, or to help determine disability/compensation.

The work of these authors with PTSD patients for many years has been exclusively with Vietnam combat veterans, who appeared for treatment nine to 19 years after their military service in Vietnam. Combatants from earlier wars still may experience some of the same psychological and physiological reactions to their wartime experiences as Vietnam veterans do, attesting to the longevity and profound effect upon the individual's ability to adjust. In former wars, these symptoms were described as "shell shock," "battle fatigue," and "war neurosis."

What do automobile accidents, rape, war, concentration camps, torture, tornadoes, collapsing buildings, or fires evoke in the victims? What are the common characteristics of stressful events that may result in a stress disorder following the event or trauma?

1. An unexplainable, unpredictable event occurs without time to prepare or react with a planned response.

2. A terrorizing fear of possible death or dismemberment grips the victim.

3. The victim is aware of a complete lack of control over either the occurrence or its result(s).

4. A sense of inability to deal with the situation or escape it, along with an abject feeling of terror, helplessness, and resignation to one's fate, encompass the victim.

5. The body, mind, and emotions respond reflexively, without conscious plans, to protect the affected person. Random activity, emotional outbursts, and

many other reactions, such as pounding heart, screams, defecation, fainting, and brief psychoses, may occur.

Those who survive the catastrophe learn profoundly and permanently, in one trial, these feelings and thoughts. Without help to unlearn the responses, they generalize over time to new situations, relationships, and behaviors that may be similar to the original trauma only in one or more cues (smells, sights, words, feelings). Survivors then react to new and different situations in the same manner as they did to the original event. Chronicity of responses to stressful cues begins at this point and, without intervention, these now ineffective responses are repeated and generalized in an automatic, unconscious way. Specific symptoms develop that represent the survivor's attempt to adjust in order to live as meaningful a life as possible while carrying this burden.

APPRECIATING THE COMPLEXITIES OF THE DISORDER

Nature of the Diagnostic Problem

The diagnosis of PTSD is at once simple and complex. The simplicity lies both in the observable psychological pain expressed by those who have experienced a traumatic event or set of events and in the common set of behavioral reactions, thoughts, and emotions shared by these survivors. The diagnostic complexities revolve around assessing intensity, chronicity, and uniqueness from other psychiatric disorders. For example, nightmares (more aptly labeled *night terrors*) may vary in level of intensity and frequency of occurrence, may have existed for many years in some people or for only a short time in others, and may include thoughts, content, and distortions that mimic phobias, paranoia, characterological disorders, or daily stress. Symptoms that are intense, frequent, chronic, and have generalized to all psychic functioning cut across many diagnostic categories. A given set of dominant behavioral symptoms can easily result in PTSD being misdiagnosed as paranoid personality disorder, schizoid personality disorder, borderline personality disorder, antisocial personality disorder, or one or more of the affective disorders. Associated features in these various disorders frequently are found in chronic PTSD. Because these features overlap with other disorders, the person experiencing PTSD may have been treated previously for depression, anxiety, alcohol/drug dependence, or antisocial behaviors. The basic trauma and resulting behavioral changes are often misunderstood and ignored, with a treatment plan prepared on the basis of an incorrect or incomplete diagnosis. A relevant differential diagnosis is necessary for proper treatment to occur; that is, symptoms specific to PTSD as opposed to another psychiatric disturbance need delineation as treaters consider pharmacological, behavioral, individual, group, and/or activity therapy. Interventions vary significantly if diagnosis suggests an anxiety (i.e., PTSD) versus a psychiatrically based (e.g., schizophrenia) disorder.

Symptoms and Signs of PTSD

In 1980 PTSD was classified officially as an anxiety disorder in the *Diagnostic and Statistical Manual of Mental Disorders* (DSM-III; American Psychiatric Association, 1980). Two subtypes were identified: *acute* and *chronic/delayed*. In the acute classification, symptoms begin within six months after experiencing the traumatic event and they last less than six months. In chronic/delayed PTSD, the symptoms begin six or more months after the trauma and last six months or more. The diagnostic criteria include the following:

a) A recognizable stressor(s) exists that would produce symptoms of significant distress in almost everyone (i.e., rape, military combat, tornados).
b) The trauma is experienced repeatedly through one or more of the following: repetitive, intrusive recollections of the traumatic event; recurrent dreams of the event; and suddenly acting or feeling as if the event were happening again because of an association with an environmental or ideational cue (e.g., similar smells, threatening thoughts).
c) The person's responsiveness becomes numb to or reduced in involvement with the external world as shown by one or more of the following: marked reduction of interest in one or more significant activities, such as jobs, spouse and children, general responsibilities; feelings of being detached or estranged from others; and constricted affect.
d) Two or more of the following symptoms, not present before the trauma, are present: a hyperalert or exaggerated startle response; sleep disturbances; guilt about surviving while others did not; memory impairment or trouble concentrating; avoidance of activities that cue recollection of the trauma; and intensification of symptoms by exposure to events that symbolize or resemble the original traumatic event (e.g., movies, funerals, guns).

Signs of PTSD seen in heavy-combat soldiers include intense and sudden vacillations among the following: impulsive acts versus inaction; rage versus kindness; hate and resentment versus love and caring; intense emotional reactions versus emotional numbness; honesty versus deception; trust versus distrust; exuberance versus despair; acceptance versus rejection of others; absolute certainty versus absolute uncertainty; strong independence versus dependency; and calmness versus extreme agitation. The patient's thoughts, feelings, behaviors, and personal standards may change moment by moment, often without the assessor knowing what cued the change. Physiological reactions (anxiety attacks, perspiration, pulse rate), social interactions with others, thoughts, and emotional reactions are usually quite intense and extreme compared to the normal range of responsiveness. In a stressful situation, all of the individual's response systems tend to react automatically and reflexively. Such seems to be the case with PTSD victims who have experienced an intense trauma that happened without warning and that they felt helpless to control or change. The extreme, intense reactions described for combat soldiers appear to apply equally to those whose trauma occurred in settings other than wars.

Formulation of Assessment and Diagnostic Strategy

Preliminary interview data establish the possibility of a PTSD diagnosis from a history identifying a recognizable stressor and physical/emotional reaction patterns linked with it. Systematic collection of other necessary information follows to assess how long the condition has existed, its intensity and severity, and what other personality characteristics may coexist with PTSD (e.g., substance abuse or dependency, personality disorder).

The basic assessment strategy begins with questions directly addressing the client's trauma, proceeds to assessing the stress and anxiety in a more general way, and then determines, on the basis of these findings, questions that can and must be answered through objective and projective tests. Measures of cognitive, personality, and social/vocational/leisure operations generally are considered because all of these functions may be affected by the trauma, especially in the chronic/delayed subtype of PTSD.

SELECTION AND ADMINISTRATION OF TESTS AND PROCEDURES

No well-established, psychometrically sound instruments exist to measure the specific characteristics of PTSD. However, there are certain core tests and procedures that provide substantial information relevant to the four questions critical in differentiating assessing trauma-related problems from other psychiatric problems:

1. Does the client exhibit PTSD?
2. Is it acute or chronic/delayed?
3. How intense is its presence?
4. Do other conditions coexist with or underpin it?

These four questions serve as an organizational strategy in the selection of particular cognitive, personality, and social/vocational/leisure measures.

Assessing the presence of PTSD begins with a structured or focused interview. Because trauma creates an uncertainty in the client as to whether he or she was the victim, the survivor, or the villain, it is important that the psychologist create an air of acceptance for the client's perception of the event and respond in a calm, interested, and caring way to allay any distrust, guilt, or anger. The interview can begin by using an "active listening" approach, aimed at eliciting the person's account of "What was the (accident, rape, combat) like for you?" This open-ended question normally evokes a flood of information and feelings. Gathering test data or demographic information too early can be ineffective and resisted by the client who feels the clinician does not care and is more interested in facts and numbers than in the client as a person who hurts and desperately seeks help. As a backdrop to the assessment process, the clinician must remember that clients seek acceptance and understanding from them rather than "good advice" and judgments, which probably have been given by friends and relatives. Building this rapport may take longer prior to beginning formalized testing than other assessment situations. Once this has been established, the client is likely to cooperate more fully, especially when the clinician also explains the value of the information obtained from interview and psychological techniques.

Precise inquiry into the presence of PTSD draws on the DSM-III criteria. A checklist such as the following facilitates this process:

1. The individual specifies a traumatic event(s) that is generally outside the range of usual human experience. ____Yes ____No

2. The traumatic event is reexperienced in nightmares/dreams, intrusive thoughts, or hallucinatory flashback experiences. ____Yes ____No

3. Numbing of responsiveness is evident in markedly diminished interest in one or more significant activites, feelings of detachment or estrangement from others, or constricted affects. ____Yes ____No

4. After, but not prior to, the traumatic event(s), the individual experiences (minimum of two): ____Yes ____No
   a. Hyperalertness/exaggerated startle response ____Yes ____No
   b. Sleep disturbance ____Yes ____No
   c. Survival guilt ____Yes ____No
   d. Memory impairment/trouble concentrating ____Yes ____No
   e. Avoidance of activities stimulating recollection of the traumatic event ____Yes ____No
   f. Intensification of symptoms when exposed to events resembling the traumatic event(s) ____Yes ____No

Initial assessment of PTSD clients further requires an understanding of their reactions to the trauma and to subsequent life and emotional changes. In addition to DSM-III criteria, it is recommended that one also meet with significant others (spouse, parents) who knew the client pre- and post-trauma. Assessing the client's functioning in all areas (e.g., intellectual, emotional, social, occupational) through discussions with significant others can corroborate the information received from the client and provide additional material. The more focused the inquiry stays on the actual traumatic event rather than on stress in general, the more credible it will be to the client. Moreover, this focus yields information that is specific and relevant to the decision of what further evaluation may be needed.

DSM-III criteria clearly delineate acute and chronic/delayed PTSD based on the amount of time elapsed since the traumatic event and on the duration of the presenting problems. The interview thus should readily provide answers to the subtype diagnosis. However, the question of the disorder's intensity or severity poses more complexities. Identifying the degree of impact from PTSD demands a multimethod approach, including evaluating the client's cognitive, emotional/personality, and social/vocational/leisure functioning.

Cognitive Functioning: A two-fold approach to assessing cognitive functioning should occur, striving to find changes resultant from the traumatic event itself or
as a result of the long-term existence of PTSD. First, some assessment of general
intellectual operations is warranted. The Shipley Institute of Living Scale provides
an estimate of the client's verbal and new-learning potentials. A more precise
intellectual measure, if needed, results from an administration of the Wechsler
Adult Intelligence Scale-Revised (WAIS-R). Second, the clinician must gauge
possible organic changes resulting from the trauma, especially with war-related or
accident-induced stress. The Trail Making Test, from the Halstead-Reitan Neuropsychological Test Battery, rapidly screens for diffuse impairment in visual scanning and/or cognitive task-shift capabilities. Should preliminary screening indicate
possible organic impairment, referral for neuropsychological testing should occur.
Information about cognitive functioning can then be compared and contrasted with
related data (e.g., school records and interviews with significant others such as
school teachers).

Emotional/Personality Operation: Judging the impact of trauma on the client
requires assessing the broader aspects of current and, if possible, long-term personality function. The clinician must examine the client's defensive style and describe
the kind, availability, and effectiveness of each strategy. Moreover, pertinent
evaluation addresses core personality characteristics involving perceptions of self
and others. Conflict areas must be identified along with some understanding of the
individual's ability to control impulses and feelings. How impulses manifest themselves, to what degree, and under what circumstances are also part of the diagnostic
process.

A three-step procedure can evaluate critical personality operations. First, a
structured or focused interview provides information about the person's level of past
and current adjustment. Second, objective personality appraisal reveals levels of
anxiety, depression, confusion, and current defensive-coping styles. Third, projective techniques yield material reflecting the impact of emotions on the individual's
ability to handle the stresses of life as well as the rigors of potential treatment.

The impact of the trauma, as perceived by the client, is explored best through
interview questions that focus on the incident and subsequent changes in the client's
functioning. How did the person respond to the trauma? What changes have
occurred? What is he or she unable to do now that was possible before the event?
How does the client see the future? The individual's appraisal of his or her emotional
state can be obtained in an interview as well. First, a mental status examination can
identify problems reflective of generalized emotional dysfunction (e.g., phobias,
perceptual disturbances). Other areas of inquiry may include questions about the
client's own as well as familial psychiatric history. Not only should the individual
under evaluation be queried, but also those who have known the client before and
after the trauma should respond to abbreviated interviews. These sources provide
crucial answers to questions arising from inconsistencies, omissions, and alter-

native perceptions during the client interviews, and thus help in selecting appropriate objective and personality assessment instruments.

The Minnesota Multiphasic Personality Inventory (MMPI) is one objective measure of personality that provides an assessment of current adaptation and adjustment to life's stressors. Emotional problems such as anxiety, unconventional life-styles (e.g., excessive drug/alcohol use), feared loss of emotional and cognitive control, severe dependency with a concomitant cry for help, and the client's style and level of coping may be assessed through this measure of personality. Objective test data should be scrutinized for signs suggesting significant impulse control problems, aggression, emotional and thinking dysfunctions, and/or disturbed interpersonal relationships; such problems necessitate further inquiry through projective assessment to gauge the degree of emotional, perceptual, or social impairment. Other indicators of the need for projective evaluation include a likely characterological personality disturbance accompanied by despair, suspicion, and confusion (i.e., borderline).

Rorschach assessment provides valuable information about the affective control present, the depth of despair evident, and the potential for confused, irrational thinking. Clues to the person's interactions with men and women, parental/authority figures, and children, as well as a sense of the individual's methods of coping with interpersonal stress, emerge from selected plates of the Thematic Apperception Test (TAT) (e.g., cards 4, 6BM, 7BM, 8GF). Finally, a general sense of how the person sees him- or herself as well as members of the opposite sex and others in general (e.g., scary, threatening, powerful) emerges from the Draw-A-Person (DAP) technique.

Social/Vocational/Leisure Functioning: Impaired social relationships serve as another indicator of PTSD, and the use of a structured interview that evaluates the presence and closeness of immediate and extended family members, spouse/friend involvement, and level of community interaction (e.g., church, civic clubs) both before and after the trauma is necessary. In the process, one looks for both the degree and the kinds of physical and emotional nurturance available to the client, as well as his or her ability to make use of the nurturance before and after the trauma.

Assessing the person's vocational history provides other critical data relevant to delineating a PTSD diagnosis, particularly with reference to the chronic/delayed subtype. Reasons for job and career change(s) and termination(s) should be identified; hence, the clinician chronicles the client's vocational behavior rather than using traditional interests/aptitude testing to assess the client's ability to integrate and commit to a work environment, whether with co-workers or alone, and to understand whether the client solves work-related problems, escapes them, or copes with them in some other way.

Finally, examining the person's use of and participation in avocational interests is relevant to a PTSD diagnosis because it, too, suggests changes in the client's behavior before and after trauma that add support to such a diagnosis. Instruments such as the Leisure Activity Blank can yield a rough measure of pre- and post-trauma avocational interests. This information may be used along with that provided by significant others aware of the individual's interests before and after the incident(s). Clinical observation indicates that PTSD clients' abilities, attitudes toward work, and job longevity are usually severely affected following a traumatic situation because of impaired interpersonal relationships, difficulties sustaining interest in specific activities, and other less understood emotional changes.

Cognitive and personality measures also yield information helpful in differentiating PTSD from other psychiatric conditions. A mental status examination focusing on the alternative anxiety disorders outlined in DSM-III serves to exclude (e.g., Generalized Anxiety Disorder) and include coexisting problems (e.g., Panic Disorder). MMPI and Rorschach personality procedures in concert with DSM-III criteria and a thorough psychosocial history can be used further in identifying inclusion and/or exclusion characteristics of personality disorders (e.g., Avoidant, Antisocial). The assessor's effort to isolate PTSD diagnostically from other conditions represents the integration of subjective and objective data derived from interview, DSM-III criteria, and psychological testing. Identifying the cardinal features of PTSD and evaluating its impact on the client's emotional, social, and occupational worlds constitute the primary task of the psychologist working to differentiate the condition from other diagnostic categories.

INTERPRETATION AND INTEGRATION OF FINDINGS

The multimethod assessment approach as delineated provides substantial information for answering the four diagnostic questions concerning the presence, subtype, and severity of the PTSD and the identification of coexisting disorders. The findings must then be integrated and interpreted in a meaningful way, and this can be accomplished by using the format outlined in Figure 1. This format involves placing all data findings in the appropriate blocks starting at the top and proceeding downward. The vital diagnostic criteria integrated in the top portion must support the DSM-III criteria for PTSD. Following the interpretation/decision steps in the right-hand column aids in this process. With respect to the question of subtype, the integration and interpretation tasks are very similar, and scanning the data placed in the appropriate block permits a quick decision.

Integrating and interpreting information related to severity and coexisting conditions involves a more complex process. However, the format in Figure 1 can facilitate this. As one places the interview findings, objective and projective test data, and information from other sources into the various blocks, a clearer diagnostic picture emerges of the client pre- and post-trauma. If this picture reveals problems largely in the post-trauma column, one likely is dealing primarily with PTSD. The severity level will depend on the number and intensity of the difficulties

FIGURE 1. FORMAT FOR INTEGRATING AND INTERPRETING PTSD DATA

PTSD	Data	Integration		Interpretation/Decision
I. Present?	A. DSM-III Criteria 1. Traumatic event(s)	(Circle YES or NO Below) NO	YES	If NO, stop. PTSD NOT PRE-SENT. If YES, proceed to 2 and 3.
	2. Nightmares, intrusive thoughts, or flashbacks	NO	YES	If NO to 2 or 3, stop. PTSD NOT PRESENT. If YES, proceed to 4.
	3. Numbing of responsiveness	NO	YES	
	4. Six other reactions	Pre-Trauma	Post-Trauma	If one or no Xs in or unique to post-trauma column stop. PTSD NOT PRESENT. If two or more Xs unique to post-trauma, PTSD PRESENT.
	a. Hyperalertness	____	____	
	b. Sleep disturbance	____	____	
	c. Survival guilt	____	____	
	d. Memory impairment	____	____	
	e. Avoidance of activities	____	____	
	f. Increase of symptoms	____	____	
II. Subtype?	A. Date of trauma B. Date of onset of symptoms C. Duration of symptoms			ACUTE if onset/duration within 6 months. CHRONIC/DELAYED if onset after 6 months and duration more than 6 months.
III. Severity? Co-conditions?		Pre-Trauma	Post-Trauma	
		POSSIBLE DATA SOURCES		
	A. Intellectual Functioning	School records, Shipley Institute of Living Scale, WAIS-R, neuropsychology tests, interviews		Check areas A-F for number and degree of problems and rate severity as: MINIMAL, MILD, MODERATE, SEVERE, or VERY SEVERE.
	B. Emotional Functioning C. Behavioral Aberrations D. Interpersonal Relations	Psychiatric history, objective/projective tests (e.g., MMPI, Rorschach, DAP, TAT), family history, social history, legal history, interviews		If pre- and post-trauma columns are similar, PTSD PLUS OTHER DISORDERS ARE PRESENT. If problems mostly in post-trauma column, PTSD PROBABLY THE ONLY DISORDER.
	E. Occupational Successes/Failures	Work experiences records, vocational history, interviews		
	F. Coping Styles	Life-adjustment history, interviews, school history, MMPI, Rorschach		
Overall Functioning and Diagnosis:				

noted in each category from *A* through *F*. On the other hand, if the pre- and post-trauma pictures are similar, revealing multiple difficulties, one probably is facing a client whose problems are severe and stem from sources in addition to or exacerbated by the identified traumatic event(s).

When addressing the various categories, it is important to remember several key aspects of PTSD clients. In the area of intellectual functioning, pre- and post-trauma differences are likely to emerge. An individual's level of abstract thinking tends to be lower post-trauma and frequently is accompanied by a decreased ability to apply cognitive skills effectively and efficiently. Organic impairment may also appear post-trauma, particularly if the trauma involves head injuries.

The emotional functioning of PTSD individuals also will differ from the pre-trauma state. Cries for help (e.g., a very high F scale on the MMPI) and severe levels of depression and anxiety (e.g., T-scores above 70 on MMPI Scales 2 and 7) are common. These responses often are accompanied by feelings of anger, guilt, confusion, fears of rejection, and losing emotional and cognitive control.

Individuals often exhibit some unusual behavior post-trauma. They may be particularly sensitive to noises similar to those associated with the traumatic experience and may exhibit a significant startle response to such sounds. To prevent themselves from being drawn back into recalling or reexperiencing the trauma, they may appear aloof, apathetic, and distant. People who knew these individuals pre-trauma usually describe them as having changed dramatically in many ways.

Establishing and maintaining social relationships present problems for persons with PTSD. Pre-trauma levels of social and community interaction frequently decrease or become more superficial in the aftermath of the incident. People with whom these individuals were once close observe such changes and often wonder what is wrong. Although trauma victims often desire acceptance and care from others and exhibit significant dependence, they are frequently afraid of becoming dependent and push others away with their behavior. These individuals vacillate in the level of commitment, consistency, and dependability they maintain in their post-trauma relationships, and such vacillation creates family problems and leads to the breakup of relationships.

Following a traumatic experience individuals often lose interest in occupational tasks and leisure activities. Problems with authority and/or maintenance of effort on the job may develop, coupled with losing a sense of purpose and meaning in work and play. Some find it difficult to be hired and remain employed, and to enjoy recreation and relaxation.

PTSD clients often exhibit similar coping styles. The most common are denial, isolation, rumination, and impulsivity. Rorschach protocols in many severely affected PTSD veterans reflect fighting and blood responses with poorly controlled color reactions. Some develop psychophysiological defenses to cope with their trauma. All of these styles typically are designed to maintain distance from others and to avoid reexperiencing the trauma; in most cases, however, they promote a chronic self-defeating behavior pattern.

The overall functioning of persons with PTSD can be described as significantly less effective and productive following the traumatic event(s). Research (Fairbank, Keane, & Malloy, 1983; Keane, Malloy, & Fairbank, 1983) has shown that PTSD veterans present an 8-2 profile on the MMPI with significantly higher elevations than well-adjusted veterans on all clinical scales except Scale 5 (Masculinity-Feminity). A number of reports in the research literature also underscore that PTSD veterans exhibit significant problems in social relationships and occupational pursuits.

The considerations outlined here should aid the evaluator in making a differential diagnosis of PTSD. If such a diagnosis exists, the integrated data will reveal the following unique signs:

1. Distinct traumatic events were present in the client's life and are identifiable.

2. Significant changes in most or all areas of functioning are detectable following the trauma.

3. The client, as well as others, can readily recognize the changes that have occurred.

4. Anxiety, fear, and guilt have prevented effective change and have left the client immobilized and prone to repeating compulsively self-defeating or limiting behaviors.

5. Current behaviors, attitudes, and feelings can be traced to the effects of the trauma by a professional person trained to assimilate the data.

COMMUNICATING RESULTS

PTSD assessment results usually are communicated to a third party. Referrals are made from many sources and for numerous reasons, including: another mental health professional seeking clarification of diagnostic possibilities and/or recommedations regarding treatment options; an attorney representing a client in proceedings related to civil or criminal issues; a court desiring information about a client prior to issuing judicial decisions; a board considering financial compensation awards for disability limitations or for occupational retraining efforts; or a client seeking understanding and guidance in resolving a long-standing, debilitating condition.

Because the PTSD diagnosis is relatively new, the clinician may need to provide the referral source with information about the symptoms and process involved in post-traumatic stress disorder. This educational effort will acquaint the recipient with an awareness of the symptoms of PTSD, how the disorder progresses, and how current behavior is related to the trauma.

A second element of communication may focus on how PTSD in a particular client differs from other diagnostic symptoms. This is especially valuable when a diagnosis other than PTSD would have profound effects on the client if decisions based on an erroneous diagnosis were to be implemented. These could include incarceration, denial of compensation or retraining, or ineffective therapeutic interventions.

Thus, a valid differential diagnosis of PTSD and the communication of assessment results comprise a demanding task. Thoroughness, accuracy, and communicating the findings in language understandable to the person receiving the report are all important; personal, financial, treatment, and rehabilitation efforts are at stake. One must, in assessing the strengths and weaknessess of the client in relationship to the PTSD condition, be diligent in reviewing the consequences of suggested recommendations. The goal is to reduce the chronic, painful stress of a person who has experienced its debilitating effects long enough.

REFERENCES

American Psychiatric Association. (1980). *Diagnostic and statistical manual of mental disorders* (3rd ed.). Washington, DC: Author.

Fairbank, J. A., Keane, T. M., & Malloy, P. F. (1983). Some preliminary data on the psychological characteristics of Vietnam veterans with posttraumatic stress disorders. *Journal of Consulting and Clinical Psychology, 51,* 912-919.

Keane, T. M., Malloy, P. F., & Fairbank, J. A. (1984). Empirical development of an MMPI subscale for the assessment of combat-related posttraumatic stress disorder. *Journal of Consulting and Clinical Psychology, 52,* 881-891.

10

Assessment of Patients with Chronic Pain

CARL J. GETTO, M.D., ROBERT K. HEATON, PH.D.

Pain is the most common reason for a person to consult a physician. Acute pain accompanied by the usual signs and symptoms of a common disease is easily diagnosed and responds to the physician's standard treatments. However, many pain problems are not diagnosed so easily and/or may be refractory to treatment. Although there may be tissue injury, the magnitude of the complaint or the degree of disability may appear out of proportion to the tissue damage that is present. Pain that has lasted more than six months and has failed to respond to standard medical treatment is defined as chronic pain. Chronic pain often becomes associated with complex emotional and/or behavioral changes, which should be considered in both the evaluation and treatment of affected patients.

Patients with chronic pain tend to be discouraged by the degree of their suffering and in turn tend to frustrate the physicians who attempt to treat them. After they have run the diagnostic and therapeutic gamut of multiple medical specialists, such individuals frequently become outcasts in the medical community. Pinsky (1978) has described chronic pain patients as having the following characteristics:

1. They have ongoing pain not due to neoplastic disease and have no significant ongoing pathophysiological mechanisms that would explain their ongoing pain.

2. They have had most, if not all, standard medical/surgical treatments without lasting success.

3. They have a relatively fixed mechanical-organic belief structure with regard to bodily functions.

4. Their chronic pain has become the central focus to their thoughts, behavior, and social relationships.

5. They may have ancillary problems involving opioid or hypnotic drug dependency.

6. These patients have a life history of difficulty forming a psychological view of life problems.

7. These patients tend to have constricted emotional functioning, impoverished family life, and difficulty verbalizing their emotions.

8. In general they are distrustful of psychiatry and psychotherapy.

113

Sternbach (1974), Fordyce (1976), and others have described a number of psychological and social factors that can contribute to the experience, expression, and maintenance of chronic pain. These factors include:

1. *Social reinforcement for behavioral expressions of pain and suffering.* The verbal or behavioral display of discomfort often evokes attention or other social reinforcements from a patient's family, friends, and acquaintances.

2. *Financial compensation for pain.* Monetary awards from workmen's compensation, social security, and personal injury litigation are contingent on the demonstration of continued suffering and disability.

3. *Obtaining "time-out" from unpleasant social or vocational responsibilities by expressions of pain and disability* (pain behavior). Relief from unwanted or burdensome responsibility can become contingent on the continued expression of pain.

4. *Emotions such as anger, sadness, or anxiety, which may be experienced by an individual as painful.* Unpleasant affects, either intrinsic to the individual or exacerbated by environmental stress such as illness or injury, influence the individuals, experience of pain and suffering.

5. *The social acceptability of pain as an "excuse" for failing to live up to the demands of society or one's own personal expectations.* Pain behavior as a manifestation of illness can serve as "validation" for the patient and society that an individual cannot be expected to assume certain responsibilities (working, parenting, etc.) that might otherwise be expected.

6. *The use of chronic pain to legitimize the procurement and use of drugs* (such as narcotics, sedative-hypnotics, and alcohol).

7. *Experiences in one's past medical history or family medical history that may serve as a model for chronic pain.* Past experience with the reinforcing aspects of the sick role, either personally or in one's family, may influence the current experience of pain or illness.

8. *Iatrogenic influences of the health-care, disability, and compensation systems.* Both rewarding and aversive experience with these systems may set expectations for what behaviors are appropriate for the patient, and may influence the future behavior of that patient with certain professionals. For example, an attorney may indicate to a patient that it is important to communicate the intensity of distress to an examining physician. This advice may then cause the patient to embellish the presentation of complaints to the physicians he or she consults.

9. *Characterological factors that predispose an individual to assume the patient role as a way of satisfying personal needs.* People with dependent personalities, for example, may find that their pain behavior is very adaptive in providing them with attention from family, friends, and health professionals.

Requests for a psychological evaluation of the patient with chronic pain most commonly comes either from a physician who has reached a diagnostic or treatment impasse or from an outside agency charged with the patient's rehabilitation. The consultation request may include the implied or explicit message that "the pain is in the patient's head," the patient is suffering from a major psychiatric disorder such as depression or hypochondriasis, or the patient is a malingerer. Although these are important considerations, experience with large numbers of chronic pain patients indicates that there rarely is a single psychological, social, or organic etiology to the pain; instead, the pain results from the complex interaction of some or all of these factors. The task of the psychological evaluation is to identify which psychological, social, and organic factors are likely contributing to the pain problem, and to estimate the extent to which those factors are involved in the etiology and maintenance of the pain in an individual patient.

Patients should be informed that the psychological evaluation is a standard and important part of the evaluation of chronic pain, as it has been the experience of most clinicians that medical problems that do not resolve quickly affect almost every aspect of the patient's life. The clinician should explain that evaluation itself has been derived from the experience of a great many other people with similar problems and is designed to obtain an in-depth understanding of this specific problem and how this individual patient is coping with it. The patient should be told that the results of the evaluation will be given to his or her primary physician to help with future treatment planning.

PREDIAGNOSTIC SCREENING

In association with any psychological evaluation of a chronic pain patient, a physician should complete a thorough physical and neurological assessment. If possible, the report of this assessment should be reviewed prior to the psychological evaluation, thus enabling the clinician to become familiar with the nature of the patient's problem, the treatments that have been attempted, and the problems encountered by the patient and the physician. It is most common for a psychological evaluation to be requested at the following points in the course of the patient's illness: 1) after initial evaluation by the patient's physician, to determine whether further physical diagnosis or treatment is reasonable; 2) prior to a major medical intervention, to help determine whether psychosocial factors would be likely to attenuate the effectiveness of such intervention; 3) after all organic diagnoses and treatment have been exhausted; and 4) in preparation for a rehabilitation program.

Patients who are referred from vocational agencies, rehabilitation programs, or attorneys may have detailed vocational assessments and employment histories available. It is useful to review these data because they are pertinent to the psychological evaluation. When insurance compensation claims or litigation have led to the evaluation, it is important to have a clear idea of what questions the psychological evaluation is expected to answer. Direct communication with attorneys, vocational counselors, or disability adjusters may be useful in this regard.

Clinicians who have never evaluated patients with chronic pain must recognize that the assessment of these patients is somewhat different from usual psychological assessments. Many chronic pain patients view the psychological evaluation as an attempt on the part of their physicians to get rid of them as patients or to convince them that the problem is entirely psychological. Patients may feel that they have failed to live up to their doctors' expectations because they have not responded to treatment. Factors such as insurance claims and litigation may complicate the evaluation further and make it difficult to obtain the patient's cooperation. Most importantly, the clinician must recognize that patients with chronic pain *hurt*. While they may understand the importance of the psychological evaluation, they continue to experience the pain and may display various pain behaviors (grimacing, wincing, holding the area that hurts, pacing, etc.) throughout the interview.

It is incumbent on the clinician to reassure the patient regarding the purpose of the evaluation.

ADMINISTERING TESTS AND PROCEDURES

From the foregoing it is apparent that the actual assessment of the chronic pain patient requires a comprehensive evaluation of the physical, psychological, and social determinants of the pain problem. Such an evaluation must include a valid examination of those psychosocial factors that are thought to contribute to chronic pain problems. The traditional, open-ended, nondirective interview may provide general information about the patient's experience of pain, the setting in which the pain occurs, and the effects of the pain in the patient's life, which ultimately may lead to speculation regarding the "psychogenesis" of the pain. However, this approach is limited by the theoretical bias of the interviewer, the lack of specifically defined factors that accurately measure the psychosocial contribution to chronic pain, and the general lack of reliability among clinicians using this approach.

The Psychosocial Pain Inventory is a standardized evaluation of many of the psychological and social factors that have been determined to contribute to chronic pain problems. Because of the problems inherent in a nondirective, nonstandardized interview format, the PSPI was designed around a structured interview format. The interview is administered to patients and their spouses conjointly. In the case of an unmarried patient, either someone who lives with him or her (such as a parent or "spouse equivalent") is interviewed or the patient is interviewed alone. Each question is asked in a prescribed manner and the patient is queried regarding a list of possible responses. The interviewer may supplement the information gained from each standardized question with more open-ended questioning about the particular issue. The inventory was designed in such a way that each factor can be numerically scored and then summed to yield a total pain score, which is intended to reflect the overall degree of psychosocial contribution to a chronic pain problem (Heaton, Getto, Lehman, Fordyce, Brauer, & Groban, 1982).

Although the PSPI at first may seem somewhat unwieldy (i.e., the inventory is lengthy and many questions must be asked in a standardized manner), it has been well accepted by patients and their spouses. Patients usually appreciate the structure of the interview and are reassured to learn that other people have had problems and concerns that are similar to their own. The format provides for a thorough, efficient evaluation of a chronic pain patient while allowing the clinician the freedom to add more detailed information when appropriate. The PSPI frequently serves to highlight areas for further investigation and attention.

The succeeding sections will describe the specific physical, emotional, vocational, and social factors that are important in the psychological evaluation of a patient with chronic pain, each of which is contained as a standardized question in the PSPI.

Physical Factors

The assessment of the chronic pain patient begins with a brief history of the pain problem. The patient is asked to explain in his or her own words how the pain began and what its course has been. Abrupt changes in the pain, as well as trends toward improvement or worsening, are noted. The total duration of the pain problem is an important factor in the evaluation, as a longer duration provides a greater opportunity for operant factors such as social reinforcement and disability income to affect the patient.

A description of the location, character and severity of the pain should also be obtained. The McGill Pain Questionnaire utilizes a 5-point scale to measure the severity of pain and provides for an analysis of a patient's painful experience through the use of multiple adjective lists, which contain sensory, affective, and evaluative descriptors of pain (Melzack, 1975).

Over the course of the pain problem, the number of physicians sought out by the patient, the number of surgeries performed, and the amount of time spent in the hospital are significant factors in the assessment. These factors may play an important role in validating the patient's pain as well as in his or her adoption of the sick role, and may add iatrogenic influences to the pain problem.

Most patients with chronic pain have received a variety of treatments, ranging from standard approaches of medications and surgery to more exotic treatments such as acupuncture. The amount of pain relief, if any, and the duration of effectiveness should be determined for each treatment. Although many clinicians believe that pain patients either fail to respond to any treatment attempted, or respond for only brief periods of time, a significant minority have had periods of significant relief in response to certain treatments. The prognosis of patients who have experienced significant relief for a period of several months is more favorable than for those who have failed to respond or who have responded only briefly to all previous therepeutic trials. A detailed review of treatment can also serve to identify those treatments that might be useful to the patient, but have been omitted previously. Such treatments may include trials of relaxation and supportive psychotherapy.

Medications, particularly narcotics and sedative-hypnotics, commonly are prescribed for patients with chronic pain. Although such drugs are useful in the treatment of acute pain problems, their utility in the treatment of chronic pain is limited. The sedative and euphoric effects of these medications are physiologically reinforcing, and physical dependence, tolerance, and withdrawal may result from chronic use. Additionally, these medications may serve to increase the attention gained from families and health professionals. A listing of all of the medications taken by a pain patient is essential to a thorough evaluation. Particular attention should be given to narcotic analgesics and sedative-hyponotics, as these are the medications that produce physical dependence. A list of the commonly used drugs in these classes is included in Question 18 of the PSPI. In addition to the *amount* of the medication consumed, the route of administration is important. Parenterally administered medications are more reinforcing physiologically and socially than are medications taken orally. If a particular medication has become an issue in the patient's relationship with his or her physician, the medication assumes additional importance.

Alcohol abuse is quite common among pain patients who use it as a sedative or analgesic. In actuality, alcohol performs neither of these functions very well, but can produce physical dependence, tolerance, and withdrawal if consumed in sufficient quantity. Continued abuse of alcohol can add to the disruption in pain patients' interpersonal relationships and can complicate treatment.

Previous experiences with painful or incapacitating medical illness, with physicians, or with medications can affect a patient's experience of subsequent painful conditions. Such direct learning may affect the patient's willingness to "give in" to pain, his or her expectations regarding the sick role, and the impact of the pain in his or her life.

Emotional Factors

Depression, anxiety, and various forms of character pathology can be important psychological factors in the genesis and maintenance of chronic pain problems. The Minnesota Multiphasic Personality Inventory (MMPI) provides a reliable measure of these factors and has been used by many researchers and clinicians working with patients having chronic pain.

A clinical assessment of depression is indicated in all patients who have chronic pain. The evaluation should include an assessment of the patient's mood and affect, vegetative signs of depression, cognitive symptoms of depression (e.g., hopelessness, helplessness, and anhedonia), and an estimate of the patient's suicidality. A past history of depression or a positive family history of depression or alcohol abuse are important in determining the relative contribution of depression to the pain problem.

In addition to the data obtained from the MMPI, the influence of tension and anxiety on the pain can be determined from the patients' responses to other questions in the standardized evaluation. Patients frequently avoid anxiety-producing situations and will report this as part of their pain behavior. For example, the patient may note that the pain increases whenever he or she faces a deadline at work or has a disagreement with his or her spouse. They may also report that relaxation or leaving a tension-filled situation decreases their pain. Some patients may even indicate that they use some form of relaxation as a pain treatment. Over time, the frequent use of pain to avoid stressful life experiences can serve as a potent reinforcer of both suffering and the chronic patient role.

A patient's motivation for change, which is an extremely important factor in any evaluation, can be explored by asking, "If you had no pain problem, or if your pain were significantly reduced, what would you do that you do not do now?" Activities are much more important than improved affective states in the patient's response. Patients are encouraged to be specific in describing the activities, which should be feasible and should be able to be accomplished with less-than-total reductions in pain. Patients who would experience no change in activities or would be obliged to participate in unpleasant activities if their pain problem improved probably have little motivation to change their present behavior. The patient who states that he eagerly would go back to work and resume some leisure activities on a limited basis has a better prognosis than one who complains that he would lose his disability and have to find a job.

Educational/Employment Factors

A significant number of pain problems result from industrial accidents or first occur within the context of some homemaking activity. The consequences of a chronic pain problem frequently involve a patient's ability to continue working at his or her previous job. Disability and compensation are factors that are implicated consistently as important in the maintenance of chronic pain problems.

In order to assess the importance of work-related factors in a patient with chronic pain, it is useful to obtain an educational and work history. Patients who maintained a consistent record of full employment (either outside the home or as a homemaker) and whose employment matched their level of education are less likely to find inactivity or decreased responsibility reinforcing. However, those patients who have work histories punctuated with multiple job changes, abrupt shifts in levels of job-related responsibility, jobs that require little or no education, or a history of previous on-the-job injuries and disability are more likely to find inactivity and avoidance of job-related stress reinforcing. A patient who has continued to work at the same job without modification over the course of a chronic pain problem is apt to have a better prognosis than someone who has modified his or her job significantly, has changed jobs, or has stopped working entirely. With this latter group it is important to assess relationships with superiors, co-workers, and subordinates, as well as job pressures for speed or perfection and job satisfaction. A patient whose pain interrupted a successful, satisfying employment experience is likely to be more motivated to return to work than is the person whose pain removed him or her from a frustrating and unpleasant job.

When asking patients how their activities would change if the pain were reduced, one should inquire specifically about plans to return to work. Further, the patient should be asked to what extent the pain would need to be relieved or what other factors would have to change to allow for a return to work. If a patient either requires complete pain relief before returning to work, intends to return to a job that is obviously unpleasant, or predicts reinjury on the job, little motivation for change can be inferred.

Social Factors

The assessment of social factors in a patient with chronic pain begins with assessing his or her pain behavior. Pain behavior that is dramatic and occurs frequently is likely to elicit attentive, sympathetic reinforcement from the environment, especially from the patient's family. Over time, such responses from others may lead the patient to define his or her role within the family solely in terms of the pain. The more a patient identifies with the pain patient role, and the more this is reinforced by others, the more unlikely that change will occur either spontaneously or in response to purely physical treatment.

Two factors are important in the assessment of pain behavior: how dramatic it is and how frequently it occurs. Patients and their spouses (or, as mentioned previously, someone else who lives with the patient, such as a parent) are asked specifically, "When you are at home and the pain is really bad, how can your family tell that you hurt?" In addition to obtaining the spontaneous answers of the patient and the spouse, it is usually necessary to ask about specific common pain behaviors such as moaning, wincing, rubbing the area that hurts, lying down, and taking medications. The behaviors included in Question 11 of the PSPI were assembled from the collective experience of several clinicians and are representative of pain behaviors most commonly engaged in by these patients.

Most patients will display a variety of pain behaviors over the course of their illness. However, those who receive significant social reinforcement for their pain behavior are likely to engage in those behaviors more frequently than individuals who do not receive such a degree of reinforcement. It is necessary therefore to ask patients how frequently each pain behavior occurs to obtain an accurate assessment of the relative importance of those behaviors. The PSPI provides norms regarding the types and frequencies of pain behaviors reported by a large sample of chronic pain patients.

Because the psychological evaluation is itself a social situation, it offers the clinician an opportunity to observe directly and record the patient's pain behavior during the interview. Pain behaviors that are dramatic, increase during the discussion of certain topics, or occur in response to the actions of the spouse are especially important in attempting to determine the behavior's significance.

Previous exposure to painful or incapacitating medical problems in members of one's family can influence a person's own adaptation to chronic pain. Thus, it is helpful to assess each patient's previous, as well as current, learning experiences with the "chronic patient" role. Examples would be a chronically ill parent or sibling or a disabled spouse who has achieved both a "favored" position regarding household chores and the general deference of other family members.

INTERPRETATION AND COMMUNICATION OF RESULTS

The results of the evaluation are most useful if they represent a comprehensive assessment of psychosocial factors important in chronic pain and if they can be quantified and compared with normative data from other patients with chronic pain. The PSPI not only allows for the standardized collection of psychosocial data, but provides the means to rate both the total psychosocial influence on the pain problem and the relative significance of each component psychosocial factor.

The total score of the PSPI has a theoretical range of O to 68 points. The mean score in normative studies was 30, with a standard deviation of 8 and a range of 9 to 54. Studies have demonstrated that PSPI total scores above 30 predict the increasing influence of psychosocial factors in a chronic pain problem and correlate with poorer response to standard medical treatment. Patients with total PSPI scores below 30 are less affected by psychosocial factors and are more likely to respond to standard medical management.

The individual items in the PSPI should be reviewed, especially for patients whose scores are above 30. The items frequently point to specific areas where treatment should be directed. For example, patients who received high scores in the work-related items may be candidates for vocational assessment and retraining. Those with high scores on the pain behavior and social reinforcement items may be candidates for an operant conditioning program. Marital problems frequently become apparent during the interview and may require specific treatment.

Data derived from the MMPI are complementary to the data obtained from the PSPI. While the PSPI measures historical, environmental, and behavioral influences in chronic pain, the MMPI provides a measure of personality pathology and frank psychiatric illness. Interpretation of the MMPI in relation to chronic pain should proceed from the interpretation of profiles rather than from elevations on particular scales. Psychotherapy and/or medication often are required for patients whose profiles suggest frank psychosis, borderline personality organization, or severe depressions. Patients with profiles suggestive of somatic preoccupation, hypochondriasis, or manipulative behavior will require different treatments than those patients without these traits. Treatment is described in detail in Fordyce (1976) and Sternbach (1974).

Following the evaluation and interpretation of the data, the results should be communicated to the patient and spouse, as well as to the patient's physician and any referral agency that may be involved. The PSPI offers a clear format for the communication of results, as it is phenomenologic in character; that is, it deals with observable events and behaviors rather than providing speculations of possible intrapsychic mechanisms that are more difficult to confirm and understand. For many patients and their families, this may be the first time they actually comprehend the impact of pain in their lives. A discussion of the specific problem areas often is useful in identifying specific treatments to be pursued.

In sum, a report based on the PSPI, the McGill Pain Questionnaire, and the MMPI is helpful in communicating with physicians and other professionals. It represents an evaluation that is both standardized and comprehensive, and provides clear statements about which psychosocial factors are important or relatively unimportant with the individual patient. The results of the evaluation can be utilized in making decisions regarding specific treatments, such as surgery or behavioral therapy, and in implementing more comprehensive treatment plans such as rehabilitation programs.

REFERENCES

Fordyce, W. E. (1976). *Behavioral methods for chronic pain and illness.* St. Louis: C. V. Mosby.

Heaton, R. K., Getto, C. J., Lehman, R. A. W., Fordyce, W. E., Brauer, E., & Groban, S. E. (1982). A standardized evaluation of psychosocial factors in chronic pain. *Pain, 12,* 165-174.

Melzack R. (1975). The McGill Pain Questionnaire: Major properties and scoring methods. *Pain, 1,* 277-299.

Pinsky, J. J. (1978). Chronic intractable benign pain: A syndrome and its treatment with intensive short-term group therapy. *Journal of Human Stress, 4,* 17-21.

Sternbach, R. A. (1974). *Pain patients: Traits and treatment.* New York: Academic Press.

11

Elements of Assessment in Cases of Sexual Dysfunction

DENNIS M. DAILEY, D.S.W.

Although sexual expression is as old as humankind itself, and so, it would seem, is sexual pain and distress, the treatment of sexual dysfunction in a structured, serious, and reasonably successful manner has a fairly short history. Helpers of varying sorts have attempted over time to assist those experiencing sexual problems, but successful outcomes and formal treatment strategies have been lacking until very recently. Affected individuals have always tried self-treatment, a few with some success, but most such attempts do not help and some even make the situation much worse.

Before discussing the psychometric evaluation of sex-related concerns, some general comments about human sexuality are required. The issue of sexuality has been treated differently than most other aspects of the human condition, largely due to the long and pervasive sexual repression that exists in Western culture. This repression has extended to care-giving professionals just as widely as to those who seek help, resulting in a systematic exclusion of the sexual dimension of personhood in assessment and treatment. For example, most assessments of individuals who seek help for life problems do not detail sexuality issues in the same way as other life-history factors that are of interest to counselors. Likewise, for persons in troubled relationships, seldom is the sexual dimension of the bond addressed to the full extent of its breadth and complexity. Occasionally the conscientious practitioner will open the issue, often asking a question such as "How is your sex life?" The typical response to such a perfunctory question would be "Oh, just fine!" Both client and counselor breathe a sigh of relief and pass on to safer issues, such as communication, conflict resolution, and so on. Obviously, the underlying dynamic is one of discomfort, often attributable to ignorance and anxiety about sex-related concerns, even though both parties maintain a calm surface (something clinicians learn in their training for when matters get a bit sticky). Most of the attention sexuality has garnered has focused on deviance. This is an important body of information, but it leaves out much of what dysfunctional sexuality can mean in the lives of people who hurt.

Being sexual or sexually experienced does not qualify as good training for professional practice. It requires an examination of one's own personal beliefs and attitudes, one's depth of knowledge, and the acquisition of specialized skills that are useful in treating adult sexual dysfunctions. Clients do not open up and share sexual material if they get the message, usually subtle, that the clinician is uptight and/or incompetent. Reaching the comfort and confidence level required to address sex-related concerns can be achieved in several ways. Attendance at a good human sexuality course during training is best. There are also workshops that can be very valuable, such as Sexual Attitude Restructuring (SAR), which force one to examine the issues of sexuality from a very personal point of view and effectively desensitize the matter. Many specifically focused workshops can follow, deepening one's knowledge, increasing comfort, and moving one toward skill expression that is useful and helpful (Gochros & Gochros, 1977).

If the practitioner does not have a thorough grounding in the human sexual response cycle, the texts of Masters and Johnson (1966; 1970) and Kaplan (1974; 1979; 1983) would be of enormous assistance. The sexual response cycle suggests that when humans are acting on their sexual needs, they progress through very clear, yet overlapping, stages: desire, excitement, plateau, orgasm, and resolution. Adult sexual dysfunctions can occur in each of these stages and require specific assessment and intervention strategies.

One may have several good tests available and be otherwise a very capable clinician, but without comfort, confidence, and competence in sex-related concerns the tests will not be used and one's helping capacities will not be particularly helpful. A beneficial test cannot be utilized unless some initial data exist that direct one in its selection and application. These kinds of data result from the very personal encounter with the client that takes place as early history is obtained.

It seems such a paradox that sexuality is a vital aspect of the human condition and has such a long history, but that attention to it has been so lacking until very recently. Once the "conspiracy of silence" was addressed and the "laughter curtain" was lifted, sexuality became a legitimate area of academic inquiry and a specialized therapeutic activity, although this does not generalize very far in the overall thrust of helping that goes on today.

The degree of past and present sexual taboo existing in our society has extended to the area of testing and measurement and has impeded careful psychometric development until very recently. The almost exponential development in psychological testing that has occurred in the last 40 or 50 years has not been accompanied by a similar growth in the measurement of sexual attitudes, behaviors, knowledge, adjustment, etc., which is testimony to the impact of sexual repression in our culture, including our professional culture.

For the purposes of discussion, most references will be made to problems that occur with heterosexuals. This is not to diminish the fact that gay individuals and couples also experience serious sexual problems. Most of what is said in this chapter applies to people, irrespective of sex-object preference.

PREASSESSMENT CONSIDERATIONS

The kinds of sexual problems that adults present can be viewed in two ways, somewhat globally. First are those disorders that manifest themselves with fairly clear behavioral symptoms. In males these are disorders of sexual desire (a situational or global lack of interest in or receptiveness to sexual expression); erectile dysfunctions (a situational or global inability to obtain or maintain an erection); ejaculatory dysfunctions (a situational or global tendency to ejaculate very quickly following arousal—once know as premature ejaculation—or an inability to ejaculate at all or only with intense, lengthy stimulation—once known as retarded ejaculation); and dyspareunia (painful intercourse). In females they comprise disorders of sexual desire; orgasmic dysfunction (never having had or having lost the capacity to experience orgasmic release); vaginismus (the involuntary contraction of the pelvic musculature that results in the vagina being impenetrable); and dyspareunia. Most of these adult dysfunctions are assessed rather straightforwardly, and the treatment of choice entails a behaviorally focused brief sex therapy.

Another set of sexual concerns also arises, sometimes co-varying with the aforementioned, which can be put into two general categories. The first is composed of sex-related concerns that arise out of traumatic life experiences such as rape, sexual molestation, coercive marital sexuality, family sexual abuse, sexual harassment, and so on. Although both sexes experience these kinds of trauma, they are more a part of women's lives and require a special sensitivity to feminism and the role of women in our society (Miller, 1976; Gilligan, 1982). The second of these categories comprises sex-related concerns that largely result from being raised and socialized in sexually repressive families and a sexually repressive society. The by-products of this environment are sexual ignorance, a good deal of internalized sexual guilt and shame, and, for some, an almost total absence of social skill and comfort with anything sexual.

Sex Problem History

There is no simple, broad-spectrum procedure dictated when adults present with sex-related concerns, partly because the issues can be highly variable and interact with other aspects of the client's life and psychological status. As a general rule there is no need for an extensive sex history; more appropriate is an overview of what the sex-related concerns and how they are experienced currently. One of the first useful steps is to take a sex problem history, which can be done in 5 or 10 minutes or stretched out over the first interview (Annon, 1974).

Description of current problem: It is not unusual for clients, especially if they are "psychology wise," to self-diagnose a problem in what seems like a very sophisticated manner. They may report "I am impotent," or "I am suffering from the trauma of incest," or "I am frigid." Unfortunately, such expressions tell a clinician very little, and thus the goal is to have the client describe the problem in concrete, behavioral terms. For example, the man who describes himself as impotent may be referring to a general sense of incompetence, both sexually and in general. When using the sex problem history this client ultimately will state that he does not have erections, either generally or situationally, that allow for satisfactory intercourse. This is concrete and behavioral, and this kind of impotence can be treated with brief sex therapy.

Onset and course of problem: The description of onset should include the client's age, whether it was gradual or sudden, the precipitating events, and any contingencies. For almost every sexual dysfunction, onset is preceded by a time when no problem existed. Precisely noting the point at which change occurred is very important. Gradual onset of anorgasmia may mean something very different than sudden onset. Likewise, almost all problems (the exception might be crisis events) have a course or process that the client should be able to note with some clarity. Information concerning the course of the disorder should cover changes over time (increase, decrease, or fluctuation in severity, frequency, or intensity) and functional relationships with other variables. Disorders of desire that have fluctuated over time are different than those that start severely and continue as such until the client comes for help.

Client's concept of cause and maintenance of the problem: This is critical information. Seldom do clients present problems for which they do not hold "private theories" of cause and maintenance, sometimes remarkably accurate, but often not so. In either case, knowing the private theory and either confirming it or reframing it is essential. Not doing so, particularly reframing, results in a client processing most of the early intervention activity through their private theory rather than through a more accurate frame of reference. (Clients who hold on tenaciously to their private theory clearly must begin the therapeutic process with reframing rather than behavioral interventions.)

Past treatment and outcomes: This portion of the sex problem history should detail any medical evaluations (specialty, date, forms of treatment, results, current medications), professional help (specialty, date, forms of treatment, results), and self-treatment (type, results). Individuals rarely seek sex therapy immediately following the onset of the problem. As a mater of fact, with sex-related concerns clients tend to wait even longer than with most other problems (no one wants to confess that they are not completely competent when it comes to sex). They have often had other experiences trying to cope with the problem, and the clinician should know that treatment history in some detail. One of the most important areas of information in this section is the matter of self-treatment. Most patients try to do something for themselves before they seek outside help, but often they are self-treating in some very nonfunctional ways. An example is the typical male with ejaculatory dysfunction (prematurity) who will often report that he tries to distract himself or monitor the level of his arousal: "Sometimes I think about my taxes, or I rehearse old war movies in my head, or I bite my lips, or I constrict my anus, or I dig my finger nails into my hands." Aside from the impossibility of enjoying sex while doing those things, they are the opposite of what he should be doing in order to maintain some ejaculatory control within normal male limits. Unfortunately it is not uncommon for a client to report that he is doing such things on the recommendation of a helping professional. He must be told specifically to stop such counter-productive behavior so that it will not obstruct the clinician's planned therapeutic intervention.

Current expectations and goals of treatment: What is important in this portion of the history is to differentiate the concrete from the ideal. For example, an impotent male may say "I want to be a great lover." Better he should be encouraged instead to say "I would like my penis to function in a manner that allows me to have sexual intercourse and enjoy it." The woman who is having difficulty with orgasm should be steered away from the goal of multiple orgasms toward the achievement of *one* (that she has for herself and not to please her partner). Reframing the heroic intent is critical, otherwise treatment will be judged as a failure (often by clinician as well as client).

Prediagnostic Screening

Physical: A critical differential diagnostic decision in the assessment of sexual dysfunction is whether the presenting problem is largely psychogenic, physiogenic, or some interaction of both. Not all sexual dysfunctions require an extensive medical examination, but some may. There is, for example, a wide range of physiological variables that can have an impact on erectile functioning, such as metabolic or hormonal imbalance, neurological damage, illness, trauma, and a variety of drugs and medications. Similarly, a gynecological workup is indicated for the woman who presents with vaginismus. If she is experiencing discomfort due to persistent infections, her vaginal musculature may contract involuntarily in antic-ipation of the pain to come. Knowing when to refer to medical personnel is largely a product of adequate preparation in the study of human sexuality and experience in the management of treatment of sexual dysfunctions.

When a medical referral is indicated, telling a client to go see his or her doctor is not enough. More effective is a call to the particular physician, in which the clinician outlines his or her concerns and notes that there is a sexual issue. This is important because many physicians have no preparation in the various aspects of human sexuality or in medical evaluations that have sexual behavior or concerns as part of the problem matrix. Some will admit this and suggest further referral; many will not. Experience usually tells the practitioner who can or cannot do the kind of evaluation that would be useful in the management of the problem, and having dependable medical referal sources is essential to the clinician who intervenes in sex-related concerns on a regular basis.

Intellectual/Educational: The concern here is not so much an evaluation of the client's intellectual level (although this may be an issue in those who are mentally retarded), but rather of the level of sexual knowledge regarding self and sexuality in general. A major erroneous assumption for many clients is that sexual experience somehow teaches people all they need to know about human sexuality. One should never be surprised (shocked perhaps, but never surprised) at the level of sexual ignorance that can occur among otherwise educated, capable adults. Recent examples in the author's experience are a 37-year-old woman who did not know what a clitoris was (and, not surprisingly, had trouble achieving orgasm), and the couple, both with Ph.D.s, who wanted to know how far into the cervix the penis generally went. This kind of ignorance, which can cause much personal and interpersonal pain, is likely to become evident in the sexual problem history.

A safe assumption is that most adults can benefit from some straightforward sex education as a part of the helping process.

Emotional: Research and clinical experience has shown that emotional states play a critical role in most sexual dysfunctions. Anxiety, fear (which can take the form of aversion and even phobia), guilt, shame, anger, and depression all have the effect of inhibiting sexual feelings and behaviors.

Anxiety, particularly the variety that arises from the demand to perform or the fear of failure, can have devastating consequences. It can interfere with the autonomic nervous system to the extent that erection or orgasm may be virtually impossible to achieve. In these circumstances the harder the affected person tries, the less successful he or she is likely to be. Women who exert extra effort to attempt an orgasm, for example, or couples who seek the elusive mutual, simultaneous orgasm, soon discover that trying harder does not produce desired results; it is difficult to be effectively sexual when one is anxious. Inhibitors include the threat of unwanted pregnancy, memories of parental censure, interruption by children, etc.

Some assessment of the client's level of depression is important if its presence is suspected. Depression has very predictable consequences in sexual functioning. Particularly influenced is the desire phase, but all stages of the sexual response cycle can be affected by depression.

Guilt, especially if excessive and irrational, can also have serious consequences for sexual functioning. If a person feels that sex is bad or dirty, or that the body is shameful, or that his or her preferences are not all right, then sexual expression often will be problematic. The clinician must be alert for the guilt/shame messages that are almost always present in the discussion of sex-related concerns.

Social: There are two aspects of the social domain that the clinician must be aware of and explore at some level in these assessments. The first is the fact that most of what we are as sexual human beings has been learned and the learning occurred in a variety of social contexts. The influence of family, peer associations in youth, new sexual themes in the general culture, and specific social/cultural imperatives that arise out of growing up in particular religious and/or ethnic contexts all strongly influence sexual learning. One cannot understand another's sexuality unless the social/cultural context is examined and used as a referent for individual growth and development.

The other aspect of the social domain to consider is that most (though not all) sexual dysfunctions occur or become apparent within a social relationship. Marriage and living together are two of the most prominent social contexts, and an assessment of dyadic stability, satisfaction, and so on is central to understanding the expression of the sexual dysfunction. Further, one of the clinician's most critical differential diagnostic judgments is whether sexual dysfunctions are symptoms of negative dyadic bonds or if they produce them, or in some cases, if a complex interaction exists. Frequently, very dysfunctional dyadic bonds, particularly those with underlying hostility must be addressed before brief sex therapy is instituted. Likewise, as sex therapy occurs, it is not at all unusual to see dyadic issues surface and require attention. Overall, it is within the context of the social relationship that the most effective intervention occurs.

ADMINISTRATION OF TESTS AND PROCEDURES

As indicated earlier, sex therapy and serious systematic attention to sex-related concerns have received a relatively recent professional focus. Further, psychometric developments in this area are even more recent. Valuable tests and procedures exist, but the breadth and depth of this area are not yet well developed (Schiavi, 1979).

Used judiciously, the tests that are available can be of substantial use in assessment and treatment plans for adults with sex-related concerns. There are no single tests or batteries that will offer a comprehensive view of adult sexual functioning or dysfunctioning, thus the critical nature of clinical decisions. The prescreening activity will often given strong clues about the direction of initial testing, and clinical management of sexual dysfunction will often suggest tests that can be used as an ongoing aspect of treatment, both for further assessment and for monitoring change over time.

Not all such cases will require testing, and intervention can proceed very effectively for them without it. The clinician, however, should develop at least a general familiarity with the tests that are available and continue to stay current. Having a grasp of the usual instances in which tests are useful and being open to their creative use constitute valuable skills in the assessment and treatment planning/management of sexual dysfunctions.

The tests that have been selected for inclusion in this chapter are not exhaustive, but represent a good sample of the materials and procedures available.

The use of a particular test without clear purposefulness will most often result in no gain, and it is through experience and clinical judgment that productive use will occur.

Physical Functioning

Few paper-and-pencil tests exist that are useful in assessing the physiological component of sexual dysfunction. However, some of the more generally used measures of neurological status or psychosomatic variables could be beneficial at later stages of assessment. In most cases of a suspected physiogenic component, the clinician is dependent on a physician's confirmation. It is thus quite important for the clinician to develop and maintain good relationships within the health-care community, particularly if one is called on frequently to assess sex-related problems.

One pervasive issue with those presenting sexual concerns is the matter of body imagery. Few people are satisfied with their bodies (especially women in our "attractive dominant" society), and yet they must be shared in order to express sexuality. The Body Attitude Scale can be useful in revealing both global and specific attitudes that clients hold toward their bodies. The need for body imagery work is quite common in the treatment of many sexual dysfunctions. The Body Contact Questionnaire provides useful information about a person's desire for body contact. In the individual who is experiencing a variety of aversive or phobic reactions, the scale can yield clues to some of the specifics that make up the dynamic. Treatment indications may also result, especially in setting hierarchies for systematic desensitization.

An interesting procedure used rather frequently with men experiencing erectile problems and those being considered for surgical penile implants is the nocturnal penile tumescence monitor (NPT). Most normal males have two to five full erections during REM sleep, and the monitor is designed to measure such involuntary reflex. The NPT usually is used in collaboration with an in-patient sleep laboratory and may be available to many clinicians on a referral basis. Some sex therapists also use a portable monitor, although there is some continuing controversy about its reliability (Wasserman, 1980).

In our fitness-conscious society there is a tendency to view persons who are not physically healthy as asexual human beings. This is patently sexually oppressive, and helping professionals are not necessarily immune to such thinking. Holding on to such beliefs usually will results in sexually oppressive behaviors towards such persons. It is highly predictable that a patient hospitalized for several months with a broken back will not be asked by any professional about concerns related to sexuality. Without heightened awareness on the part of professionals, the patient probably will leave the hospital having accepted the asexual attitudes and behaviors he or she experienced.

Intellectual/Educational Functioning

As indicated previously, the issue of interest in this context does not concern basic intelligence or educational achievement, but rather the level of sexual knowledge. (The exception is, of course, the adult who may have marginal intellectual capacity or the diagnosed mentally retarded. The implication of the latter is not that learning is impossible, but that it will take a good deal longer.) There is little question that some people can be both sexually expressive and totally uninformed; however there is also little doubt that sexuality is greatly enhanced in proportion to the knowledge one has about it.

There are a number of sex-related problems that have as their root cause sexual ignorance. An assessment of sex knowledge is important in these cases and can be especially helpful in structuring learning experiences for the person involved. Further, many sex-related concerns often are addressed exclusively in terms of increasing knowledge, which can be accomplished in a very few sessions. Two particularly useful measures are the Sex Knowledge Inventory (SKI) and the Sexual Knowledge and Attitude Test (SKAT). The SKI Form X is designed specifically for adults and assesses the general level of sexual knowledge.

Emotional Functioning

Such a substantial portion of sexual dysfunctions are caused and maintained by psychogenic factors that this category of assessment is very important and more psychometric options exist. Often the patient's "equipment" is in excellent condition and his or her "technique" superior, but sexual attitudes can keep either or both from functioning very well.

Depending on the specific case, there are several attitude measures that can be useful. The Sex Attitudes Survey provides a good global measure, as do the Heterosexual Attitude Scales and the Attitudes Toward Homosexuality Scale, depending on the sex-object preference of the client. The latter scale can also be useful in assessing the level of homophobia that may exist in heterosexually oriented individuals, if such fears/attitudes are problematic. For persons concerned about or struggling with self-pleasuring behavior, the Negative Attitudes Toward Masturbation Scale is helpful and can reveal attitudes that are often covered by the "cool" stance that most adults take towards masturbation.

In male-female relationships a good deal of sex-role socialization impacts on sexual attitudes and behaviors. Persons caught in sex-role rigidity (a significant proportion of the population) often struggle with sexual conflicts and dysfunctions. A simple example is the question of who should initiate sexual intercourse. The Bem Sex-Role Inventory and the Attitude Toward Women Scale are particularly useful in assessing the role rigidity or role stereotyping that may exist in the relationship. This is an increasingly important issue in the treatment of sexual concerns.

Anxiety over a wide range of sexual issues has a particularly destructive influence on sexual functioning. A useful test for this purpose is the Sexual Anxiety Scale, which provides some detailed data on general anxiety about sexual matters. As anxiety and guilt often covary, the Mosher Forced-Choice Guilt Inventory is a valuable adjunct to this assessment, and using the two measures together can yield some very significant insights.

An assessment of depression can be initiated in the clinical interview, but must be supported by one or more of the standard measures of depression and affect. The Generalized Contentment Scale (Hudson, 1982), a measure of non-psychotic depression, is a short test that can be used very efficiently with most of these clients. Valuable in assessment, this scale can also be used to monitor the course of the client's depressive features over time and thus keep track of clinical progress.

Finally, in those cases where aversion or phobic reactions may occur, the clinician can utilize the Sexual Pleasure Inventories and the Sexual Fear Inventories. Not only do these scales provide a useful assessment of the domains identified, but they can be very helpful in establishing hierarchies for systematic desensitization and the management of phobic responses with a variety of treatment techniques.

Sometimes sexual behavior is not impaired but the client will report very negative and sad responses to sexual experiences. The same anxieties, guilt, etc., can and do affect the subjective experience of the behavior in addition to the behavior itself. Having a clear sense of the emotional domain is a core demand in the assessment of sex-related concerns, as is a comfort level on the part of the examiner that allows for thorough exploration and skill in the use of available testing instruments.

Social Functioning

As noted previously, sexual problems frequently are presented in the context of a meaningful dyadic bond. This immediately presents a major differential diagnostic task: assessing the nature of the sexual dysfunction in terms of symptom expression and assessing the characteristics of the particular dyadic bond. Specifically, the clinician must question whether the sexual problems are secondary to a larger dyadic dysfunction or whether the sexual problems are discrete and may or may not give rise to dyadic troubles. Of course, the possibility of strong interactions in this respect is very likely. The importance of this clinical issue is fairly straightforward—if the dyadic disharmony is severe, sex therapy would best follow attempts to stabilize the dyadic crisis or chronic problem. It is very difficult to do brief sex therapy if a couple is at open war with each other.

A particularly good measure of dyadic adjustment is found in the Dyadic Adjustment Scale. This instrument is useful with married couples and other similar dyads, such as heterosexual couples who live together and homosexual couples, "whether living together or in a primary bond" (Dailey, 1979). The test provides subscale data on satisfaction, cohesion, consensus, and affectional expression. The

Index of Marital Satisfaction is a short test for assessing the severity of marital conflict and also can be used repeatedly to assess change over the course of treatment. Other tests of dyadic adjustment include An Inventory of Marital Conflicts and The Marital Communications Inventory, which are useful if the couple has particular struggles in and around communication.

There are two very good tests that examine the current sexual functioning of heterosexual couples. The Sexual Interaction Inventory provides data on both adjustment and satisfaction and yields an 11-scale profile that is highly differentiated in terms of assessment. The Derogatis Sexual Function Inventory is more oriented toward the individuals in the dyad, and its subscale domains include information, experience, drive, attitude, symptoms, affect, gender role definition, fantasy, body image, and satisfaction. If time is a consideration, the Index of Sexual Satisfaction is very efficient and is an excellent companion test to the previously mentioned Index of Marital Satisfaction. Other tests worthy of note are the Heterosexual Behavior Inventories and the Heterosexual Behavior Assessments.

If one is working with couples in premarital counseling the Reiss Premarital Sexual Permissiveness Scale is useful both in assessment as well as for exploring the sexual domain of the couples' relationship expectations.

Another clinical situation that occurs with some frequency is presented by the couple coping with the revelation that one partner is homosexually oriented. The Sexual Orientation Method is a useful testing adjunct to clinical impressions, especially if the clinician defects marked ambivalence about sex-object preference. This instrument is designed to measure male homoerotic orientation.

There are, of course, other social contexts that can and may need to be assessed, including work, leisure, extended family, etc., and much of this information can be elicited during the initial clinical interview.

INTERPRETATION AND INTEGRATION OF FINDINGS

A holistic perspective on sexual dysfunction is a prerequisite to an effective interpretation. Too often sexual problems are set apart from the other aspects of a clients, problem matrix, which can serve to diminish their importance and the attention given to them. Equally destructive is focusing on sexual issues to the exclusion of the contextual imperatives in the client's life. The best picture of sexuality emerges when one assumes that all people are sexual beings and that the sexual domain is as important as any and all others.

Physical Factors

If a physiogenic component has been established in a given sexual dysfunction, an immediate question arises—who shall treat the client? Ideally the physician and the mental health care professional work together. Each has important data to report to the other, and this needs to be done in such a way that both psychogenic and physiogenic factors are addressed in a balanced manner. Even when the primary factor(s) in sexual dysfunction can be identified as physiogenic, there is a strong probability of concomitant psychosocial components, and some physicians need assistance to keep from hearing "it's all in the patient's head." Nothing can be more powerful than a positive collaborative relationship with a competent physician when physiogenic factors are involved in sexual dysfunctions. Such relationships do not emerge automatically and need careful work, for they increase the probability that the patient will receive the best care.

Intellectual/Educational Factors

The clinician must be highly sensitive to the negative impact of sexual ignorance and its interaction with and affect on sexual problems. Most dysfunctional clients will need some kind of sexuality education, and that puts a special demand on professionals to have a mastery of sexual information. It is always frustrating to discover that sexual myths or erroneous information were passed on to a client by another professional. Advanced degrees do not make for sexual competence in clinical practice any more than sexual experience does.

Emotional Factors

Clients are not always able to be specific about their anxieties and guilt/shame feelings, and the results of testing may be especially useful in this context. The emotional component of most sexual dysfunctions must be analyzed carefully because of its frequent role in the precipitating events or contingencies surrounding sexual problems. Negative emotions (anxiety, guilt, shame, etc.) have a powerful impact on sexual attitudes and behavior.

The emotional status of clients is woven into the fabric of their essence as sexual human beings. Sometimes it is not as important to come up with a standard psychiatric diagnosis as it is to recognize the part that emotionality plays in all sexuality, whether healthy and satisfying or severly dysfunctional. That is not to say that severe psychiatric difficulties do not coexist with sexual problems, but in most cases brief sex therapy is not successful with this group of patients and intensive therapy is almost always the treatment of choice for them.

Social Factors

Information obtained about both the quality of dyadic relationships and that of sexual interaction within the relationships must be integrated in a meaningful manner or the interventions become terribly disjointed. Examining the larger context is likewise important in yielding information that may bear directly on the sexual adjustment of individuals or couples. The environmental impingements on sexual dysfunction are often the most central issues, and the ability to integrate person-in-situation is critical to accurate assessment and reduces much of clients' unwarranted self-blame.

COMMUNICATION OF RESULTS

There are basically three targets for the communication of assessment results: 1) self, 2) referring/consulting professionals, and 3) the patient/client.

"Self-talk" is a vital aspect of good clinical practice, and one must take time to sit quietly and ask, "What do I have here and how am I reacting to what I have?" Without this exercise the intervention activities tend to be aimless, and clients end up assuming a larger-than-necessary responsibility for the work. The effectiveness of this "internal communication" depends on the comfort level, confidence, and competence of the practitioner. As stated at the outset of this chapter, clinicians must work on themselves first, before dealing with sex-related concerns of others. Personal sexual histories do not suffice, and generalizations from an N = 1 are always dangerous at best.

Talking to other professionals relevant to the sexual problem presented is another delicate and important communication task. Collaborating professionals need to hear the impressions that have been gained via assessment, and the clinicians must be receptive to the adjunctive data that come from others. Without this stance, holistic service cannot be accomplished.

Finally, there is the communication with the client. In sex-related concerns it is usually helpful to reveal the assessment results directly to the client. In doing so, client perceptions (often self-diagnoses) can be confirmed or reframed early in the process. Because long-term psychotherapy is not generally the treatment of choice for most adult sexual dysfunctions, such disclosure will not impede, but more than likely will assist, the process.

Behavioral descriptions tend to be far more useful and yield much better leverage than diagnostic labels for all concerned. Avoiding terms such as *impotence, frigidity, guilt-ridden,* and so on is terribly important, as client and clinician may define and respond to them in highly divergent ways. Likewise, an avoidance of theoretical discussion is appropriate. Too often, when the practitioner does not have a good grasp of what is problematic, personally uncomfortable, etc., about the presenting problem, he or she will retreat to an intellectualized stance. This can only be unproductive, with clinician and client passing each other in a fog.

In many cases not only clinical impressions but the actual results of testing can and should be shared with the individuals involved. This may differ from other areas of psychological testing, but the activity can be applied creatively in sex-related concerns. As many of the tests used are of the self-report type, sharing the results can enhance the assessment process and be integrated directly into the course of treatment.

REFERENCES

Annon, J. S. (1974). *The behavioral treatment of sexual problems* (Vol. 1). Honolulu: Enabling Systems, Inc.

Annon, J. S. (1975). *The behavioral treatment of sexual problems* (Vol. 2). Honolulu: Enabling Systems, Inc.

Dailey, D. M. (1979). Adjustment of heterosexual and homosexual couples in pairing relationships: An exploratory study. *Journal of Sex Research, 15*(2), 143-157.

Gilligan, C. (1982). *In a different voice: Psychological theory and women's development.* Cambridge: Harvard University Press.

Gochros, H., & Gochros, J. (Eds.). (1977). *The sexually oppressed.* New York: Association Press.

Hudson, W. W. (1982). *The clinical measurement package: A field manual.* Homewood, IL: The Dorsey Press.

Kaplan, H. S. (1974). *The new sex therapy.* New York: Brunner/Mazel, Inc.

Kaplan, H. S. (1979). *Disorders of sexual desire.* New York: Simon & Schuster.

Kaplan, H. S. (1983). *The evaluation of sexual disorders.* New York: Brunner/Mazel, Inc.

Masters, W. H., & Johnson, V. E. (1966). *Human sexual response.* Boston: Little, Brown and Co.

Masters, W. H., & Johnson, V. E. (1970). *Human sexual inadequacy.* Boston: Little, Brown and Co.

Miller, J. B. (1976). *Towards a new psychology of women.* Boston: Beacon Press.

Schiavi, R. C. (Ed.). (1979). The assessment of sexual and marital function. [Special issue] *Journal of Sex and Marital Therapy, 5*(3).

Wasserman, M. D. (1980). The differential diagnosis of impotence: The measurement of nocturnal penile tumescence. *Journal of the American Medical Association, 243,* 203-242.

12

Assessment in the Treatment of Couples and Families

DANIEL C. CLAIBORN, PH.D.

The field of marriage and family therapy is characterized by a variety of theories, frames of references, and techniques, each pertaining to an extremely complex phenomenon: the relationship among complex individuals, each displaying intricate behavior patterns. The theories in the field exist at different levels of analysis as do the many assessment instruments and techniques. Few, if any, eclectic, comprehensive guides to the assessment of couples and families exist; thus, most clinicians tend to rely on a few well-practiced assessment techniques passed along in their training or picked up somewhat haphazardly as they have gained experience. In addition, most clinicians tend to use techniques that reflect their own trusted and experience-proven frames of reference.

Because of the complexity of families and the levels of organization within them, because of the limits of psychological training, and because of the tremendous variety of theoretical orientations and clinical role models, it is crucial that clinicians remain as broad and eclectic as possible as they conceptualize the problem dimensions that couples and families present them and as they learn more about and make selections among assessment techniques. This perspective helps clinicians maximize the opportunity to find a comfortable theoretical orientation and to find useful, efficient solutions to the problems presented to them. Remember the blind men touching the elephant!

This chapter is designed to give the clinician a broad and pragmatic overview of the ways couples and families can present themselves for treatment. A second purpose is to suggest certain formal and informal assessment tools that the clinician might select in accordance with the problem situation presented and the clinician's theoretical frame of reference. A model of presenting problems will be outlined, which is useful in determining the levels of severity of presenting symptoms, in prioritizing possible points of intervention, and in organizing both the clinician's inquiry into the problems of the couple or family and his or her sequencing of the treatment strategy. The tests and procedures that follow in this chapter can then be used to gather information systematically, to help clients open up to the therapist, and to generate hypotheses for the clinician's inspection. These steps then help the clinician define the problem so that it can be communicated to the clients and treated successfully, and they serve as a part of treatment itself by educating or confronting the clients with relevant realities. Finally, the tests and procedures outlined serve as a means of assessing progress as treament continues.

The brevity of this chapter and its descriptions of tests and procedures assumes first that the clinician has training in using test manuals and research articles in evaluating assessment instruments; second, that the clinician has an understanding of systems theory as applied to couples and families; and third, that the clinician has experience and training in relationship counseling, as well as an in-depth familiarity with at least one major theoretical orientation.

PREDIAGNOSTIC SCREENING

The Systems Approach

The systems approach to diagnosing and treating couples and families entails several assumptions and implications. A system (a couple or a family) can be defined as dynamic interactional flow of "relationship-defining" communication. A system is made up of communications (verbal and nonverbal behaviors influencing others) that are sent, received, and observed. These behaviors have both *content* and *contract* components. Systems operate according to rules, which are constantly changing or being reinforced by the participants in the system. In the systems approach, the clinician has the system itself as a client as well as the individuals who comprise that system, and problems are seen as lying within the system at large, though contributed to by the members. Thus, the therapist often has a dual role in treating both the system and its members.

A Model of Presenting Problems

Couples and families present themselves for a variety of purposes, including treatment of systemic problems as well as custody evaluation, divorce mediation, and the like. System problems include all sorts of unsatisfactory, frustrating interactional patterns, from dysfunctional communication to members abusing themselves or others. The following model is suggested for conceptualizing the severity and priority of presenting problems in a therapy context:

Levels of Presenting Problems

1. Particular problem issues (sex, finances, handicapped family member, job loss)
2. Poor communication
3. Dysfunctional strategies for meeting needs
4. Developmental problems in one or more members
5. Boundary problems

6. One individual severely disordered (functional psychosis, depression, substance abuse)

Couples and families can, of course, present specific problems for consultation when the members are committed to their relationships and possess good communication skills. Bibliotherapy, behavioral counseling, education, mediation, and active listening are especially appropriate therapeutic tools at this level.

Systems can present communication skills deficits, leading to frustration, alienation, misunderstandings, and low self-esteem among members. Particular issues are certain to have become problems, especially those involving sex and intimacy. Although the presenting problems often appear concrete, it is the communication skills deficits that become apparent rather quickly to the clinician. Behavioral approaches (Stuart, 1980), provocative therapy (Farrelly & Brandsma, 1974), and Satir's (1964) approach are particularly appropriate modes of intervention here, as are structured educational programs and workshops.

The category "dysfunctional strategies for meeting needs" implies broader skill deficits and deeper, more chronic patterns of dysfunctional communication than just described. This level is characterized by game-playing (Berne, 1964) and indirect maneuvering, though members play appropriate roles according to age and family status. Especially appropriate therapeutic models here are transactional analysis (Harris, 1967), provocative therapy, strategic therapy (Whitaker; Neill & Kniskern, 1982), and the approaches of Satir and Papp (1976). Additionally, it is at this level (as well as the following three) that the clinician may want to recommend individual counseling, using one of a number of models (Branden's [1973], Gestalt therapy [Polster & Polster, 1973], and rational emotive therapy [RET; Ellis, 1973]).

Clues to the presence of "developmental problems in one or more members" are often obvious and related to age, role, and normative societal functioning. Individuals experience developmental problems when they are unable to cope successfully with tasks appropriate to their age and role within the context of their society and family. An example would be the unmarried 39-year-old son living at home with his parents, who fix his meals and lay out his clothes in the morning. Fears at this level run higher, yet repressive forces and denial are stronger. These need to be taken into account by the clinician, not only in developing rapport, but in carrying out an assessment and developing a working diagnosis with the family. Of particular value here are provocative therapy, strategic therapy (Haley, 1976; Madanes, 1981), transactional analysis, and the model of Bowen (1978). Again, at this level, concurrent individual treatment of one or all system members is often recommended, and individuation and integration are often primary individual issues.

Boundary problems are "rules-roles-rigidities" issues within the system, and necessarily involve developmental, individual problems. Roles of individuals in the family are not only atypical and violate age and status norms, but have rigidified into patterns hard for anyone in the system to modify. An example would be the mother who forms an equal-status alliance with her son to punish, care for, or otherwise "parent" her husband. Observer-consultants are helpful to the clinician in diagnosing and diagramming structural configurations at this level, as well as in keeping the clinician aware of his or her effects on the structure. Especially appropriate here are the strategies of Erickson (Haley, 1973), Minuchin (1974), and Bowen.

Severely dysfunctional families often have one or more members who are severely disturbed and are highly resistant to change. Severe individual dysfunctions can include alcoholism, psychosis, and extreme forms of affective and character disorders. A multidisciplinary approach usually is recommended, hospitalization often is involved, and coordination among care-giving clinicians is crucial. Therapeutic techniques can be riskier ones, particularly if previous treatments have failed, and dramatic steps can be recommended, such as separating a member from the system for the purpose of his or her own survival. Of particular value here might be the approaches of Hoffman (1981) and Palazzoli (Palazzoli, Boscolo, Cecchin, & Prata, 1978; Tomm, 1984a, 1984b).

In this model, going down the continuum to its deeper levels, one finds dynamics more obscure and complex, problems more chronic, motivation to change more obstructed, the system more rigid, agendas more hidden, direct payoffs less visible, expression of feelings and wants less direct, frustration in meeting needs more frequent, and degree of the conscious, therapeutic "ally" in the client system diminished. Further, there are two assumptions inherent in this model: the first, that the more severe problems subsume all the less severe ones, and second, that where there are several of these problem levels present, interventions aimed at only the less severe will fail. In other words, a family assessed as having boundary problems among members also will show developmental problems, dysfunctional strategies for meeting needs, poor communication, and problems with particular issues. Also, the family presenting boundary problems, if treated only to improve their communication, will continue to suffer a good deal of their pain and frustration, as the clinician may feel increasingly defeated. The use of the assessment instruments and techniques described below can help the clinician identify the most severe level of problems with which the family is struggling, thus aiding in designing interventions appropriate to that level.

In addition to the pragmatic, clinical model outlined above, two empirically derived, process-oriented models have been developed for assessing the structure and dynamics of family systems. Each of these models applies to research and practice and makes use of empirically validated dimensions, such as cohesion, adaptability, and styles of communication and focus. These two models are the Circumplex Model, developed by Olson and colleagues (1979), and the Beavers Systems Model (Beavers, 1981). Though a full description of these useful efforts is beyond the scope of this chapter, a recent exchange of views between the two sets of model-developers serves well to highlight the differences and similarities between their assessment strategies (Olson, Russell, & Sprenkle, 1983; Beavers & Voeller, 1983). An example of research based on these models is found in Kunce and Priesmeyer (1985). Such models for the assessment of family systems may well provide alternatives to the more static and individual-focused DSM-III diagnostic framework (American Psychiatric Association, 1980), of which Fleck (1983) in particular has been critical from a family therapy perspective.

Couples

In assessing couples in particular, the following areas are useful to explore, regardless of the method or the particular tests and techniques the clinician may decide to use:

1. Each partner's stated assessment of the problem;
2. The precipitating cause for the present counseling contact;
3. The partners' motivation to stay together and work on the relationship (their level of commitment to it);
4. The implicit and explicit aspects of their contract (rules, roles, and contingencies):
   a) their expectations of each other, and
   b) their expectations of the marriage;
5. The partners' expectations of therapy (both what they expect and what they hope to accomplish);
6. Discrepancies between what the partners hoped to obtain from each other versus what they have come to expect; between what they intend versus how they behave; "survival myths" versus "survival realities";
7. The couple's roles, games, "shoulds," and "oughts" with respect to sex, conflict, power, parenting, finances, time management, parents, leisure time, etc.;
8. What the clients have tried already (and what happened);
9. Their level of communication skills, particularly their ability to listen to each other and to express feelings and wants explicitly;
10. Rigid complementarity or symmetry versus flexibility in patterns of relating;
11. The persons the partners consider significant role models for behaving in relationships;
12. Significant differences in the clients' backgrounds and values;
13. The way in which each partner handles differentness (through fighting— "who is right?"; through denial—"no difference exists");
14. Others involved in the situation (in-laws, lovers, parents, former spouses);
15. Areas of defensiveness in the relationship, as well as methods of defense and self-protection;
16. Myths each partner holds about marriage or commitment in a relationship;

17. What the relationship would be like without the problems or symptoms being presented; and
18. Strengths of each partner and of the relationship.

It is important to note that because a couple or family enters the psychologist's office as two people, three, four, or more, this does not mean they are presenting their relationship (or system) as the client. Although that is typically the case, the two individuals, for instance, each may desire or be in need of individual treatment, and enter therapy together only for convenience or anxiety reduction. If this is suspected, the clinician should ask about it directly, both in front of all members and individually. The clinician may decide to treat separate individual problems with all members of the couple or family present, but will do so then knowingly. Likewise, the clinician should ask directly about such important diagnostic signs as the presence of extrarelationship affairs, significant health or career concerns, substance abuse patterns, and any other situational variables of possible relevance. The clinician might well ask the clients for their own theories of the problems and why they think the system is still intact (if it is).

Finally, just as is the case with individuals, it is important to identify couples or families presenting themselves as a group but for reasons other than psychological treatment. At times this is obvious, as in custody evaluation or divorce mediation, but sometimes it is not so clear, such as when the family is attempting to establish one member as sick and deserving of a certain kind of treatment, consideration, or compensation. One clue to the latter in testing is, when the MMPI has been administered, finding one or more individuals' protocols showing L and K scores exceeding a T of 50 and an F score below a T of 50.

DIAGNOSTIC TESTS AND PROCEDURES

Many tests have been developed to diagnose and describe problem situations occurring with couples, families, and premarital couples as well; these can be found, for the most part, in Sweetland and Keyser (1983). The purpose of this section is to outline a number of the more useful instruments and procedures—formal tests and informal, experiential exercises, both descriptive and etiological or hypothesis generating.

Psychological testing and informal assessment procedures can help the clinician identify strategies and weaknesses of individuals and their systems. These procedures can help identify appropriate levels for intervention, as well as generate clues as to the type of intervention. Testing and experiential assessment can be used to evaluate the clients about themselves and the process of change itself. Many assessment techniques are readily adapted or evolve into therapeutic procedures. The clinician is strongly encouraged to take or directly experience him- or herself each test or procedure before deciding on its appropriateness for use with clients.

Evaluation for Psychotherapy

Descriptive Formal Testing. There are many *descriptive* tests and surveys available for use with couples and families. These generally are designed to describe from each partner's point of view the problems in the relationship or system and to rate the intensity with which each member feels each of these problems. These surveys, thus, provide a shorthand way for the clinician to gather a great deal of information about each member's perceptions of self and others in the system. Assigning these surveys is also a good way for the clinician to gauge the members' commitment to working on relationship issues, inasmuch as promptness, thoroughness, and completion/noncompletion of the surveys can be observed. Norms for comparison purposes are available for many of these instruments, helping the clinician and the clients gauge their relative levels of dissatisfaction with each other and the relationship.

The Marital Status Inventory is a 14-item true/false survey designed to evaluate a couple's divorce potential, and it has been shown to be effective for this purpose. A longer, multidimensional descriptive inventory is the Marital Satisfaction Inventory. This survey contains 280 true/false items divided into 11 nonoverlapping scales such as "Global Distress," "Affective Communication," "Sexual Dissatisfaction," and "Role Orientation." This instrument has been validated extensively and, in addition to initial assessments, is useful in monitoring progress during the course of therapy.

There are several behavioral assessment instruments in the descriptive category. The Spouse Observation Checklist (Weiss & Margolin, 1977) was developed to identify both specific reinforcing behaviors that occur with insufficient frequency and negative behaviors admitted by the spouses, and to determine the extent to which variations in these account for daily fluctuations in marital satisfaction. Weiss and Birchler's Areas of Change Questionnaire (1975) presents each spouse with identical lists of certain activities that each can use to request increases or decreases on the part of the partner and to predict their own response to these increases or decreases. The Couple's Pre-Counseling Inventory, a survey administered separately to each spouse, gathers information in 12 areas, such as positive behaviors emitted by the spouse, perceived desires of the spouse for self-change, general areas of marital satisfaction, and quality of sexual interaction.

Two other tests deserve mention here. The Parenting Stress Index (PSI) is a 151-item questionnaire completed by the parent (preferably the mother) of a particular child in a family. This instrument has been recently normed, is highly reliable, and yields stress scores with reference both to the parent and to the child with a number of subcategories under each domain. These subcategories include parent depression, lack of parent attachment, child adaptability, child depression, and child demandingness. PSI cutoff scores can help the clinician decide and communicate to the parent which areas within the system deserve attention and whether counseling intervention is warranted. In addition, one MMPI scale, Family Problems (one of the content scales), has been shown to be a reliable and valid predictor of the degree of disturbance in an individual's family (in fact, the best predictor among the MMPI scales).

After experimenting with a few of these descriptive instruments, the clinician may want to develop his or her own survey specifically designed to measure those areas of relevance and meaning within his or her own theoretical orientation.

Dynamic Formal Testing. Among formal testing instruments, those tests referred to as *dynamic* or *etiological* are designed to measure dimensions of individuals or relationships, which may help the clinician form causal hypotheses about the nature and source of the problems presented or may describe relevant traits of those individuals who are acting within the system. Five of the most useful instruments in this category are described here.

The Taylor-Johnson Temperament Analysis is a 180-item survey measuring nine bipolar traits and indicating the degree of attention required by traits rated as problematic. Further, the survey is designed so that each member of the system can use it to describe him- or herself as well as the other members and, in addition, how those other members might perceive the subject filling out the survey. When the computer-scoring service is utilized, results on 10 additional scales are available, including Potential for Marital Adjustment and Parenting Effectiveness.

The Myers-Briggs Type Indicator (MBTI), based on Jung's personality typology, is available in several forms (of varying lengths) and measures personal style on four dimensions: Extraversion/Introversion, Sensing/Intuiting, Thinking/Feeling, and Judging/Perceiving. The MBTI describes the individual taking it as falling within one of 16 "types," each with a number of strengths and weaknesses (individually, in couples and teams, in learning settings, in management of others, etc.). The philosophy behind the MBTI is that people are different in a limited number of ways and these differences are to be understood and appreciated, not confronted or changed. This test is especially well suited to helping dyads relate effectively, and a good deal of information is available relating MBTI types to occupational fit and coupling style (see Keirsey & Bates, 1978).

The FIRO-B (Fundamental Interpersonal Relations Orientation-Behavior) is a 54-item questionnaire that measures three fundamental aspects of interpersonal relationships: inclusion, control, and affection. This is another instrument that members of the system can take both to describe themselves and to anticipate how others might see them. Thus, it is an excellent instrument for stimulating openness and sharing among system members early in counseling. Clinical hypotheses are generated by contrasting scores among the members within the three dimensions measured or by comparing the contrasting scores among the three dimensions for each single individual in the system. For each of the three dimensions, a score is generated indicating the degree to which the individual expresses that dimension and the degree to which the individual wants to have that dimension expressed by others to him or her. Recently, the FIRO-B theoretical model has been presented as a framework for organizing family treatment (Doherty & Colangelo, 1984).

The Sixteen Personality Factor Questionnaire (16PF) is a 187-item survey that yields scores on 16 bipolar personality dimensions, many of which are relevant to a person's behavior in relationships. A computer-scoring service provides a "Marriage Counseling Report" based on an analysis of each partner's responses. This report can be used in premarital and marital counseling. It focuses on trait patterns that represent potential sources of conflict and generates hypotheses for follow-up by the clinician.

Finally, the Irrational Beliefs Test is a survey made up of 100 statements to which clients respond on five-point Likert-type scale. The survey measures the subject's level of agreement with 10 irrational beliefs proposed by Ellis (1973). This test is useful for higlighting different and perhaps complementary myths among family members, as well as areas of agreement in endorsing rational or irrational assumptions; thus, it can be used to identify attitudinal strengths and weaknesses in a system.

In addition to generating useful clinical hypotheses, etiological instruments can be used to stimulate and open up communication within a system, provide the members of the system with labels for their experiences and behaviors, and measure perceived progress during the course of therapy.

Descriptive Experiential Tools. Among *descriptive* experiential tools are a number of role-enactment techniques involving artistic expression and body movement activities. These are often the creations of the clinician, based on his or her experience and tailored individually to the situation and the clinician's needs in assessing the particular couple or family at hand. Notable among these techniques are family sculpting and family choreography, developed by Peggy Papp (1976). In these techniques, the members of a system sculpt the bodies of the other members, to represent metaphorically the problems as they see them, or they choreograph a sequence of movements for themselves and the other members, to tell part of a story representing their conscious and unconscious perceptions of the problem dynamics in their system.

Dynamic Experiential Activities. Although some of the descriptive experiential techniques can yield *etiological* hypotheses, several other techniques are designed particularly for that purpose. The Awareness Wheel model, developed by Miller and associates (1975) as part of a couples communication program *(Alive and Aware)*, specifies five elements present in every moment of interpersonal interaction: sense data, interpretations, feelings, intentions, and actions. The clinician can use this model to clarify elements that are not being expressed explicitly and thereby cause confusion for the communicator and others in the system. Clients can use this model themselves to examine their own feelings and motivations as well as to communicate more clearly and completely to others around them.

Neuro-linguistic programming (NLP; Dilts, Grinder, Bandler, Bandler, &

DeLozier, 1980) has given clinicians a number of useful techniques in the assessment of individuals and their systems. Among these are observing the individuals' use of eye movements and verbal predicates to indicate their preferred ways of accessing and expressing their experiences. NLP also emphasizes the importance of observing sequences of behavior, both within the individual elucidating his or her emotional responses and among individuals as they interact with each other. The extension of these diagnostic tools to therapeutic uses within the NLP framework is natural and obvious.

Recently, personal space itself has been proposed as an objective measure of the quality of a relationship. Through research two measures of the space between partners in a couple were found to correlate with marital adjustment in the expected direction, that is, the larger the space betwen spouses, the lower the marital adjustment (Crane & Griffin, 1983).

Finally, genograms of the family systems of each partner in a couple have been used to explore the patterns present in a variety of behaviors and situations (Guerin & Pendagast, 1976). The genogram is an elaborate family tree, developed by the clinician and clients, that describes chronological events such as births, deaths, marriages, and divorces in addition to other kinds of information for each individual in the family tree. This additional information includes behavioral problems, substance abuse patterns, personality traits, methods of leaving home, similarities among members, and ethics and values. Very often the process of constructing a genogram and reacting to it is of more assessment value to the clinician than the content of the genogram itself.

Evaluation for Custody Determination

The evaluation of families, particularly parents, for the purpose of determining appropriate custody disposition is a complex and sometimes frustrating process for the clinician. There are very few *tests* designed specifically to aid clinicians in this effort, and most rely on standard psychological tests in conjunction with clinical interviewing and direct observation, often in the home of each parent. The reader is referred for general consideration of custody evaluation to *Child Custody Evaluation: A Practical Guide* (Skafte, 1985) and to *Family Evaluation in Child Custody Litigation* (Gardner, 1982). Gardner has also developed a game ("The Talking, Feeling, and Doing Game") the clinician can play with children and parents to assess a number of important qualities, such as openness, criticalness, and other coping behaviors.

Bricklin has developed two instruments specifically designed for declaring a "winner" between the two parents in a custody dispute. The first, called the Perception of Relationships Test (PORT), consists of seven tasks, mainly drawings, that yield a measure of the child's perception of his or her relationship with each parent. For example, two of the tasks entail drawing the parents and putting oneself in a picture with a parent. Scoring instructions are given to help the clinician declare a "winner." The most recent instrument developed by Bricklin is the Bricklin Perceptual Scales (BPS). Using the BPS, the child responds to 64 questions, 32 pertaining to Mother and 32 pertaining to Father. For example, "If you had to memorize a long, boring poem for school, how well would Mom do at being patient enough to help you learn this?" For each question, the child responds orally in addition to punching a hole in a card along a continuum from "very well" to "not so well." Bricklin assumes that the test measures both conscious and unconscious perceptions of each parent by the child. He has designed the test to avoid asking the child direct questions about preferences between parents and to include "override factors," reflecting needs of the child so compelling that the parent who can best satisfy them receives recognition in test scoring. The BPS, as does the PORT, results in a "winner" in the custody evaluation process.

An example of a *process* rather than a testing approach for resolving child custody disputes is the team family assessment model, an example of which is described by Everett and Volgy (1983). Their team approach is designed around major family subsystems, with one team member being designated the parent-family therapist and the second team member designated the child-sibling therapist. The therapists conduct their investigation in a structured way, and in addition to evaluating specific criteria regarding stability and functioning of the family members, they focus on four systemic issues: enmeshment or cohesion in each parent's family of origin, the degree of each spouse's success in structural decoupling, patterns of structured coupling achieved by each parent, and each parent's potential for healthy recoupling.

Most clinicians find three steps important in using formal and informal (or experiential) procedures to assess couples and families: 1) experimenting with a variety of techniques for the purposes outlined at the beginning of this chapter; 2) creating a few techniques of one's own and continuing to modify these techniques based on one's experience, setting, and theoretical orientation; and, 3) combining some use of formal testing with some use of experiential activities and models.

INTERPRETATION AND INTEGRATION OF FINDINGS

The clinician should, of course, always keep in mind the limitations of tests as convenient methods of gathering relevant information, the norms on which the tests are based and their relevancy to the current situation, and the pertinent aspects of the testing situation itself (purposes for which the assessment is being carried out, emotional status of individuals being assessed, and possible ramifications of the results of such testing). This chapter assumes the clinician has a thorough familiarity with at least one major theoretical orientation and will use that orientation in a purposeful selection of assessment tactics—and yet refrain from making the scope of inquiry too narrow.

Utilizing a variety of formal and informal techniques, it is important for the clinician to look for patterns in complementary clusters of descriptors and hypotheses rather than at each individual test result and behavioral datum. As the clinician reviews each test score and behavioral observation, he or she can fit these in with other similar findings, beginning to devlop clusters that can generate hypotheses; at the same time, he or she can omit or simply make a special note of test scores or behavioral observations that seem unrelated to any other findings. Clusters and hypotheses so developed can form the foci of any written reports necessary.

It is also important that the clinician relate hypotheses emerging from the evaluation to the clients' presenting problems. This is significant in building rapport and appropriate expectations with the clients, as well as in coordinating the clinician's thinking with the client's perceptions. Testing or experiential procedures may also be appropriate as therapy progresses, to clarify developing issues, to help treatment get "unstuck," and to evaluate movement toward therapy objectives.

Finally, it is important that the clinician select as a definition of the problem one which: 1) the client can accept; 2) the clinician can treat with a maximum likelihood of success (one for which he or she has appropriate skills and expertise); 3) is at as deep a level as possible in the pragmatic model of presenting symptoms discussed earlier in this chapter; 4) is amenable to objective measurement as progress occurs during the process of treatment; and 5) if possible, fits with the clinician's theoretical orientation.

COMMUNICATING RESULTS

First of all, it is essential for the clinician to obtain the informed consent of all parties concerned before communicating results to other members within the system or to other professionals for the purposes of referral, court procedures, and so on. This informed consent should include what information is to be released, to whom, the reasons for the release, and what form (oral, written, test protocols, etc.) the released information will take.

To the Clients

It is important in communicating assessment results to the clients that the clinician describe all the aspects of the problem situation or symptom picture that he or she has observed, both the very serious and the less so. The clinician should inform the clients about the more serious dynamics present even if treatment will initially focus on less serious symptoms, unless he or she feels this would threaten rapport or initial compliance with treatment. The clinician should involve the clients actively in selecting a definition of the problem and in prioritizing the levels or facets of the problem requiring attention. This, of course, is done after the clients understand the relationship of the problems or symptoms to each other. It is important that the clinician refer the clients to other sources for special (individual) evaluations or services that the clinician cannot or does not provide.

In communicating to clients and to other professionals the clinician should use concrete examples to illustrate his or her findings and conclusions. Additionally, it is important for the clinician to explicate his or her model or theoretical frame of reference and to relate it to the methods of assessment and resultant findings.

The clinician will find, too, that the value of assessment procedures goes beyond diagnosis and hypothesis generation. All of the procedures outlined previously are valuable to treatment itself as teaching tools, as vehicles for confrontation, as means of providing language useful in labeling and discussing problems and feelings, and in stimulating and opening communication between system members and with the clinician. Some of the techniques, too, allow the clients to compare themselves with other individuals, couples, or families to develop a sense of the relative seriousness of their concerns.

To Other Professionals

In addition to using concrete examples and specifying one's own theoretical frame of reference, it is important in communicating to other professionals that the clinician specify pertinent information not obtained or observed, including significant family members unavailable for assessment. In addition, the clinician should organize written reports around hypotheses and clusters of observations and dynamics, not around individual tests, one by one.

Custody Evaluation Reports

It is incumbant on the clinician to ask assertively for relevant additional information or for additional individuals to be part of the assessment if he or she feels this is needed before making a custody recommendation. This additional information could include interviews with teachers, counselors, and babysitters, as well as records from previous therapeutic contacts, contacts with the court system, and so on. If the clinician was unable to obtain the information he or she feels might have been helpful, this fact should be stated in any communication of results to clients or other professionals, implying certain limits on the present evaluation. In communicating results of a custody evaluation, the clinician should describe each parent's assets and liabilities as a parent, sticking closely to the issue to be decided, stating explicitly the clinical conclusions and recommendations, and specifying an estimated level of certainty with regard to each conclusion. Custody evaluation reports should include a summary of the referral data, a detailed lists of clinical contacts (persons interviewed), the specific issues explored, the assesment procedures used, any other pertinent information gathered, a discussion of each parent and household, a specific set of recommendations, instructions or guidelines for executing or communicating the recommendations and a brief prognosis for the child's adjustment should the clinician's recommendations be (or not be) followed.

REFERENCES

American Psychiatric Association. (1980). *Diagnostic and statistical manual of mental disorders* (3rd ed.). Washington, DC: Author.

Beavers, W. R. (1981). A systems model of family for family therapists. *Journal of Marital and Family Therapy, 7*(3) 299-307.

Beavers, W. R., & Voeller, M. N. (1983). Family models: Comparing and contrasting the Olson circumplex model with the Beavers systems model. *Family Process, 22,* 85-98.

Berne, E. (1964). *Games people play: The psychology of human relationships.* New York: Grove Press.

Bowen, M. (1978). *Family therapy in clinical practice.* New York: Jason Aronson.

Branden, N. (1973). *The disowned self.* New York: Bantam Books.

Crane, D. R., & Griffin, W. (1983). Personal space: An objective measure of marital quality. *Journal of Marital and Family Therapy, 9*(3), 325-327.

Dilts, R., Grinder, J., Bandler, R., Bandler, L. C., & DeLozier, J. (1980). *Neuro-linguistic programming: The study of the structure of subjective experience* (Vol. 1). Cupertino, CA: Meta Publications.

Doherty, W. J., & Colangelo, N. (1984). The family FIRO model: A modest proposal for organizing family treatment. *Journal of Marital and Family Therapy, 10*(1), 19-29.

Ellis, A. (1973). *Humanistic psychotherapy: The rational-emotive approach.* New York: Julian Press.

Everett, C. A., & Volgy, S. S. (1983). Family assessment in child custody disputes. *Journal of Marital and Family Therapy, 9*(4), 343-353.

Farrelly, F., & Brandsma, J. (1974). *Provocative therapy.* Cupertino, CA: Meta Publications.

Fleck, S. (1983). A holistic approach to family typology and the axes of DSM-III. *Archives of General Psychiatry, 40,* 901-906.

Gardner, R. A. (1982). *Family evaluation in child custody litigation.* Cresskill, NJ: Creative Therapeutics.

Guerin, P. J., & Pendagast, E. G. (1976). Evaluation of family system and genogram. In P. J. Guerin (Ed.), *Family therapy: Theory and practice* (pp. 450-464). New York: Gardner Press.

Haley, J. (1973). *Uncommon therapy.* New York: Norton.

Haley, J. (1976). *Problem-solving therapy: New strategies for effective family therapy.* San Francisco: Jossey-Bass.

Harris, T. A. (1967). *I'm O.K.—You're O.K.: The psychology of human relationships.* New York: Grove Press.

Hoffman, L. (1981). *Foundations of family therapy: A conceptual framework for systems change.* New York: Basic Books.

Keirsey, D., & Bates, M. (1978). *Please understand me: Character and temperament types.* Del Mar, CA: Prometheus Nemesis Books.

Kunce, J. T., & Priesmeyer, M. L. (1985). Measuring family dynamics. *Journal of Counseling Psychology, 32*(1), 40-46.

Madanes, C. (1981). *Strategic family therapy.* San Francisco: Jossey-Bass.

Miller, S., Nunnally, E. W., & Wackman, D. B. (1975). *Alive and aware: Improving communication in relationships.* Minneapolis, MN: Interpersonal Communication Programs.

Minuchin, S. (1974). *Families and family therapy.* Cambridge: Harvard University Press.

Neill, J. R., & Kniskern, D. P. (1982). *From psyche to system: The evolving therapy of Carl Whitaker.* New York: Guilford Press.

Olson, D., Russell, C., & Sprenkle, D. (1983). Circumplex model of marital and family systems: VI. Theoretical update. *Family Process, 22,* 69-83.

Olson, D., Sprenkle, D., & Russell, C. (1979). Circumplex model of marital and family systems: I. Cohesion and adaptability dimensions, family types, and clinical applications. *Family Process, 18,* 3-15.

Palazzoli, M., Boscolo, L., Cecchin, G., & Prata, G. (1978). *Paradox and counterparadox: A new model in the therapy of the family in schizophrenic transaction.* New York: Jason Aronson.

Papp, P. (1976). Family choreography. In P. J. Guerin (Ed.), *Family therapy: Theory and practice* (pp. 465-479). New York: Gardner Press.

Polster, E., & Polster, M. (1973). *Gestalt therapy integrated.* New York: Vintage Books.

Satir, V. (1964). *Conjoint family therapy.* Palo Alto, CA: Science and Behavior Books.

Skafte, D. (1985). *Child custody evaluations: A practical guide.* Beverly Hills: Sage Publications.

Snyder, D. K. (1982). Advances in marital assessment: Behavioral, communications, and psychometric approaches. In C. D. Spielberger & J. N. Butcher (Eds.), *Advances in personality assessment* (Vol. 1, pp. 169-201). Hillsdale, NJ: Lawrence Erlbaum.

Stuart, R. B. (1980). *Helping couples change.* New York: Guilford Press.

Sweetland, R. C., & Keyser, D. J. (Eds.). (1983). *Tests: A comprehensive reference for assessments in psychology, education and business.* Kansas City, MO: Test Corporation.

Sweetland, R. C., & Keyser, D. J. (Eds.). (1984). *Test: Supplement.* Kansas City, MO: Test Corporation.

Tomm, K. (1984a). One perspective on the Milan systemic approach: I. Overview of development, theory, and practice. *Journal of Martial and Family Therapy, 10,* 113-125.

Tomm, K (1984b). One perspective on the Milan systemic approach: II. Description of session format, interviewing style, and interventions. *Journal of Marital and Family Therapy, 10*(3), 253-271.

Weiss, R. L., & Birchler, G. R. (1975). *Areas of Change Questionnaire.* Unpublished manuscript, University of Oregon.

Weiss, R. L., & Margolin, G. (1977). Martial conflict and accord. In A. R. Ciminero, K. S. Calhoun, & H. E. Adams (Eds.), *Handbook for behavioral assessment.* New York: John Wiley & Sons.

13

Evaluating Adjustment to Alternative Psychosexual Life-styles

DENNIS P. SWIERCINSKY, PH.D., CHRISTOPHER H. NORTH, PH.D.

The last 15 years have produced a growing consensus among mental health professionals that homosexuals, lesbians, and transsexuals can adjust to their alternative psychosexual life-styles and lead happy, productive lives. The American Psychiatric Association reflected this position in 1974 by removing homosexuality from the list of mental disorders and replacing it with the category Sexual Orientation Disturbance. In 1980, the Association further legitimized adjustment to homosexuality and recognized it as a potentially healthy and acceptable life-style by differentiating ego-syntonic homosexuality from ego-dystonic, and instituted the latter as a diagnostic entity in the *Diagnostic and Statistical Manual of Mental Disorders* (DSM-III; American Psychiatric Association, 1980). This decision reflects the change in diagnostic focus from determining pathological sexual orientation to evaluating an individual's adjustment to his or her sexual orientation.

Controversy remains among psychiatrists, psychologists, and other mental health workers, indeed as it does within the general population, regarding the legitimacy of psychosexual life-styles other than traditional heterosexual. Professionals who work with individuals seeking assistance in adjusting to an alternative psychosexual life-style contribute a particularly powerful influence on that adjustment. In our culture, it is fallacious to believe that the clinician can be completely objective in dealing with such matters. Professionals and clients alike are bombarded continually by subtle and sometimes not so subtle social reminders of discrimination, based on unaccepting and negative attitudes. The news media, politicians, religious leaders, teachers, and some influential mental health workers frequently and openly maintain their biases against homosexuality and other psychosexual alternatives, feeding a sense of confusion, ambiguity, and general negativity to individuals attempting to adjust to such a way of life.

Professionals who choose to accept a client for evaluation and therapy in which adjustment to alternative psychosexual life-style is an issue must be very clear in their own minds and consciences about their attitudes, acceptance, and concept of homosexuality, transsexuality, etc. It is easy to sabotage an evaluation or therapy unwittingly when, wishing to be outwardly accepting, one has failed to rearrange one's own sensibility or conceptualization. Sometimes it is best to decline to accept such a client for services if the professional feels ambivalent or confused about what the client needs. This is particularly true in the case of the client who presents a desire to strengthen heterosexual feelings in the face of emerging homosexual or at least ambiguous sexual feelings. A predominantly heterosexual person can present such a problem, but in his or her zeal to comply with the client's desires the professional may add to the magnitude of an ego-dystonic sexual identity, worsening the client's situation.

The language is powerful as it reveals one's attitudes and assumptions. What the clinician says to a client is extremely influential in shaping self-concepts, especially when that self-concept is tenuous in the face of shaky self-acceptance. There are literally hundreds of books written primarily for gay persons of which the mental health professional should be aware. *Straight Answers About Homosexuality for Straight Readers* (Loovis, 1977) is blunt and unapologetic, and probably will provide sufficient stimulus for exploring one's intrapsychic structure regarding alternative psychosexual attitudes and values. Going through the mechanics of an evaluation can be of value only to the extent that the professional interprets results for the client in a sensitive but not condescending, objective and not subtly biased, and caring but not patronizing manner.

PREDIAGNOSTIC STAFFING

Once a client has sought professional assistance in dealing with adjustment to an alternative psychosexual life-style, it must be clearly established whether or not feelings or attitudes about being different are at issue. Oftentimes, an individual may present adjustment problems in which the issue of being gay or transsexual is only concurrent—that is, not the client's primary concern. Depression due to a separation, difficulty with a variety of social or work adjustment areas, or other complex psychological problems certainly can arise and exist that are unrelated to sexual difference issues and adjustment, but one must determine early on the presence or absence of such a primary relationship. There is little doubt that presenting problems often mask underlying ones in more fundamental self-acceptance. An early assessment of this may be tentative, but the clinician must be prepared at any point during the course of treatment to address the issue of self-acceptance regarding the alternative psychosexual orientation. As this may take several sessions to be discerned, a second prediagnostic staffing may be necessary after the initial client interview.

In any event, preparing for the evaluation should take the following form. First, as emphasized previously, all professionals confronting such an evaluation and likely subsequent therapy should be well acquainted with their own feelings, attitudes, and reactions to alternative psychosexual life-styles. Second, a thorough familiarity with the procedures to be discussed in the next section must be attained. And finally, recognizing that the value of an assessment lies in the communication of its results, the clinician(s) working with the client must possess an extraordinary freedom from the encumbering social trappings of negative attitudes toward sexuality in general. Being able to talk openly, without awkward hesitations, embarrassment, or fumbling for straightforward language, is crucial in legitimizing the evaluation.

To remain within the intended scope of this chapter and to reflect a scientific validity, the following material will focus specifically on adjustment to homosexuality. The procedures can certainly be generalized to any alternative psychosexual life-style, but the bulk of research and clinical investigations have focused on the issue of homosexuality. Further, the issue of assessment here is directed essentially at the ego-dystonic/ego-syntonic dimension—not at whether the client is homosexual. Thus, instruments or test interpretations that deal with uncovering latent homosexuality are omitted.

During the initial interview with a client the adjustment to homosexuality must be assessed at least tentatively, and this often can be accomplished in a straightforward manner simply by asking the individual how he or she feels about being homosexual or about homosexual feelings. As an individual's feelings may change during the course of an evaluation or therapy, this assessment constitutes an ongoing strategy. Assuming that at some point some negative feeling about being homosexual is discovered that interferes with a broad range of adjustments, the focus of the evaluation strategy must then turn to the client's psychological capacities for making a more ego-syntonic adjustment or for maintaining such an adjustment in the face of criticism, rejection, and/or discrimination. Similarly, the strategy may need to shift the process of dealing with some secondary adjustment issue that bears on the client's homosexual identity and life-style.

Asking a person how he or she feels about being homosexual reveals nothing about the ability to come to terms with specific negative attitudes about homosexuality and the manner in which the individual has or has not resolved these concerns. Individuals unable to accept their homosexuality to some extent usually feel guilty about their impulses and ashamed of their sexual behavior. Subtler concerns may underlie a facade of well-being. These gnawing doubts may erode self-acceptance and present an obstacle to adjustment. Depression and anxiety are common secondary symptoms, resulting from fear and unacceptance of homosexual feelings. Sometimes the distress is sufficiently high to precipitate suicidal behavior or to restrict the client's ability to function at work or in other social contexts.

The DSM-III postulates that ego-dystonic homosexuality (i.e., the inability to accept one's homosexual impulses) results from an internalization of negative societal attitudes about homosexuality. A review of the connotations of the word "homosexual" in social science writings (Chesebro, 1980) revealed that many writers characterize it as a degenerate condition. Same-sex relations are described as secretive, lonely, unemotional, demanding, and neurotic. Homosexuality is regarded by many as a corrupt state. A second, widely held belief about homosexuals is that they are sex-role inverted—male homosexuals are effeminate and lesbians are overbearing (Weissbach & Zagon, 1975; Levitt & Klassen, 1974). Ego-dystonic homosexuals may have internalized one or both of these beliefs, which has implications for their experience of themselves, their relationships with others, and their conceptualization of a homosexual life-style. To evaluate adjustment to homosexuality fully, these areas of functioning must be examined for signs of impairment related to the individual's internalization of negative societal attitudes.

In ego-dystonic homosexuals, variations on the themes of degeneracy and sex-role inversion can always be found in their descriptions of themselves, of other homosexuals, and of the life-style they perceive themselves leading. In ego-syntonic homosexuals, these themes are generally absent from such descriptions. An ego-syntonic homosexual has been able to gauge these negative attitudes against self-knowledge and conclude that the attitudes do not apply. There are structural psychological differences between the two groups that result in the ego-dystonic homosexual's internalization of these attitudes and the ego-syntonic homosexual's rejection of them. These psychological differences are found in three separate, but related areas of functioning: 1) strength of ego boundaries, 2) inner resources, and 3) field dependence or independence. One of the goals for testing then, is to assess these factors. The stronger the ego boundaries, the greater the inner resources, and the more field-independent the perceptual style, the better equipped the individual is to reject negative social attitudes. In addition to assessing these structural/psychological factors, it is important to gain a more phenomenological understanding of the client's experience of self, interaction with others, and view of a homosexual life-style.

SELECTION AND ADMINISTRATION OF TESTS AND PROCEDURES

An evaluation of an individual with concerns about adjustment to an alternative psychosexual life-style must include intellectual, social, educational, and physical aspects in addition to the emotional or psychological components in order to gain a comprehensive understanding of the client's resources.

At least a brief intellectual assessment must be conducted to evaluate the client's potential for understanding the complex therapeutic discussions that will ensue, regarding how he or she can understand the internalization of attitudes and readjust cognitive structures to attain a better adjustment. The therapeutic approach, whether dynamic and insight-oriented, behavioral, or focused on cognitive restructuring, may depend on the person's conceptual reasoning potential, aptitude for making use of adjuncts to therapy such as reading, and ability to integrate perceptions from varying viewpoints and maintain a flexibility of thought. These charac-teristics are, of course, ideals for therapy, but not necessarily prerequisites to helping a homosexual individual attain a better adjustment. The mental health professional merely adjusts his or her vocabulary and expectations for interpretive complexity with regard to the client's intellectual and cognitive resources. An evaluation of the client's intellectual and cognitive resources can be attained by a variety of intellectual assessment techniques. By far the most comprehensive would be the Wechsler Adult Intelligence Scale, but selection of a briefer and less inclusive assessment may also be appropriate.

Assessing the individual's educational background complements the intellec-tual evaluations. The extent of the individual's education can offer a good clue regarding insights toward homosexuality or other socially challenged belief systems to which the individual has been exposed. Also, the educational background can indicate whether or not the individual can make use of therapeutic adjuncts such as workshops, training groups, readings, etc.

An examination of social resources is crucial in that, particularly when working with homosexual individuals, a social support system is vital. Assessing the individual's family or other social networks may also be necessary, usually accomplished most expediently through interview with the client and, if possible, other key individuals. Though interviewing family members or other significant persons in the individual's life is quite common in most psychological assessments, this is often overlooked in the case of homosexual clients due to the assumed secrecy of the life-style. The clinician should be bold in approaching this matter with the client and convey the assumption that the individual does not live in a social vacuum with regard to his or her homosexuality but has some social resource that can be evaluated and, hopefully, built upon if necessary.

Assessing the physical components that bear on adjustment to an alternative psychosexual life-style is becoming greatly more important due to the health concerns of homosexual individuals. Often the client will need an abundance of information about these health concerns as a prelude to developing a more positive self-regard. The unfortunate negative connotations in the media of venereal disease among homosexuals, such as herpes and acquired immune deficiency syndrome (AIDS), have caused considerable anxiety, which often extends to psychosexual identity in general. Thus, having the individual evaluated for physical health and supplying sufficient information regarding healthful sexual practices cannot be overemphasized as an important aspect of the evaluation and therapeutic process. Certainly, degrees of dealing with the physical health issue evolve as the therapy progresses, but must be addressed early in the evaluation to determine the need for an in-depth assessment of this area.

The examination of psychological and emotional resources is the prime focus of this chapter. For the sake of brevity but certainly not with the idea of comprehen-siveness, the remainder of the chapter will focus on approaches and interpretation of assessment procedures for evaluating the psychological characteristics and resources that require understanding for facilitating the adjustment process. The instruments recommended for use include the Minnesota Multiphasic Personality Inventory, the Rorschach or Holtzman Inkblot techniques, the Embedded Figures Test, the Homosexual/Heterosexual Differences Questionnaire, and a Q-sort technique. Each test is described regarding its application and guidelines are provided for interpretation, recognizing that the clinician may wish to implement only a few of these techniques, at least in an initial assessment, reserving the others for later use as assessment continues during therapy. Each technique offers a unique contribution to understanding the psychological factors that bear on understanding adjustment to an alternative life-style; thus, these are presented with the assumption of their complementarity, not redundancy.

Interpretation and Integration of Test Findings

The structural factors that influence one's ability to adjust to homosexuality are best understood from a variety of test instruments. As it is assumed that clinicians are familiar with the tests discussed here, the focus is on interpreting them with specific reference to adjustment to homosexuality. The first three measures discussed are used primarily to assess structural/psychological factors that predispose to an ego-dystonic or ego-syntonic adjustment. The final two are more helpful in gaining a phenomenological understanding of the client.

Minnesota Multiphasic Personality Inventory

Although the MMPI typically is interpreted configurally to gain an understanding of personality and psychological problems, several scale scores can yield prognostic information about an individual's ability to make a more ego-syntonic adjustment to homosexuality. A low L Scale, for example, would be helpful in this regard, as higher scores suggest greater social conformity and need for social approval. A score over 55T on this scale is probably maladaptive for homosexuals.

Conversely, an elevation on the K Scale (above 65T) is adaptive for these clients rather than suggestive of overdefensiveness, due to the greater degree of social disapproval homosexuals must contend with. Because of this disapproval, a higher level of defensiveness is called for. Homosexual individuals can also be expected to receive higher than average scores on Scale 4 for similar reasons. A certain amount of anger at society is healthy and expected of members of a stigmatized minority, and scores up to 75T or even 80T should not be interpreted necessarily as psychopathological. Elevations on Scales 5, 3, and 4 are often associated with ego-dystonic individuals. Lachar (1974) implies that the higher Scale 4 is relative to 3 and 5, the more frank the individual may be about adjustment to homosexuality and the greater the psychological resources. A very low Scale 4 in ego-dystonic homosexuality particularly suggests serious adjustment problems.

Other researchers have implied that a significant elevation in Scale 8 may suggest preoccupation with one's sex role as a major conflict in ego-dystonic state.

It is worthwhile to investigate subscale scores to gain a better understanding of scale elevations. On Scale 4, a high score on the Social Imperturbability subscale is adaptive for homosexuals, indicating that the individual is not bothered or upset by social disapproval of his or her behavior. A high score on the Family Discord subscale often results from familial unacceptance of the homosexual member. Elevations on Social Alienation and Self-alienation, however, suggest that the individual is not handling anger adaptively, which is resulting in feelings of alienation.

The emphasis in examining these MMPI scales in particular is relative to the assessment of ego-syntonic/ego-dystonic characteristics. Certainly these bits of information in isolation are insufficient and must be considered in view of interview or projective information as well. Clinicians must consider the complete MMPI profile in more general contexts as well as to assess other areas of psychological resources and distress factors.

A comment is offered regarding Scale 5, as it is often and erroneously associated with interpretation of homosexual meaning. A recent review by Wong (1984) points out that Scale 5 clearly fails in its purpose of assessing or "diagnosing" homosexuality, or even for measuring characteristics that differentiate males and females. Its interpretation relative to ego-syntonic/ego-dystonic meaning may also be nonexistent. As Wong states, research provides no consistent meaning for any score on Scale 5 nor has any score level been associated consistently with any serious psychological disturbance. It probably has more to do with activity/passivity than anything else.

Rorschach or Holtzman Inkblot Techniques

These tests are helpful in assessing a client's inner resources and strength of ego boundaries, two psychological factors that can be prognostic of the ability to adjust to homosexuality and to maintain that adjustment in the face of rejection or disapproval from others. As noted previously, these structural factors allow an ego-syntonic homosexual to compare negative societal attitudes about homosexuality to his or her knowledge of self and to preserve self-esteem by rejecting those stereotypes as inapplicable. A person without these resources or boundaries lacks the requisite self-understanding to compare against the negative attitudes, which in turn leaves him or her more vulnerable to internalizing those attitudes.

Inner resources refer to mature cognitive capacities (i.e., the ability to reflect on experience, to plan and organize actions, and to thinking independently). They are best assessed through the quantity and quality of human movement responses (Ms) produced in the record. Responses depicting people in happy, collaborative activities that are neither childlike nor stereotypic are signs of good inner resources. A good form quality rating (+ or o) also must accompany the response.

Strength of ego boundaries determines an individual's ability to differentiate self from others. It is conceptually related to inner resources in that the better developed or differentiated the self (the greater the inner resources) the easier it is to distinguish self from others. Strength of ego boundaries can be assessed directly in the Holtzman Technique by examining barrier and penetration scores. The general method used for determining these scores can be applied to Rorschach responses as well, in order to gain an undertstanding of how vulnerable the individual is to others' opinions, criticisms, or valuations. The strength of these boundaries is expressed symbolically through perceptual features suggestive of barriers, containers, or protective surfaces. Weaker, more permeable ego boundaries are reflected through perceptual features of penetration and disruption or erosion of outer surfaces. Percepts that include both features (e.g., a shirt with holes in it) would suggest inadequate defenses or unsuccessful attempts at defending oneself against intrusion, attack, or scrutiny. A rough estimate of the strength of ego boundaries can be obtained by comparing the number of responses suggesting barrier strength with the number suggesting penetration of those barriers. (This is done more easily with the Holtzman Technique as there are specific norms and criteria for doing so.) A high number of barrier responses suggests stronger ego boundaries or a better developed sense of self/other differentiation. A higher number of penetration responses suggests more permeable ego boundaries or a less developed sense of self/other differentiation.

Other signs that might be observed in the projective tests include possibilities of sexual confusion in human responses. These may be characteristic of ego-dystonic individuals, who may offer more responses with opposite-sex figures and opposite-sex clothing. Ego-dystonic characteristics may also be revealed in any deprecation of perceived cross-sex features. There also may be a tendency to perceive more delicately identified or ambiguously identified same-sex figures and features.

(As in the case of the MMPI, novice projective testers should avail themselves of texts relative to usual and other interpretations regarding general psychological resources or limitations.)

Embedded Figures Test

This instrument measures the extent to which an individual utilizes a field-dependent or field-independent perceptual style in processing information and making decisions. Persons employing a field-dependent style tend to internalize uncritically information from their environment, while those with a more field-independent style evaluate such information in light of internal frames of reference or self-knowledge. It is clearly more adaptive for homosexuals to utilize a field-independent style, as they are then able to compare negative societal attitudes with self-knowledge. Homosexuals with a field-dependent style are at greater risk for uncritically internalizing stereotypes and concluding that they too must be "degenerate" or "effeminate." Because being field-dependent implies powerlessness, there is a tendency to accept one's homosexual identity fatalistically and to assume a passive, often negative self-assessment. It is easy for such individuals to perceive an irreversible injustice in their homosexuality, contributing to an ego-dystonic experience.

Homosexual/Heterosexual Differences Questionnaire

This questionnaire can be devised by the examiner to assess the kinds of negative attitudes toward homosexuality that an individual has internalized. It requires the client to rate, along an 11-point scale, where a "typical" homosexual falls relative to a "typical" heterosexual along certain personality and life-style dimensions that are sensitive to popular stereotypes about homosexuality. The individual can be asked to make two sets of ratings. The first yields an understanding of how the client views homosexuals in today's society and whether he or she perceives the typical homosexual as much more effeminate, lonely, maladjusted, immoral, etc., than the typical heterosexual. The second set of comparison ratings, which require a comparison of heterosexuals and homosexuals in a society free of negative attitudes toward homosexuality, examine beliefs about innate differences that might appear regardless of social conditioning and reveal the kinds of negative attitudes that the client has internalized.

An individual can be asked to make both sets of ratings on the same form. It is the second (internalization) ratings that are prognostic of the individual's ability to accept his or her homosexuality. If the person has internalized extensive negative attitudes, it may be futile to work toward acceptance of the homosexuality without dealing with preliminary issues and values first.

In order to assist an examiner in constructing a questionnaire of this type, the directions for its administration and some sample items are included here. The examiner can add as many items as he or she wishes and may assess a narrow or broad range of attitudes about homosexuality. The examiner might also wish to add items sensitive to "positive" (though possibly stereotypic) attitudes towards homosexuals (e.g., creativity, humor, stylishness) to balance the attitude range. Such an inclusion can be powerful therapeutically in communicating to the client that attitudes about homosexuality can be positive as well as negative.

Directions for this kind of questionnaire might be as follows: "Please mark with an 'X' where you think the 'typical homosexual' would fall relative to the 'typical heterosexual' along each of the following scales." Each item's scale is provided with 1-11 points. Only the 1st, 6th, and 11th points provide a specific description, but the individual is allowed to indicate his or her standing at any of the 11 points. Three examples follow:

1	2	3	4	5	6	7	8	9	10	11

Much less masculine than the typical heterosexual   About as masculine as the typical heterosexual   Much more masculine than the typical heterosexual

1	2	3	4	5	6	7	8	9	10	11

Much less lonely than the typical heterosexual	About as lonely as the typical heterosexual	Much more lonely than the typical heterosexual

1	2	3	4	5	6	7	8	9	10	11

Much less moral than the typical heterosexual	About as moral as the typical heterosexual	Much more moral than the typical heterosexual

After the individual makes the "X" ratings, he or she should be asked to make the second set of ratings by marking with a "Y" where he or she thinks the typical homosexual would fall relative to the typical heterosexual in a society free of negative attitudes about homosexuality. These ratings provide the "internalization index" that will give psychotherapists some idea of whether it is feasible to work with the individual toward an acceptance of his or her homosexuality.

Q-sort Technique

This technique is probably the single most useful method of evaluating an individual's adjustment to his or her psychosexual life-style. It is also helpful in assessing therapy outcome with homosexual clients, particularly ego-dystonic homosexuals. General information about the Q-sort as an evaluation technique may be found in Stephenson (1953).

The technique as adapted here requires the individual to sort a deck of cards containing self-statements into piles from "least characterstic" to "neutral" to "most charactertistic" of him- or herself or a hypothetical other (e.g., a "typical homosexual"). The self-statements can be generated from theoretical information about ego-dystonic and ego-syntonic adjustments in homosexuality. Such a theory was developed by the second author of this chapter and successfully adapted to the Q-sort technique to assess an individual's adjustment to homosexuality. The Q-sort deck as it is used here consists of 57 cards; 36 of these contain self-statements drawn from areas of functioning theorized to differentiate between ego-dystonic and ego-syntonic homosexuals. Eighteen of these 36 statements reflect a more ego-syntonic adjustment, while the remaining 18 reflect a more ego-dystonic position. Each of the 18 areas of functioning and the self-statements associated with them are listed below:

I. Sexual relations: Preference for impersonal vs. intimate activities
1. My best sex is with strangers. (ego-dystonic)
2. I enjoy holding and caressing my partner. (ego-syntonic)
II. Attitudes toward masculinity and femininity: Acceptance vs. dissatisfaction
3. I feel as if I'm "less than a man." (e-d)

  4. I don't worry about how masculine or feminine I appear to others. (e-s)

III. View of normal standards: Idolization vs. disinterest
  5. I'd be a lot happier as a heterosexual. (e-d)
  6. I can be "different" and be quite happy. (e-s)

IV. Evaluation of oneself: Comparative vs. asset frame of reference
  7. I'm always sizing myself up with others. (e-d)
  8. I evaluate myself on my own terms. (e-s)

V. Freedom of self-expression: Self-monitoring vs. spontaneity
  9. I watch what I do and say around others. (e-d)
  10. I'm pretty free in what I say and do around others. (e-s)

VI. Effects of homosexuality on evaluation of self; Negative spread vs. positive spread
  11. Homosexuality has made my whole life miserable. (e-d)
  12. I have grown in some important ways from being homosexual. (e-s)

VII. Public presentation of self: "As if" behavior vs. acknowledgement of one's homosexuality
  13. I sometimes try to make others believe I'm heterosexual. (e-d)
  14. I'm quite open about my homosexuality. (e-s)

VIII. Expressing affection towards males: Comfort vs. discomfort
  15. It's hard for me to show affection for another man. (e-d)
  16. I'd like to fall in love with a man. (e-s)

IX. Life-style satisfaction: Satisfied vs. dissatisfied
  17. I like the way I live my life. (e-s)
  18. I feel lonely much of the time. (e-d)

X. Acceptance of individual differences: Intolerance vs. acceptance
  19. I take a "live and let live" attitude. (e-s)
  20. Effeminate gays bother me. (e-d)

XI. Social integration: Alienation vs. communality
  21. I feel like I live on the fringe. (e-d)
  22. I feel involved with people. (e-s)

XII. Feelings about homosexual impulses: Acceptance vs. rejection
  23. I feel badly about being attracted to men. (e-d)
  24. I have no trouble accepting my homosexual feelings. (e-s)

XIII. Personal integration of homosexuality: Integrated vs. conflicted
  25. I think of myself as a gay person. (e-s)
  26. I feel like I lead a double life. (e-d)

XIV. Feelings about self: Positive vs. negative
  27. I dislike myself. (e-d)
  28. I feel good about who I am. (e-s)

XV. Encountering negative attitudes toward homosexuality: Willingness to challenge vs. unwillingness to do so

29. It's important to change people's negative attitudes toward homosexuality. (e-s)
30. I keep quiet when homosexuality becomes a topic of conversation. (e-d)

XVI. Attitudes towards personal aging: Acceptance vs. apprehension
31. I dread growing older. (e-d)
32. There are positive aspects to aging. (e-s)

XVII. Social activities with homosexuals: Avoidance vs. valuing
33. I avoid socializing with homosexuals. (e-d)
34. Having gay friends is very important to me. (e-s)

XVIII. Effects (known or believed) of coming out on relations with family and friends: Positive vs. negative
35. My family and friends would reject me if they knew I was homosexual. (e-d)
36. Coming out to others has often improved my relationships with them. (e-s)

An individual is eventually asked to sort the deck of cards under seven different conditions: describing typical self, worst self, ideal self, a poorly adjusted homosexual, a typical homosexual, a well-adjusted homosexual, and a typical heterosexual. However, prior to this sorting, 21 more statements are generated by asking the participant open-ended questions about his or her conceptions of each of these seven sorting types (e.g., "How do you typically come across to others?", "How would you describe a well-adjusted homosexual?", "How would you describe a poorly adjusted homosexual?", etc.). The examiner selects three statements or adjectives that the client has used to describe each of these seven sorting types and adds these 21 cards to the deck, bringing the total number of cards to 57. (Thirty-six cards are thus drawn from theory and 21 are drawn from the subject's own descriptions of the seven sorting types.)

The client then sorts the 57 different cards into 11 stacks, reflecting the continuum from highly characteristic (stack 1) to neutral (stack 6) to highly uncharacteristic (stack 11) of the "type" being described in the sort. For example, the client may feel that the statement "Homosexuality has made my whole life miserable" is highly characteristic of his or her typical self and place it in a pile towad that end of the continuum. While sorting the cards again, however, this time to describe a well-adjusted homosexual, this card may be placed toward the highly uncharacteristic end of the continuum. The participant is required to place a specific number of cards in each of the piles so that the distribution of cards resembles a normal curve and thereby facilitates statistical procedures. The highest number of cards, 11 are placed in the "neutral" or "irrelevant" pile (stack 6) with progressively fewer cards being placed in the piles approaching the extremes of the continuum. The exact numbers of cards to be placed in each of the 11 piles are as follows:

Descriptor: Most characteristic					Neutral			Least characteristic		
Stack										
number:	1	2	3	4	5	6	7	8	9	10	11
Cards										
in stack:	1	2	4	7	9	11	9	7	4	2	1

The participant sorts the deck of cards seven times to reflect his conception of each of the seven sorting types (typical self, worst self, etc.). The examiner can then correlate the sortings and present the data in the form of a correlation matrix. To perform a correlational analysis of the sorts, the examiner assigns numerical values to each of the 57 cards depending on the pile in which it was placed. The numerical values are assigned to the cards as follows: Most characterstic card (stack 1) would receive a value of + 5, the second stack + 4, third stack + 3, fourth stack + 2, fifth stack + 1, and the sixth or neutral stack would receive a zero. Successive degrees of uncharacteristicness would receive values of −1 at stack 7, −2 for 8, −3 for 9, −4 for 10, and −5 for stack 11. A card's value changes from sort to sort depending on the pile in which it has been placed. The correlation between two sorts (e.g., typical self with worst self) is determined by summing the cross-products of the cards and dividing this total by the sum of the squared values of the cards. This denominator, the sum of the squared values of the cards, will always equal 260 because the same 59 cards are used in all seven sorts. To obtain the sum of the cross-products, the clinician merely multiplies the values of the card in each of the sorts and then sums these multiplied values for all 57 cards. For example, if the card "Homosexuality has made my life miserable" received a + 4 rating in the typical self sorting (it was placed in stack 2) and a −5 rating in the well-adjusted homosexual sorting (placed in stack 11), the cross product for this card would be −20. The cross products for all 59 cards are determined, totalled, and then divided by 260. The examiner can then construct a correlation matrix to examine relationships among the different sorts.

The following data are provided as an example of this procedure, gathered from an ego-dystonic homosexual (identified here as "E.D.") before and after psychotherapy. The data illustrate the usefulness of this technique for understanding changes in self-concept and assessing psychotherapeutic outcome.

As indicated in Table 1, E.D. obviously has a very low self-opinion, seeing himself as more often like his worst self and quite unlike his ideal self. He regards himself as similar to a poorly adjusted homosexual and very different from a well-adjusted homosexual. His ideal self is highly correlated with his conception of a well-adjusted homosexual, however, suggesting that he strives to become a well-adjusted homosexual. The therapist need not seek to reorient E.D.'s sexual feelings. (The correlation between his ideal self and the typical heterosexual, in fact, is much lower than that between his ideal self and the well-adjusted homosexual.) An examination of the seven cards he regarded as most characteristic of his typical self

TABLE 1

Correlations among E.D.'s Q-sort Categories before Psychotherapy

	TS*	WS	IS	PAHo	THo	WAHo	THe
TS	—	.68	−.56	.48	.02	−.49	−.03
WS		—	−.87	.72	−.07	−.77	−.13
IS			—	−.72	.00	.80	.17
PAHo				—	.02	−.85	−.04
THo					—	.10	−.08
WAHo						—	.08

*Typical Self, Worst Self, Ideal Self, Poorly Adjusted Homosexual, Typical Homosexual, Well-Adjusted Homosexual, Typical Heterosexual

before psychotherapy further reveals his sense of self-distress: 1) I don't fit in at all; 2) My homosexuality has prevented me from consummating some needs I have; 3) I'm lonely most of the time; 4) I live on the fringe; 5) I come across as well adjusted; 6) I feel closer to people I've disclosed my homosexuality to; and 7) I'm scared of becoming an old man. The picture is of someone who feels alienated from others and frustrated about his homosexuality. He apparently keeps his unhappiness to himself and has found that he can reduce his sense of alienation by disclosing his homosexuality to others.

E. D. remained in psychotherapy for eight months. Both he and his therapist agreed that he had made significant progress over the course of therapy and that he was ready to terminate. Immediately following his psychotherapy, E. D. was asked to do the same seven Q-sorts (with the same 59 cards) to compare his results post-therapy with those obtained prior to his imitations. The examiner was not his psychotherapist nor in any way related to the psychotherapist, thus minimizing the possible bias to please the therapist by exaggerating well-being.

These findings shown in Table 2 corroborate E. D.'s and his therapist's opinion that E. D. had indeed developed a better self-concept over the course of psychotherapy. He now regards himself as closer to his ideal self than to his worst self and sees himself as more like a well-adjusted homosexual than a poorly adjusted one. The data clearly indicate that E. D. now sees himself in a more favorable light. An examination of the seven cards most characteristic of his typical self post-therapy also illustrates this change in self-concept and the alleviation of felt distress: 1) I'm satisfied that I can't do any better than I'm doing right now; 2) I can be myself without worrying about it; 3) There's no reason to live my life any way other than

TABLE 2

Correlations among E.D.'s Q-sort Categories following Psychotherapy

	TS*	WS	IS	PAHo	THo	WAHo	THe
TS	—	−.54	.52	−.60	.12	.80	−.19
WS		—	−.81	.86	−.20	−.60	−.19
IS			—	−.73	.27	.65	.01
PAHo				—	−.12	−.64	−.09
THo					—	.27	.20
WAHo						—	−.13

*As in Table 1.

how I feel; 4) I accept my sexual preference; 5) Being gay is part of who I am; 6) I work hard to change people's negative attitudes toward homosexuality; and 7) I've found a balance between being self-centered and concerned with others.

Clearly the Q-sort technique can be a valuable tool for understanding how a client sees him- or herself and for assessing psychotherapeutic outcome. It is probably the best single method for assessing adjustment to alternative psychosexual life-styles. It is presented here in greater detail than the other procedures because they are much more well-documented in the psychological literature.

COMMUNICATING RESULTS

The purpose of evaluating for adjustment to an alternative psychosexual life-style is to help the client and psychotherapist understand the issues and psychological factors that must be dealt with in developing better self-acceptance. Within today's culture this evaluation rarely is based on a third-party referral, thus communication of the assessments results usually takes the form of progressing into therapy. A written summary frequently is made and highly useful as a permanent record for monitoring change. The emphasis on the Q-sort technique offers the advantage of producing statistical tables that offer a "worksheet" to share with the client. Communicating results via the Q-sort approach also relies heavily on terms and statements generated by the client him- or herself. At least 21 of the Q-sort statements are based on the client's initial responses to questions to generate the cards. Using these and showing the client how they change categories or emphases is a powerful way of showing the client how his or her own meanings have changed, much more direct than the words of the clinician alone.

Evaluation and treatment of adjustment to a homosexual orientation or other alternative psychosexual life-style requires an active, emphatic, and genuine approach by the examiner. It is an area of assessment that does not work well when the examiner is cool and distant. Also, as suggested in Chapter 11, it is often the clinician's own comfort level and self-assurance that lend the essential credibility and effectiveness of an assessment in such a sensitive area.

Despite the clinician's attempts to be accepting, enlightened, and unabashedly candid in addressing sex-related topics, there is a need to appreciate a sensibility (as Loovis calls it) about homosexuality. An essential aspect of that sensibility is the appreciation of "differentness" in a broad sense, and a recognition that that differentness seeks harmony with everyone else. Further, that "differentness" applies to something other than the mechanisms of mere physical sexual expression. An article appeared several years ago describing this sensibility, entitled "Homosexuals are not just like heterosexuals, except in bed." How often has the accepting, enlightened person remarked, "I accept you for what you are; what you do in bed is your business." The implication is, of course, that the only "difference" between the homosexual and the heterosexual exists between the sheets.

As this chapter emphasizes, by focusing on the intrapsychic peace of egosyntonicity, the professional helps a client to accept a fundamental (though not limited) differentness from most others. Feedback during the course of evaluation and therapy must seek to integrate the test signs, correlations, and adjectives within the homosexual sensibility of being different and being "okay." To accept a difference in bed but "normalcy" elsewhere eschews the wholeness and integrity of being homosexual.

REFERENCES

Chesebro, J. (1980). Paradoxical views of "homosexuality" in the rhetoric of social scientists: A fantasy theme analysis. *Quarterly Journal of Speech, 66,* 127-139.
Lachar, D. (1974). *The MMPI: Clinical assessment and automated interpretation.* Los Angeles: Western Psychological Services.
Levitt, E., & Klassen, A. (1974). Public attitudes toward homosexuals: Part of the 1971 national survey by the Institute for Sex Research. *Journal of Homosexuality, 1,* 29-43.
Loovis, D. (1977). *Straight answers about homosexuality for straight readers.* New York: Barnes & Noble.
Stephenson, W. (1953). *The study of behavior.* Chicago: University of Chicago Press.
Weissbach, T., & Zagon, G. (1975). The effect of deviant group membership upon impressions of personality. *Journal of Social Psychology, 95,* 263-266.
Wong, M. R. (1984). MMPI scale five: Its meaning, or lack thereof. *Journal of Personality Assessment, 48,* 279-284.

14

The Work Environment and Stress: Diagnosing Type A Behavior

MARY ANN STRIDER, PH.D., FRED D. STRIDER, PH.D.

In recent years, there has been an increased awareness of the role that stress plays in the etiology, pathology, and treatment of somatic and psychiatric disorders. This chapter presents an overview of the concept of stress and psychological factors in health and illness, describes current clinical approaches to the measurement of stress factors, and emphasizes one particular personality constellation in which stress can be clearly related to a physical disorder: the relationship between the Type A personality and coronary disease. The orientation is a holistic one; it is not possible to isolate single factors as causative in such a presentation. Social, situational, personality, and physical factors are interactive and deserve consideration by the clinician. In this regard, the task is to distinguish between ambitious, upwardly mobile individuals and those whose personality constellation predisposes them to heart disease.

In the early 1970s, two cardiologists, Meyer Friedman and Ray H. Rosenman, described a personality constellation that their research suggested was correlated with coronary disease (Friedman & Rosenman, 1974). In their initial formulation, they described an individual characterized by an overwhelming sense of time urgency and competitive drive. Characteristic behaviors involved pernicious ambition, pervading competitiveness, and conducting the affairs of daily life primarily and essentially in the context of urgency. This "Type A" individual's life-style was characterized by a fetish for punctuality, annoyance at being kept waiting, constant feelings of being behind, preoccupation with deadlines, irritation and anger at the inevitable delays of daily life, and persistent impatience. Particular patterns emerged, such as speech, little time for meals or relaxations, and an almost total absence of hobbies or recreation outside of competitive games or gambling. Friedman and Rosenman's Type A personality often engaged in two or more activities concurrently (polyphasic thinking), noted by a sense of preoccupation. For these individuals things worth having took precedence over more philosophical goals and

168

values, in addition to chronic dissatisfaction with current socioeconomic status and achievement, no matter how high or enviable those achievements. Research has shown that the Type A life-style is related directly to the elevation of blood cholesterol and adrenalin levels and the depletion of other hormones, all factors in turn related to heart disease.

PREASSESSMENT CONSIDERATIONS

Preassessment involves the method of contact and referral of the patient. Many times the referral source will provide some data regarding symptoms and stresses. Referrals from physicians, which are the most frequent in the experience of these authors, have the advantage of medical evaluations and responses to medical treatment along with a referral question or goal. If the individual is self-referred or referred from an employee assistance or occupational source, the psychologist must evaluate the presence or need for medical assessment. Regardless of the referral source, the aspects of stress management skills and needs should be included in the evaluation of every such patient. Prior to the initial meeting with the patient, it is most helpful to have access medical evaluations, descriptions of work-defined difficulties (if they are part of the referral presentation), and as much information about the circumstances of the referral as possible. This clarification of the reasons for referral is crucial. One should also determine whether the referral source wants recommendations. Difficulties arise when the patient's goals and those of the referral source differ significantly.

The most frequent question from a medical referral is "Can behavioral or psychotherapeutic interventions help this person manage his or her physical symptoms?" This often translates into an evaluation of stress management and the appropriateness of various treatment possibilities. When the referral comes from the patient's employer or supervisor, the most common questions involve how to improve the individual's work efficiency and whether a psychiatric disorder is involved. In this situation the psychologist may need to look beyond issues of stress management to a more extensive general clinical evaluation. A self-referral can be the most difficult of all because one has only the patient's report of current symptoms and what may be extremely biased or inaccurate evaluation of the work-related factors. During the initial contact the psychologist should address the need for information from other sources and request permission to talk with the patient's supervisor(s), spouse, and physician. From the beginning, while designing the assessment approach, it is neccessary to keep in mind whether the goal is one of prevention, assessing an acute situation, or designing a rehabilitation when the previous two stages have already occurred.

In a clinical setting, the concept of stress most commonly refers either to stimuli affecting the individual, to an inferred inner psychological state, or to a constellation of symptoms organized into a definable disorder. When the reference is to stimulus factors, the focus is frequently precipitating conditions giving rise to emotional demands (e.g., family arguments, working conditions, death of a loved one, or other psychosocial experiences). Assessment of the individual's inner state may involve evaluating physiological responses to various demanding stimulus events, general physical health, and patient attitudes and beliefs. Stress viewed as a constellation of symptoms includes diagnosed disorders (such as post-traumatic stress disorder), acutely precipitated psychiatric symptoms, and patient complaints that usually include fatigue, anxiety, headaches, backaches, heart palpitations, irritability, or unexplainable episodes of emotionality. Obviously, clinicians see many people who are not Type A personalities. In those instances, sources of stress are most likely related to recent demands for adjustment, adverse living circumstances, or personality characteristics that are no longer effective because of changes in the individual's life.

The first step in the clinical evaluation is the patient interview, usually beginning with a statement of current complaints or, if the person has no complaints, a discussion of the problems the referral source has communicated. The traditional intake interview includes discussion of current complaints/problems, their first appearance, what, if any, treatment has been attempted, the response to that treatment, and how the patient feels about these difficulties. In obtaining the necessary general developmental history, eliciting information about the patient's involvement in sports or other competitive activities, general achievement orientation, and attitudes toward competition will enable the clinician to identify factors associated with the development of the Type A personality constellation. It is important to ascertain the state of the patient's marriage or other significant relationship(s), the nature of any conflicts with family members, and the amount of time and types of activities spent with family members. Of special interest in considering the Type A personality constellation is the usual absence of sexual dysfunction or concern and the equally impressive absence of relaxation, recreation, and noncompetitive social activities.

Patient History Data

If the referral source does not or cannot provide a medical history, a release for this information should be obtained. The psychologist should also inquire into the patient's perception of his or her physical health. In some instances, for example, the physician may report concerns about hypertension, ulcers, or obesity, while the patient either denies such difficulties or regards them as inconsequential. Special attention should be directed to questions about the patient's use of alcohol, tobacco, caffeine, and prescribed, over-the-counter, and non-prescribed drugs. Self-destructive personal habits involving diet, lack of exercise, workaholism, and insensitivity to the physical signs of exhaustion and overexertion are not uncommon in this patient group.

Another focus of attention in the interview should be the patient's description of his or her job as well as attitudes and feelings about it and the work environment. Because most Type A individuals have high levels of personal investment and ego involvement in their jobs, this portion of the interview may yield especially useful information. One should particularly cover the hours they work, not only in terms of amount of time but also to discover where in the daily cycle their workload occurs. The clinician should also inquire specifically about any changes within the patient's job situation (e.g., new tasks, new supervisors, or changes such as automation). For some individuals a constant change of job setting or activity may result in extreme stress. Occupations that are innately highly stressful have one or more of the following characteristics: 1) great potential for physical danger (policeman, military); 2) high work output per time unit (short order cook); 3) lethal products of service (working with radioactive substances); 4) risk to others (surgeon, airline pilot, air traffic controller); and 5) angry and resentful social interactions with others (IRS agent, insurance claim agent, complaint department personnel). In some work situations, job expectations are unrealistic. Often patients will describe role conflicts, role ambiguity, and a dissatisfaction with their work. If the patient can articulate the job aspects that are irritating, possible changes may be readily discernible. Many times, though, careful exploration reveals "invisible entrapment," in which the patient is bound to a demanding, unrewarding job but because of personal, financial, or social obligations sees no other acceptable vocational alternatives (the "golden handcuffs" syndrome).

Persons with Type A personalities are attracted to organizations that match their attitudes and personality styles, so it is helpful to have them describe their colleagues, their employer, and the organizational climate or corporate culture. Attempts to alter Type A behavior can be complicated significantly by such factors and, in some instances, such changes may threaten the person's employability in the organization. As delineated, many of the attributes of the Type A personality style are equated with and endorsed as leading to success, particularly in high status and professional careers.

It is significant to know if physical symptoms occur at work, if a pattern to their appearance exits, and if they also occur outside of the work environment (such as on weekends or during vacations). Cognitive inefficiency at work, for example, may reveal the operation of defense mechanisms in the work setting. Anger, irritability, and symptoms of depression are of special interest as well: the presence of depressive or neurotic symptoms may suggest a "burnout" condition rather than the Type A personality syndrome. Knowing the patient's subjective experience of anger and characteristic ways of expressing it is especially useful information in the diagnosis of Type A personality.

Sleep patterns are also of clinical interest. The Type A personality frequently reports fragmented sleep, spontaneous awakenings, and difficulties in falling asleep because of emotional laden preoccupations with work situations. Episodes of suddenly precipitated exhaustion following binges of work activity may also be noted. These individuals characteristically either do not take vacations or take only "working" vacations.

During the interview the psychologist must also be aware of the patient's nonverbal communication. Movements, gestures, amount of activity, pace of speaking, "nervous mannerisms," respiration rate, and skin color may reveal underlying emotional reactions. (These authors will always remember one patient, referred by his gastoenterologist, who belched whenever asked about his situation at work.)

EVALUATION PROCEDURES

Assessment of Stress

Of major interest to the practicing clinician are currently existing measures of psychosocial stressors. In the late 1960s, Holmes and Rahe conducted a survey of the life events that Americans regarded as significantly stressful. They refined the list into 43 events, ranging from the death of a spouse to minor violations of the law, to which a "score" was assigned that reflected the degree of adaptation required by the individual. The "Holmes Scale" assumes that change, either good or bad, produces stress, which predisposes the individual to somatic or psychiatric disease. In this approach, stress is defined in terms of psychosocial experiences that require behavioral adjustment. Too many such changes in a given period of time may exceed the body's coping mechanisms and strategies and its immune response, thereby predisposing the individual to a psychological or physical disorder. The most widely used format of the Holmes Scale appears in Holmes and Rahe (1967), and is reproduced in Table 1. Obviously, a clinical understanding of the effects of stressful life events on a particular patient also involves considerations of the specific meaning that a demanding life event presents to that individual. Further modifications of the Holmes Scale and individualized applications can be found in Dohrenwend and Dohrenwend (1974).

Physiological and psychophysiological techniques have been adapted to provide a "stress profile" in which the classic physiological characteristics of stress, such as increased blood pressure, increased body metabolism, increased rates of breathing, increased heart rate, and redirection of blood flow to major muscle groups, are measured. Some patients may be able to maintain a controlled outward demeanor that masks the exessive reactivity of their cardiovascular system to situations involving competition and achievement. It is crucial when a Type A personality syndrome has been identified to refer the patient for a cardiovascular evaluation, which will assess cardiac status, characteristic patterns of physiological activity in response to stress, and propensity for coronary disease. These evaluations are best done in a cardiovascular center that has the capacity to identify patterns of response to physical and psychological demand and test for specific symptoms, such as cardiac arrhythmias, that may be the precursors of a myocardial infarction.

TABLE 1

Social Readjustment Rating Scale

Life Event	Value
Death of spouse	100
Divorce	73
Marital separation	65
Jail term	63
Death of close family member	63
Personal injury or illness	53
Marriage	50
Fired at work	47
Marital reconciliation	45
Retirement	45
Change in health of family member	44
Pregnancy	40
Sex difficulties	39
Gain of new family member	39
Business readjustment	39
Change in financial state	38
Death of close friend	37
Change to different line of work	36
Change in number of arguments with spouse	35
Mortage over $10,000	31
Forclosure of mortage or loan	30
Change in responsibilities at work	29
Son or daughter leaving home	29
Trouble with in-laws	29
Outstanding personal achievement	28
Wife begin or stop work	26
Begin or end school	26
Change in living conditions	25
Revisions of personal habits	24
Trouble with boss	23
Change in work hours or conditions	20
Change in residence	20
Change in schools	20
Change in recreation	19
Change in church activities	19
Change in social activities	18
Mortgage or loan less than $10,000	17
Change in sleeping habits	16
Change in number of family get-togethers	15
Change in eating habits	15
Vacation	13
Christmas	12
Minor violations of the law	11

300 points or more: 86% experienced a major change in their health;
150-300: 48% had a similar change; 0-150: 33% have had a similar change.

Assessment of the Type A Personality Syndrome

Newlin (1982) has carefully considered current clinical techniques for assessing the Type A behavior pattern and two primary methods emerge: the structured interview developed by Friedman and Rosenman and the Jenkins Activity Survey.

Instruction in the structure interview is available only through workshops conducted either by Drs. Friedman and Rosenman or by individuals who have been trained in the technique. The adult form of the interview (there is also a form for children) is built around 22 questions in a format designed to elicit (when a Type A individual is interviewed) loud, explosive speech, interruption of the interviewer, fist clenching, and what might best be described as "free-floating" hostility on the part of the interviewee. The content of the questions is intended to reveal self-reported instances of specific Type A behavior and focuses on four major areas: competitiveness, time urgency, impatience, and hostility. The manner in which the clinician conducts the interview is considered crucial to the accuracy of the technique.

Dembrowski and his colleagues (1978) present a detailed description of the Friedman-Rosenman interview procedures. The interviewer follows specific guidelines for clinical observation of the patient and for his or her own conduct during the interview. For example, the interviewer is instructed to note the patient's posture while waiting for the interview, his or her gait when entering the office, whether the patient sits on the edge of the chair (a hallmark of the Type A personality), the quality of the patient's handshake and eye contact, and his or her style of speech. When interviewing adults, the clinician follows a script and records the interview. Sample questions from the script follow:

> 5. Would you describe yourself as a *hard-driving, ambitious* type of *man (woman)* in accomplishing the things you want, getting things done as *quickly* as possible *or* would you describe yourself as a relatively *relaxed* and *easy-going* person?
>   a. Are you married?
>   b. How would your *wife (husband)* describe you—as *hard-driving* and *ambitious* or as relaxed and easy-going?
>   c. Has she (he) ever asked you to slow down in your work? *never?* How would she (he) put it—in *her (his) own* words?
> 10. When you play games with people your own age, do you play for the fun of it, or are you really in there to *win?*
> 19. How do you feel about waiting in lines: *Bank* lines, or *Supermarket* lines? (Rosenman, 1978, pp. 68-69)

The structured interview is scored on the basis of clinical judgments regarding both the content of the patient's responses and the style in which they are presented. In the Rosenman's (1978) presentation of the procedure, patients are classified in one of four categories: Type A-1 (extreme); Type A-2 (moderate); Type

X (no classification possible); or Type B (absence of Type A characteristics). This classification system involves a global rating (which is perhaps most appropriate for clinical and research use) of Type A or Type B, and other ratings based on the content of the patient's responses and the observation of five characteristics: 1) loud and explosive speech; 2) rapid and accelerated speech; 3) short response latency; 4) hostility; and 5) competition for control of the interview. Effective use of this interview technique is highly dependent on proper instruction, both in its format and in analyzing the results.

C. David Jenkins, in collaboration with Rosenman and Zyzanski (1972), developed a paper-and-pencil version of the structured interview that is more widely used among mental health professionals. The Jenkins Activity Survey consists of 52 multiple-choice items that can be administered in approximately 20 minutes. The questionnaire is scored on four scales: 1) Type A, 2) Speed and Impatience, 3) Job Involvement, and 4) Hard Driving and Competitive. This measure was developed such that each scale, with the exception of Type A, is independent. Scale scores are derived from weighted individual item scores and can be obtained manually or through the publisher's computerized scoring service. Although reliability estimates for the structured interview and the Jenkins Activity Survey are relatively comparable, comparisons between results of the two instruments have suggested that the Jenkins Activity Survey may be less accurate in identifying Type A personality characteristics.

Other approaches to the measurement of Type A behavior are in development. A promising method designed to assess the correspondence between the patient's self-report and perceptions of significant others is found in Newlin (1982).

INTEGRATION OF FINDINGS AND TREATMENT CONSIDERATIONS

Differential diagnosis in these cases includes discriminating stress disorders (such as acute situational reactions, post-traumatic stress disorder, and psychosomatic reactions) from psychiatric disorders in which anxiety or depression is the predominant feature. One must also differentiate between the ambitious and the coronary prone.

The Type A personality is not likely to be identified by the results of commonly used intellectual and personality assessment devices; there is no scale or profile configuration on the MMPI, for example, that reliably identifies this personality type. These individuals, however, are not immune to neurotic or psychotic disorders. When present, the usual evidence for such disorders is seen in the results of clinical psychological testing. The practicing clinician is most likely to identify candidates for the Type A classification through interview and clinical observation, seeing a combination of the following factors: tension, depression, anger, vigor, fatigue, confusion, denial of cardiac illness, an accumulation of stressful life events, and often a combative, competitive orientation to the events of daily life. Positive findings on appropriate assessment measures mandate referral for a complete extensive cardiovascular and physiological examination.

Differentiation between the ambitious and the coronary prone presents some difficulties, especially when evaluating young, intelligent, well-educated persons. Most successful people who are well organized, goal directed, and who have been well socialized by their families and the American educational system will show some Type A characteristics. They do not, however, demonstrate them to the extent or degree that the true Type A personality shows in interview or reveals in responses to the Jenkins Activity Survey. The usual purpose of an evaluation is to determine the presence of a disorder and to recommend a program of remediation. Treatment of the Type A personality involves special procedures and the collaboration of cardiologists. The clinician must communicate findings in ways that will enlist the cooperation of the patient in referral to appropriate medical specialists and to individuals or settings in which coherent programs of psychological and medical intervention are available. Effective treatment of the Type A personality transcends the usual dimensions of psychotherapeutic intervention.

Treatment of the Type A Personality

In their initial presentation of Type A characteristics, Friedman and Rosenman (1974) outlined a program of modification of this personality style, emphasizing what they termed *drill* (practicing a given activity until a counter habit is established) and *reengineering* (the modification of life-style so that one's existence is more leisurely and gratifying). Patients were encouraged to learn new behaviors—to discontinue polyphasic thinking, to listen without interrupting, to read books that required concentration, to savor food—and to "drill" themselves until these new habits were established in their daily lives.

The "reengineering" components of this approach involved replacing traditional competitive and materialistic goals and values with standards that emphasize being rather than having, living by the calendar instead of the stopwatch, and ensuring that each day contains something of psychological or personal value. The Type A individual was encouraged, for example, to have a retreat at home, to avoid irritating people, and to plan some idleness in every day. Specific suggestions included: beginning the day in a humane way, with enough time for dressing, breakfast, and being with one's family; avoiding overscheduling; taking long lunch breaks (avoiding mixing business with food); keeping one's desk clear (especially of accumulated long-range tasks, which signal guilt and obligations); and restructuring trips and vacations.

Most recently, Friedman and Ulmer have emphasized procedures that alleviate free-floating hostility and self-destructive orientations (factors that recent research has revealed) in addition to competitiveness and time urgency. They have summarized the results of the San Francisco Recurrent Coronary Prevention project begun in August of 1977 in their new book *Treating Type A Behavior and Your Heart* (1984).

In that study, 1,012 post-infarction patients were recruited and assigned randomly to three Sections. Section I patients attended 90-minute meetings with cardiologist counselors every two weeks for three months, monthly for three months, and then at two-month intervals for the duration of the study. Every few months a psychiatrist or psychologist met with the group and offered counseling for the concerns the patients might have about their cardiovascular illness, but all counselors avoided dicussing or counseling about Type A behavior. Section I patients were counseled to avoid: 1) the ingestion of one meal rich in either vegetable or animal fat; 2) participation in any form of severe physical exercise; 3) ingestion of caffeine or alcohol; 4) high altitudes; and 5) prolonged exposure to cold. All participants had quit cigarette smoking at least six months prior to the study.

Section II patients received essentially the same advice and counseling as did those in section I, plus counseling aimed at the basic dimensions of Type A behavior. The ranges of such counseling are related in detail in chapters designated "Alleviating Your Sense of Time Urgency," "Alleviating Your Free-Floating Hostility," and "Alleviating Your Self-Destruct Tendency."

The Section III group is described as a control/comparison group. In their summary of results, Friedman and Ulmer report evidence obtained from questionnaires that the Section II participants made significant improvement in altering their Type A behavior and had significantly fewer new heart attacks (three times as many new heart attacks occurred in the Section III group as in the Section II group). Analysis of data after one year suggested that participants enrolled in either of the counseling sections appeared to be receiving statistically significant protection against instantaneous cardiac death. Participants enrolled in Section II and thus receiving behavioral as well as cardiological counseling suffered significantly fewer new nonfatal heart attacks than Section III comparison subjects. After three years, Friedman and Ulmer determined their data established that 1) Type A behavior had been modified, and 2) modification of Type A behavior prevented recurrent heart attacks. The authors conclude that Type A behavior thus becomes the first of all the commonly accepted coronary risk factors to be directly demonstrated as bearing not just associational but causal relevance to clinical coronary disease. Follow-up studies are targeted to ascertain whether the study participants who changed their Type A behavior maintain the change after discontinuation of counseling, and how many heart attack survivors, as well as still-healthy Type As, will be able to alter their behavior by themselves, following proper instructions but without participation in counseling sessions.

REFERENCES

Dembrowski, T. M., Weiss, S. M., Shields, J. L., Haynes, S. G., & Feinleib, M. (Eds.). (1978). *Coronary-prone behavior.* New York: Springer-Verlag.
Dohrenwend, B. S., & Dohrenwend, B. P. (1974). *Stressful life events: Their nature and effect.* Chicago: Aldine Publishing Co.

Friedman, M., & Rosenman, R. H. (1974). *Type A behavior and your heart.* New York: Alfred A. Knopf.

Friedman, M., & Ulmer, D. (1984). *Treating Type A behavior and your heart.* New York: Alfred A. Knopf.

Holmes, T. H., & Rahe, R. H. (1967). The Social Readjustment Rating Scale. *Journal of Psychosomatic Research, 11,* 213-218.

Jenkins, C. D., Rosenman, R. H., & Zyzanski, S. J. (1972). *The Jenkins Activity Survey for Health Prediction.* Unpublished manuscript.

Newlin, D. B. (1982). Modifying the Type A behavior pattern. In C. J. Golden, S. S. Alcaparras, F. D. Strider, & B. Graber (Eds.), *Applied techniques in behavioral medicine* (pp. 169-190). New York: Grune & Stratton.

Rosenman, R. H. (1978). The interview method of assessment of the coronary-prone behavior pattern. In T. M. Dembrowski, S. M. Weiss, J. L. Shields, S. G. Haynes, & M. Feinleib (Eds.), *Coronary-prone behavior* (pp. 55-69). New York: Springer-Verlag.

15

Identifying and Understanding the Learning Disabled Adult

LAWRENCE C. HARTLAGE, PH.D.

During the more than 20 years since Kirk (1963) first used the term *learning disability,* there have been literally thousands of scientific papers describing this condition as it relates to school-age children. In recent years there has been increasing recognition that, like those without learning disabilities, children with learning disabilities generally become adults.

Although the learning disabled adult is essentially the same individual as the learning disabled child who has reached the end of school age, there are important differences in how the problems related to learning disabilities are recognized and handled. The school-age child with learning disabilities is often identified through his or her inadequate performance within the structured requirements of educational expectancies based on age or grade placement, but the adult rarely functions in such a structured expectancy milieu and so may not be recognized as suffering from a learning disability. Further, the child with learning disabilities is exposed to regular evaluations and testings, with diagnostic support from psychologists and other specialists and with treatment support from a cadre of special educators and resource personnel from such diverse areas as speech, hearing, physical therapy, and reading, all functioning within an administrative structure geared toward meeting the total educational, psychological, and psychosocial needs of the child. Adults with similar learning disabilities, on the other hand, rarely have access to those constant diagnostic or treatment resources as they struggle to meet the demands of competitive employment, additional education, and social adjustment. They are thus at considerable risk for having problems resulting from their learning disabilities and their struggle goes unrecognized and unaided.

There is also the matter of differential social consequences of learning disabilities in children as opposed to adults. Children with learning disabilities who are perceived by parents and teachers as working diligently, if without success, at school tasks are viewed with a tolerant and sympathetic gaze, even if their learning disabilities are unrecognized or undiagnosed. Learning disabled adults who fail to meet work or social expectancies are not so likely to be viewed with tolerance by employers who must meet production standards or by colleagues and spouses who depend on the individual for meeting their needs.

In light of traditional estimates of learning disability incidence involving up to 25% of the school-age population (e.g., Klasen, 1972), the potential incidence of undiagnosed learning disabilities in the post-school-age among children who suffered with this condition during school years suggests that learning disabled adults represent a substantial segment of the population.

The Nature of the Diagnostic Problem

Unfortunately, learning disabilities do not represent a disease or condition that can be diagnosed with a single clinical or laboratory test. Unlike syphilis or tuberculosis, a positive reading is not confirmatory; unlike alleged paternity, a negative laboratory result does not prove absence. Even in the realm of mental tests, it is easier to infer mental retardation or schizophrenia from a test result, especially if confirmed by behavioral data, than it is to infer learning disabilities from the same data base. A particular diagnostic difficulty involves the fact that learning disabilities are confined in terms of discrepancies between two sets of tests, without any demonstrated scientific rationale for why this discrepancy constitutes the existence of a learning disability. Specifically, by both federal law (PL 94-142) and statutes in most states, a learning disability is presumed to exist when achievement (measured by proper tests) falls a specific level below ability (measured by proper tests), provided that a number of specific causal factors have been excluded. Although the etiology is presumably neurologic, there is no specific scientific model for exactly what neurophysiological process constitutes a learning disability. The clinician in essence works on a diagnosis-by-exclusion basis: if a child does poorly on achievement tests and there is no evidence of mental retardation or a perceptual or emotional cause for this poor performance, then learning disability may be considered as a possible etiology.

From a clinical perspective, this diagnostic process is made especially complex by the fact that learning disability takes many forms, each existing in varying degrees of severity and some with several subtypes. In addition, the intellectual level of the adult with a learning disability is related to the extent to which a learning disability affects either global or specific aspects of performance and adjustment. Further, there is a possibility that once formal education has been completed or terminated a learning disability may not present any signs or symptoms, even though still present in the same form and of the same severity as when its symptoms were more manifest. Finally, there may be some defensiveness among adults about admitting to having a learning disability, whether for fear of being considered "stupid" or "weird," and so they may be quite guarded about seeking evaluation for the problem. Not uncommonly, there may be such denial and defensiveness that sometimes it may be best to approach the issue via indirect interview and testing techniques. Examination of these issues may help lay the basis for considering the selection of an assessment strategy.

Learning Disability Types and Subtypes

It is traditional to classify learning disabilities according to which academic skill is impaired. Since reading constitutes the cornerstone of most educational programs, a reading disability exerts a substantial impact on academic progress and is perhaps for this reason the learning disability most diagnosed and studied. Dyslexia, or poor reading, is the most commonly reported learning disability and has been recognized since the 19th century as having some neurological basis. There appear to be at least two major subtypes of dyslexia, classified according to whether the difficulty lies with verbal sequencing or with spatial recognition. Difficulty with verbal sequencing as a manifestation of dyslexia has been diagnosed according to several schemata, variously referred to as dysphonetic dyslexia (Boder & Jarrico, 1982); spatially competent dyslexia (Bannatyne, 1968); or dyslexia resultant from left cerebral hemisphere dysfunction (Hartlage, 1984). Difficulty with spatial recognition of words has been referred to as dyseidetic dyslexia (Boder & Jarrico, 1982); verbally competent dyslexia (Bannatyne, 1968); and dyslexia secondary to right cerebral hemisphere dysfunction (Hartlage, 1982).

In addition to this processing dichotomy, dyslexia has also been categorized as congenital versus acquired, with the congenital type generally considered more selective and specific than the acquired, which presumably results from insult to the central nervous system and thus may involve areas other than those uniquely concerned with reading. Within the congenital category there are ranges of expressivity, and some cases apparently self-resolve around puberty while others are present throughout life. Acquired dyslexia is often diagnosed as a combination disorder, such as "acquired dyslexia with (or without) aphasia" or "acquired dyslexia with dyscalculia." The severity of acquired dyslexia will depend, in part, on how much cortical tissue has been compromised and the involvement of the damaged tissue in reading, and so may affect verbal sequencing, spatial recognition, or both of these aspects of reading.

There is also a form of dyslexia occasionally referred to as "secondary dyslexia" (e.g., Hartlage, 1980); this condition generally involves impaired reading in combination with impaired language processing, including either comprehension, expression, or both.

A learning disability less common than dyslexia but not infrequently seen involves mathematical processing disorders, generally referred to as *dyscalculia*. As with dyslexia, essentially two major types appear: one involving logical mathematical reasoning (sequential dyscalculia) and the other, spatial organization (spatial dyscalculia). As with most forms of dyslexia, there is no specific anatomic or etiologic basis for dyscalculia, but its sequential form frequently has symptoms that suggest processing disorders of the left cerebral hemisphere, and the spatial form often has features suggesting processing impairment of the right cerebral hemisphere. Dyscalculia, like dyslexia, varies in levels of severity, but one does not find the breadth and depth of research on this condition as has been dedicated to dyslexia.

Other learning disabilities tend to be mixed or seen in combination with one or more processing disorders. Spelling problems, occasionally manifest as dysgraphia, frequently occur in conjunction with those involving either expressive language, reading, receptive language, or combinations of these problems. Some combinations of disorders tend to occur in clusters, as in Gerstmann's syndrome, but in many cases the individual has a unique configuration of processing difficulty that defies classification under meaningful generic categories. Thus, whether the suspected learning disability produces a single problem, such as reading, or possible multisystem difficulties, the clinician must carefully develop diagnostic statements concerning the condition to avoid oversimplified conclusions about the nature of the problem.

Among adults, the most common causes for learning disability evaluations involve changes in work or educational settings. A worker whose learning disability may not have influenced performance on a previous job may, on promotion or transfer, find substantial problems in handling the requirements of a new job. As mentioned earlier, sometimes these problems will be expressed in psychological or medical symptoms as presenting complaints, and without sensitivity to the possibility of a learning disability the problem may be overlooked and misdiagnosed. Another common cause of adults being seen for learning problems is related to attempts to seek further education. In such cases, there is likely to be considerably more candor in the presentation of the problem, with a definite educational goal and focus reflected in the referral question. Another occasional cause of adults requiring evaluation for learning disorders involves acquired disorders of learning, such as might be occasioned by neurological problems like head injury or cerebrovascular accident. Obviously, the nature of the presenting problems, the ultimate goal of the evaluation, and the intended recipient of the findings will be of consequence in determining the selection of evaluation instruments and strategies.

SELECTION OF EVALUATION PROCEDURES

Both as the first step in reaching a diagnosis and for developing a relevant intervention strategy, it is important to obtain a measure of the patient's global level of intellectual functioning. For this purpose, as well as to derive somewhat more specific information about the relative efficiencies of language versus nonlanguage abilities, the Wechsler Adult Intelligence Scale-Revised (WAIS-R) is most appropriate. Next, a measure of academic achievement is needed, both to determine whether a learning disability exists and, if one does, to determine its nature. A number of achievement tests may be used; one of the simpler and most commonly used of these, the Wide Range Achievement Test-Revised (WRAT-R), is in many cases adequate for this purpose.

For comparison of results from achievement test scores with IQ test scores, it may be helpful to convert both measures to percentiles, especially in cases where the different tests have different means and standard deviations. By keeping in mind that many IQ and achievement tests with mean 100 and standard deviation 15 include the standard score range 90-110 ("average" or between the 25th and 75th percentiles), this may make it easy to compare performance on tests expressed in T-score, stanine, or other measurement units with standard score measurement units.

In the event that a comparison of results from the intelligence and achievement tests reveals no evidence that achievement scores are substantially lower than IQ scores, it may be appropriate in some cases to discontinue the examination at this point. It is not uncommon for adults who recollect having experienced academic difficulties during school years to question whether they may have some type of learning disability, and this preliminary comparison may be sufficient to clarify this question.

Although considering grade-level performance in specific achievement areas may be helpful (e.g., in planning further education or career possibilities), one must keep in mind that the high school graduate of average (i.e., IQ-100) mental ability typically obtains achievement levels of around the 10th grade. Therefore, a mere consideration of grade-level achievement can suggest false positive diagnoses of learning disabilities.

At somewhat lower IQ levels (e.g., around 90), it is not uncommon for achievement to fall below the eighth-grade level. Inspection of the standard scores will demonstrate that for a young adult such an achievement level is within one or two standard score points of expectancy based on an IQ score of 90. Considered from another perspective, an IQ of 90 lies at the 25th percentile; that is, one of four individuals in the general population may be expected to function at or below this level. Thus an adult at the lower end of the normal IQ range, perhaps a high school graduate, who has academic skill levels below the eighth-grade level is not necessarily suffering from a learning disability so much as a mild global mental deficit.

Following the development of an IQ score and an achievement score for reading (word recognition), arithmetic, and spelling, the inspection of any discrepancies between the expectancy level based on IQ standard scores and the specific academic deficit areas will help identify the learning disability if one is found to be present. Because various states may have different eligibility criteria for the magnitude of discrepancy between IQ and achievement area standard scores required to document a learning disability, and because federal criteria for this purpose are in a state of evolution, some clinical judgment may be necessary. In general, at least one standard deviation between IQ and academic skill standard score should be present before a diagnosis of learning disability can be considered, and other exclusionary conditions besides perceptual acuity may need to be taken into account. For example, if a 23-year-old individual with an IQ score of 95 shows computational skills at the late third-grade level (i.e., approximately what might be expected in mild mental retardation), a level almost two standard deviations below the measured IQ, but dropped out of school in mid-third-grade, dyscalculia cannot be inferred even though the statistical difference in scores might suggest such a possibility.

Thus tests by themselves, though generally necessary to establish a diagnosis of learning disability, may not be sufficient for such purposes. Once an area of deficit has been identified, however, and possible extraneous causes have been excluded, further testing may be helpful in clarifying the exact nature and extent of the identified learning disability. Assume, for example, that an apparently normal young adult shows presumptive evidence of dyscalculia, manifested in a WRAT-R arithmetic score that is considerably below both IQ level and performance levels on academic measures of reading and spelling. The next step might be to compare the WRAT-R arithmetic score with the score obtained on the WAIS-R Arithmetic subscale, to determine whether the difficulty involves both spoken/sequential and visual/spatial calculation or is limited to the format and processing required for one or the other tests.

In the case of an individual with adequate intellectual ability but impaired performance on reading/word recognition, the next step in the diagnostic evaluation might involve testing for receptive picture recognition, as with the Peabody Picture Vocabulary Test-Revised, to measure possible sight-sound processing difficulties. If this ability is intact, speech sounds recognition may be assessed, using a measure such as the Aphasia Screening Test (from the Halstead-Reitan Neuropsychological Test Battery) to determine whether the reading disorder may be part of a more global language disability. In each successive step, the focus is on identifying the specific disability and on refining the way or ways in which it impairs the individual from functioning effectively in given vocational or sociopersonal contexts.

With the learning disabled adult, it is especially relevant to consider interest to aptitude patterns, which can provide clues to possible educational or vocational goals. Inventories such as the Strong-Campbell Interest Inventory or the Kuder Preference Record-Vocational, when combined with patterns of strength reflected in psychometric and achievement testing, can help identify areas of vocational potential that would be compatible with the individual's intact abilities and would likely provide satisfaction.

As the reader may have noted, the strategies for assessing learning disabilities bear a striking resemblance to those developed in this volume's chapter on neuropsychological assessment, which covers such tests and their use in considerably more detail. Because the identification of the learning disabled adult may be conceptualized as a subarea of adult neuropsychological assessment, it is appropriate at this point to shift from purely identification-focused approaches to how the clinician can best apply the findings from such approaches to an understanding of and intervention with the learning disabled adult.

INTERPRETATION AND INTEGRATION OF FINDINGS

Whatever the nature and severity of an adult's learning disability, the absolute level of intellectual functioning, whether independent of or related to the learning disability, is an extremely important consideration in the interpretation and integration of findings. In considering a 30-point standard score discrepancy between intellectual ability (IQ) and reading level (Achievement Quotient), for example, the handicapping effect will be quite different for an individual with an IQ score of 95 as opposed to 140. The individual with the lower score (95) IQ may be limited to reading at or below the fourth-grade level, a dramatic handicap for training in work settings that require reading and interpretation of manuals, printed instructions, or educational material. Conversely, the individual of superior global mental ability (IQ-140) with the same 30-point discrepancy could feasibly handle college-level reading. The impact of global mental ability on both the areas of function impaired by a learning disability and the areas of comparatively intact function needs to be taken into account in developing an understanding of the individual and for formulating appropriate counseling, intervention, or planning.

Unlike the psychoeducational assessment of learning disabilities in children, which is often focused on identifying deficit areas in order to implement remediation, the interpretation of findings for the learning disabled adult centers more on determining *strengths,* which can be utilized for vocational or continuing education planning. A learning disability involving dyscalculia, for example, even in an individual of high mental ability, would argue against preparation for or success in a career such as accounting or engineering. In an individual of average mental ability, such a disability might preclude work as a bookkeeper, timekeeper, rate clerk, or actuary, and possibly some sales positions (such as insurance). Focus on the disability thus leads at best to the exclusion of undesirable or unattainable educational or vocational goals. By focusing on strengths, however, the clinician can help the learning disabled adult to capitalize on intact assets, whether verbal, spatial, manipulative, and so on. An individual with average or above average visuospatial abilities (as reflected, for example, in a good WAIS-R Performance IQ), but with a reading or language disability, could plan career goals to include such vocational areas as drafting, art, and, if accompanied by intact manipulative skills, skilled trades.

A most important caveat applies to the implications of findings for remedial intervention with adults. Though it may be tempting to follow the psychoeducational forms often used with children, which involve diagnosing the learning disability to try to treat it, such approaches are especially limited in their applicability to adults. In most cases it is prudent to assume that if an adult has a residual learning disability involving reading, spelling, or counting, which has resisted years of formal attempts at educational amelioration, no quick solution may be expected from new efforts to correct the disorder. Indeed, such an approach may serve only to further the feelings of frustration or possibly even worthlessness in an adult accustomed to failure resulting from the learning disability.

Frequently, the individual who has been identified as a learning disabled child may experience few obvious problems as an adult. This apparent good fortune, however, usually reflects the individual's intuitive avoidance of career activities in which the skills impaired by the learning disability are important. Not uncommonly, a child with a form of language disorder, such as dyslexia, may achieve adult career success and personal satisfaction in a work context where the need for deficient skills are minimized, as in landscaping, skilled trades, or technical work. Similarly, the child who suffered from poor visuospatial skills with attendant learning difficulties may mature to success in a verbal profession, be it law, teaching, selling, broadcasting, clerking, or whatever is compatible with his or her intellectual and educational level. The "Peter Principle," whereby individuals presumably rise in vocations to their level of incompetence, may in many cases reflect the manifestations of learning disabilities in adults. The reading- or language-disabled person who has achieved vocational success as a welder, for example, and then is promoted to a leadership role in which language and reading skills are important may for the first time as an adult suffer an apparent reappearance of the learning disability.

COMMUNICATING RESULTS

In the interpretation of evaluation results to learning disabled adults, there is considerable potential for a constructive and helpful focus. In many cases, the adult seen for such an evaluation is self-referred, having become aware of an adverse effect of the learning disability on some aspect of vocational or personal adjustment. In these cases the focus on positive findings that document the existence of a learning disability comes as no particular surprise and frequently provides the patient with a welcomed reason for the difficulties. It is not uncommon for such individuals to express relief that their problems are not due to emotional factors or diminished mental capacity.

For relatives, spouses, and occasionally supervisors and teachers, a somewhat different focus concerning the disability may be appropriate. Though highlighting the individual's abilities rather than his or her deficits is normally a good strategy, there may be substantial benefit to the learning disabled adult if the clinician helps significant others in the patient's life to understand that some areas of deficit performance are due to a learning disability. It is not uncommon for others to perceive the problems resulting from a learning disability as stupidity, hysteria, lack of maturation or diligence, or signs of lacking clear goals. The wife who interprets her husband's lack of verbal expressiveness as neurotic shyness or lack of interest in her can be helped to understand that his verbal expressive dysfluency represents a manifestation of language learning disability rather than volitional action. Similarly, an employer who regards a worker as careless because of frequent miscalculations may be helped to recognize this poor performance as a manifestation of dyscalculia, which is beyond the employee's control.

Constructively accentuating positive skill areas in subsequent vocational or educational planning helps the patient avoid a sense of frustration when realizing that certain vocational or educational goals may not be feasible. Although most adults recognize, on the basis of their academic, social, and work history, that some plans may not be realistic for them, the occasional learning disabled adult may cling to a hope—perhaps engendered by overly optimistic accounts of cures—that a diagnosis may open the way to a cure. By directing attention to positive applications of intact abilities and skills, the clinician can deter possible disappointment.

In communicating findings to the patient, it is obviously important to be realistic about the prognosis. As mentioned previously, a learning disability that has resisted earlier long-term attempts at amelioration is not likely to be obviated by any short-term intervention and in most cases will not improve dramatically through new intensive long-term programs. Accordingly, the clinician must carefully avoid an overly optimistic communication that could convey the message that, now that the problem is understood, something can be done to change it. In fact, what more often can and should be changed is the patient's orientation, building strengths rather than dwelling on the limiting effects of the learning disability.

A number of years ago, the words to a then-popular song suggested that you've got to accentuate the positive, eliminate the negative, and latch on to the affirmative. While no doubt a worthwhile maxim for many people, it may represent an approach uniquely applicable for communicating evaluation findings to the adult with a learning disability.

REFERENCES

Bannatyne, A. (1968). Developmental dyslexia: A new approach. In H. Myklebust (Ed.). *Progress in learning disabilities* (Vol. 1). New York: Grune & Stratton.

Boder, E., & Jarrico, S. (1982). *The Boder Test of Reading-Spelling Patterns—Manual.* New York: Grune & Stratton.

Hartlage, L. C. (1980, July). *Developmental aspects of brain-behavior relationships.* Paper presented at the North Atlantic Treaty Organization Conference on Neuropsychology and Cognition, Augusta, GA.

Hartlage, L. C. (1984, October). *Neuropsychological substrates of dyslexia and related learning problems.* Paper presented at the annual meeting of the International Orton Society, Winston-Salem, NC.

Kirk, S. A., & Becker, W. (Eds.). (1963). *Proceedings of the Conference on children with Minimal Brain Impairment, University of Illinois, Urbana.* Chicago: National Society for Crippled Children and Adults.

Klasen, E. (1972). *The syndrome of specific dyslexia.* Baltimore: University Park Press.

16

The Adult Vocational Rehabilitation Assessment

DENNIS P. SWIERCINSKY, PH.D., TERRIE FISK, M.A.

Employment is the primary goal of vocational rehabilitation programs, which generally are aimed at individuals who have failed initially to enter the job market unassisted or who are unable to reenter at a level or position held prior to a current physical or mental incapacitation. Specifically, clients seek public, or sometimes private, agency vocational rehabilitation assistance for the following reasons: 1) to find appropriate employment; 2) for assistance in learning marketable job skills; 3) to receive financial aid for returning to school or entering job-training programs; 4) for guidance in locating additional sources of help for physical or mental problems that interfere with the capacity to find and maintain employment; 5) for assistance in making career choices; and 6) for obtaining diagnoses regarding the disability to establish eligibility for public financial aid when one cannot return reasonably to competitive work. With employment as the primary goal, the psychological evaluation process and accompanying report are uniquely geared toward addressing fundamental questions: Can this individual work in the competitive job market? Which career area is he or she best suited for? What are the training and educational needs for suceeding in the job that this person must fulfill? What will it take, financially, physically, intellectually, and psychologically for this client to attain a realistic job goal?

The vocational rehabilitation services client often is one who has tried to succeed on his or her own for many years, attempting to find and keep good-paying and satisfactory jobs or hoping to get the education or skill training that will improve overall job marketability. The client seeks vocational rehabilitation assistance when a career change is necessitated by a significant and disabling life experience (i.e., a physical or mental disability) that interferes with vocational attainment. In many cases, the client may not have the requisite financial resources for commercial job placement agencies, private rehabilitation agencies, job training centers, or school. An alternative is the state-supported vocational arm of the social and rehabilitation

188

services, an agency that usually is well equipped to handle a variety of services for the disabled.

A disability is a prerequisite for vocational rehabilitation. Most agencies have established criteria that define the severity of a disability, and in cases of emotional or intellectual disability it is often up to the psychologist to determine whether a client meets those criteria. Once the standards have been satisfied, the assessment can address fundamental issues of employment: interests; intellectual, emotional, and achievement resources; training and educational needs; and psychological stability and resources.

The types of disability presented in a vocational rehabilitation assessment are varied. Somatic, visual, and hearing impairments are typical problems. Post-stroke victims or those with other physical illnesses, either in remission or recovery, that leave residual impairment frequently are represented as well. Head-injured or other organic-brain-disordered persons and the learning-disabled are being accepted by such agencies. Individuals presenting histories of serious social adjustment problems or emotional disorders are also seen. (Chapter 8 in this volume discusses some of the special assessment concerns important in the evaluation of physically disabled clients.)

This chapter focuses on the variety of psychological testing that a psychologist could be asked to perform in a vocational rehabilitation assessment—within a private setting, an institution, or as a referral from a state agency. Frequently, state vocational rehabilitation programs contract with psychologists from the private sector to perform evaluations within the psychologist's expertise. In addition, a variety of concurrent assessments may be requested for the client from a spectrum of practitioners. Counseling and clinical psychologists are used as the needs of the client demand. A neuropsychologist, for example, may be called on in cases of suspected learning disability or organic brain impairment, or vocational counselors may become involved with the client who lacks direction in pursuing interests.

A typical psychological assessment in this context consists of a basic evaluation of intellectual potential; career interests, goals and related values; emotional stability; and fundamental skills relevant to potential jobs (e.g., reading level, mathematics skill, ability to follow sequences of instructions, manual dexterity, etc.). Usually, a comprehensive yet brief evaluation battery must be selected based on agency needs as well as appropriateness for the client. The psychological evaluation is usually an initial step in the client's progression through the vocational rehabilitation agency, and may even be a precursor to an extended (up to three weeks) work-sample evaluation program.

It is impossible to provide definitive guidelines within the scope of this chapter as the nature and depth of the clinician's involvement with vocational rehabilitation varies considerably. In any case, fundamental information must be obtained, either entirely by the clinician or through additional resources such as social workers, teacher's reports, and the results of tests already performed by other providers.

In addition to the more-or-less typical vocational rehabilitation clients described earlier, a recent, growing area of concern in employment, particularly for the young man or woman first entering the job market, is the effect of learning disability on job potentials. Many agencies now include this diagnosis as a legitimate problem, where once it was denied as ineligible. A neuropsychologist frequently is sought to help identify and circumscribe organically based learning difficulties, which influence the client's work and training potentials, job adjustment, and career directions. The neuropsychologist will see a spectrum of individuals who have been identified as or are suspected of having a significant learning disability and/or cognitive deficit associated with brain maldevelopment or trauma (accidents, injuries, illness).

The vocational programs candidate frequently presents the dilemma of having struggled (for any number of reasons) through high school and currently struggling to find or keep work, succeed in college, or receive adequate job training. As such, he or she presents the psychologist with a variety of concerns about job placement, further education, qualification for services, realistic future financial security, and so on. Overall, the individual and agency rely on the psychologist to provide insight into the client's learning and work potentials and the psychological-emotional factors that may negatively influence job prospects, as well as helping the client clarify his or her career needs, values, and interests—fitting all the information into realistic statements about career future.

Prediagnostic Staffing

The prediagnostic staffing begins with the delineation of the client's and agency's needs. This information guides the psychologist in selecting appropriate test instruments, formulating the focus of testing, and anticipating the structure of the report. Public vocational assistance agencies require a diagnosis based on established criteria, and further require that the report address these criteria and other specified diagnostic questions. The psychologist's primary task is to answer the agency's questions regarding the client's acceptability for services and then offer relevant information obtained from the testing to determine the best direction for working with the client, once accepted for help.

In the prediagnostic staffing, the psychologist reviews the school, job, rehabilitation, and medical records available on the client. This information is so valuable that it may need to be requested before the actual testing session for a thorough review. The school record may provide past intelligence test scores, a record of placement and performance in learning-disabled, personal-social adjustment, or remedial classes, and make reference to identified academic or behavioral problems. Job history records indicate what attempts the individual has made toward finding a job and establishing a career, and the resulting level of success. If the individual has previously sought assistance from rehabilitation agencies, this information is helpful to evaluate job potential stability. The psychologist may wish to learn whether any prior rehabilitation experience was helpful, in what way, and if not, why not. Social histories give information about the client's economic and educational background, which suggest the career values and expectations that the individual may hold. Medical records should be reviewed for results of neurological and physical examinations, significant injuries, indications of prenatal or birth trauma, present physical and health-related limitations, and current prescribed medications. Examining these materials prior to seeing a client greatly facilitates the pretesting interview in which the history is completed.

The psychologist must gain an overall impression of the client from the history and records. The greatest predictor of cognitive potential, adjustment, personality, coping resources, etc., is past behavior. The individual seeking vocational rehabilitation services comes to the agency with traits and characteristics that likely will not change despite the onset of an adventitious disability that changes many employment considerations and prospects.

On the basis of the information obtained from and about the client, the psychologist formulates hypotheses regarding the client's affective, intellectual, psychological, physical, social, and cognitive functioning, as well as possible career values and interests. Specifically, the examiner forms ideas about how the client may respond to specific tasks, which areas of work may pose the greatest difficulty, which areas of concern may require more intensive follow-up questioning or testing, and what are the client's intellectual and emotional response styles. These hypotheses or questions are then used to select relevant tests to evaluate the client objectively for a comprehensive vocational rehabilitation assessment.

It is important to recognize at the outset that the employment goal in vocational rehabilitation is not at all easy. Individuals seeking help are usually in the most disadvantaged position for competitive employment. This factor alone is stressful for the client and often compounds the primary disability. Therefore, the psychological assessment must be as sensitive and predictive as possible. It is foolish to identify an intellectual strength and then recommend a vocational setting that is otherwise inconsistent with a behavioral trait clearly evidenced in the history but not apparent on immediate testing. The tendency to focus on intellectual strengths and recommend placements where the disability will be minimal or negligible, without considering all other relevant factors such as interests, values, or emotional functioning, is a common fallacy and the source of great frustration in vocational rehabilitation.

ADMINISTRATION OF TESTS AND PROCEDURES

Based on the psychologist's understanding client and agency needs, a battery of tests is chosen. The standard battery for vocational rehabilitation services typically includes a neurological and physical-symptom screening and measures of intelligence, academic achievement, vocational interests, personality, and auxiliary issues specific to the case at hand. These data are then combined with the history to form a comprehensive picture of the client and to make the most useful recommendations. Clinicians may prefer to use measures other than the ones described, but the intention is to highlight here the core tests most frequently used and accepted by referring agencies.

Physical Evaluation

Usually, for the psychologist's purposes, a physical description of the client relating to motor performance, range of motion, limiting neurological/physical/ health characteristics, and other similar information is obtained from past records, concurrent examinations from other professionals, and from the personal report of the client. Although direct evaluation in this area is usually outside the scope of the psychologist, the information is crucial and will preclude recommendations that are inconsistent with physical and neurological characteristics. The Quick Neurological Screening Test is an excellent procedure for evaluating a wide range of sensory and motor functioning, relevant not only for evaluating aspects of brain functioning, but for gaining an impression of physical capabilities as well. As usual, a holistic approach is stressed as the psychologist attempts to integrate all relevant information in making diagnoses and recommendations. Subtle physical limitations, though often not the primary disability and which may be easily missed, still must be recognized (cardiovascular anomalies, diabetes, diseases/conditions that produce abnormal fatigue, etc.).

Intellectual Evaluation

The Wechsler Adult Intelligence Scale-Revised (WAIS-R) assesses diverse cognitive skills and brain-behavior functional areas, including abstract reasoning, sequential planning, and problem solving; immediate and delayed short-term memory; language comprehension and production; visual-spatial processing, reasoning, and manipulation; perceptual-motor speed and coordination; attention skills; and arithmetic reasoning.

The WAIS-R is a comprehensive tool, providing a global picture of the individual's intellectual functioning as well as strengths and weaknesses in specific areas. Typically, levels of verbal and spatial skills are expected to be essentially equivalent and individually consistent across the component measures. Therefore, significant inter- and intrasubtest deviations are flags for potential problem areas. The learning disabled individual, for example, might be expected to show a significantly lower score on one or two components while the other component scores remain consistent and in the average or higher range of functioning.

The WAIS-R can be the foundation of the vocational rehabilitation assessment. The wealth of data yielded is often overlooked when only the summary IQ scores are reported. Every subtest produces information that is predictive of job potential or capability. Although it is usually not the psychologist's role as a consultant to make a specific job recommendation, it is essential to predict a category or range of categories for appropriate jobs, given the test results. To accomplish this, the examiner should use the Holland typology (1973) to scan career categories and see if the client's intellectual skills (considering other disabilities) suggest a specific job area, such as mechanical versus social.

Examiners should be familiar with the works that elaborate on WAIS-R subscale interpretations. Zimmerman and Woo-Sam's (1973) text as well as Kaufman's (1979) work on the WISC-R provide insight and research relevant to gaining maximum information from the one to two hours usually spent administering and scoring the WAIS-R.

The Shipley Institute of Living Scale is a measure of conceptual reasoning for verbal and sequential abstractions. In one section the examinee is required to identify conceptual associations among word sets, which yields the individual's level of verbal functioning and vocabulary resources. The second section requires the subject to comprehend then complete logical sequences in lexical and numerical abstractions, which purports to measure abstraction capabilities. Together, the verbal and abstraction sections combine to form a modified ratio to indicate the client's ability for conceptual thought. Understanding someone's ability in this cognitive mode has far-reaching implications for job performance potentials. An individual who is highly limited in simultaneous or sequential thinking and in general fluidity of thought likely will experience performance problems where more than one task is involved or where anything beyond the most concrete decisions and judgments must be made. Such a client could not be recommended for positions of higher responsibilities where it is essential to make decisions quickly and accurately.

The Quick Test offers a gross estimation of intellectual functioning that requires no reading and little time to administer. Similarly, the Peabody Picture Vocabulary Test-Revised (PPVT-R) measures expressive communication skills, and thus is an excellent measure of verbal intelligence for individuals who experience a cognitive and/or organically based difficulty in expressing their ideas and communicating their intentions, or in reading. Such tests are particularly useful for persons with reading and communication disorders such as dyslexia, dislabia, and aphasia to gain an uncontaminated estimate of their overall intellectual potential. The Quick Test and the PPVT-R are usually unnecessary if the full WAIS-R can be administered without major deviations from normal procedures.

Achievement and Educational Evaluation

The most widely used assessment for academic achievement is the Wide Range Achievement Test-Revised (WRAT-R), covering reading, arithmetic, and spelling. This instrument provides the clinician with information regarding the overlearned material acquired in these basic school-related verbal areas. One anticipates normally that level of achievement, as expressed in normative percentiles, will be consistent with intellectual learning potential. Therefore, when achievement in any area measured by the WRAT-R is lower than would be expected given the individual's measured (WAIS-R) cognitive potential, the clinician must probe further for clarification. Such a finding might relate to a localized brain trauma, developmental learning disability, or unspecified underachievement. Regardless, this is a crucial determinant of the individual's past learning history and strongly suggests future learning/achievement expectations.

The WRAT-R is another test often overlooked for its wealth of information aside from yielding grade or percentile achievement levels. Quality and speed of spelling as well as the nature of errors can provide a sensitive predictor of learning potential. Errors reflecting a phonemic impairment are much different than those reflecting lack of education; the latter can be more easily corrected. Reading performance (speed, ability to sound-out unfamiliar words, and errors) can provide clues regarding a client's ability to read job-related material or to accomplish classroom learning. Arithmetic skill is vital for handling money or the kinds of statistical reports required in many jobs. In addition, the test as a whole also provides insight into effective learning modes.

Another instrument assessing achievement is the Peabody Individual Achievement Test (PIAT), which provides an overview of academic achievements in math, reading comprehension, word recognition, spelling, and general information. The purpose of the test is to identify areas of potential academic weakness for more in-depth evaluation and remediation. As with the WRAT-R, the PIAT can offer clues about the kinds of learning problems *across* verbal areas whereas the client may recognize global deficits *in* one or more verbal areas. Through such tests the clinician can provide insight into the presence and nature of any deficits while indicating how and to what degree they might influence career choices. As an example, individuals with math deficits have difficulty succeeding in sales and clerical positions that require quick mental mathematical calculations.

Vocational Interest Tests

It is usually beneficial to clients to assist them in sorting through the alternatives in career/job selection by obtaining a measure of their interests. The task is to strike a balance between the individual's career interests, values, goals, and work abilities. Frequently the client is unclear about how these elements merge into a job decision. Similarly, clients may feel uninformed about their skills and the job options available to them. Vocational interest measures are devised to help individuals in this search.

The majority of frequently used interest measures have adopted the Holland (1973) typology for classifying careers. This greatly enhances clients' understanding of career options by first showing them what their interest patterns reveal about the kinds of careers they seek, the work environments they prefer, the degree of freedom/responsibility they require, etc. Next, career areas are categorized within the interest areas, providing specific career directions (i.e., Artistic—advertising executive, language teacher, musician). From this perspective it becomes easier for the client to sort through career options. Even if a disability precludes realistic consideration of a particular career, the testing still provides interest-area information relevant to further work with the client.

The widely used Strong-Campbell Interest Inventory (SCII) assess an individual's interest in many job, leisure, home, value, and social areas to determine whether interests are significantly similar to those of individuals in a variety of fields. The theory is that if one has interests similar to those of individuals who are happy and successful in a specific career, then perhaps one also is suited for that career. However, the careers assessed are those that require at least four years of postsecondary schooling. The SCII also categorizes interest preferences within the Holland career typology: Realistic (hands-on, concrete, conventional); Investigative (scientific, abstract, introspective); Artistic (unstructured, creative, non-physical); Social (humanistic, responsible, interactive); Enterprising (persuasive, influential, achieving); and Conventional (well ordered, conforming, concrete). Career options are categorized along these areas as well so that individuals can scan specific careers within their highest interest areas to discern the career options thought to be most suitable for individuals with that specific interest profile.

The Career Assessment Inventory operates on the same principle of measuring and categorizing interest areas along the six Holland code types, and therefore also provides substantial information regarding career interests and options. It differs from the Strong-Campbell in that the careers along which individuals are compared require a high school degree and a maximum of two years additional post-high-school training, whereas the SCII careers usually require a minimum of a bachelor's degree.

John Holland, originator of the respected theory of career and interest categorization, developed a simple career interest instrument called the Self-Directed Search, which is self-explanatory, produces a quick interest profile, and includes information about how the individual can learn more about career areas. What it lacks in depth it makes up for in ease of use and availability.

Frederic Kuder developed two career assessment instruments that require the individual to make a series of choices between pairs of careers. The resulting profile ranks the person's stated career interest and illustrates the quality of fit between his or her interests and those of individuals in various career areas. These measures, the Kuder Occupational Interest Survey, Form DD, and the Kuder General Interest Survey, Form E, differ from the Strong-Campbell in test structure and layout of information. Whereas the SCII has the individual indicate preferences among career titles, Kuder believed that examinees bring too many stereotypes and misperceptions to their interpretations of career titles for the latter to be valid. Instead the Kuder measures require subjects to make statements about interest areas across hobbies, school activities, job tasks, preferred work environments, etc. The client's interest profiles are ranked according to their fit with the interest profiles among people of different occupations. It further includes preferences regarding college majors, and is therefore frequently used by counselors in college settings.

The clinician also must go beyond interest measures to explore career values and needs. Several instruments are available including the Hall Occupational Orientation Inventory (HOOI) and the Minnesota Importance Questionnaire. Such instruments examine the fit between the individual's abilities and needs and the job requirements and reinforcers. The HOOI specifically adapts Maslow's personality need theory to occupational choices. Worker traits considered crucial are aptitude, temperament, physical capabilities, interests, feelings about working conditions, education, and training. Whether the clinician chooses a structured needs measurement device or probes for such information in histories and other measurement sources, it is clear that the client benefits from this understanding of worker-job fit, and the procedure further assures more realistic job-career recommendations.

Finally, resources are available to the clinician and client that help further elaborate on the variety of careers available. The *Dictionary of Occupational Titles* (U.S. Department of Labor, 1977) is a standard reference for career information. Its two volumes present career titles both in alphabetical order and also categorized along worker traits of data-people-things. The *Occupational Outlook Handbook* (U.S. Department of Labor, 1984) provides educational requirements, job outlook, and other relevant statistics on over 800 common career areas, which facilitates realistic discussions about the likelihood of success and the prerequisites for entry. Of course, the vocational rehabilitation client poses unique restrictions on determining appropriate career goals. Nevertheless, as thorough an uncovering as possible needs to be undertaken to seek the broadest range of possibilities for a client.

Assessment of Learning Styles

The assessment of learning styles is a new area of exploration in the field of vocational counseling, pursued in recent years primarily by educators but also by industrial psychologists. The value of learning-style assessment rests in its ability to help an individual better understand the optimal conditions under which the greatest amount of learning can occur. It is known, for example, that learning disabled individuals often do not learn in conventional ways, but rather develop alternate strategies for coping with academic demands. It would be of interest to evaluate whether their preferences reflect their actual learning modes. The clinician can recommend methods for utilizing the person's most effective learning strategies and ways to compensate for learning weaknesses. Two of the better-researched instruments for this purpose are the Learning Styles Inventory (LSI) and the Productivity Environmental Preference Survey (PEPS). Both instruments assess preferences across 22 learning conditions: noise level; light; temperature; design; motivation;

persistence; responsibility; structure; learning alone versus peer-oriented; authority; learning in many ways; auditory, visual, kinesthetic preference; food intake; evening, morning, late morning, or afternoon learner; mobility needs; and parent-figure or adult-figure oriented.

Personality and Emotional Functioning Test

Depending on the nature of the rehabilitation, the clinician may require clarification on personality traits and dynamics, which can shed more light on the client's needs and can help in differential diagnosis. For example, an individual suffering from a serious depression may experience diminished learning potential due to slow thinking and poor concentration. Learning disabled individuals may present personality conflicts and negative self-image attitudes that impede learning and frustrate remedial interventions. Personality measures offer crucial information regarding an individuals tolerance for stress, preferred coping strategies, orientation toward others, grip on reality, and ability to perceive and comprehend social interaction sequences accurately.

A commonly used personality measure is the Minnesota Multiphasic Personality Inventory (MMPI), which assesses the client's affective, psychological, and social-interpersonal functioning. Significant elevations along clinical scales may indicate the existence of an influential, negative personality characteristic that has a harmful impact on the individuals cognitive functioning. Some individuals present a fairly average cognitive skill profile and limited learning deficits but nonetheless seem unable to find and/or maintain succesful employment. In such a case, the MMPI may provide clues to disruptive underlying psychological conflicts. Referring agencies specifically request information about clients' potential for work adjustment, which specifically addresses the individual's emotional stability. Poor coping through somatization, chronic depression, conflict with authority, excessive need gratification, and low self-esteem seriously influence a client's job success prospects. Clinicians often use the MMPI to help differentiate functional versus organic impairments. Lowered intellectual functioning across IQ subtests is more common among depressed individuals than head-injured, who frequently show greater inter- and intratest scatter. Similarly, the validity scales can add insight regarding the client's request for services. A clinically elevated F Scale and low K Scale may suggest a wish to be seen as needy, wanting to depend on the care of others rather than to assume more responsibility for one's own life.

Clinicians also choose projective devices, such as the Rorschach and the Thematic Apperception Test, to uncover the presence and nature of personality conflicts that may not be apparent in objective, structured measures. Well-guarded individuals frequently are able to hide significant conflicts from objective tests like the MMPI, but provide clues on more projective measures. Further, objective measures provide quantitative information and do not indicate the nature of the conflict to the degree that the projective device offers.

Neuropsychological Tests

Neuropsychological testing offers an overview of the individual's cognitive, motor, and perceptual functioning that serves as a basis for comparison with their scholastic achievements and potentials. A neuropsychological test profile gives a picture of the client's learning potential for various kinds of information, whereas achievement tests demonstrate recall of overlearned information. Learning disabled individuals, for example, show a significantly higher *potential* for learning than is illustrated in their actual achievements in specific areas. Similarly, various forms of brain trauma show unique patterns of cognitive deficits across various tests, and the neuropsychologist evaluates the test findings in search of configurations and information specific to the client's learning styles.

There are two batteries typically used in clinical settings: the Halstead-Reitan Neuropsychological Test Battery and the Luria-Nebraska Neuropsychological Battery. (Readers are refered to Chapter 7 in this volume for more detail regarding neuropsychological assessment.) The value of such assessment in the vocational rehabilitation is in delineating the cognitive strengths and weaknesses that bear on job performance. Such evaluation is indicated in the case of clients referred because of central neurological impairment.

INTERPRETATION AND INTEGRATION OF FINDINGS

The interpretation of the test findings essentially flows from the referral questions. Typically the clinician seeks to establish a diagnosis regarding the client's eligibility for services if the referral comes from a public assistance agency. Usually, there is a need to establish the client's acceptance into a category of learning disabled, physically handicapped, emotionally disabled, or mentally retarded.

Based on the client's pattern of cognitive skills and deficits, personality indicators, vocational interest areas, and pertinent historical data, the psychologist combines the information to answer the referral questions. This compilation must address work and training potentials, readiness for work, suggested job training areas, educational needs, presence of personality conflicts that may impede training, education, or work placement, and the need for additional testing, career counseling, or psychotherapy.

COMMUNICATING RESULTS

In communicating a client's test profile, findings should be presented in a positive light, emphasizing strengths that can be built on as well as reasonable recommendations for remedial activites to strengthen areas of weakness. The client should derive from the evaluation a realistic and nondefensive view of him- or herself and come away with specific and concrete ideas about appropriate job directions.

At this time the clinician can challenge career goals or expectations that are not supported by the client's capabilities or are a function of misrepresentations. If a client cannot be predicted to succeed in law school, for example, the counselor can present other legal career options or branch into career areas that are consistent with client expectations, values, interests, and abilities. Similarly, the psychologist can affirm current career decisions and support and client's training/educational process before referral agencies.

The testing, interpretation, and report writing should be singularly directed toward providing useful information about the client, in an edifying and constructive way, with an emphasis on employment prospects. Having struggled to find and keep good jobs or to make it through school, many vocational rehabilitation clients often harbor the fear or believe that they are either retarded, lazy, or unusual in some way. The clinician has a fourfold responsibility in the use of the testing process. First, the results are derived to help the client to better understand his or her overall cognitive functioning and important personality factors, and the career issues that influence potential for success in work and training. Second, the clinician looks for career and educational avenues that fit the client's abilities and interest and in which the client can find success. Third, the clinician's honest appraisal is necessary when the client does not appear to meet the agency's criteria for services. On occasion, the clinican may be the one who must state that the person is likely disabled to the extent that he or she cannot hold competitive jobs and should be considered disabled for work. Finally, the clinician must extend him- or herself beyond the requirements to inform the agency and client when other forms of assistance are warranted and where additional therapeutic resources may be found.

REFERENCES

Holland, J. L. (1973). *Making vocational choices: A theory of careers.* Englewood Cliffs, NJ: Prentice-Hall.
Kaufman, A. S. (1979). *Intelligent testing with the WISC-R.* New York: John Wiley & Sons.
United States Department of Labor. (1977). *Dictionary of occupational titles* (4th ed.). Washington, DC: U.S. Government Printing Office.
United States Department of Labor. (1984). *Occupational outlook handbook.* Washington, DC: U.S. Government Printing Office.
Zimmerman, I. L., & Woo-Sam, J. M. (1973). *Clinical interpretation of the Wechsler Adult Intelligence Scale.* New York: Grune & Stratton.

17

Forensic Issues: Assessments in Litigation

CHARLES J. GOLDEN, PH.D., MARK R. LOVELL, PH.D.

As the discipline of clinical psychology has evolved over the last 40 years, the psychologist's role in the legal arena has assumed increasing importance. This has been evidenced by a large increase in the number of those professionals who now dedicate a significant amount of their time to forensic work. The well-trained psychologist has much to offer in assessment for litigation, and such expert testimony has become particularly valuable in clarifying issues pertaining to personal injury compensation, competency to stand trial, and responsibility for crime. The use of psychological assessment in legal proceedings has become especially valuable to both defense and prosecuting attorneys because of the "data-based" nature of this form of evaluation, which can provide the court with a more objective appraisal of mental state than traditional psychiatric assessment.

This chapter emphasizes objective evidence because of the unique contribution that the psychologist can make in this area. Traditional psychiatric or psychological testimony has been based largely on opinion, depending solely on the degree to which the expert could convince the court that he or she was more qualified (or important) than the experts on the other side of the case. This made decisions on such issues difficult for the court, as well as often becoming a test of showmanship rather than expertise. When objective data can be employed, however, the focus of the legal argument relies instead on debates about the validity and reliability of the data and the methods with which they are interpreted. The psychologist is in an ideal position to produce and interpret objective data, which can enhance significantly the role of such an expert witness if these approaches are used appropriately.

The involvement of psychologists in litigation proceedings represents a challenging, exciting new area, one which requires preparation and study beyond that which is provided in typical graduate training programs. To this end, this chapter discusses issues of importance to psychologists who aspire to utilize their assessment skills in the legal arena. However, it must be emphasized that due to the "springboard" nature of this text and the complex and multifaceted nature of litigation assessment, the following discussion serves as a "primer" on the subject and speaks to general issues rather than addressing specific legal questions. Individuals interested in additional reading in the area are advised to seek out more in-depth discussions (Sales, 1977; Ziskin, 1981; Blau, 1984).

PREDIAGNOSTIC SCREENING

Understanding Legal Issues and Definitions

The most basic prerequisite for an individual who wishes to perform forensic assessment is an adequate understanding of legal statues in the state(s) in which he or she will be practicing. Without such an understanding, the psychologist is likely to provide the referring source (the attorney or court) with information that may not answer directly the referral question. For example, because the legal criteria for determination of competence to stand trial differ from state to state, an evaluation conducted to determine competency in Nebraska may necessitate an entirely different assessment focus from that required in another state. More specifically, though Nebraska requires the assessor to answer at least 14 specific questions ranging from whether the defendant understands the crime with which he or she is charged to whether the defendant can decide upon a plea, such findings may be of little value in deciding this issue in a state that utilizes criteria that are not as well articulated.

The need for this understanding has gained greater importance as psychologists have become involved in increasingly complex issues and as state laws have become increasingly divergent. One state may require the psychologist only to reach the conclusion that is the most *likely* (whether or not the probability of that conclusion is particularly high), another may require the most likely conclusion with more than a 50% probability, and a third may require near certainty (usually 80% or more probability). In a recent trial, a psychologist made a complete shambles of her own conclusions by noting that she did not believe that anyone could conclude anything on the basis of the data available, but that the opposing witness's explanation was more likely than the other (though in her opinion of low probability), perhaps to avoid a further argument. Under the rules of that state, the psychologist in effect had testified (quite unintentionally) for the other side, and attempts to withdraw or modify the statement after she finally understood the law were in vain. In many cases, only a knowledge of the law can produce phrasing that is most effective in communicating one's true opinion.

If courtroom testimony is required during the legal proceedings it is essential that the psychologist has at least a basic understanding of courtroom protocol. The expert witness who feels comfortable in the courtroom environment presents his or her findings in a more convincing manner than the witness who is uneasy in this milieu.

Understanding Diagnostic Issues

Although the psychologist involved in litigation must have at least a basic grasp of legal protocol, it is far more important that he or she thoroughly understand the particular assessment issues for a specific case. Because most attorneys have only a minimal understanding of psychodiagnostics, they cannot always clearly articulate what type of psychological assessment they want for a client. For this reason, the psychologist should meet with the attorney prior to undertaking a given case. If one does not understand exactly the reasons for an evaluation and what information is necessary for a court decision, one may fail to seek or recognize appropriate data or may subject the patient needlessly to tests unrelated to the case. The lawyer may need to be apprised of the psychological issues or the potential limits of psychological testimony, as the psychologist may be asked to address points that are either inappropriate or cannot be discussed because no information exists. Such early consultation with the attorney must include as detailed historical records as possible as well as access to independent sources of data (family, significant others, etc.). It is also extremely important prior to testing and testimony that the psychologist discuss the questions that the attorney will ask during the proceedings. This will help to avoid the embarrassment of being asked questions one is not prepared to answer or the frustration of not being asked questions that elicit data or opinions one considers important to the case.

Beyond these general comments regarding pertinent diagnostic issues, it must be emphasized that because the psychologist who desires to expand his or her practice to include forensic assessment will often be asked to render a diagnosis of the client in question, an excellent understanding of current psychiatric diagnostic criteria is also necessary. In view of the current, nearly universal acceptance of the *Diagnostic and Statistical Manual of Mental Disorders* (DSM-III; American Psychiatric Association, 1980) criteria for psychiatric diagnosis, a thorough understanding of this manual is a prerequisite to successful and responsible legal testimony. As DSM-III diagnoses are made primarily on the basis of historical data, the forensic psychologist must have a good understanding of the client's history prior to actual psychological testing and must integrate the psychological test data within this framework. The psychologist who attempts to present a diagnostic opinion that does not take the client's history into consideration is likely to lose credibility when historical information is produced by the opposition that is in conflict with his or her professional opinion. This investigation should involve not only a detailed investigative interview with the client but should also seek to obtain information from potentially corroborating sources such as the client's family and employer.

ADMINISTRATION OF TESTS AND PROCEDURES

As noted, the use of objective psychological tests can aid immeasurably to the influence of the psychologist in the forensic situation. Indeed, it is the skill at objective assessment that differentiates the testimony of the psychologist from that of the psychiatrist, social worker, or general physician. Testing can also provide a good counter to the testimony of the neurologist, neurosurgeon, or radiologist in cases concerning the effects of brain injury, especially in mild cases, which are the ones most likely to be contested. Rarely are the arguments in these cases over injuries that are so clear and severe that anyone can see them.

Selection of Tests

Following the meeting with the referral source and the delineation of pertinent assessment issues, the next step in the process involves the selection of psychologi- 'cal tests that best address these relevant diagnostic questions. Although seemingly a simple process, the selection of assessment instruments is extremely important in forensic cases and should be completed only after giving careful consideration to several issues.

First, the tests should provide information that is readily understandable to the attorney, the judge, and/or the jury. As these individuals are not likely to be well versed in the interpretation of psychological tests, assessment instruments yielding information that requires a lengthy elaboration by the psychologist in order to be understood will serve only to confuse others involved in the legal process. For this reason, tests that are "face valid" should be employed whenever these tests are otherwise psychometrically viable. The exception occurs when the client might be expected to "fake" the test results, which becomes harder to guard against the more open the test is to understanding and manipulation. The ideal test offers some balance between the extremes of obvious and esoteric interpretation.

Another important issue is the test's defensibility in court. Using thoroughly researched psychological tests is recommended over the use of experimental or obscure procedures. Because objective psychological tests are more likely to have documented psychometric properties such as reliability and validity, these mea- sures are easier to defend under cross-examination and are therefore recommended over more subjective assessment procedures. Objective psychological tests have the added advantage of specific criteria for interpretation provided in the form of numbers and ratios. This information is likely to have a much greater impact on a judge or jury than test results that depend on the expert witness' subjective evalua- tion.

In additional to considerations of test interpretability and defensibility, it is also very important for the psychologist to have a good understanding of the strengths and weaknesses of the procedures used. Given that the forensic psychol- ogist's testimony almost always will be pitted against that of an opposing expert witness, perhaps with similar training in psychodiagnostics, the adversary witness will likely help the opposing attorney pinpoint possible weaknesses in the psychol- ogist's selection and interpretation of assessment instruments. In other words, the psychologist is involved in a contest in which each side will try to demonstrate more competence in the area than their opponents. Being able to defend the use and interpretation of the test in court presupposes not only a thorough understanding of how the test was developed and standardized but also an understanding of appropriate subjects and a thorough knowledge of the research, both positive and negative. There is the underlying assumption, of course, that whoever has given the test has adhered scrupulously to the standardized procedures for administration and scoring.

Finally, since all tests have strengths and weaknesses, redundancy in testing is often useful. This is especially true in more subtle cases, where the concurrence of several methods that use different approaches or have different theoretical or empirical underpinnings can strengthen any argument considerably.

Because legal clients referred for psychological evaluation may have sustained some form of trauma resulting in psychological and/or neuropsychological symptoms, the forensic psychologist must have a thorough understanding of how these somatic problems affect the individual in emotional and cognitive spheres. This is particularly important in cases where brain impairment is suspected because information gained from psychological assessment must often be integrated with other neurodiagnostic information, such as CT scan, X-ray, angiographic, and myelographic data. Failure to take this information into account when formulating an assessment strategy can result in a focus on irrelevant issues and, hence, a less-than-adequate evaluation. It is also important to be aware of such factors as visual or auditory impairment and physical diseases, such as diabetes or some forms of chronic pain, which could affect psychological adjustment or cognitive performance.

Periodically, the forensic psychologist is asked to answer questions regarding a client's level of intellectual or cognitive functioning. This form of evaluation is most likely to arise when a client's competence to stand trial is questioned or when the issue of diminished capacity is raised. Obviously, if the accused is found to be severely mentally retarded, his or her sentencing is likely to be viewed differently than that of an individual with above-average intellectual abilities. Hence, intellectual evaluation may be useful and even necessary in certain legal situations, though it may not be adequate in more complex cases that hinge on the client's ability to perform certain acts or to understand specific circumstances. Intellectual evaluation also is not adequate by itself when the question of brain impairment has been raised. In cases where it is determined that an intellectual evaluation will provide useful information to the referring attorney, the Wechsler Adult Intelligence Scale-Revised (WAIS-R) should be employed. The test represents the standard for intellectual assessment and is well accepted in forensic situations.

Neuropsychological Tests

The use of neuropsychological tests in legal cases has increased dramatically over the last ten years. This increase in popularity has been due no doubt, at least partially, to the demonstrated usefulness of this form of assessment in answering questions related to personal injury and competence to stand trial. In general, there are two major approaches to neuropsychological assessment that are currently popular in the United States: 1) the clinical or qualitative approach, and 2) the actuarial or quantitative approach. The clinical approach emphasizes a qualitative analysis of performance and the selection of tests depends on the suspected deficit. This approach to assessment has the advantages of flexibility and of providing a detailed description of individual strengths and weaknesses. However, the qualitative approach relies on subjective clinical interpretation rather than on comparing performance to statistically determined standards, and hence is particularly vulnerable to attack in the legal arena. As a qualitative approach to neuropsychological assessment can involve any number of individual test procedures, specific instruments will not be highlighted here. (Readers interested in learning more about individual neuropsychological tests and their appropriate uses are advised to consult Heilman & Valenstein [1979] and Lezak [1983].) It must be emphasized, however, that the use of individual measures of "organicity" such as the Bender-Visual Motor Gestalt Test do not provide sufficient information to warrant their use in forensic situations. In many cases the qualitative approach will resemble standard neurological assessment procedures, and thus may be difficult for the psychologist to uphold effectively against opposing testimony by a neurologist; when all other factors are equal, physicians carry more clout in legal arenas.

On the other hand, the quantitative or actuarial approach provides empirically derived standards for comparing the client's performance to that of "normal" individuals. This approach has obvious advantages in that it provides the attorney, the judge, and the jury with numerical cutoffs for substantiating the presence or absence of brain impairment, and the results of the evaluation can be presented in a concise, clear-cut manner. At present, there are two popular neuropsychological assessment approaches that were developed along primarily quantitative lines: the Halstead-Reitan and the Luria-Nebraska neuropsychological batteries.

The Halstead-Reitan Neuropsychological Test Battery for Adults is comprised of 13 tests and is designed to be employed with persons aged 15 and older. This battery was developed originally by Ward Halstead in 1949 and has been modified since by Reitan (1955). The tasks that make up the battery include the Category Test, Tactual Performance Test (Time, Memory, and Localization), Speech-Sounds Perception Test, Rhythm Test, and Finger Tapping Test. From these five tests, which yield seven scores, an Impairment Index can be calculated to provide a general indication of level of brain dysfunction. For each test within the battery, cutoff scores are available for determining normal and abnormal performance. The Halstead-Reitan battery is useful in forensic work in that it represents a standardized, data-based approach to assessment; however, it does not lend itself readily to qualitative interpretation.

The Luria-Nebraska Neuropsychological Battery (LNNB) allows for quantitative assessment of brain function while also emphasizing qualitative interpretation of test performance. This battery consists of 11 scales, which provide information on motor, tactile, auditory, visual, memory and intellectual functioning as well as receptive and expressive language abilities. The inclusion of writing, reading, and arithmetic scales allows for a direct assessment of educationally related skills. In addition to providing qualitative information on performance, the Luria-Nebraska has several other advantages in legal situations. First, the cutoffs for identifying brain impairment are adjusted for the client's age and educational background, which allows for a more sensitive appraisal of brain impairment free of these extraneous factors. Second, the individual items that comprise the LNNB are arranged hierarchically, with later, more complex items requiring a combination of abilities tapped by earlier, simpler items. This format allows for a direct assessment of malingering or exaggeration of injury by allowing the examiner to compare a client's performance on earlier items with that on later, more complex items. Individuals who perform adequately on the more difficult items after having difficulty on the previous simpler ones are not likely to have a true organic deficit.

Personality Tests

Frequently a forensic psychologist is asked to provide the attorney or the court with information concerning a client's emotional condition. This form of evaluation is most often requested when the issue of competency to stand trial or responsibility for a crime is raised. However, information on emotional adjustment is also crucial in personal loss cases, because many individuals suffer emotionally from the physical injuries received in automobile accidents, industrial mishaps, and the like. (For a discussion of emotional sequelae to physical injury, see Chapter 9.)

Although currently there are hundreds of psychological tests that purport to measure some aspect of personality, relatively few of these instruments are "data-based" approaches, but instead are interpreted subjectively. This has limited the amount of research studies that have been undertaken to attest to their usefulness. As mentioned earlier, employing psychological tests that have not been investigated rigorously can seriously undermine the attorney's defense or prosecution efforts and hence should be avoided. Conversely, tests that have been researched thoroughly can provide the attorney with extremely useful information.

No doubt the most popular personality test in forensic assessment situations traditionally has been the Minnesota Multiphasic Personality Inventory (MMPI). The MMPI has several attributes that make it ideally suited for forensic use. First, the validity scales provide direct information on whether the client is endeavoring to fabricate or deny psychiatric symptoms in an attempt to influence the outcome of the legal process. Second, clinical scales provide a broad range of information on both level and type of psychiatric disturbance. This allows for answering questions concerning competency to stand trial and non-responsibility for a crime, as well as making the index applicable to personal injury cases where emotional sequelae of a traumatic event are suspected.

Another personality test that traditionally has enjoyed widespread popularity in forensic cases is the Rorschach. This projective instrument has been utilized by psychologists for many years and is still considered by many to be a necessary component in any complete psychological assessment. Although earlier scoring and interpretation strategies for the Rorshach were highly subjective and hence somewhat difficult to defend in court, the system proposed by Exner (1974) provides empirically based criteria for scoring and interpretation, which increases considerably the usefulness of this test in court. Another property that makes the Rorschach useful in court is that this instrument is difficult to fake. Because the test stimuli are ambiguous and only a minimum of information is given to the subject prior to administration, the client is not likely to know how to fake responses in any coherent manner.

A number of other personality tests have been utilized in forensic assessments with less success than the MMPI and the Rorschach. For example, the use of the Thematic Apperception Test (TAT) and the Draw-A-Person Test (DAP) in forensic situations has been criticized due to the inherently subjective manner in which these techniques are scored and interpreted and the consequent low reliability and validity of these procedures. As mentioned throughout this chapter, the use of projective psychological tests in legal cases can lead to reliance on data that are not easily defended in court and result in information that is not readily understandable to the judge and/or jury. Therefore, the use of these procedures is not encouraged. (See Rabin, 1968 for a review of these tests.)

Tests of Competency

Determination of competency to stand trial represents a very important step in the legal process, especially in criminal trials. Though standards for competency may vary among states, there are some common procedures that are often employed. Historically, decisions concerning competency were based on English common law, which requires that a defendant must be capable of defending him- or herself in court. This rather vague notion has been translated into three criteria: 1) the defendant must be aware of the nature of the legal process; 2) the defendant must recognize the consequences of conviction; and 3) the defendant must be able to assist legal counsel in his or her defense. Traditionally, in making these decisions the court based its subjective opinion in part on the subjective opinion of mental health professionals. More recently attempts have been made to standardize this process.

The Competency Screening Test (CST) consists of 22 sentence completion items that focus on various courtroom situations. Each item is scored on a three-point scale ranging from "appropriate" to "poor." As the CST is primarily a screening device it should not be used to make final decisions but rather to suggest which clients need additional competency evaluation.

The Competency to Stand Trial Assessment Instrument (CAI) was designed to provide for an in-depth interview with the client that focuses more on the legal aspects of competence than the CST. The client is rated on 13 different areas that deal with understanding different aspects of the trial process. The individual is rated on a six-point scale ranging from "no incapacity" to "unrateable." The CAI may be a useful instrument because potentially it can aid the court in quantifying the degree to which an individual is competent to stand trial. However, its effectiveness has yet to be established by independent researchers.

The Interdisciplinary Fitness Interview is a new instrument designed to involve both the mental health professional and the lawyer in the interview process. The scale consists of three major sections: legal issues, psychopathology, and overall ratings by each of the professionals. This test presents an interesting approach but is still too new at the time of this writing to allow any conclusions about its efficacy.

This chapter has identified only the major highlights and practices of forensic psychology. It should be emphasized that these assessments vary from others not so much in the instruments and approaches used (any test can be employed as long as it fulfills the described considerations) as in the application of these instruments to the very specific questions that can be posed in the legal situation. Thus, the psychologist involved in this work must thoroughly understand the legal issue in question and be able to translate the issue(s) into questions that can be answered by psychological evaluation. In turn one must translate the data obtained into language that answers the legal questions directly, and then defend these conclusions against both direct and indirect challenge that is conceived not to establish psychological conclusions but to influence the legal decision of a judge and jury.

REFERENCES

Blau, T. H. (1984). *The psychologist as expert witness*. New York: John Wiley & Sons.
Bukataman, B. A., Foy, J. L., & DeGrazia, E. (1971). What is competency to stand trial? *American Journal of Psychiatry, 127*, 1225-1229.
Exner, J. E. (1978). *The Rorschach: A comprehensive system*. New York: John Wiley & Sons.
Heilman, K. M., & Valenstein, E. (Eds.). (1979). *Clinical neuropsychology*. New York: Oxford University Press.
Lezak, M. D. (1979). *Neuropsychological assessment*. New York: Oxford University Press.
McGarry, A. L. (1972). *Competence to stand trial and mental illness* (DHEW Publication No. HSM 73-9105). Washington, DC: U.S. Government Printing Office.
Rabin, A. I. (1968). *Projective techniques in personality assessment: A modern introduction*. New York: Springer.
Robey, A. (1965). Criteria for competency to stand trial: A checklist for psychiatrists *American Journal of Psychiatry, 122*, 616-622.
Sales, B. D. (Ed.). (1977). *Psychology in the legal process*. New York: Halstead Press.
Ziskin, J. (1981). *Coping with psychiatric and psychological testimony* (Vol. 1). Venice, CA: Psychology and the Law Press.

Appendix:
Test Directory and Index

209

ANXIETY SCALE FOR THE BLIND   *Richard E. Hardy*

Measures manifest anxiety among blind and partially sighted individuals 13 years of age and older. Recently modified for adults. Used for clinical evaluations by psychologists, psychiatrists, and trained counselors.

A 78-item, true-false test. The individual is given a roll of tickets to be placed to the right or left of the table to indicate true or false as the items are read aloud. Time of administration varies. Originally developed for use in residential schools with students of high school age, it is useful in other contexts as well. The test is still experimental in nature and must be used only by psychologists, psychiatrists, and other qualified counselors. Administration is untimed and varies. Examiner required and evaluated. Not suitable for group use. The scale costs $4.00. *Publisher:* American Foundation for the Blind

ARTHUR POINT SCALE OF PERFORMANCE, FORM I
Grace Arthur

Measures intelligence of children and adults. Used as a nonverbal supplement to the highly verbalized Binet tests, especially with people having language, speech, emotional, or cultural problems.

The ten nonverbal task assessment subtests are Mare-Foal Formboard, Seguin-Goddard Formboard, Pintner-Paterson 2-Figure Formboard, Casuist Formboard, Pintner-Manikin Test, Knox-Kempf Feature Profile Test, Knox Cube Imitation Test, Healy Pictoral Completion Test 1, Kohs Block Design Test, and Porteus Mazes. Particularly useful in supplementing the Binet scale in cases where the environmental conditions have varied widely from those of the average child. The comparison is of value whether it confirms the Binet ratings or shows a disparity in verbal and nonverbal development. Examiner required and evaluated. Not suitable for group use. Complete kit (including all tests, 50 record cards, and manual) costs $395.00. *Publisher:* Stoelting Co.

ATTITUDE TOWARD WOMEN SCALE   *J. T. Spence and R. Helmreich*

Assesses vocational, educational, social, and intellectual roles of women, including their freedom and independence, interpersonal relationships, and sexual behavior. Used to determine both male and female attitudes toward female roles.

A self-report inventory consisting of 55 items categorized into six groups: vocational, educational, and intellectual (17 items); freedom and independence (4 items); dating, courting, and etiquette (7 items); drinking, swearing, and dirty jokes (3 items); sexual behavior (7 items); and marital relationships and obligations

Refer to page(s):	*Test Title*

(17 items). Items consist of declarative statements with four response alternatives (agree strongly to disagree strongly). Each item scored 0 to 3 (0 reflects most traditional, conservative attitude and 3 reflects the most liberal, profeminist attitude). Score obtained by summing values for individual items according to scoring key identifying most conservative choice. Administration is untimed and varies. Examiner evaluated. Hand- or machine-scored. Separate machine answer sheets are available. *Source:* Available from Selected Documents in Psychology, American Psychological Association, 1200 Seventeenth Street, NW, Washington, DC 20036.

131

ATTITUDES TOWARD HOMOSEXUALITY SCALE
A.P. MacDonald, Jr.

Measures subject's attitudes toward homosexuality, regardless of their own sexual orientation. Used with widely divergent populations, especially college students and faculty.

A self-report, 28-item inventory with nine scale positions for each item. Subject responds on a nine-point scale (strongly agree to strongly disagree). Three forms are available: General (Form G), Lesbian (Form L), and Male (Form M). Resulting score is the total score for all items. Suitable for group use. Examiner evaluated. Administration is untimed and varies. *Source:* Available from Publications Office, Center for the Study of Human Sexuality, 4105 Medical Parkway, Suite 205, Austin, Texas 78756.

12, 84

BECK DEPRESSION INVENTORY   *Aaron T. Beck*

Measures the degree of depression of adolescents and adults. Used for treatment planning and evaluation in mental health settings.

A 21-item, multiple-choice and true-false inventory assessing individual complaints, symptoms, and attitudes related to their current degree of depression. Scales include sadness, pessimism, sense of failure, lack of satisfaction, guilty feelings, sense of being punished, self-dislike, self-accusations, suicidal wishes, crying spells, irritability, withdrawal, and indecisiveness. Questions are presented on an eighth-grade reading level. Administration is untimed and requires approximately 15-20 minutes. Examiner required. Not suitable for group use. Consult publisher for costs. *Publisher:* Center for Cognitive Therapy

131

BEM SEX-ROLE INVENTORY (BSRI)   *Sandra L. Bem*

Measures masculinity and femininity of adults. Used for research on psychological androgyny.

A 60-item, paper-pencil measure of integration of masculinity and femininity. Items are three sets of 20 personality characteristics: masculine, feminine, and neutral. Subjects indicate on a seven-point scale how well each characteristic describes them. The inventory is untimed and requires approximately ten minutes. Materials include a 30-item short form. Self-administered and hand-scored. Suitable for group use. A specimen set (including manual, key, and tests) costs $8.50; manual, $8.00; key, $1.00; 25 expendable inventories, $3.25. *Publisher:* Consulting Psychologists Press, Inc.

BENTON REVISED VISUAL RETENTION TEST
Arthur Benton

Measures visual memory in individuals aged eight years to adult. Used as a supplement to usual mental examinations and in experimental research.

A ten-item paper-pencil test assessing visual perception, visual memory, and visuoconstructive abilities. Items are designs that are shown to the individual one at a time. The individual studies the design and reproduces it as exactly as possible on a blank sheet of paper. Administration is untimed and requires approximately five minutes to complete. Materials include design cards, and three alternate and equivalent forms, C, D, and E. Examiner required and evaluated. Not suitable for group use. The complete set, including manual, design cards (three forms combined), and 50 record forms, costs $21.00. *Publisher:* The Psychological Corporation

THE BLIND LEARNING APTITUDE TEST (BLAT)
T. Ernest Newland

Evaluates the academic aptitude of blind children aged 6-16 years. Sixty-one item, verbal-touch test of tactile discrimination involving patterned dots and lines on 61 embossed plastic pages. The examiner guides the child's hand over the pages and the child describes what he or she feels. Administration requires 20-45 minutes. Examiner required and evaluated with the aid of a hand key. Not suitable for group use. The complete set, including the examiner's manual, testing book, embossed pages, and 30 record forms, costs $50.00. *Publisher:* University of Illinois Press

BODY ATTITUDE SCALE   *R. Kurtz and M. Hirt*

Measures global attitudes toward the outward form of a person's body on three primary attitude dimensions: evaluative (good-bad), potency (strong-weak), and activity (active-passive). Used in assessment of adults of various ages and backgrounds with or without physical or psychological disorders.

A self-report scale rating 30 different body concepts (parts) on a modification of the Osgood semantic differential—a seven-point bipolar adjective scale (1 = most negative, 4 = neutral, 7 = most positive). Adjective scales for each dimension are summed to obtain

Refer to page(s):	*Test Title*

item score for each concept on each dimension, which can be summed across the 30 body concepts to obtain a composite global body attitude score, a potency body attitude score, and an activity body attitude score. Administration is untimed and varies. Examiner evaluated. *Source:* Author: available from R. Kurtz, Dept. of Psychology, Washington University, St. Louis, Missouri 63130.

130
BODY CONTACT QUESTIONNAIRE (BCQ)
Marc H. Hollender

Measures an adult's wish to be held and the wish to hold. Used in clinical evaluation.

A self-administered questionnaire with 12 items embedded in a matrix assessing strength of the wish to be held and 12 assessing strength of the wish to hold. Separate questionnaires for men and women. Subjects (who should be alone when answering) rate each statement on a 1-5 scale (never to always or equivalent categories). Administration is untimed and requires approximately ten minutes. Hand- or computer scored. Suitable for group use, if monitored. *Source:* Author; requests for questionnaire should be directed to Marc H. Hollender, M.D., Department of Psychiatry, Vanderbilt University School of Medicine, Nashville, Tennessee 37232.

82
BOSTON DIAGNOSTIC APHASIA EXAMINATION
Harold Goodglass and Edith Kaplan

Assesses the functioning of adult aphasic patients. Used for clinical evaluations.

A multiple-item, oral response, paper-pencil, and task performance test yielding 43 scores that relate to recognized aphasic syndromes: severity rating, fluency, auditory comprehension, naming, oral reading, repetition, paraphrasia, automatized speech, reading comprehension, writing, music, parietal; plus 7 ratings: melodic line, phrase length, articulatory agility, grammatical form, paraphrasia in running speech, word finding, and auditory comprehension. The 80-page text, *The Assessment of Aphasia and Related Disorders,* serves as the test manual and includes information on the nature of aphasic deficits, common clusters of defects, statistical information, administration and scoring procedures, and illustrations of test profiles that correspond to major aphasic syndromes. Administration is untimed and varied. Examiner required and evaluated. Not suitable for group use. Complete set (including text, 16 stimulus cards, and 25 test booklets) costs $37.50. *Publisher:* Lea & Febiger; distributed by The Psychological Corporation

Test Title

BRICKLIN PERCEPTUAL SCALES: CHILD-PERCEPTION-OF-PARENTS-SERIES   *Barry Bricklin*

Measures a child's (aged four years or older who is able to understand instructions) conscious and unconscious perceptions of each parent in the areas of competence, supportiveness, follow-up consistency, and possession of admirable traits (e.g., altruism, friendliness, trustworthiness). Used by mental health professionals (trained in test administration) to assist in custody decision making to designate which parent more frequently acts in a child's best interests.

A nonverbal test consisting of 64 cards (items), with 32 pertaining to the mother and 32 pertaining to the father. Makes use of a continuum stimulus that elicits verbal and nonverbal responses. Instructions for administering the test and an "invisible" grid, which scores the card automatically as the child responds to it, are printed on the cards. Administration is untimed and requires approximately 30-45 minutes. Examiner required. Not suitable for group use. A starting set (including six sets of testing cards and manual) costs $44.00. *Publisher:* Village Publishing

CALIFORNIA PSYCHOLOGICAL INVENTORY (CPI) *Harrison G. Gough*

Assesses normal adult personality as an aid to educational, clinical, counseling, and vocational guidance. Used to assist counselors of nonpsychiatrically disturbed adolescents and adults by measuring personality characteristics important for social living and social interaction.

A 480-item, paper-pencil test of 18 socially desirable behavioral tendencies: dominance, capacity for status, sociability, social presence, self-acceptance, sense of well-being, responsibility, socialization, self-control, tolerance, good impression, communality, achievement via independence, achievement via conformance, intellectual efficiency, psychological-mindedness, flexibility, and femininity. Administration is untimed and requires approximately 45-60 minutes. Self-administered. Available in Spanish, French, Italian, and German. Hand-scored. Counselor's kit (including 5 reusable tests, 25 answer sheets, 25 profiles, a set of stencils, and manual) costs $25.00. *Publisher:* Consulting Psychologists Press, Inc.

CAREER ASSESSMENT INVENTORY (CAI) *Charles B. Johansson*

Evaluates career goals of students (Grade 8 through high school) and adults who want immediate, noncollege-graduate business or technical training. Used for employment decisions, vocational rehabilitation, and self-employment.

Test Title

A 305-item, paper-pencil test in a five-response Likert format. Covers six General Occupational Themes (Holland's RIASEC), 22 Basic Occupational Interest Scales, and 91 Occupational Scales. Administration is untimed and requires approximately 20-35 minutes. Self-administered. Suitable for group use. Available in French and Spanish. Computer-scored. A specimen set (including manual and both a narrative and a profile answer sheet, each of which contain test items) costs $14.25; a narrative or profile answer sheet via mail-in (including test items and report), $2.45-$8.25 each; 25 narrative or 25 profile Arion II or MICROTEST (IBM PC or PC/XT) answer sheets, $7.50; scoring/reporting via Arion II, $2.45-$8.25 per test; via MICROTEST, $1.60-$4.50 per test. *Publisher:* NCS Professional Assessment Services

COLOURED PROGRESSIVE MATRICES   *J.C. Raven*

Assesses the mental ability of young children (aged 5-11) and adults who are mentally subnormal or impaired. Used for school and clinical counseling, and research.

A 36-item, paper-pencil nonverbal test consisting of design and pattern problems printed in several colors, including the two easiest sets from SPM-1938, plus a dozen additional items of similar difficulty. In each problem the subject is presented with a pattern or figure design that has a part missing and selects one of six possible parts as the correct one. Examiner required. Administration is untimed and requires approximately 15-30 minutes. Suitable for group use above age eight. Hand-scored. Standard norms developed in Great Britain. Specimen set (including 1 book of tests and 12 combined Coloured Matrices and Crichton Vocabulary Scale Forms) costs $16.00; 10 test booklets, $87.00; plastic marking key, $12.00. *Publisher:* H.K. Lewis & Co. Ltd.; U.S. Distributor—The Psychological Corporation

THE COMPETENCY SCREENING TEST (CST)   *P.D. Lipsitt, D. Lelos, and L.A. McGarry*

Assesses defendants for whom the issue of competency has been raised. Used to identify those for whom competency might be a significant issue.

A 22-item, sentence-completion instrument that focuses on various courtroom situations. Each item is given a score ranging from 0 to 2 with a response of 2 indicating an appropriate response to the sentence stem and 0 indicating a poor response. A score of 1 is given to responses that are not clearly appropriate or inappropriate. Scoring decisions are made by comparing the client's response to examples provided in the handbook, and the total score is obtained by summation of the item scores. Cutoffs are provided for determination of competency. *Source:* Administration, scoring, and interpretation guidelines are provided in *Competency to Stand Trial and Mental Illness: A Monograph Series,* available through the Superintendent of Documents, U.S. Government Printing Office, Washington, D.C.

THE COMPETENCY TO STAND TRIAL ASSESSMENT INSTRUMENT (CAI)   *A.L. McGarry*

Assesses defendant's ability to understand and cope with the trial process. Used as the basis for an in-depth interview with a client, focusing more on the legal standards of competency than The Competency Screening Test (CST) or more traditional, psychopathologically based evaluation procedures.

A semistructured interview that rates the defendant in 13 areas that range from the degree of capacity to appraise available legal defenses to the individual's motivation for cooperation in his or her defense. Subject is rated in each area on a 6-point scale, with a rating of 1 being indicative of total capacity, 5 indicating no capacity, and 6 indicating that the client is unrateable in that assessment area. Scoring is by comparison of the defendant's responses to examples listed in the manual. Examiner evaluated. Not suitable for group use. *Source:* A copy of this instrument and scoring and interpretation information are provided in *Competency to Stand Trial and Mental Illness: A Monograph Series,* available through the Superintendent of Documents, U.S. Government Printing Office, Washington, D.C.

COMPLEX FIGURE TEST (CFT)   *Andre Rey*

Assesses brain damage in individuals aged 16 years and over. Used to investigate perceptual organization and visual memory in brain-damaged subjects in clinical settings and research.

Figure consists of 18 areas (units), each of which is appraised for accuracy, as well as its relative position within the whole design. Materials consist of blank typewriter-size paper and five or six colored pens or pencils. The examinee's task is to copy a complex figure while the examiner notes the subject's copying sequence. Usually followed by one or more recall trials after design is removed. Scoring is based primarily on the sequence in which the lines of the figure are drawn, as well as omissions and interruptions of a line within the figure. An accuracy score, based on a unit scoring system, gives an overall evaluation and provides a measure of how well subject reproduces the design, regardless of sequence, for both copying and memory trial. Each unit receives a maximum of two points, and the maximum total score is 36 points (average adult = 32 points). Administration is untimed, but time to completion is recorded. Examiner required and evaluated. *Publisher:* SWETS Test Services (The Netherlands); U.S. distributor— SWETS North America, Inc.

COUPLE'S PRE-COUNSELING INVENTORY
Richard B. Stuart

Assesses problem areas of married couples beginning counseling. A comprehensive revision of The Marital Pre-Counseling Inventory used in counseling as the basis for planning specific therapeutic strategies and tactics.

Scales cover areas such as conflict management, personal moods, counseling goals, and power balance. An accompanying guide offers instructions on scoring, interpretation of interventions, and selected statistics on validity and reliability. Sets of 25 only (including guide) cost $16.95. *Publisher:* Research Press

DEROGATIS SEXUAL FUNCTIONING INVENTORY
(DSFI)   *Leonard R. Derogatis*

Measures and describes the quality of an adult's sexual functioning. Used for counseling.

Ten multiple-item, paper-pencil subtests assess the following factors related to an individual's sexual functioning: information, experience, drive, attitude, psychological symptoms, affects, gender role definition, fantasy, body image, sexual satisfaction. Scaled scores from each subtest are combined to derive an overall sexual functioning score. Norms available separately for men and women. Examiner required and evaluated. Administration is untimed and requires approximately 30-40 minutes. Ten reusable test booklets cost $30.00; 30 expendable test booklets, $33.00; 50 answer sheets, $9.00; 50 score/profile forms, $10.00; manual, $4.00. *Publisher:* Clinical Psychometric Research

DRAW-A-PERSON (DAP)   *William H. Urban*

Assesses processes and functions, such as developmental level and personality functioning, of individuals aged five years and older. Used in clinical evaluations as a diagnostic, therapeutic, and screening device.

A projective technique, utilizing freehand pencil and crayon drawings of a person. Examiner required and evaluated. Time varies. Not suitable for group use. Draw-A-Person Catalogue for Interpretative Analysis costs $12.40. For cost of drawing forms and protocol booklets contact publisher. *Publisher:* Western Psychological Services

DYADIC ADJUSTMENT SCALE   *Graham B. Spanier*

Assesses the quality of marriage and similar dyads; evaluates dyadic adjustment; and determines the degree of troublesome dyadic differences, interpersonal tensions and personal anxiety, dyadic satisfaction, dyadic cohesion, and consensus on matters of importance to dyadic functioning. Used with married or unmarried cohabiting couples as part of an interview schedule and in research as either a global assessment of marital functioning or for research in a particular area (i.e., using only that or those subscales that affect a specific research area).

A 32-item, paper-pencil instrument measuring four empirically verified components (subscales): dyadic satisfaction, dyadic consensus, dyadic cohesion, and affectional expression. Subjects rate 30 of the items on a five-, six-, or seven-point scale (e.g., always agree to always disagree, all of the time to never, extremely unhappy to perfect) and two items yes/no. Administration is untimed and requires only several minutes. Self-administered. Suitable for group use. Examiner evaluated. *Source:* (1976, February). *Journal of Marriage and the Family,* pp. 15-28.

157, 159-160   EMBEDDED FIGURES TEST (EFT)   *Herman A. Witkin*

Assesses cognitive styles and functions in perceptual tasks of older children, adolescents, and adults. Used in counseling and research.

A 12-item, verbal-manual test of perceptual processes, including field dependence-independence. Performance related to analytic ability, social behavior, body concept, and preferred defense mechanisms. Materials include cards with complex figures, cards with simple figures, and a stylus for tracing. A stopwatch is also required. Manual includes instructions and information for the children's (CEFT) and group (GEFT) versions, as well as for the EFT. Tasks require subject to locate and trace a previously seen simple figure within a larger complex figure. Two separate forms are available for test-retest. Examiner evaluated. Not suitable for group use. Administration is untimed and requires approximately 10-45 minutes. Test kit (including card sets, stylus, and 50 recording sheets) costs $13.00; manual, $5.25. *Publisher:* Consulting Psychologists Press, Inc.

60   EYSENCK PERSONALITY INVENTORY (EPI)   *H.F. Eysenck and S.B.G. Eysenck*

Measures extraversion and neuroticism, the two dimensions of personality that account for most personality deviance. Used for counseling and clinical evaluation of high-school and college students and adults, and research.

A 57-item, paper-pencil, yes-no inventory measuring two independent dimensions of personality: Extraversion-Introversion and Neuroticism-Stability. A falsification scale provides for detection of response distortion. Scores are provided for three scales: E-Extraversion, N-Neuroticism, and L-Lie. Available in equivalent Forms A and B for pre- and post-testing and Industrial Form A-1. College norms are presented in percentile form for Forms A and B separately and combined. Adult norms are presented for Form A-1.

Refer to page(s):	*Test Title*

Self-administered. Suitable for group use. Available in Spanish. Administration is untimed and requires approximately 10-15 minutes. Hand-scored. Computer-scoring available. Specimen set (including manual and one copy of all forms) costs $3.00; 25 inventories (specify Form A, B, or A-1), $3.75; keys, $2.00; manual, $2.00. *Publisher:* Educational and Industrial Testing Service

99

FULL RANGE PICTURE VOCABULARY TEST
(FRPV)   *R.B. Ammons and H.S. Ammons*

Assesses individual intelligence in individuals two years of age and older. May be used for testing special populations such as physically handicapped, uncooperative, aphasic, or very young subjects.

A 50-item test of verbal comprehension. Items are matched on 16 cards. Subject points to one of four drawings that best represents a particular word. Subject may also respond by indicating yes or no as the examiner points to each drawing. No reading or writing is required of the subject. Administration is untimed and requires approximately 5-10 minutes. Materials include two parallel forms, A and B, which use the same set of stimulus plates. Scoring is by hand key. Examiner required and evaluated. Not suitable for group use. Set of plates with instructions, norms, and sample answer sheets costs $15.00. *Publisher:* Psychological Test Specialists

144-145

FUNDAMENTAL INTERPERSONAL RELATIONS ORIENTATION-BEHAVIOR (FIRO-B)   *Will Schutz*

Measures both children's and adult's characteristic behavior toward other people. Used in individual and group psychotherapy, executive development programs, and as a measure of compatability in relationships.

A 54-item, paper-pencil test measuring six dimensions of behavior toward others: expressed inclusion, expressed control, expressed affection, wanted inclusion, wanted control, and wanted affection. Optional materials include the FIRO-BC, a form developed for use with children. May be self-administered, although an examiner is recommended to assist in the assessment/interpretation. Suitable for group use. Administration is untimed and requires approximately 20 minutes. Hand-scored. A sample set (including test key and self-scoring test with profile and interpretation) costs $2.25; 25 tests (specify FIRO-B or FIRO-BC), $4.00. *Publisher:* Consulting Psychologists Press, Inc.

69

GENERAL APTITUDE TEST BATTERY (GATB)
U.S. Employment Service

Measures vocational aptitudes of literate adolescents (from Grade 9) and adults who need help in choosing an occupation. Used for counseling.

A 434-item, paper-pencil test consisting of 284 multiple-choice, 150 dichotomous choice (same-different) questions and two dexterity form boards. Twelve subtests measure nine vocational aptitudes: General Learning Ability, Verbal, Numerical, Spatial, Form Perception, Clerical Perception, Motor Coordination, Finger Dexterity, and Manual Dexterity. Raw scores are converted to aptitude scores by use of conversion tables. Occupational Aptitude Patterns (OAP) indicate the aptitude requirements for groups of occupations. There are 66 OAPs covering 97% of all nonsupervisory occupations. The GATB is scored in terms of OAPs. A letter grade of "H"(High), "M"(Middle), or "L"(Low) is assigned for each OAP. Results of the battery indicate the individual's likelihood of being successful in the various occupations. Administration is untimed and requires approximately one hour. Examiner required. Suitable for group use. Available in Spanish and French. May be either hand- or computer-scored. Use in the U.S. must be authorized by State Employment Security Agencies, and in Canada by the Canadian Employment and Immigration Commission. Directions for administration and scoring are in the current edition of the *Manual of USES,* available from the Superintendent of Documents, U.S. Government Printing Office, Washington, D.C. 20402. 250 answer sheets (including 25 identification sheets) cost $20.00; scoring stencil, $5.50; computer scoring, $1.25. *Publisher:* U.S. Department of Labor

196

HALL OCCUPATIONAL ORIENTATION INVENTORY
(HALL)   *Lacy G. Hall and Randolph B. Tarrier*

Assesses students' (Grade 3-Adult) psychological needs that are correlated to worker traits and job characteristics identified by the U.S. Department of Labor, emphasizes the many possibilities for their future, and encourages the broadening of their perceptions of potentials and priorities. Used for career planning and vocational guidance.

A multiple-item, paper-pencil test, based on the personality need theory and adapted to the area of occupational choice. Focuses on 22 job and personality characteristics (e.g., creativity, aspiration, monetary concern, physical abilities). Available in 3 levels: 1) Intermediate (Grades 3-7), school-focused to complement awareness/development programs; 2) Young Adult/College (high-school and college students and professionals), special focus on jobs and occupations; 3) Adult Basic (reading-handicapped adults), world-of-work orientation and controlled readability levels. Level 2 is longer than 1 and 3, and separate inventory booklets, interpretive folders, and response sheets are available for each level. A carbon response sheet cumulates responses in clusters, facilitating students' understanding of response patterns. The HALL Career Education Reader, a supplement to the interpretive folder, details DOT occupations, which utilize many of the HALL scales according to relative education/training requirements. Self-administered and suitable for group use. Examiner evaluated. Administration is timed and requires 30-40 minutes. Hand- or computer-scored. Videotape training film and scoring service is also available. 20 inventory booklets cost $15.50; 20 interpretive folders, $9.00; 20 response sheets, $9.00; counselor's manual, $7.00. *Publisher:* Scholastic Testing Service

8, 69, 83, 84, 86,   HALSTEAD-REITAN NEUROPSYCHOLOGICAL TEST
106, 184, 198, 205   BATTERY FOR ADULTS   *Reitan Neuropsychological Laboratories and others*

Assesses neuropsychological functioning, brain function and dysfunction, in adults. Used for clinical evaluation.

A battery of tests, including the Halstead Neuropsychological Test Battery, the Wechsler Adult Intelligence Scale, the Trial Making Test, the Reitan-Indiana Aphasia Screening Test, the Minnesota Multiphasic Personality Inventory, and various tests of sensory-perceptual functions. Administration is untimed and varied. Examiner required and evaluated. Not suitable for group use. Materials include category test projection box with electric control mechanism and projector, 208 adult category slides in carousels, Tactual Performance Test (10-hole board, stand, 10 blocks), manual finger taper, tape cassette for speech-sounds perception test, Tactile Form Recognition Test, and manual for administration and scoring. Components may be ordered separately. Complete battery costs $1,106. *Publisher:* Reitan Neuropsychology Laboratory

92-93, 94   HAPTIC INTELLIGENCE SCALE   *Harriet C. Shurrager and Phil S. Shurrager*

Measures the intelligence of blind and partially sighted adults. Used as a substitute for or supplement to the Wechsler Adult Intelligence Scale.

Contains seven nonverbal (except for instructions) task assessments. The tests are Digit Symbol, Object Assembly, Block Design, Plan-of-Search, Object Completion, Pattern Board, and Bead Arithmetic. Wechsler's procedures were followed in establishing age categories and statistical treatment of the data. The test is timed and requires 90 minutes. Examiner required. Not for group use. Complete kit (including 25 record blanks, testing materials, manual, and carrying case) costs $475.00. *Publisher:* Stoelting Co.

Test Title

HETEROSEXUAL ATTITUDE SCALES (HAS)
C.H. Robinson and J.S. Annon

Assess adults' attitudinal or emotional responses to specific sexually related activities and experiences alone and in conjunction with a heterosexual partner. Used clinically to pinpoint sexual experiences and activities that may elicit positive or negative attitudes within the subject, clarify generalized positive and negative sexual attitudes, index relative emotional responses to stimuli for possible covert procedures, reveal relevant current or historical information, and order and select appropriate treatment strategies; measures changes in attitudinal responses to particular sexual activities as the result of specific therapeutic procedures.

Consists of two scales (one for males and one for females), each of which contain 77 items rated by subjects on a seven-point scale (dislike very much to like very much). Self-administered. Comparison between partners frequently suggests relevant therapeutic intervention points. Often used in conjunction with the Heterosexual Behavior Inventories. Examiner evaluated. Administration is untimed and varies. One-24 scales cost $.50 each; 100, $.35 each. *Publisher:* Enabling Systems, Inc.

HETEROSEXUAL BEHAVIOR ASSESSMENTS   *P.M. Bentler*

Assess heterosexual behaviors of adults. Used as a hierarchy in desensitization therapy or as an assessment of behavioral change resulting from therapy.

A self-report, Guttman-type scale consisting of 21 classes (long form) or 10 classes (short form). Two versions (one for males and one for females) are available. Number of items endorsed by subject provides the total score. Several items are specific to either male or female. Administration is untimed and varies. Examiner evaluated. *Source:* Author: available from P.M. Bentler, Dept. of Psychology, University of California, Los Angeles, California 90024.

HETEROSEXUAL BEHAVIOR INVENTORIES (HBI)
C.H. Robinson and J.S. Annon

Assess range of adults' sexual behavior repertoire and the frequency, if at all, in which they engage in specific sexual activities alone and with a heterosexual partner. Used clinically to ascertain subjects' heterosexual behavior repertoires and changes in their sexual behavior.

Consists of two inventories (one for males and one for females), each of which contain 77 items that subjects rate on a four-point scale according to the frequency that they engage in a particular behavior (i.e., 0 times, 1-3 times, 4-10 times, 11 or more times). Subjects check an additional column if they consider the

           Test Title

sexual activity to be a regular sexual behavior. Often used in conjunction with the Heterosexual Attitude Scales. Self-administered. Examiner evaluated. Administration is untimed and varies. One-24 inventories cost $.50 each; 100, $.35 each. *Publisher:* Enabling Systems, Inc.

     HISKEY-NEBRASKA TEST OF LEARNING APTITUDE
Marshall S. Hiskey

Evaluates learning potential of deaf children (ages 2½-18½) and those with hearing, speech or language handicaps. Used to establish how deaf individuals compare with those who can hear.

A battery of 11 subtests measures visual-motor coordination, sequential memory, visual retention or stimuli in a series, visual discrimination and matching. The tests are Bead Patterns, Memory for Color, Picture Identification, Picture Association, Paper Folding Patterns, Visual Attention Span, Block Patterns, Completion of Drawings, Memory for Digits, Puzzle Block Picture Analogies, and Spatial Reasoning. The test is untimed and requires approximately 50-60 minutes. Scales have norms for comparing hearing and deaf children. Examiner required and evaluated. Not suitable for group use. Complete set (including all materials, manual, and record forms) costs $96.00. *Publisher:* The Hiskey-Nebraska Test

     HOLTZMAN INKBLOT TECHNIQUE (HIT)   *W.H. Holtzman*

Assesses individual personality of subjects aged 5 years-adult. Used for diagnosis and therapy planning.

A 45-item projective measure of personality. Items are inkblots to which examinee gives one response each. Some inkblots are asymmetric and some are in one color other than black. An objective scoring system has been developed. Materials include two alternative and equivalent forms, A and B, for a total of 90 stimulus cards. Examiner required and evaluated. Not suitable for group use. Untimed. Complete set (including 45 inkblots, 25 record forms with summary sheets, scoring guide) of Form A or B costs $137.50; Forms A & B combined, $260.00; monograph, $40.00. *Publisher:* The Psychological Corporation

     ILLNESS BEHAVIOR QUESTIONNAIRE   *Issy Pilowsky and Neil Spence*

Assesses patients' attitudes, ideas, affects, and attributions relevant in relation to illness and measures their responses to their health status. Used in psychiatric in-patient settings (including patients with somatic disease), in general hospitals to delineate the psychosocial dimension of physical disease in patients with a mixture of problems, in clinical settings as a screening instrument, and in research to assess attitudes to illness and related areas of patients with physical complaints.

A 62-item, self-report, yes/no questionnaire consisting of seven scales (General Hypochondriasis, Disease Conviction, Psychological vs. Somatic, Focusing, Affective Inhibition, Affective Disturbance, Denial, and Irritability), two second-order factors (Affective State and Disease Affirmation) that combine various scale scores, a discriminant function (likelihood of a conversion reaction), and the Whiteley Index (likelihood of hypochondriacal syndrome). A parallel Form B is available for use in nonclinical settings. Translations into most major languages. Administration is untimed and usually requires less than 15 minutes. Hand-scored. Examiner evaluated. *Source:* (1984). *General Hospital Psychiatry,* 6, 123-130; direct reprint requests to Professor I. Pilowsky, The University of Adelaide, Royal Adelaide Hospital, Adelaide, South Australia 5000.

133

INDEX OF MARITAL SATISFACTION (IMS)   *W.W. Hudson*

Measures degree or magnitude of discord or dissatisfaction (but not source or cause) that adult partners experience with the interpersonal component of their relationship. Used to monitor, guide, and evaluate clinical treatment.

A self-rating, 25-item scale positively and negatively worded. Part of a set of seven short-form measurement scales, the Clinical Measurement Package. Administration is untimed and varies. Examiner evaluated. *Source:* Author: available from W.W. Hudson, School of Social Work, University of Hawaii, Honolulu, Hawaii 96822.

133

INDEX OF SEXUAL SATISFACTION (ISS)   *W.W. Hudson*

Measures degree or magnitude of discord or dissatisfaction (but not source or cause) that adult partners experience with the sexual component of their relationship. Used to monitor, guide, and evaluate clinical treatment.

A self-rating, 25-item scale, both positively and negatively worded. Part of a set of seven short-form measurement scales, the Clinical Measurement Package. Administration is untimed and varies. Examiner evaluated. *Source:* Author: available from W.W. Hudson, School of Social Work, University of Hawaii, Honolulu, Hawaii 96822.

69

THE INTEREST CHECK LIST (ICL)
U.S. Department of Labor

Determines an individual's employment interests. Used as a guide to vocational counseling and self-assessment of adults.

A 210-item, paper-pencil checklist of sample tasks that have

Refer to page(s):	*Test Title*

been keyed to the work groups listed in the *Guide for Occupational Exploration*. Permits the evaluation of applicants' likes and dislikes, leading to an understanding of why they are interested in the subjects indicated. Especially useful for persons who have no firmly stated interests or who are not aware of the variety of existing occupations. Self-administered. Suitable for group use. Administration is untimed and requires approximately 20 minutes. Handscored. Available in Spanish. May be acquired through State Employment agencies only. *Publisher:* U.S. Department of Labor

208   INTERDISCIPLINARY FITNESS INTERVIEW (IFI)
Stephen L. Golding, Ronald Roesch, and Jan Schreiber

Assesses defendant's behavioral, emotional, communicative, and cognitive capacities, covering domains of both psychopathology and law from the perspective that psychiatric symptoms are deemed to be relevant only if they interfere with the defendant's participation in his or her specific trial situation. Used as an alternative to The Competency Screening Test (CST) and The Competency to Stand Trial Assessment Instrument (CAI) by legal experts in collaboration with mental health professionals to provide the basis for a structured interview and rating system to reach decisions about a defendant's competency. Used in research.

Scale consists of three major sections: 1) legal issues, 2) psychopathological issues, and 3) overall evaluation by each examiner separately. *Source:* (1984). *Law and Human Behavior, 8*(3, 4), 331-334.

133   AN INVENTORY OF MARITAL CONFLICTS   *D.H. Olson and R.G. Ryder*

Obtains five interaction data on conflict resolution and decision-making process in couples. Used for research and diagnostic purposes and possible evaluation of process change resulting from treatment.

Consists of 18 vignettes (12 conflict items and six nonconflict items) describing various types of marital conflicts usually relevant to couples. On each item, subject responds to four specific questions concerning conflict (who is primarily responsible, acceptance or rejection of suggested way to resolve it, if it existed previously, and if other couples experience the same). Couples individually respond on separate forms, after which they discuss each conflict situation and jointly decide who is primarily responsible and which of two ways best resolve it. Discussion is taped (30 minutes or less), coded on 29 categories in an interaction coding system objectively measuring the interaction process, and analyzed by computer. Data are also obtained from the individual or joint response forms. Administration is untimed and varies. Examiner evaluated. *Source:*

Refer to page(s):	*Test Title*

Author: available from D.H. Olson, 32-28 Birchtree Lane, Silver Springs, Maryland 20906.

145   IRRATIONAL BELIEFS TEST   *R.G. Jones*

Measures personality, interests, and attitudes. Used in clinical settings for assessment, diagnosis, and treatment and in industrial, personal, marriage, and family counseling.

Incorporates empirical relationships between scales and other conditions such as stress, pathology, personality, motivation, organization roles, and decision styles. Provides scores and a narrative report based on a factor-analytic model and three broad dimensions derived from Ellis' Rational Emotive Therapy. Examiner required and evaluated (sales restricted to qualified professionals). Mail-in service costs $12.00. *Publisher:* Test Systems International

174, 175, 176   JENKINS ACTIVITY SURVEY   *C. David Jenkins*

Identifies adults with the "coronary-prone behavior pattern" or "Type A" behavior. Used for research and clinical screening.

A 52-item, paper-pencil test of several aspects of Type A behavior, including speed and impatience, job involvement and hard driving, and competitive. Items include questions about behavior found useful in medical diagnosis. Scores associated with future risk of heart disease. Untimed. Self-administered. Suitable for group use. Scoring service available. Twenty-five questionnaires (with scoring service fact sheets) cost $21.00; 10 questionnaires (with prepaid scoring certificates), $120.00; manual, $8.00. *Publisher:* The Psychological Corporation

94, 97   KAHN INTELLIGENCE TEST (KIT:EXP): A CULTURE-MINIMIZED EXPERIENCE   *T.C. Kahn*

Assesses individual intelligence of subjects from infant to adult. Used for the blind, deaf, or those from different educational and cultural backgrounds.

A performance measure of several aspects of intelligence, including concept formation, recall, and motor coordination. Special scale for assessment of intelligence with blind subjects is included. Requires no reading, writing, or verbal knowledge. Uses same materials as the Kahn Test of Symbol Arrangement (KTSA): 16 plastic objects and a cloth strip containing 15 equally sized segments. Manual contains instructions on obtaining mental age, IQ, or developmental level. For use only by psychologists, psychiatrists, counselors, and others with comparable training. Administration is untimed and requires approximately 15 minutes. Examiner required and evaluated. Not suitable for group use. Hand scored. Complete set (including plastic objects, felt strip, storage box, manual, and 50 copies of record sheets) costs $52.00. *Publisher:* Psychological Test Specialists

97   KOHS BLOCK DESIGN TEST   *S. C. Kohs*

Measures intelligence for persons with a mental age of 3-19 years. Used in testing individuals who have language and hearing handicaps, as well as the disadvantaged and those who do not speak English.

A multiple-item, task-assessment test consisting of 17 cards containing colored designs and 16 colored blocks, which the subject uses to duplicate the designs on the cards. Performance is evaluated for Attention, Adaptation, and Auto-Criticism. Results are claimed to be less affected by school training than the Binet tests. This test is also included in the Merrill-Palmer and Arthur Performance Scales. Administration is timed and requires up to 40 minutes. Examiner required and evaluated. Suitable for group use. Complete kit (including blocks, cards, manual, and 50 record blanks) costs $55.00. *Publisher:* Stoelting Co.

195   KUDER GENERAL INTEREST SURVEY, FORM E
             Frederic Kuder

Assesses students' preferences for various activities related to ten general interest areas. Used with students (Grades 6-12) to guide their educational planning toward future employment.

A 168-item, paper-pencil test measuring preferences in ten general interest areas: outdoor, mechanical, scientific, computational, persuasive, artistic, literary, musical, social science, and clerical. Scoring and profile construction can be done by student. Sixth-grade reading level required. Self-administered. Suitable for group use. Administration is untimed and takes approximately 30-40 minutes. May be scored by hand or machine. A specimen set costs $6.25; complete set (including materials and scoring for 25 students), $26.50. No charge for general manual if requested when ordering. *Publisher:* Science Research Associates, Inc.

195   KUDER OCCUPATIONAL INTEREST SURVEY, FORM DD
             (KOIS)   *Frederic Kuder*

Measures how an individual's interests compare with those of satisfied workers or students in a number of occupational fields. Used with high-school and college students (Grades 11-UP) and adults for career planning, vocational guidance, and academic counseling.

A 100-item, paper-pencil inventory assessing subjects' interests in areas related to occupational fields and educational majors. Each item lists three activities, and subjects indicate which they like best and which they like least. Compares subjects' interests with those of satisfied workers in 126 specific occupational groups and satisfied students in 48 college major groups. All respondents receive scores on all scales. The report of scores lists scores on occupational and college major scales separately, in rank order for each student. The interpretive leaflet helps subjects to understand and use scores. Optional interpretive guides include *Expanding Your Future* (interpretation and use of scores for students) and *Counseling with the Kuder Occupational Interest Survey Form DD* (for counselors). Sixth-grade reading level required. Self-administered. Suitable for group use. Administration is timed and requires 30-40 minutes. Computer scoring available. A specimen set (including survey booklet, interpretive leaflet, general manual, and scoring for one individual) costs $6.50; materials and scoring for 20 persons, $66.00. No charge for general manual if requested when ordering. *Publisher:* Science Research Associates, Inc.

69, 184

KUDER PREFERENCE RECORD, VOCATIONAL, FORM CP   *Frederic Kuder*

Evaluates occupational interests of students and adults. Used in vocational counseling and employee screening and placement. Identifies reading subject areas of special interest.

The 168-item paper-pencil test measures interests in ten occupational areas: outdoor, mechanical, scientific, computational, persuasive, artistic, literary, musical, social science, and clerical. Subject uses pin to indicate a "most liked" and "least liked" activity for each group of three activities. High school reading level required. Self-administered and scoring is by hand key. Suitable for group use. Specimen set is $6.30; no charge for manual if requested when ordering. *Publisher:* Science Research Associates, Inc.

196-197

LEARNING STYLES INVENTORY (LSI)   *Joseph S. Renzulli and Linda H. Smith*

Assesses the methods or ways through which students (Grades 4-12) prefer to go about learning subject matter content. Used to assist teachers in individualizing the instructional process.

A 65-item, paper-pencil inventory assessing student attitudes toward nine modes of instruction: projects, drill and recitation, peer teaching, discussion, teaching games, independent study, programmed instruction, lecture, and stimulation. Classroom learning experiences associated with the modes are described, and students indicate their reactions to each activity along a five-point scale, ranging from "very unpleasant" to "very pleasant." A teacher form is included. Teachers respond to items that parallel those of the student form in terms of how frequently each activity occurs in the classroom. The resulting profile of instructional styles can be compared to individual student preferences to facilitate a closer match between how teachers instruct and the styles to which stu-

Test Title

dents respond most favorably. Administration is untimed and varies. Examiner required. Suitable for group use. All forms are prepared on optical scanning sheets and are computer scored. A specimen set (including one teacher form and one student form) costs $7.50; class set (30 student forms, one teacher form, and computer scoring), $18.50. *Publisher:* Creative Learning Press, Inc.

LEISURE ACTIVITIES BLANK (LAB)   *George McKechnie*

Assesses an adult's past and future leisure and recreation activities. Used for research and counseling.

A 120-item, paper-pencil test of recreational time use. Items are a list of activities to which respondents indicate the extent of past participation and expected future participation. Responses are scored on six Past Scales: Mechanics, Crafts, Intellectual, Slow Living, Sports, and Glamor Sports; and eight Future Scales: Adventure, Mechanics, Crafts, Easy Living, Intellectual, Ego-Recognition, Slow Living, and Clean Living. There are two validity scales. Self-administered. Suitable for group use. Administration is untimed and requires approximately 15-20 minutes. Hand-scored. A specimen set (no key) costs $5.75; manual, $5.25; 25 tests, $3.50; 25 profiles, $3.00; plastic scoring stencils, $18.50. *Publisher:* Consulting Psychologists Press, Inc.

LEITER INTERNATIONAL PERFORMANCE SCALE
(LIPS)   *Russell G. Leiter*

Measures intelligence and mental age for all individuals 2-18 years old including the deaf, cerebral palsied, non-English speaking, and culturally disadvantaged in a nonverbal task assessment test.

The subject is required to match blocks with corresponding characteristic strips positioned in a sturdy wooden frame. The difficulty of the task increases at each level. The categories measured are: Concretistics (matching of specific relationships), Symbolic Transformation (judging relationships between two events), Quantitative Discriminations, Spatial Imagery, Genus Matching, Progression Discriminations, and Immediate Recall. Test materials include three trays of blocks and strips that make up 54 subtests. Tray 1 covers years 2-7, Tray 2 covers years 8-12 and Tray 3 covers years 13-17. Instructions for all age levels are delivered by easily learned pantomime. Testing time is approximately 45 minutes. The LIPS yields Mental Age and I.Q. The Binet-type year scale has four tests at each year level from year II through year XVI and six tests at year XVII. Examiner required and evaluated. The test kit (including 3 trays, wooden frame, carrying case, 100 record cards, and manual) costs $525.00. *Publisher:* Stoelting Co.

Test Title

LINCOLN-OSERETSKY MOTOR DEVELOPMENT
SCALE   *William Sloan*

Measures motor development of children aged 6-14 years. Used to supplement information obtained from other techniques concerning intellectual, social, emotional, and physical development.

A 36-item test, covering the areas of static coordination; dynamic coordination; speed of movement and asynkinesia (finger dexterity); eye-hand coordination; and gross activity of hands, arms, legs, and trunk. Both unilateral and bilateral tasks are involved. Items, arranged in order of difficulty, include tasks such as walking backwards, touching fingertips, making a ball, putting matchsticks in a box, balancing a rod vertically, and balancing on tiptoe. The manual includes a complete analysis of test results obtained from boys and girls aged 6-14 years for each item of the scale, percentages passing each item at each age level, correlation of item-scores with age, percentile norms of both sexes (separately and combined), and odd-even reliability for boys and girls. Examiner required and evaluated. Untimed. Not suitable for group use. A complete kit (including all test materials, 50 record blanks, and manual) costs $105.50. *Publisher:* Stoelting Co.

LURIA-NEBRASKA NEUROPSYCHOLOGICAL BATTERY *Charles J. Golden, Thomas A. Hammeke, and Arnold D. Purisch*

Assesses a broad range of neuropsychological functions for persons age 15 and older. Used to diagnose specific cerebral dysfunction and to select and assess rehabilitation programs.

A verbal, observational test, consisting of two forms: Form I (269 items) and Form II (279 items). Both forms assess a wide range of cognitive functions in the following scales: Motor, Rhythm, Tactile, Visual, Preceptive Speech, Expressive Speech, Writing, Reading, Arithmetic, Memory, Intellectual, Pathognomonic, Left Hemisphere, and Right Hemisphere. Form II contains the additional scale, Intermediate-Term Memory. The battery ($1\frac{1}{2}$-$2\frac{1}{2}$ hours in duration) has the ability to diagnose the presence of cerebral dysfunction, as well as to determine lateralization and localization. Form I may be computer scored or hand keyed. Form II is scored by computer only. Examiner required. Not for group use. The test materials include six stimulus cards, one tape cassette, and a few commonly available items such as a comb, a quarter, and a stopwatch. A manual provides instructions for administering the test, evidence of reliability and validity, interpretive guides, and copies of the *Administration and Scoring Booklet* and the *Patient Response Booklet*. The *Administration and Scoring Booklet* includes the Profile Form and Computation of Critical Level Tables. It is used to record all scores during the administration and provides the verbal instructions to be read to the patient. *The Patient Re-*

sponse Booklet is provided for those items requiring written answers. Complete kit for both forms consists of a manual, all stimulus cards, tape cassette, 100 administration and scoring booklets, and two computer-scored answer sheets. Form I costs $205.00; Form II costs $210. *Publisher:* Western Psychological Services

84, 86   LURIA'S NEUROPSYCHOLOGICAL INVESTIGATION
Anne-Lise Christensen

Diagnoses type and severity of brain injury as a basis for planning rehabilitational measures for brain-damaged adults.

Oral response and task assessment test that begins with a structure for preliminary conversation with the patient and goes on to measure the following neurological areas: motor functions, acoustico-motor organization, higher cutaneous and kinesthetic functions, higher visual functions, impressive speech, expressive speech, writing and reading, arithmetical skill, mnestic processes, and intellectual processes. Examiner required and evaluated. Not suitable for group use. Untimed. Materials include a set of cards, manual, and text. Contact distributor for cost. *Publisher:* Munksgaard—distributed by The Australian Council for Education Research Limited

133   THE MARITAL COMMUNICATIONS INVENTORY
Millard F. Bienvenu, Sr.

Assesses communication of adults in a troubled marriage and identifies communication problems. Used to stimulate group discussion in marriage enrichment programs and increases awareness of positive and negative communication patterns.

A 46-item, paper-pencil questionnaire, covering areas of feelings, emotions, economics, communication patterns, and behaviors, plus an optional socioeconomic survey. Separate forms for male and female. Both husband and wife answer questions by indicating frequency of communication in each area. Self-administered. Examiner evaluated. Suitable for group use. Hand-scored. A specimen set (including manual, one male and one female form, and key) costs $2.00; manual, $2.00; 10 questionnaire forms (5 male, 5 female), $5.00. *Publisher:* Family Life Publications, Inc.

143   MARITAL SATISFACTION INVENTORY (MSI)
Douglas K. Snyder

Identifies separately for each spouse the nature and extent of marital distress. Used in marital and family counseling.

A 280-item (239 for couples with no children), paper-pencil, true-false test, providing information from each spouse concerning nine basic measured dimensions of their marriage: affective communication, problem solving communication, time together, disagreement about finances, sexual dissatisfaction, role orientation, family history of distress, dissatisfaction with children, and conflict over childrearing. A validity scale and a global distress scale that measures each individual's overall dissatisfaction with the marriage are also included. After answer sheets are scored, results of both spouses are recorded on the same profile, graphically identifying the areas of marital distress. Each spouse's scores can be both individually evaluated and directly compared, facilitating diagnostic and intervention procedures. Group mean profiles (with case illustrations) for each sex are provided for couples seeking general marital therapy or divorce, with specific sexual dysfunctions or distress concerning childrearing, and physically abused wives. Administration is untimed and requires approximately 30-40 minutes. Hand-scored; computer scoring available. A complete kit (including manual, 50 administration reusable booklets, 500 answer sheets, 500 profile forms, one set of scoring keys, and two computer-scored answer sheets) costs $60.00. *Publisher:* Western Psychological Services

143   MARITAL STATUS INVENTORY (MSI)   *D. Russell Crane and D. Eugene Mead*

Assesses thoughts and actions toward divorce and evaluates a couple's divorce potential. Used in counseling to predict divorce or nondivorce outcome, diagnose relationships, and select style, pace, and type of treatment (e.g., divorce adjustment vs. marital therapy), and for research purposes.

A 14-question, true/false, self-report scale inquiring into specific thoughts and behaviors believed to represent progressive steps toward divorce. Scores range from 0 to 14, with higher scores indicating greater marital instability. Examiner evaluated. Suitable for group use. Administration is untimed and varies. *Source:* (1984). *Journal of Marital and Family Therapy, 10,* 305-312.

117, 122   McGILL PAIN QUESTIONNAIRE   *Ronald Melzack and W.S. Torgerson*

Measures pain in individual patients. Used in clinical evaluation as an aid in diagnosis and prognosis, and as a possible experimental tool for the study of anesthetic and analgesic drug effects on pain experience.

A brief 20-item questionnaire containing a checklist of words that describe pain (e.g., pulsing, tender, fearful, numb), a drawing of the human figure, a pain index describing intensity of pain and rated on a six-point scale from 0 (no pain) to 5 (excruciating), a frequency checklist of pain (e.g., brief, periodic, constant), and space for examiner's notations. Administration is untimed and varies. Examiner required and evaluated. Can be adapted to computer analysis. Not suitable for group use. *Source:* (1971). *Anesthe-*

siology, 34(1), pp. 50-59. Available from Ronald Melzack, Professor, Psychology Dept., McGill University, 1265 Dr Penfield Ave., Montreal, Quebec H3A 1B1, Canada.

144   MEYERS-BRIGGS TYPE INDICATOR (MBTI)   *Isabel Briggs Meyers and Katherine C. Briggs*

Measures personality dispositions and interests of adolescents (Grades 9-12) and adults, based on Jung's theory of types. Used in personal, vocational, and marital counseling; executive development programs; and personality research.

A paper-pencil test of four bipolar aspects of personality: Introversion-Extroversion, Sensing-Intuition, Thinking-Feeling, and Judging-Perceptive. Subjects are classified as one of two types on each scale. Two forms are available: Form F (166 items) and Form G (126 items) that eliminates 40 items not scored on the four standard scales. Heavily influenced by Jungian theories of personality types and the ways in which these types express their personality traits through perceptions, judgments, interests, values, and motivations. A booklet, *Introduction to Type,* describes each type and includes information on vocations and interpretation. A theoretical background in dynamic psychology is helpful in maximizing the benefits of research compiled for the test. Self-administered. Administration is untimed and takes approximately 20-30 minutes. Suitable for group use. Hand-scored. Counselor's kit (specify Form F or G), which includes manual, *Introduction to Type,* five tests, and 25 answer sheets and report forms, costs $30.00. *Publisher:* Consulting Psychologists Press, Inc.

60   MILLON BEHAVIORAL HEALTH INVENTORY (MBHI)
                  Theodore Millon, Catherine Green, and Robert B. Meagher

Assesses attitudes of physically ill adults (aged 18 years and up) toward daily stress factors and health-care personnel. Used for clinical evaluation of medical patients for possible psychosomatic complications.

A 150-item, paper-pencil, true-false inventory with scales covering eight basic coping styles (e.g., cooperation), six psychogenic attitudes (e.g., chronic tension), three psychosomatic correlatives (e.g., allergic inclinations), and three prognostic indexes (e.g., pain treatment responsivity). Examiners must be experienced in the use of clinical tests. Self-administered. Suitable for group use. Administration is untimed and requires approximately 20 minutes. Scoring and interpretation available from NCS via mail-in, Arion II, and MICROTEST (IBM PC or PC/XT) to administer via pencil and paper, then score/report with microcomputer. A specimen set (including interpretive answer sheet with test items and manual) costs $17.50; 1-4 mail-in interpretive prepaid answer sheets, including interpretive report, $15.50 each; 1-3 packages of Arion II answer sheets, $7.50 each; 1-4 Arion II scores/reports per month, $15.50 each; ten MICROTEST assessment software, including test items, scoring, and reporting, $12.00 per test; 25 MICROTEST answer sheets, $7.50. *Publisher:* NCS Professional Assessment Services

13, 60

MILLON CLINICAL MULTIAXIAL INVENTORY (MCMI)   *Theodore Millon*

Diagnoses emotionally disturbed adults (age 18 years and older). Used only with psychiatric, emotionally disturbed populations to screen individuals who may require more intensive clinical evaluation and treatment and to evaluate those who have psychological or psychiatric difficulties.

A 175-item, paper-pencil, true-false test covering three categories: eight basic personality patterns (DSM-III, Axis II) reflecting a patient's lifelong traits existing prior to the behavioral dysfunctions, three pathological personality disorders (DSM-III, Axis II) reflecting chronic or severe abnormalities, and nine clinical symptom syndromes (DSM-III, Axis I) describing episodes or states in which active pathological processes are clearly evidenced. Examiner must be experienced in the use of clinical tests. Self-administered. Suitable for group use. Administration is untimed and requires approximately 25 minutes. Scoring and interpretation available from NCS via mail-in, Arion II, and MICROTEST (IBM PC or PC/XT) to administer via pencil and paper, then score/report with microcomputer. A specimen set (including interpretive answer sheet with test items and manual) costs $17.75; 25 reusable hand-scoring test booklets, $6.00; 25 hand-scored answer sheets, $5.00; answer keys (21 transparent overlays) with manual, $36.00; 1-4 mail-in profile prepaid answer sheets, including profile report, $5.85 each; 1-3 packages of Arion II answer sheets, $7.50 each; 1-4 Arion II scores/reports per month, $5.85 each; ten MICROTEST assessment software, including test items, scoring, and reporting, $4.35 per test; 25 MICROTEST answer sheets, $7.50. *Publisher:* NCS Professional Assessment Services

80

MINI-MENTAL STATE   *Marshall F. Folstein, Susan E. Folstein, and Paul R. McHugh*

Assesses cognitive function, disturbance, and change and evaluates severity of cognitive impairment. Used in clinical settings for serial and routine testing, by professionals (e.g., lawyers, judges, social workers) to estimate subject's competency, and in teaching residents a method of cognitive assessment.

A brief examination consisting of eleven questions and concentrating only on cognitive aspects of mental functions (excludes those concerning mood, abnormal mental experiences, and form of thinking). Divided into two sections: one (requiring only vocal responses) covering orientation, memory, and attention (maximum

Refer to page(s):	*Test Title*

score is 21), and a second score covering ability to name, follow verbal and written commands, write a sentence spontaneously, and copy a complex polygon (maximum score is nine). Administration is untimed and requires approximately 5-10 minutes. Examiner required. *Source:* (1975). *Journal of Psychiatric Research, 12,* 189-198.

196   MINNESOTA IMPORTANCE QUESTIONNAIRE
                   (MIQ)   *Work Adjustment Project*

Measures vocational needs of adults and relates them to occupational reinforcers. Used to assess need-reinforcer correspondence as a supplement to standard measures of occupational interests and abilities.

A multiple-item, paper-pencil inventory in two forms: Paired Form (102 items) that presents pairs of vocational needs statements, to which examinees indicate the more important need in each pair, and the Ranked Form (42 items) that presents vocational need statements in groups of five, which examinees rate according to importance for each group. Both forms measure the need dimensions of ability, utilization, achievement, activity, advancement, authority, company policies and practices, compensation, coworkers, creativity, independence, moral values, recognition, responsibility, security, social service, social status, supervision-human relations, supervision-technical, variety, and working conditions. Provided for each examinee is a computer-generated profile and interpretation that includes scores on each dimension (Ranked Form also includes Autonomy Scale) in the form of a profile, correspondence of examinee's need pattern to Occupational Reinforcer Patterns (ORPs), lists (50 each) of occupations with ORPs most similar and least similar to the examinee's MIQ profile, predictions of job satisfaction for each listed occupation, references for further information, a validity score, and an error factor for each score. Self-administered with clinical supervision. Restricted to APA members. Suitable for group use. Available in Spanish and French. Computer-scored. Administration is untimed and varies. For each form (specify Ranked or Paired) 10-99 booklets cost $.40 each; 10-499 answer sheets, $.05 each; computer scoring, $1.30 per report. Technical manual available at no charge to qualified users. *Publisher:* Vocational Psychology Research, University of Minnesota

7, 14, 36, 37, 38,   THE MINNESOTA MULTIPHASIC PERSONALITY
40, 42, 57-59, 67,   INVENTORY: THE INDIVIDUAL FORM (MMPI)
68, 69, 71, 84, 93,   *Starke R. Hathaway and Charnley McKinley*
94, 97, 98, 107,
108, 109, 110, 118,   Assesses individual personality. Used for clinical diagnosis
119, 121, 122, 142,   and research on psychopathology.
                          The Inventory is available in four different administration

formats. The Group Form consists of 566 true-false items written at a 6th-grade reading level. Form R covers 14 basic scales with the first 399 test items. The Card Form consists of 550 statements which the examinee sorts in three groups—true, false, or cannot say. The Audiocassette Version contains the entire Group Form on audio tape; responses are recorded on Group Form answer sheets.

The scales included on the hand-scored version cover: L (Lie), F (Infrequency), K (Defensiveness), Hs (Hypochondriasis), D (Depression), Hy (Hysteria), Pd (Psychopathic Deviate), Mf (Masculinity-Femininity), Pa (Paranoia), Pt (Psychasthenia), Sc (Schizophrenia), Ma (Hypomania), Si (Social Introversion), A (Anxiety), R (Depression), Es (Ego Strength) and MAC (Mac-Andrew Addiction). Additional scales are available with computer scoring. Test time is 45-90 minutes. Examiner required and evaluated. Available in 45 languages. For cost information and various services/reports write to distributor. *Publisher:* University of Minnesota Press—Distributed by NCS Professional Assessment Services

MINNESOTA RATE OF MANIPULATION TESTS
Employment Stabilization Research Institute, University of Minnesota

Measures finger-hand-arm dexterity. Used for employee selection for jobs requiring manual dexterity, and in vocational and rehabilitation training programs.

The five test battery measures: Placing, Turning, Displacing, One Hand Turning and Placing, and Two Hand Turning and Placing. Materials consist of two test boards, each with 60 round holes in four rows, and 60 round blocks, painted orange on the top half and yellow on the lower half. Two blocks are transferred from one board to the other, being turned and moved in various ways. The subject is then instructed to transfer all pegs back to the board using only one hand. In the turning test, the pegs are left in the board and the subject removes each block one at a time with one hand, turns it over, transfers it to the free hand and replaces it in the same position on the board. All tests are timed (10 minutes each) and repeated for four complete trials. The Displacing and Turning Tests are suitable for use with the blind. Examiner required and evaluated. Suitable for group use. Blocks, 50 individual record forms, two test boards, and a manual are included in a vinyl carrying case for $181.00. *Publisher:* American Guidance Service

MINNESOTA TEST FOR DIFFERENTIAL DIAGNOSIS OF APHASIA *Mildred Schuell*

Assesses adults' language disturbance due to brain damage. Used as an aid in classifying patients and determining prognosis.

Subject responds to questions and cards presented by the

examiner, who then evaluates disturbances in hearing, seeing, and reading; speech and language; visuomotor and writing; and disturbances of numerical relationships and arithmetic processes. Examiner required and evaluated. May be administered over several sessions, depending on patient's fatigue. Administration is open-ended and untimed. Not suitable for group use. Hand-scored. Manual costs $2.00; two packets of cards, $10.00; 25 tests, $6.00; Differential Diagnosis of Aphasia with the Minnesota test, $7.95. *Publisher:* University of Minnesota Press

132   MOSHER FORCED-CHOICE GUILT INVENTORY
(FCGI)   *D.L. Mosher*

Assesses three separate aspects of guilt: sex guilt (SG), hostility guilt (HG), and morality guilt (MG). Used to measure adults' personality disposition of guilt rather than the feeling state.

A self-report inventory consisting of pairs of answers to a series of incomplete sentence stems. Two available versions: Male (150 items) and Female (78 items). Subjects select one of two answers that best applies to them. Administration is untimed and varies. Examiner evaluated. *Source:* Author: available from D.L. Mosher, Department of Psychology, University of Connecticut, Storrs, Connecticut 06268.

13, 67, 68   MULTIPLE AFFECT ADJECTIVE CHECK LIST
(MAACL)   *Marvin Zuckerman and Bernard Lubin*

Measures anxiety, depression, and hostility in high school and college students and adults. Used for clinical evaluation and research applications.

A 132-item, paper-pencil inventory of adjectives. Available in three forms: Today Form, measuring current affect states with instructions to check those adjectives that describe how the subject feels at the time of testing; In-General Form, instructing subjects to check those adjectives that describe a more general state of their feelings; a computer-scored form, allowing for verbally presented instructional sets and providing scores for A-Anxiety, D-Depression, and H-Hostility. The Today Form is sensitive to changes in affect resulting from examination anxiety among college students, perceptual isolation, therapy sessions, combat training, and intake of alcohol. College student and adult job applicant norms are presented in the form of T-Score equivalents. Means and standard deviations are presented for a variety of clinical groups and experimental situations. Self-administered. Examiner scored. Administration is untimed and requires approximately five minutes for each form. Suitable for group use. Hand-scored; computer scoring available. A specimen set (including manual and one copy of all forms) costs $3.25; 25 check lists (specify Today or In-General Form), $3.75; 100 computer check lists (IBM 1231), $14.50; 25

recording forms, $2.00; keys, $2.00; manual, $2.00. *Publisher:* Educational and Industrial Testing Service

NEGATIVE ATTITUDES TOWARD MASTURBATION SCALE *P.R. Abramson and D.L. Mosher*

Assesses attitudes toward masturbation. Used with normal adults, patients with sexual dysfunctions, and psychiatric populations to determine attitudes toward masturbation.

A self-report, 30-item scale rated on five points (strongly agree to strongly disagree). Yields three factors (positive attitude, false beliefs about the harmful nature, and personally experienced negative affects) associated with masturbation. Administration is untimed and varies. Examiner evaluated. *Source:* Abramson, P.R., & Mosher, D.L. (1975). Development of a measure of negative attitudes toward masturbation. *Journal of Consulting Clinical Psychology, 43,* 485.

NON-LANGUAGE MULTI-MENTAL TEST *E.L. Terman, W.A. McCall, and J. Lorge*

Measures basic intelligence of illiterate or language-handicapped individuals (Grade 2 and above), including those who do not speak English or who are deaf. Used to determine linguistic handicaps.

A multiple-item picture test of abstract thinking and relationships of pictorial symbols. Adaptable for either simple verbal or pantomime directions. Administration is flexible. Materials include Forms A and B (verbal or pantomime) with instructions. Administration is untimed and requires approximately 30 minutes. Examiner required. Suitable for group use. Hand scored. Specimen test costs $4.00; 35 tests (Form A or B), $15.00. *Publisher:* Institute of Psychological Research, Inc.

PARENTING STRESS INDEX (PSI) *Richard R. Abidin*

Assesses stressor, stress reaction, and parent-child interaction problems; measures relative magnitude of stress in a parent-child system, and identifies sources of stress by administration to parents (especially with target children aged three years and younger) with a minimum fifth-grade reading level. Used in medical settings, such as private practice pediatric groups, well-child clinics, and agencies providing early intervention service, and by pediatricians and other physicians as a screening tool.

A self-report, 120-item questionnaire containing three scales (main stressor domains): Child Characteristics (consisting of six subscales examining characteristics such as child's adaptability, mood, and reinforcement of parent), Parent Characteristics (consisting of seven subscales measuring characteristics such as parents'

Refer to page(s):	*Test Title*

depression, sense of competence, and social isolation), and Life Stress (optional, consisting of life events and providing an index of parent stress outside of parent-child relationship). Parents rate 101 items 1-5 (strongly agree to strongly disagree) and 19 optional yes or no, according to whether the event has occurred within the past year. Administration is untimed and requires approximately 20-30 minutes. Examiner evaluated. Suitable for group use. Hand-scored. A set (including manual, two reusable test booklets, ten answer sheets, and ten profile sheets) costs $18.50 (plus $2.00 postage); manual, $8.00; reusable test booklet, $3.50; answer sheets, $.75 each; profile sheets, $.10 each. *Publisher:* Pediatric Psychology Press

194
PEABODY INDIVIDUAL ACHIEVEMENT TEST
(PIAT)   *Lloyd M. Dunn and Fredrick C. Markwardt, Jr.*

Provides an overview of individual scholastic attainment in children ages 5 and up. Used to screen for areas of weakness requiring more detailed diagnostic testing.

The 402-item test consists of mathematics (84 items), reading recognition (84 items), reading comprehension (66 items), spelling (84 items), and general information (84 items), including science, social studies, fine arts and sports requiring 30-50 minutes. Examiner required and evaluated. Not suitable for group use. Derived scores are grade equivalents, grade percentile ranks, age equivalents, age percentile ranks, and standard scores by age or grade. Materials (including two easel kits containing test plates, 25 record booklets, and a manual) cost $72.50. *Publisher:* American Guidance Service

94, 98, 99, 184, 193
PEABODY PICTURE VOCABULARY TEST-REVISED
(PPVT-R)   *Lloyd M. Dunn and Leota M. Dunn*

Measures hearing vocabulary for standard American English, estimates verbal ability and scholastic aptitude in children ages 2½ and up. Used with non-English speaking students; to screen for mental retardation or giftedness; as a part of a comprehensive battery; and to screen applicants for jobs requiring good aural vocabulary.

The untimed 175-item "point-to" response test measures receptive vocabulary in English. Test items, arranged in order of increasing difficulty, consist of plates of four pictures. Subjects are shown a plate and asked to point to the picture which corresponds to the stimulus word. Only those plates within a subject's ability range are administered. Age-based norms include: standard scores, percentile ranks, stanines, and age equivalents. Examiner required and evaluated. Complete kit includes: 175 test plates bound in an easel, manual, 25 individual record forms, and shelf box for $34.00.

| *Test Title*

Available in two forms, L and M. Special Plastic Plate Edition available. *Publisher:* American Guidance Service

PERCEPTION-OF-RELATIONSHIPS-TEST *Barry Bricklin*

Illuminates certain key aspects of the child's interaction patterns with each parent. Used with children (aged three and up) and adults by mental health professionals (trained in test administration) in custody decision making to yield a designation of the better primary caretaking parent.

Highly correlated with The Bricklin Perceptual Scales: Child-Perception-of-Parents-Series. Validated by comparisons to independent clinical material, interview material, other tests, and designations by judges as to better primary caretaking parent in adversary cases. Administration is untimed and requires approximately 20 minutes. Examiner required. Suitable for group use. Test is described in the Bricklin Perceptual Scales: Child-Perception-of-Parents-Series manual. *Publisher:* Village Publishing

PERKINS-BINET TEST OF INTELLIGENCE FOR THE BLIND, FORMS N & U *Carl Davis*

Assesses both verbal and performance functions of low-vision and blind children (age three and over) and adults. Used for clinical evaluation.

A test of learning ability consisting of two forms: Form N (for totally blind subjects aged four-adult) and Form U (for subjects, aged three-adult, with usable vision). Both forms consist of both verbal and nonverbal stimuli. Yields mental age and intelligence quotient. Uses items from Interim Hayes-Binet, Stanford-Binet, and the Williams Test of Intelligence for the Blind. Administration requires approximately 90 minutes. Examiner required. Not suitable for group use. Currently out of print. For more information contact publisher. *Publisher:* Perkins School for the Blind

PORCH INDEX OF COMMUNICATIVE ABILITY (PICA) *Bruce E. Porch*

Evaluates the ability of aphasic adolescents and adults to communicate with other people. Not recommended for children under 12 years of age. Used to measure changes in functioning due to time, treatment, and surgery for diagnosis and therapy.

A 180-item, paper-pencil verbal test of nine modalities of communication: writing, copying, reading, pantomime, verbal, auditory, visual, gestural, and graphic. Items are scored for accuracy, responsiveness, completeness, promptness, and efficiency. Administration is untimed and requires approximately 30-60 minutes. Examiner required and evaluated. Not suitable for group use. Materials include ten pairs of test objects, plastic stimulus cards, and graphic test sheets. A fibertip pen is required for graphic items. A complete kit for 25 subjects (including test items and sheets, stimulus cards, manuals, test format booklet, profiles, and carrying case) costs $128.50. *Publisher:* Consulting Psychologists Press, Inc.

97, 98

PORTEUS MAZES   *S.D. Porteus*

Assesses mental ability of verbally handicapped subjects of all ages. Used in anthropological studies and in research on the effects of drugs and psychosurgry.

A nonlanguage test of mental ability. Items are mazes. Materials include the Vineland Revision, the basic test consisting of 12 mazes; the Porteus Maze Extension, a series of eight mazes designed for retesting and not intended for use as an initial test; and the Porteus Maze Supplement, designed for a third testing in clinical and research settings. Examiner required and evaluated. Administration is untimed and requires approximately 25 minutes per scale. Not suitable for group use. Basic sets (including mazes and 100 score sheets) cost $62.50 for Vineland Revision, $46.00 for Porteus Maze Extension, and $42.50 for Porteus Maze Supplement; manual is $24.00. *Publisher:* The Psychological Corporation

196-197

PRODUCTIVITY ENVIRONMENTAL PREFERENCE SURVEY (PEPS)   *Rita Dunn, Kenneth Dunn, and Gary E. Price*

Assesses the manner in which adults prefer to function, learn, concentrate, and perform in their occupational or educational activities. Used for employee placement and counseling and office design to provide a basis for supervisor- or instructor-individual interaction in the ways that permit each person to concentrate best and allow instructors or supervisors to group individuals or design work settings based on similarity among productivity elements.

A 100-item, paper-pencil, Likert-scale inventory measuring the following environmental factors related to educational or occupational activities: immediate environment (sound, temperature, light, and design), emotionality (motivation, responsibility, persistence, and structure), sociological needs (self-, peer-, authority-oriented and combined), and physical needs (perceptual preferences, time of day, intake, and mobility). Respondents indicate whether they agree or disagree with each of the 100 statements about ways people like to work or study. Computerized results are available in three forms: individual profile (raw scores for each of the 20 areas, standard scores, and a plot for each score in each area), group summary (identifies individuals with significantly high or low scores and groups with similar preferences), and a subscale summary. May be self-administered. Suitable for group use. Administration is untimed and requires approximately 20-30 minutes.

Specimen set (manual and answer sheet) costs $11.00. *Publisher:* Price Systems, Inc.

PSYCHOSOCIAL PAIN INVENTORY (PSPI)   *Robert K. Heaton, Ralph A.W. Lehman, and Carl F. Getto*

Assesses psychosocial factors considered to be important in maintaining and exacerbating chronic pain problems of adults. Used in treatment of chronic pain patients.

An eight-page, multiple-item, paper-pencil inventory evaluating the following factors: several forms of secondary gain, the effects of pain behavior on interpersonal relationships, the existence of stressful life events that may contribute to subjective distress or promote avoidance learning, and components of past history that familiarize the patient with the chronic invalid role and with its personal and social consequences. Ratings also consider the fact that patients differ in the degree to which they are likely to be influenced by potential sources of secondary gain. A total score is obtained, with high scores on the inventory predicting poor response to medical treatment for pain. Examiner required and evaluated. Not suitable for group use. Administration is untimed and varies. A test kit (including 25 test forms, one set of scoring instructions, and one copy of the initial research paper on the inventory by Dr. Heaton et al.) costs $13.50. *Publisher:* Psychological Assessment Resources, Inc.

PURDUE PEGBOARD TEST   *Developed by Purdue Research Foundation under the direction of Joseph Tiffin*

Measures adolescents' and adults' hand-finger-arm dexterity required for certain types of manual work, for example, dexterity needed in assembly work, electronic production work, and similarly related jobs. Used in educational and industrial settings for the selection of business and industrial personnel and high-school shop trainees.

A multiple-operation manual test of gross- and fine-motor movements of hands, fingers, arms, and fingertips. Tasks test gross-motor ability (moving hands, fingers, and arms) and fingertip dexterity ability (controlling manipulative movements of small objects). Five separate scores can be obtained for the right hand, left hand, both hands, right and left and both hands, and assembly. Materials consist of a test board with two vertical rows of holes and four storage wells holding 50 pegs, 40 washers, and 20 collars. To test the right hand, the subject inserts as many pegs as possible in the holes, starting at the top of the right-hand row. Left-hand test uses the left row, moving from top to bottom. Both hands are then used together to fill both rows from top to bottom. Administration is timed and requires 5-10 minutes. Examiner required. Suitable for group use. Hand-scored. A complete set (including board, and

Refer to page(s):	*Test Title*

manual) costs $179.00; 100 profiles, $44.00; complete replacement set (pegs, washers, collars), $48.00; manual, $10.00. *Publisher:* Science Research Associates, Inc.

192   QUICK NEUROLOGICAL SCREENING TEST   *Harold M. Sterling, Margaret Mutti and Norma V. Spalding*

Assesses neurological integration as it relates to the learning abilities of children, teenagers, and adults.

The test is a multiple task, nonverbal test of 15 functions, each involving a motor task similar to those observed in neurological pediatric examinations. The areas measured include: maturity of motor development, skill in controlling large and small muscles, motor planning and sequencing, sense of rate and rhythm, spatial organization, visual and auditory perceptual skill, balance and cerebellar-vestibular function, and disorders of attention. Examiner required and evaluated. Testing time is approximately 20 minutes. Scoring occurs simultaneously and neurodevelopmental difficulties result in an increasingly larger numerical score. A test kit (including manual, 25 scoring forms and 25 geometric form reproduction sheets) costs $20.50. *Publisher:* Academic Therapy Publications

193   QUICK TEST (QT)   *R.B. Ammons and C.H. Ammons*

Assesses individual intelligence in individuals ages 2 and older. May be used for evaluation of severely physically handicapped, those with short attention spans, or uncooperative subjects.

The 50-item test of general intelligence has subject look at plates with four line drawings and indicate which picture best illustrates the meaning of a given word. Answers are usually given by pointing. Requires no reading, writing or speaking. Usual administration involves presentation of 15 to 20 of the items and takes 3-10 minutes. Items are administered until there have been six consecutive passes and six consecutive failures. Examiner required and evaluated; scoring is by hand key. Materials include plates with stimulus pictures, and three alternate forms. Complete Kit (including manual, 3 plates, 100 record sheets, instruction cardboard, and item cardboard) costs $16.00. *Publisher:* Psychological Test Specialists

133   REISS PREMARITAL SEXUAL PERMISSIVENESS SCALE   *Ira L. Reiss*

Measures adolescents' and adults' degree of acceptance of kissing, petting, and coitus, given various degrees of affection in a heterosexual relationship. Used in clinical and research settings.

Two 12-item scales (one for males and one for females) that are individually answered. Hand- or machine-scored. Response analysis, using Guttman scaling program of the SPSS statistical package.

Administration is untimed and requires approximately 5 minutes. Suitable for group use. Examiner evaluated. *Source:* (1967). Ira L. Reiss. *The Social Context of Premarital Sexual Permissiveness* (pp. 211-214). New York: Holt, Rinehart and Winston, Inc.

70   REVISED MINNESOTA PAPER FORM BOARD TEST
Rensis Likert and W.H. Quasha

Measures ability of adults to visualize and manipulate objects in space. Used for selection of applicants for jobs requiring mechanical-spatial ability.

A multiple-item, paper-pencil test of spatial perception. Applicant is required to visualize the assembly of two-dimensional geometric shapes into a whole design. Related to both mechanical and artistic ability. Materials include two sets of equivalent forms: AA and BB (for hand scoring) and MA and MB (hand or computer scoring). Examiner required. Suitable for group use. Administration is timed and requires 20 minutes. Available in a French-Canadian edition. Keys for hand scoring Form MA or MB IBM 805 answer documents (including manual) cost $6.00; 25 Form AA or BB tests (including manual and key), $16.00; 25 Form MA or MB test booklets for use with separate answer documents, $20.00; 50 Form MA or MB IBM 805 answer documents, $12.00; Examination kit (including one each of materials for all forms), $10.00. *Publisher:* The Psychological Corporation

81-82, 85   REY AUDITORY-VERBAL LEARNING TEST   *André Rey*

Measures immediate memory span and retention following interpolated activity, provides a learning curve, reveals learning strategies (or their absence), and elicits tendencies of retroactive and proactive interference and to confusion or confabulation on memory. Used in clinical evaluations.

A five-trial learning format using three 15-word lists (A, B, C). List A is presented with recall five times (Trials I-V). After one presentation of List B, there is a sixth recall trial of List A. (List C is used only when either A or B list is spoiled by interruption, improper administration, or subject's confusion or premature response). Examiner notes words in the order recalled, subject's pattern of recall, association of two or three words, and whether the subject's procedure is orderly. Each trial is scored by the number of words correctly recalled. A total score (sum of Trials I-V) can also be calculated. Examiner required and evaluated. Not suitable for group use. Administration is untimed and requires approximately 10-15 minutes. *Source:* Lezak, M. (1983). *Neurological Assessment* (2nd ed.) (pp. 422-429). New York: Oxford University Press.

Test Title

RORSCHACH PSYCHODIAGNOSTIC TEST
Hermann Rorschach

Evaluates personality through projective technique in individuals ages 3 and older. Used in clinical evaluation.

The test is a ten card oral response projective personality test. The subject is asked to interpret what he sees in ten inkblots, based on the assumption that the individual's perceptions and associations are selected and organized in terms of his motivations, impulses, and other underlying aspects of personality. Extensive scoring systems have been developed. Although many variations are in use, this entry refers only to the Psychodiagnostic Plates first published in 1921. Materials include: inquiry charts, tabulation sheets, and set of 10 inkblots. Set of 10 Kodaslides of the inkblots may be imported on request. Trained examiner required. Examiner evaluates responses. Contact distributor for cost. *Publisher:* Hans Huber-distributed in U.S. by Grune & Stratton

ROSENZWEIG PICTURE-FRUSTRATION STUDY (P-F)
Saul Rosenzweig

Measures aggression in personality of individuals aged four years through adult. Used in clinical counseling.

An eight-page leaflet series, paper-pencil test of an individual's response patterns to everyday frustration or stress. Consists of 24 cartoon pictures, each of which depict two persons in a frustrating situation, with one being the frustrator. Requires subject to write or tell the first response that comes to mind for the anonymous frustrated person in the second picture. Measures three types of aggression (obstacle-dominance, ego-defense, and need-persistence) and three directions of aggression (extraggression, imaggression, and intraggression). Nine factors, derived by combining the types and directions of aggression, constitute the score. For optimal scoring, individual administration is followed by inquiry. Available in three formats: C (ages 4-13 years), T (ages 12-18 years), and A (18 years and older). A separate manual supplement, used in conjunction with the basic manual, is available for each format. Administration is timed and requires 15 minutes. Hand-scored. Kit (including basic manual, manual supplement, 25 test booklets, and 25 scoring sheets—specify A, T, or C) costs $26.00. *Publisher:* Psychological Assessment Resources, Inc.

ROTTER INCOMPLETE SENTENCES BLANK
Julian B. Rotter

Assesses personality of adolescents and adults in a 40-item paper-pencil test. Items are stems of sentences to be completed by the subject. Responses may be classified into three categories: unhealthy responses, neutral responses, and positive or healthy responses. Self-administered. Examiner evaluated with scoring by hand key. Suitable for group use. Materials include a High School, College, and Adult Form. Twenty-five blanks (specify High School, College, or Adult) cost $6.00; manual costs $10.00. *Publisher:* The Psychological Corporation

195   SELF-DIRECTED SEARCH (SDS)   *John L. Holland*

Identifies appropriate vocational options and aids adolescents (Grade 10-UP) and adults to explore their work worlds. Used for vocational guidance counseling and personnel work to stimulate discussion of vocational problems.

Multiple-item, paper-pencil test of six interest types: realistic (R), investigative (I), artistic (A), social (S), enterprising (E), and conventional (C). An eight-page brochure discusses personality characteristics associated with the six groupings and gives suggestions on exploring career possibilities; a 16-page assessment booklet enables subjects to evaluate their own abilities and interests; and an eight-page occupations finder provides descriptive codes for about 500 occupations (95% of U.S. labor force). Examinees obtain a three-letter code reflecting their major interest types. This code can then be used to identify appropriate vocational options. A separate form (Form E), available for examinees with a limited command of written English, yields simplified two-letter codes. Self-administered. Suitable for group use. Available in Spanish and Vietnamese. Administration is untimed and requires approximately 2-3 hours. Hand-scored. A specimen set (including assessment booklets [Form E also], an occupations finder, jobs finder, and the 8-page brochure) costs $3.75; manual, $8.75. *Publisher:* Consulting Psychologists Press, Inc.

84   SELF-RATING DEPRESSION SCALE   *William W.K. Zung*

Assesses intensity of depressive symptoms of subjects of all ages (except the extremely debilitated), but is best suited for those aged 20-64 years. Used for clinical diagnosis and research on depression for both clinical and measurement purposes.

A 20-item, paper-pencil measure of anxiety. Each item is a specific characteristic of depression. Subject checks "None or A Little of the time," "Some of the time," "Good part of the time," or "Most or All of the time" for each item, according to their feelings the week before taking the test. Administration is untimed and requires approximately five minutes. Examiner required and scored. Suitable for group use. Available in Chinese, Czech, Dutch, French, German, Italian, Japanese, Slovak, Spanish, Swedish, and Thai. Hand scored. The test booklet, consisting of a sample test, scoring transparency, 12 test/answer sheets, and information, is available free of charge from either the author or CIBA Pharmaceutical Company. A booklet *Current Concepts: How Normal is*

Refer to page(s):	*Test Title*

Depression? serves as the manual and is available from the author or the publisher, UpJohn Laboratories. *Publisher:* William W.K. Zung

131

THE SEX ATTITUDES SURVEY (SAS)   *G. McHugh and T.G. McHugh*

Taps adolescents' and adults' basic personal attitudes towards all aspects of human sexuality and energizes the issue of sex attitudes to promote understanding, sharing, and growth. Used in classrooms, marital and pre-marital counseling, adult sex education, counselor/teacher training, sexual enrichment, and marriage enrichment.

A 107-item test with statements about issues, such as intercourse, sex roles, sex dreams, homosexuality, and heterosexuality, to which subjects respond on the basis of strength of agreement/disagreement. Responses can be connected to form a profile for comparison between individuals for the purpose of determining specific disagreements. Manual contains in-depth discussion of items, their intent, and options in counseling and teaching. Suitable for group use. A specimen set (including manual and two forms) costs $2.00; 10 forms, $5.00; 25 forms, $10.00; manual only, $1.00. *Publisher:* Family Life Publications

131

SEX KNOWLEDGE AND ATTITUDE TEST (SKAT)
Howard I. Lief and David Reed

Assesses individuals' (aged 18 and older with more than a high-school education) sexual knowledge and attitudes. Used as a research and educational tool.

A 106-item, paper-pencil test consisting of two sections: sexual knowledge and sexual attitudes. The sexual knowledge section contains 71 items (50 scored and 21 that are teaching items). Sexual attitudes section contains 35 items (32 scored) in four subsections: heterosexual relationships, sexual myths, abortion, and auto-eroticism. Using medical students for the norm, attitudes are measured for "conservatism" vs. "liberalism." Available in Spanish. Self-administered. Suitable for group use. Administration is untimed and requires approximately 30-45 minutes. Hand- or computer-scored. Test booklet costs $1.00; answer sheet, $.25; manual, $2.50; norms booklet, $.25; set of scoring keys, $3.00; sexual performance evaluation, $2.00; and set of SKAT related articles, $3.00. *Publisher:* Marriage Council of Philadelphia

131

SEX KNOWLEDGE INVENTORY-FORM X (SKI-X)
Gelolo McHugh

Assesses knowledge of and attitudes toward sexual behavior of adolescents (Grade 10-UP) and adults and aids teachers and counselors in dispelling sexual myths and teaching facts and facilitates discussion of basic sex facts and the emotional aspects of sexuality. Used for marital and premarital counseling, college and high-school sex education, and counselor-educator training.

An 80-item, paper-pencil test consisting of multiple-choice items. Materials include reusable test booklet, manual, answer sheets, and see-through scoring key. The test is included in the Complete Specimen Set, Premarital Set, and Sex Educators and Counselor's Package. Administration is untimed. Examiner evaluated. Hand-scored. A specimen set (including manual, one test booklet, two answer sheets, and key) costs $7.00; 1-9 test booklets, $1.35 each; 10 answer sheets, $4.00; key, $5.00; manual, $5.00. *Publisher:* Family Life Publications, Inc.

132   SEXUAL ANXIETY SCALE   *M. Obler*

Measures cognitively experienced social and sexual anxieties of adults. Used in clinical evaluations.

A self-report scale consisting of 22 items ranging from anxiety experienced during contact with a member of the opposite sex to intravaginal penetration. Separate forms for males and females. Administration is untimed and varies. Examiner evaluated. *Source:* Author: available from M. Obler, Dept. of Educational Services, Brooklyn College, Brooklyn, New York 11210 or on microfilm at The New School for Social Research Library, 65 Fifth Avenue, New York, New York 10003.

132   SEXUAL FEAR INVENTORIES (SFI)   *J. S. Annon*

Assess relative degree of fear or other unpleasant feelings an adult may associate with sexually related activities and experiences and measure changes in attitudinal responses to particular stimuli as the result of specific therapeutic procedures. Used clinically to pinpoint sexual stimuli that elicit anxiety, clarify generalized sexual anxiety sources, determine specific sexual fears, index relative emotional responses to stimuli for possible hierarchy construction for such procedures as systematic desensitization and covert sensitization; pinpoints and orders specific areas for therapeutic intervention when used in conjunction with the Sexual Pleasure Inventories and comparing fear-pleasure responses.

Consists of two inventories (one for males and one for females) and 130 items taken from a variety of sources (e.g., sexual hierarchies created for use with covert therapeutic procedures, various sexual attitude scales). Items comprise four conceptually different areas: general in nature (items 1-30; e.g., nude art), involving subject personally (items 31-60; e.g., talking about sex to others), concerning social relationships (items 61-80; e.g., telephoning a female), and consisting of physical contact (items 81-130; e.g., kissing a female goodnight). Items describe objects, events, or

Test Title

situations of varying degrees of sexual salience. Administration is untimed and varies. Examiner evaluated. One-24 inventories cost $.50 each; 100, $.35 each. *Publisher:* Enabling Systems, Inc.

133 SEXUAL INTERACTION INVENTORY *Joseph LoPiccolo*

Evaluates sexual adjustment of adult heterosexual couples. Used in clinical settings for diagnostic treatment planning in cases of heterosexual dysfunction, assessment of treatment outcome, and evaluation of normal level of heterosexual adjustment in deviant sex offenders, and for research on nonclinical samples as a measure of sexual adjustment.

Consists of 17 heterosexual behaviors described in words and illustrated with pictures. For each behavior each member of couple responds to six questions that assess actual frequency of occurance, desired frequency of occurance, pleasure, desired pleasure, perception of spouse's pleasure, and desired spouse pleasure. Five scales for the male and five for the female (frequency dissatisfaction, self-acceptance, pleasure mean, perceptual accuracy, and acceptance of mate) and a summary scale (total disagreement) are derived from questions to give an overall measure of sexual adjustment. Scale scores are plotted on an MMPI-style graph. Administration is untimed and requires approximately 30 minutes. Examiner evaluated. *Source:* Author: a packet (including two inventories, ten answer sheets, manual, and journal articles) costs $10.00; available from Joseph LoPiccolo, Ph.D., Department of Psychology, Texas A & M University, College Station, Texas 77843-4235.

133 THE SEXUAL ORIENTATION METHOD *M.P. Feldman, M.J. MacCulloch, V. Mellor, and J.M. Pinschof*

Assesses the relative degree of homo- and hetero-erotic orientation of men who show homosexual behavior. Used to evaluate the response of adult male homosexual patients to treatment (not intended to detect homosexuality in subjects who are not known to have homosexual characteristics).

A self-report questionnaire presented at random in pairs with a total of 120 pairs (1-60 concerning attitudes to males; 60-120 concerning attitudes to women). Subjects respond with one of six adjectives (interesting, attractive, handsome, hot, pleasurable, and exciting) to two concepts: "Men are sexually to me . . ." and "Women are sexually . . ." Five scale positions (very attractive to very unattractive) are used for each adjective. Derived from the Semantic Differential Technique of Osgood. Administration is untimed and varies. Examiner evaluated. *Source:* (1966). *Behavior Research and Therapy, 4,* 289.

           Test Title

       SEXUAL PLEASURE INVENTORIES (SPI)   *J. S. Annon*

Assess relative degree of arousal or other pleasant feelings an adult may associate with sexually related activities and experiences. Used in clinical settings to identify positive sexually related activities and experiences, index relative change in emotional responses to particular stimuli as the result of therapeutic procedure, and (when used in conjunction with the Sexual Fear Inventories) serve as a prime assessment measure for identifying and ordering specific sexual areas for therapeutic intervention.

Self-report inventories consisting of two inventories (one for males and one for females) and 130 items in four areas: general in nature, involving subject personally, concerning social relationships, and consisting of physical contact. Administration is untimed and varies. Examiner evaluated. One-24 inventories cost $.50 each; 100, $.35 each. *Publisher:* Enabling Systems, Inc.

    SHIPLEY INSTITUTE OF LIVING SCALE   *W. C. Shipley*

Measures the intellectual ability and impairment of adults and adolescents aged 15 years and older. Used for clinical assessment and counseling purposes in a wide variety of clinical, educational, personnel, and counseling settings.

A 60-item, paper-pencil test measuring vocabulary and logical sequencing (abstract thinking) abilities. Yields both an IQ estimate and a Conceptual Quotient (CQ) that expresses the extent to which the person's abstract thinking falls short of vocabulary. The CQ is particularly useful for assessing current impairment of intellectual functioning. Standardized on over 1,000 subjects. Examiner required. Suitable for group use. Administration is timed and requires 20 minutes. Hand- or computer-scored. Microcomputer diskette (for IBM PC or XT with 128K memory) administers, scores, and prints complete interpretation. A kit (including 100 tests, key, and manual) costs $33.00; diskette (25 uses), $119.50. *Publisher:* Western Psychological Services

       SHORT PORTABLE MENTAL STATUS QUESTIONNAIRE (SPMSQ)   *Eric Pfeiffer*

Assesses and determines the degree of organic brain deficit in the elderly. Used for clinical evaluations to determine extent of patient's self-care capacities.

A 10-item questionnaire in which the examiner asks the questions (e.g., today's date, day of the week, the current U.S. president's name) and the subject responds orally. First nine are scored correct or incorrect; item 10 is scored correct if first nine are scored correct and incorrect if there is an error in the series or unwillingness to attempt the series. Corrections for scoring according to race (white/black) and level of education (grade school only,

through high school, beyond high school). Administration is untimed. Examiner required and evaluated. Not suitable for group
use. *Source:* (1975). *Journal of the American Geriatrics Society,*
23(10), 433-441; includes the questionnaire and instructions for
administration, scoring, and evaluation.

60, 97, 145   SIXTEEN PERSONALITY FACTOR QUESTIONNAIRE
Raymond B. Cattell and IPAT Staff

Evaluates the normal personality of adolescents (16 years-UP)
and adults. Used in diagnostic and therapeutic settings to measure
anxiety, neuroticism, rigidity, and other behavior trends; by business and industry to predict important job-related criteria, such as
length of time an employee will probably remain with the company,
sales effectiveness, work efficiency, tolerance for routine, and personnel selection and placement; by educators and school psychologists to counsel college-bound and university students and identify
students with problems (e.g., potential dropouts, drug users, low
achievers); for marriage counseling; and psychological research on
personality.

A paper-pencil test measuring levels of 16 primary personality
traits: emotional maturity, assertiveness, shrewdness, tension, self-
sufficiency, intelligence, seriousness, conscientiousness, shyness,
tough-mindedness, suspiciousness, imaginativeness, self-assurance, conservatism, self-control, and reserve. Five forms are
available: Forms A and B (seventh-grade reading level) consist of
187 items each, Forms C and D (sixth-grade reading level) consist
of 105 items each, and Form E (third-grade reading level) consisting
of 128 items in a forced-choice format with large type and shorter,
more concrete items. Computer-analyzed reports include the narrative scoring report (provides a complete report for each individual, including descriptions of all significant personality
characteristics and relevant vocational and occupational comparisons), the personal career development profile (provides information about individual strengths, behavioral attributes, and
gratifications to accomplish personal career development objec-
ties), the Karson clinical report (provides an in-depth analysis of
underlying personality dynamics in clinical terms for use in psychiatric and psychological applications), and the marriage counseling
report (examines individual and joint strengths and weaknesses in
the personality organization of two individuals). Handbook is primary source of technical information, including summary of occupational profile data for use in vocational and rehabilitation
counseling. Manual gives information on administration, scoring,
and interpretation of Forms A, B, C, and D. Form E has separate
manual. A videotape recording of Form A test booklet in American
sign language and a cassette tape of Form E are also available.
Examiner required. Suitable for group use, as well as individual and

self-administration. Available in Spanish and German. Administration is untimed and requires approximately 45-60 minutes. Introductory kit (including manual, key, norms, one reusable test booklet, answer sheet, profile sheet, and second-order worksheet) costs $11.40 for Form A and $10.15 for Form E; 25 reusable test booklets (specify Form A, B, C, or D), $14.25; 50 machine-scorable answer sheets (A, B, C, or D), $6.50; 50 hand-scoring answer sheets (A, B, C, D, or E), $5.50; 50 profile sheets, $5.40; handbook, $12.50. *Publisher:* Institute for Personality and Ability Testing, Inc.

94

SLOSSON INTELLIGENCE TEST (SIT)/SLOSSON ORAL READING TEST (SORT)   *Richard L. Slosson*

Measures the mental age, IQ, and reading level of children and adults. Used by psychologists, guidance counselors, special educators, learning disabilities teachers, and remedial reading teachers to provide a quick assessment of a person's mental abilities.

The 195-item oral screening instrument (approximately 10-20 minutes in duration) consists of questions arranged on a scale of Chronological Age from one-half month to 27 years. A Basal Age is established at the point before which the subject gives an incorrect answer after giving at least ten correct answers in a row. Additional credit is then added for correct answers given above the Basal Age. The Basal Age plus added months credit are used to determine mental age and IQ. Norms provided include: percentiles, Normal Curve Equivalents, Stanine Categories, and T-Scores. The results can be used to predict reading achievement, to plan educational programs, to predict to success and acceptance in college, to screen students for reading disabilities, and as an IQ test for the blind. Also includes the Slosson Oral Reading Test (SORT), which yields a reading grade level from primer into high school based on the ability to pronounce words at different levels of difficulty. Also used to identify reading handicaps. SIT item analysis available to identify strengths and weaknesses in eight learning areas. Examiner required and evaluated. Not suitable for group use. Computer scoring offers two options: a service that requires sending input data sheets to Slosson, and diskettes for Apple II +, TRS-80 Model III/IV, 4P and IBM Compatible (MS-DOS). A complete kit (including manual of questions, directions, 1981 norms tables, 50 SORT tests, 50 SIT score sheets, and vinyl binder) costs $35.00; computer scoring is $5.00 per pupil (1-10) and $4.00 per pupil (10 or more); 50 input data sheets, $7.00; diskettes (including manual and extra back-up diskette), $195.00. *Publisher:* Slosson Educational Publications, Inc.

Refer to page(s):	*Test Title*

81, 97

STANDARD PROGRESSIVE MATRICES (SPM-1938)
J. C. Raven

Measures individuals' (ages 8-65) mental ability through assessment of nonverbal abstract reasoning tasks. Used for school and vocational counseling and placement.

A 60-item, paper-pencil nonverbal test consisting of five 12-problem sets. In each problem, the subject is presented with a pattern or figure design that has a part missing. The subject then selects one of six possible parts as the correct one. The patterns are arrayed from simple to complex. The test is often used with the Mill Hill Vocabulary Scale. Examiner required. Suitable for group use. Standardized in Great Britain. Administration is untimed and requires approximately 45 minutes. Hand- or computer-scored. Examination kit (including test booklet, answer document, key, and appropriate sections of manual) costs $15.00; scoring key (including appropriate sections of manual), $12.00. *Publisher:* H.K. Lewis & Co., Ltd.; U.S. Distributor—The Psychological Corporation

184, 195

STRONG-CAMPBELL INTEREST INVENTORY (SCII)
E. K. Strong, Jr. and David P. Campbell

Measures occupational interests in a wide range of career areas requiring, for the most part, advanced technical or college training. Used to make long-range curricular and occupational choices, as well as for employee selection and placement, and vocational rehabilitation placement.

The 325-item paper-pencil multiple-choice test asks the examinee to respond either "like," "indifferent," or "dislike" to items covering a broad range of familiar occupational tasks and day-to-day activities. General topics include: occupations, school subjects, activities, amusements, types of people, preference between two activities, and "your characteristics." Testing time is approximately 30-40 minutes. Responses are then analyzed by computer to yield a profile that presents scores on a number of scales and offers interpretive advice. Specifically, the respondent is scored on: Six General Occupational Themes (based on Holland's RIASEC themes), 23 Basic Interest Scales (measuring strength and consistency of specific interest areas), and 162 Occupational Scales (reflecting degree of similarity between respondent and people employed in particular occupations). The scoring services also provide 11 additional non-occupational and administrative indexes as a further guide to interpreting the results. Computer scoring required and available from a number of sources (test results available immediately via ARION II Teleprocessing). Self-administered. Suitable for group use. Available in Spanish. Contact publisher for costs. *Publisher:* Stanford University Press

Refer to page(s):	*Test Title*

70   SYMBOL DIGIT MODALITIES TEST   *Aaron Smith*

Measures individual brain damage in persons 8 years old and up. Used to screen and predict learning disorders and to identify children with potential reading problems.

The test is a multiple-item test in which the subject is given 90 seconds to convert as many meaningless geometric designs as possible into their appropriate numbers according to the key provided. Useful as a screening device when group-administered; may be individually administered with an oral presentation for those who cannot take written tests. Since numbers are nearly universal, the test is virtually culture-free. Standardized on more than 3,600 boys and girls ages 8-17 years and 431 adults ages 18-75 years with norms given for each year by sex. Examiner required. Scoring is by hand key. Complete kit (includes 100 tests, key and manual) is available for $29.00. *Publisher:* Western Psychological Services

98   TACTUAL PERFORMANCE TEST (TPT)   *Ward Halstead and Ralph Reitan*

Assesses a range of perceptual-motor and visuospatial abilities, adaptation to novelty, tactile form discrimination, kinesthesia, coordination of movement of arms and hands, visuospatial imagery, incidental memory, frustration tolerance, and possible verbal encoding of the tactile-spatial input, of subjects all ages. Used in a variety of neuropsychological applications, such as in the evaluation of central nervous system integrity and as a basis for making inferences concerning an individual's pattern of behavioral strengths and deficits. Included as one of the tests in the Halstead-Reitan Neuropsychological Test Battery.

A complex, multiple-task test using a modification of the Seguin-Goddard Formboard. Materials consist of a board with ten holes cut in various geometrical shapes and ten blocks of corresponding shapes. When in place, the blocks are raised above the board's surface to facilitate test performance. After being blindfolded the subject's task is to place the blocks into their correspondingly shaped holes as rapidly as possible in three trials: using preferred hand, nonpreferred hand, and both hands. Scoring is based on the time required for each trial, plus total time. The blindfold is then removed and the subject is required to draw the board and blocks in their proper places as best remembered. Two additional scores are derived: Memory (number of blocks remembered) and Localization (number of blocks placed in their correct order). No time limit is specified, but subjects should be able to place all of the blocks in approximately ten minutes. Examiner required and evaluated. Not suitable for group use. Complete set costs $99.25. *Publisher:* Reitan Neuropsychology Laboratory

Refer to page(s):	*Test Title*

94   TACTUAL PROGRESSIVE MATRICES (TMP)   *Frank Raven*

Measures abstract reasoning of children and adults. Used for assessment of the blind.

A nonverbal test that is a tactual adaptation of the Raven Progressive Matrices. Subject is required to select a tactual pattern to complete a series of progressive patterns. In addition to forms for children aged nine to 15 years, a 25-item short form is available for use with adults. For more information and costs consult publisher. *Publisher:* Human Sciences Research Council

146   TALKING, FEELING, AND DOING GAME   *Richard Gardner*

Enhances a child's interest and elicits revelations that would not otherwise be obtainable, thus providing insights into the child's psychodynamics. Used in therapy as a catalyst to engage the resistant child in therapeutic interchanges; in group psychotherapy (up to four or five players); and in the treatment of children with MBD.

A standard board game, using dice and cards and utilizing token reinforcement. Both child and therapist throw the dice, in turn, move the pieces from square to square, and select a talking, feeling, or doing card (depending on the color of the square on which the piece lands). The questions and directions in each set of cards range from the least anxiety provoking (e.g., "How old are you?") to the moderately anxiety provoking (e.g., "What's the worst thing a boy can say to his mother?"). The child's responses are generally revealing of those psychological issues that are most important at the time. Other elaborations (e.g., a spinner) enhance the child's interest and enjoyment. Administration is untimed. Examiner required. Sale limited to mental health professionals. The complete set (including board, tokens, cards, and spinner) costs $19.75. *Publisher:* Creative Therapeutics

144   TAYLOR-JOHNSON TEMPERAMENT ANALYSIS
Robert M. Taylor and Lucille P. Morrison

Measures common personality traits to assist in assessing individual adjustment and formulation of overall counseling of adults and adolescents aged 15 years and older. Used for clinical assessment of personality; premarital, marital, and family counseling; and educational and vocational guidance.

A 180-item, paper-pencil test consisting of two editions: Regular (ages 15 years-adult) that requiress an eighth-grade reading level, and Secondary (ages 11-19 and adult poor readers) that requires a fifth-grade reading level. The Regular edition has a special feature allowing "criss-cross" testing where questions are answered as applied to self and again as applied to significant other, thereby adding the dimension of interpersonal perception to coun-

Refer to page(s):	*Test Title*

seling. Secondary edition is presented in direct question format with simplified vocabulary and is not designed for "criss-cross." Evaluation is presented as bipolar graphs of trait pairs: nervous/composed, depressive/light-hearted, active-social/quiet, expressive-responsive/inhibited, sympathetic/indifferent, subjective/objective, dominant/submissive, hostile/tolerant, and self-disciplined/impulsive. Publisher's computer service provides evaluation on the additional scales of emotional pressure (stress), adequacy of self-image (self-esteem), preference for privacy, outwardly poised, alienating, passive-aggressive, potential for marital adjustment, parenting effectiveness, leadership, and sales. Self-administered. Administration is untimed and requires approximately 20 minutes. Available in Spanish, French, German, and Portuguese. Basic package (including manual, handscoring stencils, pens, ruler, 5 test booklets [Regular or Secondary], 50 handscoring answer sheets, and 50 profiles) costs $70.00; manual only, $50.00. *Publisher:* Psychological Publications, Inc.

97

TEST OF NONVERBAL INTELLIGENCE (TONI)
Linda Brown, Rita J. Sherbenou, and Susan J. Dollar

Provides a language-free measure of intelligence and reasoning of individuals (ages 5-86 years). Used with subjects suspected of having difficulty in reading, writing, listening, or speaking, including the mentally retarded, stroke patients, bilingual and non-English-speaking persons, the speech or language handicapped, and the learning disabled.

A 50-item response test assessing intellectual capacities in a format completely free of reading, writing, and verbalizing. The examiner pantomimes the instructions, and the subject points to the selected answer. Test items use abstract symbols to present a variety of reasoning tasks arranged in increasing order of complexity and difficulty. Yields a TONI quotient and percentile ranks, accurately discriminating between retarded and normal subjects. Available in two equivalent forms. Suitable for group use. Examiner required. Administration is untimed and requires approximately 20-30 minutes. Hand scored. Complete kit (including manual, picture book, 50 Form A answer sheets, 50 Form B answer sheets, and a storage box) costs $69.00. Components available for separate purchase. *Publisher:* PRO-ED

12, 13-14, 15, 24, 27, 28, 29, 30, 31, 32, 36, 37, 38, 40, 43, 69, 84, 93, 96, 99, 107, 109, 197, 207

THEMATIC APPERCEPTION TEST (TAT)
Henry Alexander Murray

Assesses personality in individuals ages 14-40 through projective technique focusing on dominant drives, emotions, sentiments, complexes, attitudes, and conflicts.

Twenty-item projective-type test in which a subject is shown pictures one at a time and asked to make up a story about each picture. The examiner records the subject's stories for later analysis. The projective test seeks to measure, among other things, the subject's temperament, level of emotional maturity, observational ability, intellectuality, imagination, psychological insight, creativity, sense of reality and factors of family and psychic dynamics. Generally the subject is asked to make up stories based on ten cards in each of two sessions. A trained examiner is required. Testing time is one hour per series. Examiner required and evaluated. Not suitable for groups. Specimen set is available for $11.50; manual $1.50. *Publisher:* Harvard University Press

83   TOKEN TEST FOR CHILDREN   *Frank DiSimoni*

Measures functional listening ability in children aged 3-12 years and identifies receptive language dysfunction. Used in language therapy.

A 20-item test in which the child arranges wooden tokens in response to the examiner's oral directions. Results can be used to indicate a need for further testing of lexicon and syntax or to rule out language impairment in a child having reading difficulties. The test is not appropriate for deaf subjects. Examiner required and evaluated. Not suitable for group use. Administration is untimed and requires approximately ten minutes. Materials include 20 tokens, manual, and 50 scoring forms. Complete set costs $30.00. *Publisher:* DLM Teaching Resources

82   VISUAL FORM DISCRIMINATION   *Arthur L. Benton*

Assesses complex visual form discrimination and short-term visual recognition memory and evaluates the extent to which brain damage has impaired an individual's ability to discriminate visual forms. Used for clinical evaluations of brain-damaged patients of all ages.

A multiple-choice test composed of 16 items ranging in level of difficulty. Includes two demonstration-practice items. Scored in terms of the number of wholly or partially correct responses. No corrections in score for age, educational level, or sex required. Data collected on patients with brain disease show a relatively high frequency of defective performance, with those having posterior right hemisphere lesions showing the highest frequency of defect. Administration is untimed and requires approximately 15 minutes. Examiner required and evaluated. Not suitable for group use. The 176-page manual, *Contributions to Neuropsychological Assessment—A Clinical Manual* (Benton, Hamsher, Varney, & Spreen, 1983), must be ordered separately. Consult publisher for cost. *Publisher:* Oxford University Press

            Test Title

WASHINGTON PSYCHOSOCIAL SEIZURE INVENTORY (WPSI)   *Carl B. Dodrill*

Evaluates psychological and social concerns, gives standardized findings approximating those obtained from a detailed professional evaluation, and provides economical, systematic, and objective evaluation of the extent of psychosocial problems in areas important for adolescent (16 years and over) and adult epileptics. Used in clinical settings to ascertain a patient's clinical condition by patterns of profile elevation and to assist in rapidly obtaining an overview of difficulties in psychosocial adjustment, and in research to evaluate treatment effectiveness and change in epileptic patient population (e.g., effects of anticonvulsants, surgery for epilepsy, operant conditioning for seizure control, and identification of epileptics with special needs).

A 132-item inventory covering eight clinical scales: Family Background (interpersonal problems pertaining to parents, school, and peers during childhood), Emotional Adjustment (e.g., depression, tension, inability to think clearly, somatic concerns, poor self-image), Interpersonal Adjustment (e.g., comfort in social situations, existence of close personal friends), Vocational Adjustment (e.g., view of employment status), Financial Status, Adjustment to Seizures, and Medical Management (reactions to attending physician and medication), and Overall Psychosocial Functioning (single global index including items from other seven scales). Three validity scales are Scale A—No. Blank (number of items left blank), Scale B—Lie, and Scale C—Rare Items (items endorsed by no more than 15% of the patients). Items answered "yes" or "no," according to self-perceived, usual feelings and actions of respondent. Administration is untimed and requires approximately 15-20 minutes. Examiner required and evaluated. Suitable for group use. Tape cassette (25 min.) is available for patients who cannot read. Spanish edition available. *Source:* (1980). *Epilepsia, 21,* 123-135; for further information, contact the Epilepsy Center, Department of Neurological Surgery, University of Washington School of Medicine, Seattle, Washington 98104.

WECHSLER ADULT INTELLIGENCE SCALE (WAIS) *David Wechsler*

Measures intelligence in adults and adolescents aged 16 years and older. Used for clinical assessment.

Consists of 11 subtests divided into two major divisions yielding a verbal IQ, a performance IQ, and a full scale IQ. The Verbal section consists of the following subtests: Information, Comprehension, Arithmetic, Similarities, Digit Span, and Vocabulary. The Performance (nonverbal) section consists of the following subtests: Digit Symbol, Picture Completion, Block Design, Picture Arrangement, and Object Assembly. Some units require verbal

Refer to page(s):	*Test Title*

responses from the subjects and others require the subjects to manipulate test materials to demonstrate performance ability. Raw scores are converted into scale scores after the subject's performance has been recorded and scored on the provided answer form by the examiner. Examiner required and evaluated. Not suitable for group use. Available in Spanish. Administration is untimed and requires approximately one hour. A basic set (including all necessary equipment, manual, 25 record forms, not including attaché case) costs $120.00; 25 supplementary record sheets, $7.00; attaché case, $40.00. *Publisher:* The Psychological Corporation

12, 13, 15, 36, 37,
38, 40, 43, 56-57,
66, 80, 81, 84, 85,
106, 109, 182, 184,
185, 192-193, 194,
204

WECHSLER ADULT INTELLIGENCE SCALE-REVISED (WAIS-R)   *David Wechsler*

Assesses intelligence in adolescents and adults. The 11 subtests divided into two major divisions yield a verbal IQ, a performance IQ and a full scale IQ for persons age 16 and older. The Verbal section of the WAIS consists of the following subtests: Information, Comprehension, Arithmetic, Similarities, Digit Span and Vocabulary. The Performance or nonverbal section of the test consists of the following subtests: Digit Symbol, Picture Completion, Block Design, Picture Arrangement, and Object Assembly. Some units of the test require verbal responses from the subjects and others require the subject to manipulate test materials to demonstrate performance ability. Testing time is 75 minutes. Raw scores are converted into scale scores after the subject's performance has been recorded and scored on the provided answer form by the examiner. The WAIS-R is a revision of the 1955 WAIS edition. Examiner required and evaluated. Not suitable for group use. Available in Spanish. The complete set (including all necessary equipment, manual, 25 record forms, and carrying case) costs $135.00; without carrying case, $120.00. *Publisher:* The Psychological Corporation

81, 84, 85

WECHSLER MEMORY SCALE   *David Wechsler and C.P. Stone*

Assesses memory functions of adults. Used for clinical evaluation of subjects with special problems, such as aphasics, elderly, and organically brain-injured.

A brief, seven-subtest scale yielding a memory quotient. Materials include two alternate forms: Form I and II. Examiner required and evaluated. Not suitable for group use. Administration is untimed. Examination kit (including manual, design card for both forms, and record form for both forms) costs $6.00; 50 record forms (specify Form I or II), $17.00; manual, $4.50. *Publisher:* The Psychological Corporation

WIDE RANGE ACHIEVEMENT TEST-REVISED (WRAT-R)
Joseph F. Jastak and Sarch Jastak

Measures the basic educational skills of word recognition, spelling and arithmetic, and identifies individuals, ages 5 and older, with learning difficulties. Used for educational placement, measuring school achievement, vocational assessment, job placement and training.

The three paper-pencil subtests (50-100 items per subtest) assess the coding skills of: Reading (recognizing and naming letters and pronouncing printed words), Spelling (copying marks resembling letters, writing name and printing words), and Arithmetic (counting, reading number symbols, oral, and written computation). Timed administration is 10 minutes per subtest. Test consists of two levels printed on the same form: Level I for ages 5-11 and Level II for ages 12-adult. Optional word lists for both levels of the reading and spelling test are offered on plastic cards, and a recorded pronunciation of the lists is provided on cassette tape. The tape itself can be used to administer the spelling section. A One Level edition is available for clinicians and teachers who are willing to spend more time in testing in order to be able to analyze error patterns. A Large Print edition is available for those who require magnification of reading material. Normed for age rather than grade for better accuracy. In conjunction with other tests, such as the Wechsler Scales, WRAT-R is useful for determining personality structure. Restricted to Educational and Psychological professionals. Examiner required and evaluated. Spelling and Arithmetic subtests are suitable for group use. Reading subtest must be individually administered. The cost of the manual is $13.65; 50 test forms cost $9.75. *Publisher:* Jastak Associates, Inc.

Publisher Index

ACADEMIC THERAPY PUBLICATIONS, 20 Commerical Boulevard, Novato, California 94947; (415)883-3314

AMERICAN FOUNDATION FOR THE BLIND, 15 West 16th Street, New York, New York 10011; (212)620-2000

AMERICAN GUIDANCE SERVICE, Publisher's Building, Circle Pines, Minnesota 55014; (800)328-2560, in Minnesota (612)786-4343

AUSTRALIAN COUNCIL FOR EDUCATIONAL RESEARCH LIMITED (ACER), Radford House, Frederick Street, Hawthorn, Victoria 3122, Australia; (03)818-1271

CENTER FOR COGNITIVE THERAPY, 133 South 36th Street, Room 602, Philadelphia, Pennsylvania 19104; (215)898-4100

CLINICAL PSYCHOMETRIC RESEARCH, 1228 Wine Spring Lane, Towson, Maryland 21204; (301)321-6165

CONSULTING PSYCHOLOGISTS PRESS, INC., 577 College Avenue, P. O. Box 60070, Palo Alto, California 94306; (415)857-1444

CREATIVE LEARNING PRESS, INC., P.O. Box 320, Mansfield Center, Connecticut 06250; (203)423-8120

CREATIVE THERAPEUTICS, P.O. Box R, Cresskill, New Jersey 07626; (201)567-8989

DLM TEACHING RESOURCES, P.O. Box 4000, One DLM Park, Allen, Texas 75002; (800)527-4747, in Texas (800)442-4711

EDUCATIONAL AND INDUSTRIAL TESTING SERVICE (EdITS), P.O. Box 7234, San Diego, California 92107; (619)222-1666

ENABLING SYSTEMS, INC., P.O. Box 2813, Honolulu, Hawaii 96803; (808)545-2646

FAMILY LIFE PUBLICATIONS, INC., Box 427, Saluda, North Carolina 28773; (704)749-4971

GRUNE & STRATTON, INC., Orlando, FL 32887-0018; (800)321-5068, (305)345-4100

HARVARD UNIVERSITY PRESS, 79 Garden Street, Cambridge, Massachusetts 02139; (617)495-2600

HISKEY-NEBRASKA TEST, (THE), 5640 Baldwin, Lincoln, Nebraska 68507; (402)466-6145

HUMAN SCIENCES RESEARCH COUNCIL, Private Bag X41, 0001 Pretoria, South Africa; (012)28-3944

INSTITUTE FOR PERSONALITY AND ABILITY TESTING, INC. (IPAT), P.O. Box 188, 1602 Coronado Drive, Champaign, Illinois 61820; (217)352-4739

INSTITUTE OF PSYCHOLOGICAL RESEARCH, INC., 34 Fleury Street West, Montreal, Quebec, Canada H3L 159; (514)382-3000

JASTAK ASSOCIATES, INC., 1526 Gilpin, Wilmington, Delaware 19806; (302)652-4990

MARRIAGE COUNCIL OF PHILADELPHIA, INC., 4025 Chestnut Street, Suite 210, Philadelphia, Pennsylvania 19104; (215)222-7574

NCS PROFESSIONAL ASSESSMENT SERVICES, P.O. Box 1416, Minneapolis, Minnesota 55440; (800)328-6759, in Minnesota (612)933-2800

OXFORD UNIVERSITY PRESS, 200 Madison Avenue, New York, New York 10016; (212)679-7300

PEDIATRIC PSYCHOLOGY PRESS, 320 Terrell Road West, Charlottesville, Virginia 22901; (804)973-5680

PERKINS SCHOOL FOR THE BLIND, 175 North Beacon Street, Watertown, Massachusetts 02172; (617)924-3434

PRICE SYSTEMS, INC., P.O. Box 3067, Lawrence, Kansas 66044; (913)843-7892

PRO-ED, 5341 Industrial Oaks Boulevard, Austin, Texas 78735; (512)892-3142

PSYCHOLOGICAL ASSESSMENT RESOURCES, INC., P.O. Box 98, Odessa, Florida 33556; (813)977-3395

PSYCHOLOGICAL CORPORATION, (THE), A Subsidiary of Harcourt Brace Jovanovich, Inc., 7500 Old Oak Boulevard, Cleveland, Ohio 44130; (216)234-5300

PSYCHOLOGICAL PUBLICATIONS, INC., 5300 Hollywood Boulevard, Los Angeles, California 90027; (213)465-4163

PSYCHOLOGICAL TEST SPECIALISTS, Box 9339, Missoula, Montana 59805; no business phone

REITAN NEUROPSYCHOLOGY LABORATORY, 1338 East Edison Street, Tucson, Arizona 85719; (602)795-3717

RESEARCH PRESS, Box 317760, Champaign, Illinois 61820; (217)352-3273

SCHOLASTIC TESTING SERVICE, INC. (STS), 480 Meyer Road, P.O. Box 1056, Bensenville, Illinois 60106; (312)766-7150

SCIENCE RESEARCH ASSOCIATES, INC. (SRA), 155 North Wacker Drive, Chicago, Illinois 60606; (312)984-7000

SLOSSON EDUCATIONAL PUBLICATIONS, INC., P.O. Box 280, East Aurora, New York 14052; (800)828-4800, in New York (716)652-0930

STANFORD UNIVERSITY PRESS, Stanford, California 94305; (415)497-9434

STOELTING COMPANY, 1350 S. Kostner Avenue, Chicago, Illinois 60623; (312)522-4500

SWETS TEST SERVICES, P.O. Box 517, Berwyn, Pennsylvania 19312; (215)644-4944

TEST SYSTEMS INTERNATIONAL, P.O. Box 18347, Wichita, Kansas 67218; (316)262-0102

UNITED STATES DEPARTMENT OF LABOR, Division of Testing, Employment and Training Administration, Washington, D.C. 20213; (202)376-6270

UNIVERSITY OF ILLINOIS PRESS, 54 E. Gregory Drive, Box 5081, Station A, Champaign, Illinois 61820; institutions (800)233-4175, individuals (800)638-3030, or (217)333-0950

UNIVERSITY OF MINNESOTA PRESS, 2037 University Avenue S.E., Minneapolis, Minnesota 55414; (612)373-3266

VILLAGE PUBLISHING, Furlong, Pennsylvania 18925; (215)794-7418

VOCATIONAL PSYCHOLOGY RESEARCH, UNIVERSITY OF MINNESOTA, Elliott Hall, 75 East River Road, Minneapolis, Minnesota 55455; (612)376-7377

WESTERN PSYCHOLOGICAL SERVICES, A Division of Manson Western Corporation, 12031 Wilshire Boulevard, Los Angeles, California 90025; (213)478-2061

ZUNG, WILLIAM W. K., M.D., Veterans Administration Medical Center, 508 Fulton Street, Durham, North Carolina 27705; (919)286-0411

General Index

263

About the Contributors

MELVIN BERG, PH.D. is a staff psychologist at Colmery-O'Neil Veterans Administration Medical Center in Topeka, Kansas, where his work focuses on diagnosis and inpatient treatment of borderline and psychotic adults. Formerly, he was the coordinator of psychological services for children at the Topeka State Hospital. Dr. Berg, who obtained his doctoral degree in clinical psychology from Michigan State University, is a graduate of the postdoctoral training program in clinical psychology at The Menninger Foundation and is currently studying at the Topeka Institute for Psychoanalysis. He has published articles on borderline psychopathology, testing, and the diagnostic process.

DANIEL C. CLAIBORN, PH.D. is a certified and licensed psychologist in Kansas and Missouri and has been providing family counseling services since 1970. He is a graduate of Vanderbilt University and the University of Missouri-Columbia, and a member of the American Psychological Association, the American Society of Clinical Hypnosis, and the American Association for Marriage and Family Therapy. Dr. Claiborn consults with various hospitals and corporations, and has presented papers and workshops nationally on individual, group, and family psychotherapy. He has also taught doctoral practica in family therapy at the University of Missouri-Kansas City.

DENNIS M. DAILEY, D.S.W. is Professor of Social Welfare in the School of Social Welfare at the University of Kansas. He received his doctoral degree in social work from Washington University in St. Louis. In addition to his responsibilities in teaching and research, he travels extensively, giving workshops and institutes on a broad range of topics in the area of human sexuality, and has a limited private practice as a certified sex therapist. Dr. Dailey has published numerous articles, book chapters, and monographs in sexology, and currently writes a column in an international journal, *The Renal Family.* His research and writing interests lie in the influence of sex-role socialization on clinical judgment, sexual issues in the sexually oppressed groups, and sexuality education for helping professionals.

TERRIE FISK, M.A. is a Ph.D. candidate in counseling psychology at the University of Kansas where she is completing her dissertation researching the efficacy of computer remediation of specific cognitive deficits among chronic alcoholics. She is also specializing in neuropsychological and vocational assessment and rehabilitation and is the cognitive remediation trainer in the *Brain Training* neuropsychology treatment program providing cognitive and psychological services to brain-injured individuals. She has served as coauthor for a book entitled *Computer Programs Reference Guide For Cognitive Remediation* (in press).

NANCY J. GARFIELD, PH.D. is a certified psychologist in Kansas and director of training and a staff psychologist at the Colmery-O'Neil Veterans Administration Medical Center in Topeka, Kansas. She received her Ph.D. in counseling psychology from the University of Missouri-Columbia. Dr. Garfield works with Vietnam veterans in individual and group therapy. She is a coinvestigator of the research project "Characteristics of Vietnam Veterans" and a coauthor of a "A Study of Posttraumatic Stress Disorder in Vietnam Veterans," published in the *Journal of Clinical Psychology.*

CARL J. GETTO, M.D. is Assistant Professor of Psychiatry and director of the pain treatment program at the University of Wisconsin-Madison. He received his M.D. from Loyola University Stritch School of Medicine and did his psychiatric residency at the University of Colorado. Dr. Getto has worked as a consulting psychiatrist in multidisciplinary pain clinics at the University of Colorado and the University of Wisconsin, and has lectured and written extensively on the psychiatric evaluation and treatment of patients with chronic pain. He is currently the associate dean of the University of Wisconsin Medical School and director of clinical affairs at University of Wisconsin Hospital and Clinics.

CHARLES J. GOLDEN, PH.D. is past president of the National Academy of Neuropsychologists, serves on the board of directors of the American Board of Clinical Neuropsychology, and edits the *International Journal of Clinical Neuropsychology.* Dr. Golden received his Ph.D. in clinical psychology from the University of Hawaii and currently holds diplomates in both clinical psychology and clinical neuropsychology. He is on the editorial board of the *Journal of Consulting and Clinical Psychology, Computer in Human Behavior,* and the *Journal of Psychoeducational Assessment.* He has published over 100 articles and books in the areas of assessment, including several papers on forensic issues.

LAWRENCE C. HARTLAGE, PH.D. is Professor of Neurology, Professor of Pediatrics, and head of neuropsychology at the Medical College of Georgia. His graduate degrees are from the University of Louisville. He has served as president of the National Academy of Neuropsychologists and the American Psychological Association Division of Clinical Neuropsychology, and as general editor of the *International Journal of Clinical Neuropsychology.* Dr. Hartlage's publications include more than 150 books, chapters, and articles dealing with various aspects of testing and assessment.

ROBERT K. HEATON, PH.D. is Associate Professor of Psychiatry and director of the neuropsychology laboratory at the University of Colorado School of Medicine. Dr. Heaton received his Ph.D. in clinical psychology from the University of Washington. He has published extensively in the field of neuropsychology and is a diplomate in neuropsychology in the American Board of Professional Psychology and the American Board of Clinical Neurospychology.

MARK R. LOVELL, PH.D. is a post-doctoral fellow in neuropsychology at the University of Nebraska Medical Center where he also completed his clinical internship. He received his Ph.D. in clinical psychology from the University of Health Sciences/The Chicago Medical School. Neuropsychology is a long-standing area of interest of Dr. Lovell's, and he has recently coauthored an article on the topic in the *Journal of Nervous and Mental Disease.*

WILLIAM J. LYNCH, PH.D. is the program director of the brain injury rehabilitation unit and directs the assessment unit of the Menlo Park Division of the Palo Alto (California) Veterans Administration Medical Center. He received his Ph.D. in clinical psychology from the University of Tennessee, Knoxville. He completed an internship at the University of Tennessee Center for Health Sciences Department of Psychiatry in Memphis where he began to specialize in clinical neuropsychology. Dr. Lynch has published articles dealing with the relationship of personality factors to outcome of lumbar disc surgery, the development of a standard problem list for traumatically brain-injured patients, the use of microcomputers in cognitive rehabilitation, and the role of the neuropsychologist in cognitive rehabilitation. He is the author of a number of book chapters dealing with neuropsychological assessment and rehabilitation. His research interests are in the area of developing microcomputer-based screening measures for detecting and differentiating dementia.

CHRISTOPHER H. NORTH, PH.D. has recently received his doctoral degree from the University of Kansas. Dr. North completed a clinical internship at the University of Texas Health Science Center at San Antonio. His research interests are in the area of ego-dystonic and ego-syntonic adjustments to homosexuality.

CARROLL D. OHLDE, PH.D. is a certified psychologist who received his Ph.D. in counseling psychology from the University of Kansas. He serves as a staff psychologist on the Vietnam Unit at the Colmery-O'Neil Veterans Administration Medical Center where he coordinates the inpatient program designed to treat post-traumatic stress disorder (PTSD). While working in this position since 1982, Dr. Ohlde coauthored studies on PTSD and served as a co-investigator on a research project assessing characteristics of Vietnam veterans. He has also served as a consultant to other inpatient PTSD treatment programs and as a faculty member at VA regional workshops on PTSD.

TOM W. PATTERSON, PH.D. is chief of psychology services at the Colmery-O'Neil Veterans Administration Medical Center in Topeka, Kansas. His work with PTSD has included individual and group psychotherapy, treatment program building and consulting, workshops and lectures throughout the United States consulting with Vietnam veteran organizations, and research. Dr. Patterson is a consulting editor to the *Journal of Personality Assessment*.

THOMAS REILLY, PH.D. is Assistant Professor of Psychology at the University of Kansas. Dr. Reilly received his Ph.D. in clinical psychology from the University of Kansas and completed his clinical internship at the Greater Kansas City Mental Health Foundation. He teaches courses in assessment and supervises the assessment and psychotherapy work of graduate students in clinical psychology. He is certified in Kansas.

DOUGLAS E. ROBBINS, PH.D. is a post-doctoral fellow in neuropsychology at the University of Nebraska Medical Center where he also completed his clinical internship. He received his Ph.D. in clinical psychology from the University of Wisconsin-Milwaukee. Dr. Robbins' interests include not only the area of neuropsychology, but psychological assessment in general. At the present time he is involved in the development of a rehabilitative assessment center specializing in the treatment of neurological, psychiatric, and chronic pain patients who present with multiple disorders.

ANDREW H. SCHAUER, PH.D. is assistant chief of psychology services at the Colmery-O'Neil Veterans Administration Medical Center, Topeka, Kansas. Assigned to an acute inpatient ward, he works with Vietnam veterans displaying residuals of PTSD and other behavioral difficulties. He coordinates a three-year long research project examining intellectual, personality, and interpersonal characteristics of Vietnam veterans. Psychological assessment with this population is also a special interest of his. In addition to these areas, Dr. Schauer serves as psychological test review coauthor for the *Journal of Counseling and Development* and has had articles covering various assessment topics accepted for publication.

FRED D. STRIDER, PH.D. is Professor of Medical Psychology in the department of psychiatry of the University of Nebraska College of Medicine. He is Director of Allied Professional Services and chief of the clinical psychology section of the Nebraska Psychiatric Institute. Dr. Strider's research interests include behavioral medicine, mental retardation, and the use of self-regulation therapies in the treatment of psychosomatic and stress disorders.

MARY ANN STRIDER, PH.D. is Assistant Professor of Medical Psychology in the department of psychiatry of the University of Nebraska College of Medicine. She is assistant director of the Psychological Assessment Center of the Nebraska Psychiatric Institute. She holds a master of science degree in industrial psychology, a doctoral degree from the University of Nebraska at Lincoln, and obtained postdoctoral training in neuropsychology. Dr. Strider is certified as a clinical psychologist by the Nebraska State Board of Examiners of Psychologists and is in the *National Register of Health Service Providers in Psychology.* Her research interests include development of neuropsychological assessment methods, behavioral medicine, and the assessment and treatment of psychosomatic disorders. She is currently active in stress management and the application of behavioral medicine procedures during the care of patients undergoing bone-marrow transplantation.

DENNIS P. SWIERCINSKY, PH.D. is a nationally recognized clinical neuropsychologist who is in private practice in the Kansas City area and directs a comprehensive treatment program for head-injured persons. His specialty in rehabilitation includes ten years of experience in vocational rehabilitation, sexual dysfunction, and neurofunctional assessments. He has published extensively and taught at California State University, Kansas University, and Texas A & M University in the area of psychological test theory and construction and has written an automated neuropsychological test battery that is familiar to many clinicians using computerized testing. His many published works in psychodiagnostics include a *Manual for the Adult Neuropsychological Evaluation,* which has been used extensively for training student neuropsychologists. Dr. Swiercinsky received his Ph.D. from the University of Kansas and is a professional member of the International Neuropsychological Society and the National Academy of Neuropsychologists.